AMERICAN REBEL

ALSO BY MARC ELIOT

Reagan: The Hollywood Years

Jimmy Stewart: A Biography

Cary Grant: A Biography

*Song of Brooklyn: An Oral History
of America's Favorite Borough*

*Death of a Rebel: Starring Phil Ochs
and a Small Circle of Friends*

*Down Thunder Road: The Making
of Bruce Springsteen*

Roconomics: The Money Behind the Music

Walt Disney: Hollywood's Dark Prince

The Whole Truth

To the Limit: The Untold Story of the Eagles

*Down 42nd Street: Sex, Money, Culture,
and Politics at the Crossroads of the World*

AMER

THE LIFE OF CLINT EASTWOOD

AMERICAN REBEL

MARC ELIOT

 Harmony Books · New York

Copyright © 2009 by Rebel Road, Inc.

All rights reserved.

Published in the United States by Harmony Books, an imprint of the Crown Publishing Group, a division of Random House, Inc., New York.

www.crownpublishing.com

Harmony Books is a registered trademark and the Harmony Books colophon is a trademark of Random House, Inc.

Library of Congress Cataloging-in-Publication Data is available upon request.

ISBN 978-0-307-33688-0

Printed in the United States of America

DESIGN BY ELINA D. NUDELMAN

10 9 8 7 6 5 4 3 2 1

First Edition

For XIAOLEI

You go to an Eastwood movie with definite expectations. From the comically crude . . . to the gentler epithets of his later films, you know what you're going to get and, even more important, what you're *not* going to get. You're not going to get everything.

—Molly Haskell

Clint Eastwood is a tall, chiseled piece of lumber—a totem pole with feet . . . Eastwood seems to be chewing on bullet casings.

—James Wolcott

Eastwood has a particular grace, every inch that of a "star," in the old sense . . . the taut, lean, powerfully built body, the sensitively chiseled unsmiling face, a voice surprisingly soft, the shock of tawny hair, the lithe walk (the most distinctive of any actor's since Fonda's), the famous squint and glacial eyes which . . . produce a certain inarticulate melancholy.

—Robert Mazzocco

People can know him for years and never be sure of what he's thinking. He's one of the warmest people in the world, but there's a certain distance, a certain mystery to him.

—Sondra Locke

There is something intransigently irreducible in Eastwood, some corner of his soul that no shrink can penetrate . . . Clint Eastwood is an interesting screen personality because his essence is more interesting than his existence. The screen functions to freeze life styles into myth rather than to adjust life forces into art. The beauty of actors is that they are basically vain enough and stupid enough to allow themselves to be embalmed for the edification of their audience.

—Andrew Sarris

I'm an actor playing roles; all of them and none of them are me.

—Clint Eastwood

CONTENTS

I grew up watching movies in an era when there wasn't even television, nothing else even to listen to. I was shaped by John Ford, Howard Hawks, Preston Sturges, those were the guys, plus a ton of other people we don't know the names of who made "B" movies.

—Clint Eastwood

Clint Eastwood stands tall among the most popular and enduring stars Hollywood has ever produced. He has been making movies for more than fifty years, ranging from small, meaningless, and forgettable parts as a Universal Studios contract player to acting in, as well as producing and directing, many Oscar-caliber blockbusters that will one day, sooner rather than later, take their place among the best-loved American movies.

Early in his career, Clint spent seven and a half years costarring in TV's *Rawhide*, and his Rowdy Yates became one of the most popular TV cowboys of the late 1950s and early 1960s.* By the time *Rawhide* ended its eight-season run he had also become an international movie star, following his appearance in three wildly popular spaghetti westerns made and distributed throughout Europe; when they were finally released in America, they made him a big-screen star in the States as well. For the next quarter-century Clint appeared in dozens of entertaining movies that made him a household name anywhere in the world that films could be seen. He was undoubtedly a crowd-pleaser, but at the time the Hollywood elite considered his movies too genre-heavy to be Oscar-worthy.

Then in 1992 Clint produced, directed, and starred in *Unforgiven*, a western to (literally) end all westerns, made by his own production company, Malpaso, that he had created to operate as a ministudio in the service of its resident star. *Unforgiven* won four Academy Awards, including two for Clint (one for Best Director and one for Best Picture), and the Midas-touch Oscar-style was suddenly his; nearly everything he made for the next fifteen years was deemed award- or

---

*The show ran eight seasons, with only twenty-two episodes in its debut year as a mid-season replacement. The show made thirteen episodes in its final season. Seasons two through seven had full-season commitments.

nomination-worthy by the Academy, including *Million Dollar Baby, Mystic River, Flags of Our Fathers, Letters from Iwo Jima,* and *Changeling.* Throughout Hollywood's post-studio era, the first rule of filmmaking has been that youth equals box office—young people go out to the movies, older audiences stay home and watch them on cable and DVD. It is, therefore, even more remarkable that he made all of these movies past the age of sixty.

Perhaps more than for any other Hollywood star, the double helix that is Clint's creative and real-life DNA is so intertwined it is nearly impossible to separate the off-screen person from the on-screen persona. The two feed off each other so thoroughly, it is often difficult to tell where the lives of the characters in his movies end and the life of the man playing them begins.

In the movies that he has thus far acted in, produced, or directed, in various combinations wearing one or more of these hats, three essential Clint Eastwood screen personae continually reappear. The first is the mysterious man without a past who is resolute in his loneness, the Man with No Name, who appeared in the three Sergio Leone westerns—*A Fistful of Dollars, For a Few Dollars More, The Good, the Bad and the Ugly*—then reappeared slightly altered in *Hang 'Em High* and *The Outlaw Josey Wales,* and took several other guises and variations all the way through to *Unforgiven.* The second persona is "Dirty" Harry Callahan, whose essentially nihilistic loner personality continually reemerges up to and including *Gran Torino.* And finally, there is the good-natured redneck, who uses his fists the way a more thoughtful person uses words and who makes his first appearance as Philo Beddoe in *Every Which Way but Loose* and returns again and again on the way to *Pink Cadillac.*

All three characters in their various incarnations are viscerally connected to the real-life Clint. All three are quintessential loners, unlike any other in the canon of American motion pictures. The other cinematic "men alone" who most immediately come to mind are not really loners at all—that is to say, they are loners Hollywood style, buffered with the idealized images of the actors who played them. Probably mainstream films' greatest "loner" is Gary Cooper as the isolated sheriff in Fred Zinnemann's *High Noon* (1952). Yes, Will Kane heroically stands alone to face his enemies, but in truth he is not alone at all, as in the end he relies on the love of his wife, and her reluctant use of a gun that saves his life; and when all the fighting has ended, the two of them ride off together into the sunset. Another who comes to mind is Humphrey Bogart's Rick Blaine, the neutral American caught in the crosswinds of World War II in Michael Curtiz's *Casablanca* (1942). He proudly boasts that "I stick my neck out for nobody" and then does precisely that for the woman he loves, in this case Ingrid Bergman, in an act so unselfishly noble that the very idea that he was ever a loner is so absurd it becomes laughable. James Bond appears to be the ultimate loner, but we now know that he lost his one true love early on and both seethes with revenge and longs with lust, no longer for any single woman but, apparently, all of womankind. On a nobler plane, Charlton Heston in Cecil B. DeMille's *The Ten Commandments* (1956) is isolated from his family, his people, his land, and his heritage. Yet he still needs someone to lean on, in this case the Almighty himself, who provides the love, guidance, and moral sustenance that establish quite profoundly that even Moses did not go it alone.

Clint's movie characters need nothing and no one more than or beyond themselves. Whether he is surrounded by vicious killers or predatory women (oftentimes one and the same), faceless adversaries (as opposed to the Man with No Name), by serial man-hunters pursued and ultimately defeated by someone dirtier (and therefore stronger) than they are, or even by buddy-buddy orangutans, the Man with No Name, Dirty Harry, and Philo Beddoe all arrive alone at the start and leave alone at the end. They rarely, if ever, win the heart of any woman because they almost never pursue women. On the few occasions when a Clint character reluctantly finds himself to be involved with one, the relationship remains distant, cynical, unromantic, and for the most part nonintimate; the so-called love story is always the least interesting part of any Clint Eastwood movie. His loners are unable, unwilling, and therefore unavailable to fulfill the wishes of those men or women who want to be with him, but not of those in the audience who dream of being like him. With this brand of character, Clint delivered something original and provocative to American motion pictures.

In real life, too, Clint has frequently been described as something of a loner, even in his early and undistinguished film appearances, even when married and playing the role of the happy Hollywood husband. All through his first marriage's thirty-one years,* there were loud whispers that he was not the family man he appeared to be but a lone-wolf womanizer—a role certainly not unique in a town that sees womanizing as something glamorous, even heroic, and where the locker-room lingo of beer-boosted braggadocio is often raised to the level of bad poetry. Perhaps the label stuck harder to him because of how closely his few on-screen romances overlapped with his many real-life ones. Clint's off-screen life has always been filled with women, some might say too many, others might say none really at all. While married to Maggie Johnson, he fathered a child out of wedlock, the first of four,† and took numerous lovers. Several of them were costars, in affairs that often began when production on the film commenced and ended after the final shot was completed. Relatively late in his game, at age sixty-six, he finally married, for only the second time, twelve years after his divorce from Maggie became finalized, to a woman thirty-five years younger than himself, this time finding some measure of peace and happiness.

In his salad days he hung out in the seedy bars in and around San Francisco, drinking, playing jazz on house pianos, and in the vernacular of that time and those places, kicking ass in barroom brawls, whose circumstances and resolutions would later be reprised in many of his films. A tough guy in real life, Clint easily and realistically played the tough guy on film, someone who usually settles disputes with a knock-down, drag-out brawl or, as in *A Fistful of Dollars*, *Dirty Harry*, and many others, with cinema's classic metaphorical extension of the fistfight, the final, decisive shoot-out.

Perhaps even more compelling than any of his movie roles (but what also makes them so compelling) is how Clint the real-life loner

---

*Clint and Maggie Johnson, his first wife, were married in 1953, separated in 1978, and divorced in 1984.

†One with Roxanne Tunis, one with Frances Fisher, and two with Jacelyn Reeves. His total of seven children are Kimber Eastwood (born June 17, 1964), Kyle Eastwood (born May 19, 1968), Alison Eastwood (born May 22, 1972), Scott Eastwood (born March 21, 1986), Kathryn Eastwood (born February 2, 1988), Francesca Fisher-Eastwood (born August 7, 1993), and Morgan Eastwood (born December 12, 1996).

struggled to find his way out of his own emotional wilderness. He was a child of the Depression, whose parents wandered from town to town to try to make ends meet. Not long after he finished high school, he was drafted into the army and fell in with a bunch of other tough young would-be actors, all of whom grew up in or near Southern California and quickly discovered they had what it took—rugged good looks—to make easier money as contract players, in the desperate declining days of studio-dominated moviemaking, than they could pumping gas.

After his discharge he followed their lead, but his emerging talent quickly separated him from the two he became closest to—Martin Milner and David Janssen—and the rest of the pack. Milner's undistinguished career in movies led to an even less distinguished, if steady, one on television with *Route 66* (1960–64) and *Adam-12* (1968–75); Janssen briefly hit pay dirt on TV as Dr. Richard Kimble in the mid-1960s (1963–67), only to see his post-*Fugitive* career devolve into increasingly mediocre work. But Clint used the time he spent on TV as a film school. Amid tired and bored union men moving wagon trains onto and off of Universal's back lot, he studied everybody and everything and learned not only how to make movies (*Rawhide*, a one-hour TV western series, cranked out a minimovie every week, thirty-nine weeks a year) but how to make them fast and cheap, telling a concise and comprehensible story, often the same one over and over with slight variations; these stories had a logical beginning, an action-filled middle, and a morally uplifting, perfectly plot-resolved end.

Years later, after establishing himself as a bankable star on the big screen, Clint finally got the chance to direct. Early on he had felt that that was where the real action was in movies, that it was ultimately better to play God than to play parts. Along the way to achieving that goal, he met Don Siegel, who would direct him in five films, *Coogan's Bluff* (1968), *Two Mules for Sister Sara* (1970), *The Beguiled* (1971), *Dirty Harry* (1971), and *Escape from Alcatraz* (1979). These films greatly influenced Clint's own early directorial style, especially their collective belief in human nobility as the ultimate redemptive force. Clint would, however, eventually shrug off nobility and redemption as his own style continued to develop and he realized these themes were not just overly derivative, but the least interesting aspect of what he wanted to put on film—less-plot-dependent movies that were, in truth, feature-length, complex character studies of the leads he played, men who were aloof, estranged (from women and from the larger social order), detached, and embittered, up to and including Clint's portrayal of Walt Kowalski in *Gran Torino*, a dark and chilling film where self-forgiveness and relief come in the form of self-sacrifice, in a single overwhelming (and shocking) attempt to connect in order to redeem another human being. As a showcase for his directorial style and his maturation as an actor—he was seventy-eight when he made it—*Gran Torino*, with no female romantic lead, no comic relief, and until the end, no obviously redemptive qualities in its leading character, perfectly caps the arc of Clint's unique acting and directing style and his auteur's quest to celebrate the loner as the ultimate hero, even (or especially) into old age. By doing so Clint demonstrated, once again, how unlike any other contemporary filmmaker or film actor he always had been.

Always unwilling to talk about his films as anything but entertainments, and even less willing to discuss his private life beyond delivering a certain set of rote answers to the press when promoting his latest film, the clues to who he is and what he does are, nevertheless, found not only in the content of the movies he makes but also within the context of the life he has led, beyond the PR pale, indeed in the symbiotic relationship between the two. He is a man who makes his living making the movies that in turn make the man. He is an American artist whose films are at once great entertainments and cautionary tales, and, as all great movies are, both windows and mirrors. They offer glimpses into his private contemplations even as they reflect universal truths to audiences everywhere.

What follows, then, is an examination of Clint Eastwood, the man he is and the artist he became, seen through the window of his real life and reflected again in some of the most offbeat, disturbing, provocative, and entertaining American films ever made.

PART I

FROM AIMLESS TO ACTOR

ONE

My father always told me you don't get anything for nothing, and although I was always rebelling, I never rebelled against that.

—Clint Eastwood

The boy who would one day become famous for playing the Man with No Name did not have a well-defined self-image or a strong role model to follow growing up. In his formative years his father, forever in search of a steady job during the Great Depression, developed a deceptive California suntan, the mark of a hardworking outdoor laborer trying to avoid poverty rather than a man of sun-worshipping leisure and privilege.

Clinton and Francesca Ruth (sometimes recorded as Margaret Ruth, although she only used Ruth as her given name) were two good-looking California kids who met while attending Piedmont High School in Oakland. They dated each other and married young, before the market crashed, and took with it their romantic dream of the good life. Ruth's family was Dutch-Irish and Mormon with a long line of physical laborers, including pickup fighters, lumberjacks, sawmill operators, and an occasional local politician. She graduated from Anna Head School in Berkeley, where she had been transferred to from Piedmont just before her senior year—a move that may have been prompted by her parents' concern over an intense relationship she had begun with her high school sweetheart, Clinton Eastwood. Clinton was a popular, well-liked boy with strong American roots; his ancestors were pre–Revolutionary War Presbyterian farmers and men who sold goods by traveling from town to town, their carts bearing inventory samples such as women's underwear and soap used to elicit orders from their customers. In the days before mail-order catalogs, most goods were sold this way outside the big American cities.

Despite Ruth's parents' attempts to put some distance between her and the economically deficient Clinton, upon graduating from high school they were married, on June 5, 1927, in a ceremony held at Piedmont's interdenominational church. Both newlyweds were lucky enough to find enough work to keep them going during the first years of their marriage. Ruth eventually landed a job as an accountant for an insurance company, and Clinton found one as a cashier. When the stock market crashed in October 1929, they clung to these jobs tenaciously.

Almost three years after their marriage, on May 31, 1930, Clinton Jr. was born. The boy weighed a whopping eleven pounds, six ounces, and was nicknamed "Samson" by all the nurses at San Francisco's St. Francis Hospital.

At about this time Clinton Sr. managed to land a job selling stocks and bonds. At a time when stocks and bonds had been rendered all but worthless, Clinton was following the family tradition; he was now a glorified cart-man, weaving from town to town looking for those few elusive customers with enough cash to invest in their own future and therefore in his. That he got by at all was likely due to his natural charm and good looks.

But even those could only get him so far, and soon Clinton was selling refrigeration products for the East Bay Company, a position whose long-range prospects were little better than those of a seller of stocks and bonds. People had to have enough money to buy food before they could invest in ways to keep it cold. So in 1934, after the birth of their second child, a girl they named Jeanne, Clinton took to a more itinerant life, moving the family by car to wherever he could find pickup work. In a couple of his earliest recollections, Clint later said of those times:

> Well, those were the thirties and jobs were hard to come by. My parents and my sister and myself just had to move around to get jobs. I remember we moved from Sacramento to Pacific Palisades just [so my father could work] as a gas station attendant. It was the only job open. Everybody was in a trailer, one with a single wheel on one end, and the car, and we were living in a real old place out in the sticks . . .

> My father was big on basic courtesies toward women. The one time I ever got snotty with my mother when he was around, he left me a little battered.

The attendant job was at a Standard Oil station on Sunset Boulevard and Pacific Coast Highway, near a stretch of Malibu beach that was rapidly becoming the suburb of choice for the nouveau riche of the Hollywood film industry—one of the few businesses that actually benefited from the Depression. Films were both cheap and fanciful, the ultimate escape for those who could not afford to live out the American dream themselves but loved watching others do it for them on-screen. Those who lived in this part of town drove big cars that used a lot of gas, so Clinton had plenty of work. For the time being it was a good enough living if not exactly a great life. From the money he made he was able to rent a small house in the lush, hilly Pacific Palisades.

On his off days Clinton and Ruth took their children to one of the public beaches adjacent to Malibu for an afternoon of sun and swimming. One day Clinton, who was an excellent swimmer, dove into a wave with Clint sitting in the saddle of his shoulders. Big Clint came back up but little Clint didn't. After a few heart-stopping moments Ruth saw her boy's foot sticking up and bobbing in the water. She screamed. With some help from alert nearby swimmers, Clinton was able to pull him up. Afterward Ruth sat in the cool muddy turf with her little Clint and splashed him playfully to make sure he wouldn't become afraid of the surf.

A year later, in 1935, the gas station job dried up, and the Eastwoods were once more on the move. They gave up the house in Pacific Palisades and took a smaller one for less rent in Hollywood, a few miles farther inland. Soon afterward they swung back north to Redding, then to Sacramento, then to the Glenview section of the East Bay of San Francisco. Finally they settled back down in the Oakland-Piedmont area, where Clinton worked a series of dead-end jobs. Clint, by now, had attended several schools, necessitated by the family's continual relocations. "I can't remember how many schools I went to," he later recalled. "I do remember we moved so much that I made very few friends." In 1939, after their long loop through the tough times of California, the family settled long enough for young Clint, now nine, to enroll in Piedmont Junior High School.

Following the December 7, 1941, Japanese attack on Pearl Harbor, America's entry into World War II brought new defense-driven work.

Clinton managed to secure a draft-exempt job in the shipyards with Bethlehem Steel, and Ruth found day work at the nearby IBM center.

On the brink of adolescence, six-foot Clint was the tallest boy in his class; he would reach his full height, six four, by the time he graduated from high school. He was also, by all accounts, one of the best-looking students. He had inherited his father's strong, broad shoulders, rugged good looks, and seductive half-closed eyes. He had a finely shaped, aristocratically turned-up nose and a thick bush of brown hair that fell in a curly dip over his forehead. The look was tough, but he was shy, likely the product of his family's vagabond journey through the Depression years. Being left-handed also made him feel like an outsider, as his teachers forced him to use his right hand.

He enjoyed playing high school sports—his height made it easy for him to excel at basketball—but that did little for his social skills. His teachers warned his parents that he had to be brought out of his shell if he was to make something of himself. One of them, Gertrude Falk, who taught English, had the class put on a one-act play and cast a reluctant young Clint in the lead. He was less than thrilled.

> I remember Gertrude Falk very well. It was the part of a backward youth, and I think she thought it was perfect casting . . . she made up her mind that I was going to play the lead and it was disastrous. I wanted to go out for athletics; doing plays was not considered the thing to do at that stage of life—especially not presenting them before the entire senior high school, which is what she made us do. We muffed a lot of lines. I swore [at the time] that that was the end of my acting career.

Clint also didn't do well academically, and his schoolmates and teachers considered him something of a "dummy." Besides sports, the only other subject that held any interest for him was music—not the kind of big-band sound that was popular with the older kids, but jazz. He liked to play it on the piano, something that he correctly believed enhanced his attractiveness to girls. He even learned the current pop tunes that he had no use for but that made them flock around him.

> When I sat down at the piano at a party, the girls would come around. I could play a few numbers. I learned a few off listening to records

and things that were popular at that era. I thought this was all right, so I went home and practiced . . . I would lie about my age and go to Hambone Kelly's. I'd stand in the back and listen to Lu Watters and Turk Murphy play New Orleans jazz . . . I grew up listening to Ella Fitzgerald and Nat King Cole . . . Lester Young, Charlie Parker, Dizzy Gillespie, Miles Davis, Clifford Brown, Fats Navarro, Thelonious Monk, Erroll Garner.

And he loved cars. For $25 Clint's father bought him a beat-up 1932 Chevy to help him keep his paper route job. Clint nicknamed it "the Bathtub" because of its missing top. Its best accessory was, of course, the girls. The Chevy, which didn't last very long, was only the first of a long line of his beat-up cars. To pay for them all and the gas and repairs, Clint took extra after-school jobs on top of his paper route. He worked at the local grocery and as a caddy at the golf course; he baled hay on a farm in nearby Yreka, cut timber near Paradise, and was a seasonal forest firefighter. All these jobs were purely physical, the type of work he could forget about as soon as he punched out. But they were time consuming and exhausting, even for a young and strong teenage boy. They left him even less time for his studies at Piedmont High, and when his parents and school authorities realized he wasn't going to graduate with a regular academic degree, he transferred to the Oakland Technical High School, a vocational training institute where he would specialize in aircraft maintenance. This would give him his best chance, upon graduation, to attend the University of California, which had an affiliated program with the high school, or to land a well-paying job.

After school Clint hung with a crowd of tough-looking teens decked out in leather and T-shirts, with greased-back long hair. All strong, tall, and lean, they tucked cigarettes behind their ears and held bottles of beer in one hand while they drove, usually to the local dives where the hottest girls hung out. And they were all into jazz. Most often they found themselves at the Omar, a pizza and beer dive in downtown Oakland where Clint liked to play jazz on a beat-up old piano in the corner. Whenever he could, he would go to hear Dizzy Gillespie, Coleman Hawkins, Flip Phillips, Lester Young, or Charlie Parker. Sometimes they played alone in the small dark clubs that dotted the streets of Oakland; sometimes they performed together at the Shrine Auditorium, where the heavily mixed crowd regularly gathered to see and hear them.

It was Parker, more than all the others, who opened his eyes to the new music's emotional power. As Clint later told Richard Schickel, "I'd never seen a musician play with such confidence. There was no show business to it in those days, and this guy just stood and played, and I thought, God, what an amazing, expressive thing." His cool, aloof sound held great appeal for Clint.

He was nineteen when he finally graduated from Oakland Tech in the spring of 1949. By then, he had grown tired of school and often cut classes to hang out with boys, among whom he was the only one still in school.

Meanwhile the war's end had brought new prosperity, especially along the rapidly growing Pacific coast, where jobs were plentiful, wages generous, and mobility upward. Clinton Sr. found work with the California Container Corporation, was quickly caught up in the flow of automatic promotions, and soon was offered a major managerial post in the company's main plant, in Seattle. Together he and Ruth and fourteen-year-old Jeanne packed up the house and loaded the car for the drive to Seattle.

Clint didn't want to go, and because he had graduated, he said he didn't have to. Harry Pendleton's parents agreed to let him stay with them for a while. Harry and Clint had been friends since junior high school and long hung with the same crowd. With his family in Seattle, his education finished, and no clear plan for the future, Clint was, in his own words, "really adrift." He found a job on the night shift at Bethlehem Steel, tending the blast furnaces, then moved to the day shift at Boeing Aircraft. For the next two years these hard and charmless jobs kept him in cars, girls, and music, allowing him to roam aimlessly through his early twenties unfocused and unconcerned, the perfect West Coast rebel without a care.

Then, in 1950, border hostilities broke out in Korea, and the United States began a massive buildup of forces in Seoul. Knowing his A1 military status made him a prime target for the draft, Clint's unlikely next goal was to go back to college, to get a student exemption. He moved up to Seattle and in with his parents to enroll at Seattle University. He figured he might major in music, since nothing else held any appeal. But his grades weren't good enough, and he was told he'd have to attend junior college as a nonmatriculated, part-time student, which would not be enough to earn him the draft exemption. He then moved back to Oakland and made a last-ditch personal appeal to his local draft board, to convince them he had every intention of attending college full time.

The board took him the following month.

In the spring of 1951, he spent his last free nights getting drunk and listening to music at the local dives, before reporting, hung over and hell-bent, for basic training at Fort Ord, near the Monterey Peninsula. As far as he was concerned, he didn't need any training. What could the army teach him that at the age of twenty he didn't already know?

Plenty, as it turned out, although not at all in the ways he might have expected.

TWO

Basically I was a drifter, a bum. As it has turned out, I'm lucky because I'm going to end up financially well-off for a drifter. But that really doesn't change things . . . You can only dig so many holes in the ground.

—Clint Eastwood

The army quickly altered the rhythm of Clint's life, from the jazzy syncopation of his unstructured days and nights to the beat of a military march. He was stationed at Fort Ord, near the Monterey Peninsula, for six weeks of basic training. To everyone's surprise but nobody more than himself, his natural physical abilities gave rise to talk among the drill sergeants that he should be sent to Officer Training School—a suggestion he rejected out of hand. He had been drafted for the obligatory two years and didn't want to spend one second longer in uniform. *No problem,* they told him. *So be ready for more training and toughening up before you're shipped off to Korea.*

Only something he had written down on his induction papers saved him from that grim assignment. When asked to mention any special skills, he had put down "swimming." The camp brass had made note of it, and when he completed basic, they assigned him to permanent duty as a lifesaving swimming instructor at the Fort Ord Division of Faculty. The boy who had almost drowned in the Pacific and done so poorly in school was now assigned to teach the army how to swim. That kind of irony helped produce what would one day be known as the Eastwood smirk—an ambiguous squint-eyed half-smile that said nothing and everything at the same time.

This "Clint luck," as his friends always called it, didn't stop there. His placement at the base pool brought him into frequent contact with Special Services, the army division created during World War II to utilize the popularity of Hollywood celebrities inducted into the service. Knowing that killing off movie stars was not the best PR or economic move, the army segregated them into Special Services and gave them essentially (but not always) a free ticket, most of the time saving them from active duty and using them for as much publicity and as many recruiting opportunities as they could. They spent most of their ample free time swimming. His real job was to save them from drowning.

On duty, Clint met several young Hollywood contract players, including Martin Milner, John Saxon, and David Janssen, and dozens of other future familiar film and TV faces all congregated around the pool, turning it into a gathering spot for drinks and small talk, lacking only girls to complete the cool social scene. WACs assigned to the base were everywhere but were not allowed to fraternize with the men at the pool or after hours.

Clint became friends with the exceptionally good-looking Janssen, who had played football for Fairfax High School in Hollywood before a serious knee injury ruined his chances of playing college sports and steered him instead into acting. Clint and Janssen shared an athletic bravado cut with strong sexual appetites, which made them legends of a sort on base. They were privy to and took full advantage of the pleasures of the young, single women at the nearby nightclubs, soldier-lovers who were sweet, plentiful, willing, and available. Another noncom who became a friend of Clint was Irving Lasper, a photographer who told him he had the kind of face the movies—or more accurately, the men who made them—would love. Clint shrugged off the suggestion, having no interest in that business.

Clint also got close to many of the musicians assigned to the unit, including Lennie Niehaus, an alto sax player who had worked with Stan Kenton and now played at the base's junior NCO (noncommissioned officers) mess hall four nights a week. Clint managed to talk his way into the hall's bartending job so that after lounging by the pool all day he could hang back, drink for free, and listen to Niehaus blow his horn. He became so close with these members of the Special Services that he became an unofficial member by association, which meant the officers in charge either didn't know or didn't care that he slept past reveille. He didn't do much KP or much of anything except sit by the pool, and work at the club at night, and come and go from the base at will.

He often took overnight excursions by himself to explore the gorgeous coastal scenery that he had loved since childhood. In the emerald expanse of Carmel, a sleepy enclave 120 miles south of San Francisco, he enjoyed hearing jazz played in the local clubs that also attracted some of the best-looking women north of L.A. They always took to the surf wearing as little as possible to allow themselves to soak up the famous California sun. So for Clint, it was women during the day, jazz at night.

Another job assigned to Clint—after all, he wasn't exactly over-loaded—was base projectionist for the Division Faculty classrooms. "One of my auxiliary jobs, besides swimming instructor, was to project training films for the soldiers. I kept showing [John Huston's 1945] *The Battle of San Pietro*, one of my favorites, which I must have seen around fifty times during my two years in the service." Watching it over and over again, Clint could not help but break down the mechanics of the movie, how it was put together, the rhythm of the shots, the camera angles, Huston's off-screen narration.

Out of this fascination with movies came a new friendship with Norman Bartold, another noncom actor, who had a small part in one of the new pictures Clint was assigned to screen, H. Bruce Humber-stone's *She's Working Her Way Through College* (1952), a Ronald Reagan vehicle costarring Virginia Mayo in one of her leggy imitation–Betty Grable roles. Clint enjoyed hanging out with Bartold, to talk about how the movie was made as well as what it was like to work with the luscious Mayo.

The few times Clint voluntarily wore his uniform off the base was to gain free passage on a military aircraft, which came in handy whenever he wanted to visit his parents in Seattle, and a girl he had met off base who also happened to live there. One day in the fall of 1951, he hooked up with a twin-engine Beechcraft. At the last minute he changed plans and chose instead a Douglas AD naval attack bomber because its return flight schedule would give him a little extra time in Seattle. But on its way back to the base the plane developed engine trouble and ran out of gas, forcing it to belly-flop into the ocean along Point Reyes, just off the coast of Marin County. Here Clint's swimming abilities kicked in—he was able to dislodge himself from the flooded fuselage and make it to the surface. Not too far away he saw the pilot bobbing in the water. Both then swam to shore, which was four, seven, or more miles away (depending upon the several and highly varied published accounts of this incident).

By overstaying his time in Seattle—spending it not with his parents but with the girl—Clint had technically violated his leave and nearly drowned. Although in later years he underplayed the incident, likely because of its decidedly unheroic backstory, he did occasionally talk about this early adventure but always matter-of-factly. Still, the momentary drama would later be useful for publicity purposes when he became an action star.

The crash also introduced him to a bit of momentary fame. Although he didn't feel especially heroic, just Clint-lucky to be alive, the local press lauded him as a hero for surviving the crash and, in accounts, helping to rescue pilot Lieutenant F. C. Anderson (who was actually rescued separately). Clint was portrayed heroically, photographed on the scene bare-chested and dripping wet, looking for all the world like a hero. But the episode also introduced him to the very real notion of mortality. Defiantly looking into the face of death would have a powerful and lasting effect on him.

Although Clint never left the States while in the service, several of the fellow recruits who did basic training with him were sent overseas and saw action in the war. One was Don Kincade, whom he had known since high school. Immediately after being discharged in January 1953, Kincade enrolled in the University of California at Berkeley on the GI Bill. That spring Clint hitched a ride to Berkeley to visit him.

Kincade, who was by now dating a sorority girl, offered to set Clint up on a blind date with her best friend. He assured Clint he wouldn't be disappointed; Maggie Johnson was a beauty—tall, good face, terrific body. And, he added, she was dating someone else, so this would be a guaranteed one-shot affair.

As it turned out, Clint and Maggie hit it off, and when the weekend came to an end, they promised to try to get together in the fall, when Clint's active service time was up and Maggie had graduated and returned to live with her parents in Alhambra, a suburb of Los Angeles.

She quickly got rid of the other guy.

As his tour of duty wound down, Clint gradually reverted to the easy syncopations of pre-army days. After two years of his laid-back conscription, he had little "military" to get rid of. He had long ago let his hair grow out, rarely wore a uniform, and more or less came and went as he pleased. By the time of his summer 1953 discharge, he had already made plans to return to Seattle, where a cushy civilian job as a lifeguard was waiting for him. Only he didn't go, at least not for long. Staying for just a few days to visit his parents, he quickly took off for Los Angeles to be with Maggie Johnson.*

Down in L.A. Clint trudged through a series of day-to-day jobs until he landed a full-time one managing a building on Oakhurst Drive, several miles south of Beverly Hills, which he supplemented by working at a Signal Oil gas station. Hoping college credits would help him get a better job, he started taking classes in business administration at City College in downtown L.A., on the GI Bill. School still bored him, and just to break things up he sat in on a few acting seminars with Chuck Hill, one of many noncom show-business dreamers he had met at Fort Ord.

Hill was a gay man who had slipped through the screening processes of the wartime military. What would, years later, be known as the "don't ask, don't tell" philosophy was actually in full, if unofficial, effect in the 1950s. Even if homosexuals wanted to enter the military, the military wanted nothing to do with them, partly, as the bizarre thinking of the day went, because they wouldn't be able to fight as well among other males or control themselves in the communal shower rooms. Hill, who wanted a show-business career working behind the scenes, had spotted Clint and was struck by his good looks, and told him to look him up after his discharge, which Clint did while he was pumping gas.

Because this was Los Angeles, essentially a one-industry town, every college and university had drama and film departments superior to those of any other institution outside of L.A. At Los Angeles Community College (LACC) George Shdanoff was on the teaching staff. Shdanoff was a practitioner of the methods of Michael Chekhov, who in turn was a disciple of the Stanislavsky "Method" school of acting, and his was the class that Clint and Hill sat in on. Unfortunately, much

---

*A story keeps popping up that has Clint staying a bit longer, getting a Seattle girl pregnant, and borrowing money from his parents to pay for an abortion, all of which hastened his decision to get out of town, but no hard and detailed evidence of it can be found.

of what Shdanoff offered was wasted on Clint, who at the time was not all that introspective, an aspect crucial to the Method. Most of the time he just sat there among the more serious acting students who tried to absorb the daily theoretical lectures.

Meanwhile Clint reconnected with Maggie Johnson, who had relocated to Altadena, about ten miles out of L.A. in the San Bernardino mountains, with a spectacular view. There she had found a job as a manufacturer's representative for Industria Americana. They started seeing each other on a regular basis, and soon the subject of marriage came up. In early 1950s America "nice" girls only dated "good" men with an implied promise of a ring for their finger. With her solid upper-middle-class background, Maggie's choice of Clint as the one to fulfill her dreams might seem a bit odd, even more so because, by every account, she was the aggressor. Maggie was pretty, from a good family, and nothing like the easy women he had been with during his army stint. Marriage to the right girl was what he thought he was supposed to do. So he did it.

On December 19, 1953, Clinton Eastwood Jr. married Maggie Johnson in South Pasadena before a Congregational minister, the Reverend Henry David Grey. After a brief honeymoon in Carmel, Clint resumed his studies and his part-time gig at the filling station and Maggie went back to work. The only difference was that now she could properly move into Clint's small house on South Oakhurst.

Soon enough, though, Clint's new and quite normal life would take a dramatic and unexpected turn that had very little to do with married life but a whole lot to do with, of all things, making movies.

THREE

I had a premonition that acting might be a good thing for me. I had done some of it in school and little theaters in Oakland, but I never did take it seriously then. I got serious after a director talked to me about my chances.

—Clint Eastwood

Nineteen fifty-four was a pivotal year in American movies. Without question the explosive Marlon Brando as Terry Malloy in Elia Kazan's *On the Waterfront* made a huge mark on the popular mores of American male youth. Brando would win the Best Actor Oscar for his indelible performance and change forever the notion of what a movie leading man could look like, sound like, behave like, and be. The role as written may not have been earth-shattering—it had classic Hollywood plot devices of attempting to change the world while managing to win the heart of the prettiest girl in the neighborhood. But the way Brando brought it to life on the screen surely was.

In the aftermath of Brando's performance, Hollywood saw a policy shift in the casting departments of the major studios. Now they all wanted their leading men to be beautiful but rebellious American youths. At first this policy would work against Clint, who was cool and laid back more than burning and restless. But Brando's youth and brooding appeal would nevertheless lay the foundation for Clint's unique brand of hero, even as the young, handsome gas station attendant with only the slightest interest in acting and even less in the movies was about to be discovered by the men who made the movies.

The details surrounding Clint's signing with Universal Pictures have always been murky, in numerous slightly differing (and at times overlappingly repetitious) accounts of the actual events. Clint himself has remained vague even about the details of what attracted him to the movie business. One reason is his natural reticence to talk about his personal life, but perhaps he also wishes, maybe needs, to take the focus off the overly eager women, the gay men, and the singularly opportunistic "suits" who helped launch his career.

What is certain is that, as 1954 began, Clint was attending classes at LACC while working at the gas station, and Maggie was continuing at her full-time job and earning additional income doing part-time modeling work. Also that Arthur Lubin, a short, stubby, hustling con-tract director at Universal—best known at the time for his insanely popular Abbott and Costello films and the *Francis the Talking Mule* series—was looking for someone to help boost his standing at the stu-dio. He needed a project or a star that would help him up the prestige-and-profit ladder. According to Lubin, "Someone took me to meet Clint at the gas station." Very likely it was Chuck Hill, looking to secure a position at Universal as well and figuring that Lubin might be interested in Clint and return the favor.

Under the shrewd machinations of Lew Wasserman, Universal had moved into TV production earlier than most of the other major stu-dios. They were still trying to compete with television, an increas-ingly losing proposition, rather than become a profitable partner in it. In the early 1950s Wasserman had created a self-contained TV unit, called Revue, to produce shows exclusively for the small screen. To find, train, and develop new young talent to appear on television (something most major motion picture stars were still reluctant to do), Wasserman approved the creation of the Universal Talent School (UTS), offering in-house "acting" classes run by coach Sophie Rosen-stein. The school's mandate was to discover new talent, to bring young actors up to professional speed, and when they were ready, to sign them to the studio at relatively cheap and long-term contracts and use them either in movies (part of the lure) or, more likely, in TV.

UTS was not all that easy to get into. Admission was determined by a complex multiaudition process. Only two applicants were allowed to audition every day, and only the best were even awarded a screen test. A handful were picked to attend the school and of those about one in sixty were actually given a Universal contract for up to $150 a week, for which they were to appear in whatever productions they were assigned.

Lubin insisted that the school give Clint an immediate audition, even though he was not exactly the next Brando the studio was look-ing for; an intense actor who gave off a lot of heat fueled by his repres-sive darkness. Clint had none of it. Nor was he the usual beautiful, romantic type that the studio could always use as screen filler and never seemed to find enough of who had some actual talent, like Rock Hudson and Tony Curtis.

Moreover, Clint had no real experience as an actor. He didn't know how to move like a movie performer, how to react, how to talk, how to "think" for the camera, or how to smile for a close-up. The smile thing was a special problem; Clint's teeth were yellow, too small, and curved inward, which caused him to smile with his lips closed—something the movie camera did not show well. Too good-looking to be a character actor but not good-looking enough to be a traditional leading man (according to the conventional studio wisdom), he was the least likely prospect for a screen test.

But somehow Lubin made it happen. When Clint saw his audition film, he knew immediately how badly he had come off. "I thought I was an absolute clod. It looked pretty good, it was photographed well, but I thought, 'If that's acting, I'm in trouble.' " Nonetheless, seventeen days later Universal signed him to a provisional seven-year learning contract starting at $75 a week.

He quit his gas station job and began taking full-time classes at UTS. To his surprise, these lessons—essentially teaching how to look good in front of a camera without tripping over your own feet (or your lines)—were infinitely more valuable to him than had been the internal agonies of his Michael Chekhov–based acting-class theoreticals. All of it meant nothing to him.

Besides taking classes, Clint worked out at the studio gym and kept his eye on the gorgeous young starlets all over the place. All the young female students of the UTS, he quickly found out, were single, hot, and available. According to one of them, wannabe sex kitten and B-movie starlet Mamie Van Doren, a demi-Monroe whose career never fully blossomed (she would appear with Clint in Charles Haas's 1956 *Star in the Dust*, in which she was the costar, he a walk-on), sex was rampant among the students, and she and Clint had spent more than one afternoon in her dressing room contributing to the count.

Clint, who had thus far refused to get his teeth fixed or darken his brown hair (to match Hudson's and Curtis's blue-black), had no problem attracting and sleeping with many starlets besides Van Doren. As far as he was concerned, he had no reason not to, least of all his marriage. Now in this new world of plenty, his marriage was, to him, like being on a diet in the biggest candy store in the world. Years later Clint would tell one writer that "the first year of marriage was terrible. If

I had to go through it again, I think I'd be a bachelor for the rest of my life. I liked doing things when I wanted to do them. I did not want any interference . . . One thing Meg [Maggie] had to learn about me was that I was going to do as I pleased. She had to accept that, because if she didn't, we wouldn't be married."

In a rare interview in 1971 Maggie seemed to confirm Clint's continuing independence when she described his behavior this way: "He is very much a twentieth-century cowboy. We're not advocates of the total togetherness theory. I happen to like women with their own thing. I admire individuality and am not of the theory that 'I'll be an individual and you stay home.' " Whether out of choice or necessity, she had found a way to rationalize what both of them instinctively knew; that for Clint the notion of marital fidelity never held much sway. That he came home at all was what mattered to Maggie, and sooner or later he always did. Still, the unspoken-of friction it caused between them was palpable. Maggie, raised to be a traditional wife, understandably did not take easily to her husband spending his days among young and beautiful and (she suspected) easy girls in the glamorous world of sexy movie make-believe, with nothing to show for it—at least nothing she could see.

When he wasn't sneaking off with one starlet or another, Clint passed the time on the lot walking among the soundstages, where he'd often run into other recently signed actors, like John Saxon, Marty Milner, and David Janssen, his buddies from Fort Ord. The four would-be actors enjoyed hanging out at the studio in the daytime and in local bars at night; and occasionally on weekends, when the gas station called, he went back and filled in for a day or two, as he was always in need of extra cash.

In class, Clint's teacher Katherine Warren was joined by Jack Kosslyn, who brought in a parade of famous actors, including the great Brando himself, whose mere presence was a thrill and whose message to the students was not to try to "act," but just to get on the soundstage and let "it" happen (whatever "it" was supposed to be). Something and someone had, at last, made sense to Clint, and he concentrated on his acting with a seriousness and intensity he had not shown before.

By May 1954 he was considered good enough to try for a real film, at an increased salary of $100 a week. At the same time he signed with a manager-agent, none other than Arthur Lubin, who was eager to get Clint out of the classrooms and into some films. The first picture Lubin wanted him to try out for was *Six Bridges to Cross*, which would be the first for the brooding, ethnic, East Coast, and utterly charming newcomer Sal Mineo. But despite Lubin's enthusiasm, *Bridges's* director, forty-four-year-old Joseph Pevney, was not impressed with Clint, dismissing him as a nonactor; despite Lubin's pushing, Pevney refused to use Clint even in any background shots. In truth Pevney, like most of the directors at Universal, thought the talent school concept was a dumb throwback to the days when studios and training *mattered*. Journeymen like Pevney did not want the studio to supply him with students for his film; he preferred *real* actors.

Lubin continued to try to get Clint a part in any film, even as he worked on a number of other, peripheral studio assignments. Lubin was, at the time, busy in postproduction on his latest talking-mule franchise, *Francis in the Navy*. He used Clint's voice for some looping (overdubbing) and put him in a few crowd scenes, along with Milner and Janssen. Despite his microscopic participation, Lubin gave Clint on-screen billing, his name appearing at the end of the back-of-the-film cast list.

Not until May 1954 did Clint make his film debut as a real character in a real part (still uncredited), in actor-turned-director Jack Arnold's *Revenge of the Creature* (1955),* a sequel to his unexpectedly huge hit of the year before, *Creature from the Black Lagoon*, which no doubt benefited from the big-screen hot fad of the time, 3-D. In his only scene as a lab technician, opposite the film's star—western, war, and horror film staple (and former husband of Shirley Temple) John Agar—Clint's unnamed character discovers a missing rat that has conveniently parked itself in his lab coat.

The scene was shot in a single day (July 30, 1954) and was the first of a series of nondescript studio-assigned parts that included a role as "First Saxon" in the borderline sexploitation flick *Lady Godiva of Coventry*† (directed by Arthur Lubin, starring Maureen O'Hara and Rex Reason); in *Tarantula* (1955), another Jack Arnold film, Clint

---

*Year of release. Unless otherwise indicated, all dates of films are release rather than production dates.

†Aka *21st Century Lady Godiva*.

played an air force pilot assigned to kill the giant, irradiated insect-gone-wild. He got a half-minute of screen time playing a laboratory assistant, in service to Rock Hudson, in *Never Say Goodbye*, a 1956 medical melodrama about an insanely jealous doctor (directed by Jerry Hopper, featuring Janssen in a solid supporting role.)* Hopper suggested to Clint that he wear glasses to help him create a character, in the time-honored notion of no small parts, only small actors. The suggestion, and the attention given to Clint in his relatively tiny screen appearance, made Hudson furious. Always an insecure actor, Hudson insisted that his character—a doctor, after all—should be the one to wear the glasses.

Clint then did two more blink-and-you-miss-him roles, one in Pevney's 1956 star vehicle for granite-faced Jeff Chandler, *Away All Boats* (Pevney was incensed at having been forced this time by the studio to use Clint, who is barely visible in the film—in one scene he calls for a "medic"), and a bit-bit in Charles Haas's *Star in the Dust* (1956), a western starring Agar. "They made a lot of cheapies in those days, a lot of B pictures," Clint later recalled. "I'd always play the young lieutenant or the lab technician who came in and said, 'He went that way,' or 'This happened,' or 'Doctor, here are the X-rays,' and he'd say, 'Get lost, kid,' I'd go out, and that would be the end of it."

Over the course of eighteen months, Clint received good reports that had resulted in an increased salary of $125 a week. But on October 23, 1955, he was unexpectedly and unceremoniously let go by Universal because, the executives said, he just didn't have the right look. They especially objected to his teeth and a rather prominently protruding Adam's apple. Janssen was also let go, because of his receding hairline and distracting facial tics (which would serve him well in his portrayal of Richard Kimble on the 1960s classic TV series *The Fugitive*). The studio also released a young Brando look-alike who, unfortunately, they felt couldn't act his way out of a paper bag, or control his real rage and channel it effectively onto the screen, an unknown by the name of Burt Reynolds.

After their dismissals, Reynolds and Clint went out to the parking

---

*It was a remake of *This Love of Ours* (1945), directed by William Dieterle and starring Claude Rains in the role now handed to Hudson.

lot together and found that Burt's name on his reserved space was already being stenciled over for western TV series up-and-comer Clu Gulager. Clint's was still there. "Don't worry," Burt said to Clint. "I may learn to act someday, but you'll never get rid of that Adam's apple."

Clint was not prepared for this unexpected turn of events. He had been sure he had a future at Universal, so sure that he and Maggie moved to better quarters. The Villa Sands, at 4040 Arch Drive, just off Ventura Boulevard, was close enough to the studio that Clint could walk to work on a slow day. The one-bedroom apartment offered a communal pool for its tenants to share; at $125 a month, a relatively expensive rental for California in the 1950s. Clint had heard about it through a couple of his UTS classmates who lived there, young starlets-in-the-making Gia Scala and Lili Kardell.

Soon after Clint moved in, Bill Thompkins came down from Seattle and took an efficiency in the complex, as did Bob Daley, who'd moved to L.A. via Chicago, Texas, and California and was currently working at Universal's budget department dealing with production schedules and costs. Daley and Clint had met before, at the studio, but now, as neighbors, became friends and joined the Villa Sands–Universal youthful associate social scene, where no one was over twenty-eight, everyone was good-looking, loose, and into jazz that played all day, thanks to a phonograph someone had rigged at one end of the pool.

Needing work, Clint went back to day jobs, mostly digging swimming pools and other such work, all of it off the books so he could collect unemployment. He auditioned for the other studios, using a scene from Sidney Kingsley's *Detective Story*, which he had practiced at UTS, playing the part that Kirk Douglas had done in the film version.

For Clint, neither a sentimentalist nor an especially high achiever at this point, that might have been it for him and the movies, had it not been for the incessant drive of Arthur Lubin, who remained steadfast in his belief that he could do for Clint Eastwood what director Douglas Sirk had done for Rock Hudson. Eight of Sirk's biggest 1950s films had featured Hudson, beginning when the actor was still an unknown contract player as the romantic lead opposite Piper Laurie in *Has Anybody Seen My Gal?* (1952). By the time they had made their last movie together, *The Tarnished Angels* (1958), Hudson was a major Hollywood star.*

Lubin, who did not have the success or the talent of Sirk, admired him less for his movies than for his relationship (whatever it might have been) with Hudson. Lubin believed that he too could become an important director working with the right actor, and that Clint was that actor. Likely Lubin's attraction to Clint had as much to do with his being gay as with his opinion of Clint's abilities. Homosexuality was not unusual in Hollywood. (Both Hudson and Sirk were gay, although there is no evidence that they were ever actually involved.) But in the simplest terms Lubin wanted to continue his professional association with Clint (who had shown no signs of being anything but a raging heterosexual) as a way to remain relevant in his life while making both of them stars.

Meanwhile, Maggie suffered a life-threatening bout of hepatitis. Because she and Clint had no medical insurance, it hit them hard financially as well as emotionally. He continued to dig ditches for swimming pools and, thanks to Lubin's unerring drive, landed a couple of minor TV bits—too small to actually be called parts—that helped him get by. His motorcycle abilities got him a quick shot on *Highway Patrol*, a vehicle for Broderick Crawford that introduced the aging Academy Award–winning actor to television viewers. Crawford, an alcoholic, had a habit of trimming his lines down to a sentence or two because he couldn't memorize them or easily read them off cue cards. Clint had only one quick scene with him but it was enough for him to realize how excessive most dialogue really was (despite the negative reason for it in this case). And, although his part was minuscule, Clint actually received a piece of fan mail.

He landed a bit in another series, *TV Reader's Digest*, based on the popular magazine, but that was it. After Maggie's recovery, money was so tight that she had to return quickly to her day job and take on addi-

---

*The eight films were *Has Anybody Seen My Gal?*, *Taza, Son of Cochise* (aka *Son of Cochise*) (1954), *Magnificent Obsession* (1954), *Captain Lightfoot* (1955), *All That Heaven Allows* (1955), *Never Say Goodbye* (1956; Sirk was uncredited, Hopper was listed as the official director), *Battle Hymn* (1957), and *The Tarnished Angels*. After *Imitation of Life* (1959) Sirk retired under circumstances that remain unclear and permanently moved to Switzerland.

tional part-time work doing showroom modeling of bathing suits; the long hours wreaked havoc on her feet. She also managed to find occasional TV work as living wallpaper for Jimmy Durante's semiregular popular Sunday-night variety show.

Meanwhile Clint's only link to show business, Lubin, often took him to dinner when Maggie had to work late and invited him to informally join his social entourage of mostly gay companions.

At the end of 1956, when his initial contract with Lubin was up, Clint opted to let it expire, for a reason that even Lubin could not argue with: nothing was happening in his career. Clint replaced Lubin with Irving Leonard, whom he had met during his time at Universal and who, leaving the studio, had become a business manager specializing in actors who needed help handling their finances. Leonard often found parts for his clients who didn't have agents, including a grateful Clint. Since in Hollywood someone could be poor one day and rich the next, Leonard could sign unknowns and bank on them while also banking for them. Leonard had noticed Clint at Universal, and when the young actor approached him, Leonard took him on. Soon afterward Leonard landed a position at Gang, Tyre & Brown (later Gang, Tyre, Ramer & Brown), a law firm that specialized in film clients, and brought Clint along with him. Once he had settled in, Leonard hooked Clint up with Ruth and Paul Marsh, who ran a small PR firm for actors and actresses that included a fair share of wannabes.

Lubin, meanwhile, disappointed and maybe even a little heartbroken, was determined to find a way to get Clint back, or at least to have him around. In the summer of 1956 Lubin landed his next assignment, at RKO, directing *The First Traveling Saleslady* and he quickly offered Clint a small part. It paid him little money but was his chance to get back into films.*

The First Traveling Saleslady was a western comedy starring Ginger Rogers, Carol Channing, Barry Nelson, and the up-and-coming James Arness. (Arness's friendship with John Wayne would result in his landing the starring role, after Wayne turned it down, in what would become the longest-running TV western series, *Gunsmoke*.) It was by far Clint's biggest movie role to date, with a couple of comedy bits and

---

*Clint received $750 for the film.

service as a love interest for Rogers. Clint had no use for the script, had no sense of comedy, and didn't particularly like to play "love" roles, but when Lubin told him that after seeing the daily rushes, RKO was considering offering him a player contract, he was encouraged.

The contract never materialized, but Lubin did get another part for Clint—his fourth with Lubin—in his next film for RKO, *Escapade in Japan*, essentially an adventure movie intended for children. This time Clint played a soldier named, of all things, Dumbo, who leads two young boys on a runaway trip to Japan. The film almost didn't open because prior to its release the cash-strapped studio was sold. Ironically, *Escapade* eventually reached theaters through a distribution agreement with Universal. But it made little difference which studio released the film; it was a complete failure at the box office.

With no prospects Clint, desperately in need of cash, this time took a weekend job as a sweeper at the Mode Furniture Factory in South L.A. while continuing to dig swimming pools during the week. As 1958 bled into 1959, he got an audition for *The Spirit of St. Louis*, the story of Charles Lindbergh's 1927 heroic solo transatlantic flight. Called in to try out, Clint was optimistic about his chances, believing he physically resembled the real Lindbergh; but when he arrived, he found himself among hundreds of Lindbergh look-alikes. The role eventually went to Jimmy Stewart, who was twice as old as Lindbergh. Nonetheless Stewart could command the lead because he was a star. That was the kind of world Hollywood was, a world built on star power, a world Clint really wasn't a part of.

He next landed a minor supporting role in William Wellman's *Lafayette Escadrille,** conceived as a swan-song reflection of Wellman's own life both in the military and in motion pictures. Wellman, known as "Wild Bill" for his aviator heroics during World War I, was a veteran director whose career reached all the way back to the silent era, highlighted by his direction of 1927's *Wings*, winner of the first Oscar for Best Picture by the newly formed Academy of Motion Picture Arts and Sciences. The film looked to be one of the bigger releases of 1958 after hot new actor Paul Newman was rumored to have signed on to play Thad Walker, the Wellman-like lead. Newman, however, decided at

---

*Aka *C'est la Guerre*, aka *Hell Bent for Glory* (UK), aka *With You in My Arms*.

the last minute to pass in favor of playing Brick in Richard Brooks's film version of Tennessee Williams's *Cat on a Hot Tin Roof.* Wellman had difficulty replacing Newman; finally Warner, the studio that was producing the film, pushed contract player Tab Hunter on him. Wellman had originally picked Clint out of a cattle-call audition (the only way he could get into any studios in those days), principally because Wellman felt he would play well in a supporting role behind Newman. But against the weaker Hunter, Clint was too imposing. His role went instead to a smaller and darker actor, none other than David Janssen. Clint wound up as part of the background, living scenery with no dialogue. This film too went nowhere and did nothing to advance Clint's marginal career.

So it was back to digging more pools. Increasingly he spent his nights at a local bar among friends and on at least one occasion venting his frustrations by getting into a pretty nasty brawl. Clint could take care of himself, and from all accounts the other guy came off much worse.

Not long afterward Clint, via Leonard, heard about a cheapie independent that was being made at 20th Century–Fox's facilities (they would produce but not distribute the film) by first-time director Jodie Copelan, a post–Civil War action movie called *Ambush at Cimarron Pass.* Clint tried out for and landed the part of one of the villains, an ex-soldier loyal to the South. He got paid $750 for it; the lead, career villain Scott Brady, cast here as the hero, managed to get $25,000. For some reason Copelan wanted Brady, even if his high fee ate into production values, like extras to fill out the vapid wide screen. And horses, the lack of which made the film, ostensibly a western, look a bit odd. (A plot line was developed that they had been stolen by thieves, which might have made a pretty good film.) After the film opened, Clint got a positive single-line review in *Variety*—"fine portrayals also come from Margia Dean, Frank Gerstle, and Clint Eastwood"—but the film was a bomb. Later on Clint would describe *Ambush at Cimarron* as "the lousiest western ever made."

With nothing happening in his film career, Clint gave serious thought to returning to college full time, getting a degree in something, anything, and then finding a steady job with decent pay. Still, he couldn't completely give up trying to make it in the movies and signed up for more acting lessons (a thriving storefront business in Hollywood, then and now). Mostly these classes were like health clubs for actors, a place to work out with a scene or a monologue to keep the chops tight. One of Clint's classmates, Floyd Simmons, who was also a casual friend from the studio, suggested to Clint that he needed a better agent, and sent him to his own, Bill Shiffrin, who signed him.

Shiffrin specialized in "beefcake," brawny good-looking young men who could play romantic leads in B-movies without looking too ridiculous when they tried to "act." A bent-nose kind of guy who prided himself on being able to handle himself in a rough situation (as the actors he repped did on-screen), Shiffrin represented Vince Edwards and Bob Mathias. (Edwards, dark and angry-looking, would eventually gain fame on TV as Ben Casey, a dark and angry-looking doctor.) Mathias had won the Olympic gold medal in the decathlon in London in 1948 and again in Helsinki in 1952 (the only person at the time to ever accomplish that feat); in 1954 he'd starred in a film about his own early life, Francis D. Lyon's *The Bob Mathias Story*, in which he played himself. Before he knew it, a film career, if not a star, was born. He knocked around B-films for a few years, proving to everyone that he had no acting ability whatsoever, then turned to politics and served four terms as a Republican congressman for California's San Joaquin Valley.

Through the grapevine of agents, Shiffrin had heard about a new one-hour western series that CBS was planning, to follow up on the enormous ratings success of *Gunsmoke*. *Gunsmoke* had begun as a radio drama in 1952, a creation of producer-writer-developer Charles Marquis "Bill" Warren, director Norman MacDonnell, and writer John Meston. Put on the air by CBS head William Paley, it quickly became a sensation. *Gunsmoke* spawned dozens of similar "adult" westerns on all three networks. CBS wanted to find another one just as good (and just as profitable).

The producer of the new series, Robert Sparks, an executive at CBS in charge of filmed programming, and principal writer Warren began the search for an actor who could make the series his own. Casting was crucial to a TV series's success, more than a film's, because of its recurring nature. The right star, like Arness, could make a bad series. The wrong star could kill a good one.

In the new series, each season a bunch of wranglers would move a herd of cattle north, and the episodes would tell the stories of their adventures during the journey. The format was already in use quite successfully on NBC's *Wagon Train*, in which passengers moved every season from the East Coast to the West. Paley wanted something that combined *Gunsmoke*'s drama with *Wagon Train*'s expanse.

Neither Sparks nor Warren was a newcomer to series TV. Warren, who had had the original idea for *Gunsmoke*, had met and to some extent been mentored by the great American writer F. Scott Fitzgerald while in college at Maryland, where he made All-American as a football player, when Fitzgerald was living in the area. Heavily influenced by the romance of Fitzgerald's addictive personality, Warren became a heavy drinker and a barroom tough guy, neither of which got him anywhere in school. Upon graduation in 1934, Warren took off for Hollywood (à la Fitzgerald), determined to break into the film industry and make a name for himself, to succeed where Fitzgerald had failed. After service in World War II as a navy commander, he found success as a pulpy western serial writer for *The Saturday Evening Post*. Many of his stories were adapted and made into novels, and some into movies. Forever in need of money (and booze), Warren moved into television, where he became a favorite of Bill Paley, the chairman and founder of CBS. After conceiving *Gunsmoke*, Warren could do no wrong, and the new series was his for the asking.

He had originally called his new pilot script *The Outrider*, but Paley rejected the title, believing no one would know what it meant except outriders (the cowboys who rode outside a herd and kept it moving). Instead he suggested *Rawhide*, a meaningless term—a strip of leather— that had been the title of a successful 1951 Henry Hathaway western that starred Tyrone Power. Paley liked it because it immediately evoked "western" to him and also because a lot of what eventually became *Wagon Train* on TV had been loosely based on the original story of that film.

Robert Sparks, as a program executive, had specialized in westerns, most notably 1957's slick and highly entertaining *Have Gun—Will*

Travel, a Saturday-night half-hour hit show starring movie veteran Richard Boone in the role of Paladin, the intellectually superior, highly cultured gun-for-hire. Paley assigned Sparks to work with Warren on the proposed new series.

Warren, for his part, had just directed a feature film called *Cattle Empire* (1958), written by his frequent partner and co-writer (Warren was uncredited), Hungarian émigré Endre Bohem. It was about the troubles of life on a cattle drive and starred Joel McCrea, one of Hollywood's best-known and best-liked cowboy heroes. The film owed a lot to Howard Hawks's great *Red River* (1948), which starred John Wayne and Walter Brennan and made young Montgomery Clift a star.

Warren was a big fan of Clift's style of acting, soft-spoken and good-looking, tough but not bullying, and sensitive in a youthful and appealing way. Knowing that Clift, now one of the biggest (and most difficult) actors in Hollywood, would not do TV, Warren wanted an actor who captured Clift's qualities in *Red River* to balance off the tough, grizzled leader of the drives, Gil Favor, to be played by Eric Fleming, thirty-four years old and properly grizzled. He resembled a young Ben Gazzara with his face swollen after a fistfight. Heavier and a couple of inches taller than Clint, his acting style was thought of in Hollywood as less Method than maniac. Once cast in the role, he believed he *was* Gil Favor.

As Sparks and Warren continued their search for an actor who could support Fleming, Shiffrin believed there might be something in *Rawhide* for his new client, Clint Eastwood. Unknown to him, Clint was already on the trail of the show via a young woman he'd known from back in his Universal days. Sonia Chernus was a former script reader for Arthur Lubin who now did that same job for him at CBS. She was one of the few women Clint associated with during that period who became a friend rather than a lover. She had met and become friends with Maggie as well.

Perhaps Clint was aware of *Rawhide* through Lubin; perhaps Chernus heard about it and thought of him; or perhaps Clint had been sniffing around Lubin's new production setup at the network, where Lubin had made it clear Clint was always welcome, in the hopes of finding some acting work. Whatever the actual details were (no one, including Clint, seems to remember exactly), Chernus managed to convince Sparks—who had seen hundreds of actors and was frustrated at not being able to find a costar for *Rawhide*—to at least see Clint for a few minutes.

The meeting, spontaneous and casual, took place in the CBS hallway, with Chernus standing between the two men as they briefly spoke. Sparks asked Clint what specifically he had done. Clint mentioned a few projects, including *Ambush at Cimarron Pass*. He was relieved when Sparks said he hadn't seen it but worried when Sparks said he would take a look at it as soon as possible.

Sparks casually asked Clint how tall he was, and Clint told him he was six foot four. Sparks then invited him into his office, while Chernus remained outside. Sparks introduced Clint to Charles Warren. They talked for a while about *Rawhide* and how they saw it with two leads, one younger, one older. When the meeting ended, both Sparks and Warren promised to take a look at *Ambush at Cimarron Pass* (something that could not have made Clint happy) and get in touch with his agent, Shiffrin, sometime that week. Chernus, who was waiting outside in the hallway, walked Clint back outside to his car and told him to relax, hang loose, that she would let him know as soon as she heard something.

Later that same day Clint received a call from Shiffrin saying he had heard from Sparks and Warren. They weren't interested in screening the film but did want to screen-test him for the younger lead, Rowdy Yates, as soon as possible. The next day Clint found himself back at CBS. He was sent to wardrobe to be outfitted in western garb, introduced to Fleming, and given a scene to study.

After Clint left, Sparks and Warren watched the screen test dozens of times. Warren liked the similarities he saw in Clint's audition to Clift's performance in *Red River*. Sparks, however, was less impressed and was leaning toward another actor, Bing Russell. CBS executive Hubbell Robinson, in charge of all the network's programming, had been sent from New York City by Paley specifically to sit in on all the casting decisions for *Rawhide*; he had the final say and sided with Warren, believing Clint was the right actor to play Rowdy Yates.*

*Neil "Bing" Russell, the father of actor Kurt Russell, was later cast as Deputy Clem Foster in *Bonanza*, a role he played from 1961 until the series ended a decade later.

A week later he got the phone call telling him the good news. Just like that, Clint had landed a starring role in a major network TV series. The first episode of *Rawhide*, "Incident of the Tumbleweed Wagon," aired at eight o'clock on Friday night, January 9, 1959, sandwiched between two of CBS's biggest winners, the enormously popular *Hit Parade* and *The Phil Silvers Show*.

Rawhide proved a smash in its first season. For the next seven years it was a staple of American weekly television viewing* and along the way made cathode-cowboy stars out of its two male leads.

---

*In its first full season the show was moved up to 7:30. In 1963 it was moved to Thursdays at 8:00. In 1964 it moved back to Fridays at 7:30. In 1965 it was moved to Tuesdays at 7:30.

FOUR

I was set to direct a segment of Rawhide *once in those days but it never came about. I think some other actor had tried and run way over budget so they wouldn't let me try.*

—Clint Eastwood

PREVIOUS PAGE: *As Rowdy Yates in* Rawhide

Whend Clint got his first look at the advance fall 1958 schedule of TV shows and didn't see *Rawhide* anywhere on it, he broke out in hives. Filming the first episodes had been a difficult and awkward process; everybody was just beginning to get to know one another, and the kinks were still being worked out of the characters and scripts. Worse, even after production began, the network couldn't make up its mind whether the show should be an hour or a half hour or even on the air at all. Warren had wanted a full hour and a half, which Paley might have actually gone for if Phil Silvers wasn't doing as well as he was in the coveted Friday-night prime-time nine o'clock slot.

In 1958, in what was supposed to have been *Rawhide*'s first season, a little less than one-third of all prime-time network TV shows (30 out of 108) were westerns; that was a problem. Advertisers felt the market was oversaturated and preferred a new genre of shows that was about to break big, crime and law-and-order programs. Nine one-hour episodes had been completed (the producers figured on the middle ground; one hour could easily be cut down to a half hour or expanded to ninety minutes); the network had spent a fortune shooting on location in Arizona; Warren had hired his old friend Andrew V. McLaglen (veteran film actor Victor McLaglen's son) to come in and direct a couple of episodes on a play-or-pay basis; and some of Hollywood's biggest, if slightly over-the-hill, movie stars, including Dan Duryea, Troy Donahue, Brian Donlevy, and Margaret O'Brien, appeared in guest roles. Yet the network remained divided over the fate of *Rawhide*.

Weeks of delay passed into months. Clint became notably frustrated as his big break seemed to be slipping away, and at times he was visibly angry. He'd be in a restaurant and in the middle of a conversation might clear the table with his arm, sending everything on it crashing to the ground. One night he had such a severe anxiety attack that ambulances came screaming up Ventura Boulevard to his home. When they arrived, they gave him a bag to breathe into until he was able to regain his equilibrium.

Other programs were offering Clint small parts, most of them arranged by Lubin, and he could have taken at least one major film role.* But by contract, he could not accept any other work on television or in the movies that CBS did not first approve, and they were stingy with their potential star-in-the-making. When the Broadway team of Howard Lindsay and Russel Crouse offered him the starring role in a big-screen adaptation of the novel *Tall Story*, the network forced him to turn it down. The role went instead to Tony Perkins.

For Christmas 1958 Clint and Maggie decided to take a train to Piedmont, to visit friends and his family who had moved back from Seattle. Clint was looking forward to the peace and quiet of the scenic ride, hoping to get away from everything. On the way, while on board the train, a telegram arrived for him stating that *Rawhide* had been put on the January replacement schedule and that on the first day of the new year he was to report for the resumption of production. Paley had overridden everyone else and insisted the show be added in a one-hour version to the midseason schedule. Clint whooped when he read the news, and then ordered a bottle of champagne for himself and Maggie. The celebration lasted the rest of the way to Piedmont.

On January 1 Clint joined the cast in Arizona, where the show's permanent outdoor set had been erected. Besides Rowdy Yates and Gil Favor, the series's other regular characters included an Indian scout, a cook, his helper, and some "grizzled" cowhands, as the production notes describe them. The scout was played by Sheb Wooley, an actor/country singer who had made an indelible impression as one of Frank Miller's gang of killers in Fred Zinnemann's iconic 1952 western *High Noon*. Wooley had worked for Warren before, and the two had become friends. Warren had insisted Wooley be given his part on the show. For the cook, Wishbone, intended as comic relief, Warren turned to Paul Brinegar, and as the cook's helper, Mushy, James

---

*Clint did get permission to play a navy lieutenant in a 1958 segment of *Navy Log* and appeared in an episode of *Maverick*, a top-rated TV western. The episode, "Duel at Sundown," was directed by Lubin, who pulled some strings at CBS to get them to let Clint appear.

Murdock. Steve Raines and Rocky Shahan became, respectively, cowhands Jim Quince and Joe Scarlett.

But perhaps the biggest single ingredient in making the show a hit was Dimitri Tiomkin's *Rawhide* theme. In the 1950s and 1960s, every TV show had to have identifiable theme music that opened and closed it under the credits. Many of these signature show themes went on to become pop-culture classics—*I Love Lucy's* bouncing Latin-tinged theme, the whistle at the beginning of *The Andy Griffith Show*, the brassy horns of *The Dick Van Dyke Show*, the thunderous theme of *Bonanza*, the high-stringed opening of *The Fugitive*, and the pulse-pounding Lalo Schifrin theme for *Mission Impossible*. Tiomkin's theme song for *High Noon* had won him and his writing partner Ned Washington a Best Song Oscar (while he won a solo Oscar for Best Score); now he reteamed with Washington to create the *Rawhide* theme, with its unforgettable "Roll 'em, roll 'em, roll 'em, keep those dogies rollin' . . . *Rawhiiide* . . . ," sung by Frankie Laine, sounding as if he were being dragged to the electric chair. The song was so energetically catchy, it became a hit single and helped make *Rawhide* a welcome weekly guest in living rooms across the country.

In the beginning, *Rawhide* was unquestionably Fleming's show. He was the star, hero, leader of the herders, narrator, and main interest of the story lines of many early episodes. Clint, meanwhile, played his mostly silent (at first) sidekick, rough, tough, cute, and slim, with a fast gun and faster fists. But as soon as the executives at CBS, especially William Paley, saw the first show, they knew they had found something special in their new leading man—not Fleming but Clint—who brought something to *Rawhide* that Fleming didn't, or couldn't: youthful appeal, in the new culture that had grown up in the aftermath of Brando, James Dean, and Elvis Presley. Young boys *and* girls quickly became the main demographic of the show, and Clint, not Fleming, was the reason. By the end of the first year his $600-a-week salary was doubled, and by the end of the show's run he was making six figures annually.

After his second season on *Rawhide*, Clint felt secure enough in CBS's projection of a long run that he bought a house in Sherman Oaks near Beverly Glen Boulevard—a vast improvement in neigh-·borhood and living quarters, and with a pool all his own. Maggie retired from her various jobs and devoted herself to turning their new house into a real home. But even with paintings, photos, and furniture, one essential of their new life was missing for her. Married seven years now, Maggie was, at her husband's insistence, still childless.

At least one reason may have been psychological. Clint told biographer Richard Schickel that the lingering insecurity of being a Depression baby, of having to watch his parents struggle to keep food on the table and clothes on their backs, had affected all the Eastwoods. The sentiments sound genuine, but his star was on the rise, and money, fame, and stability tend to allow one to conquer one's childhood fears and rages. While Clint's fears may have been so deeply embedded that physical security could never adequately make up for what he lacked in childhood (a childhood that wasn't all *that* bad, considering the times), more likely, something was fundamentally wrong with the marriage.

Despite his newfound fame, money, and home, Clint's sexual appetites remained unchecked and unclassifiable; the only measure of morality he understood or was willing (or perhaps able) to respect was discretion. In a February 1974 *Playboy* magazine interview, Clint indirectly alluded to an understanding between him and "Mags" (or "Mag" as he sometimes called her) about the special openness of their marriage. The *Playboy* interviewer, film critic Arthur Knight, asked Clint about his "fairly open relationship with Mag," to which he replied, "Sure. Oh, yeah, we've always had—I'd hate to say I'm a pioneer with women's lib or whatever, but we've always had an agreement that she could enter any kind of business she wanted to. We never had that thing about staying home and taking care of the house. There's always a certain respect for the individual in our relationship; we're not one person. She's an individual, I'm an individual, and we're friends . . . I'm not shooting orders to her on where she's supposed to be every five minutes, and I don't expect her to shoot them at me." When asked if he preferred blondes like Maggie, Clint replied, "For marriage, no. For fooling around, sure, fooling around a little, hanky-panky, you know, sitting in the saloon with that old patter, 'Do you come here often' . . . I think friendship is important. Everybody talks about love in marriage, but it's just as important to be friends."

If this sounded a bit disingenuous, it's because Clint was fairly certain Mags would never talk in public about such things. Instead, a combination of denial and rationale served as her survival mechanism. At least part of the problem was that his new success allowed Clint to slide into the saddle of the emerging sexual zeitgeist of the 1960s, while Maggie remained firmly planted in the uptight culture of the 1950s. Nonetheless, each satisfied some need in the other that allowed them, despite Clint's indiscretions, to continue to operate as a couple, as parents without children, as friends, or perhaps more accurately, as parents to each other.

As Clint's star continued to rise, one relationship that he had no interest or need in maintaining was with Bill Shiffrin. Once Clint had gotten what he wanted from Shiffrin, as with Lubin, he simply—some might say coldly—moved on. After all, Shiffrin had benefited from Clint's being hired to play Rowdy Yates rather than actually causing it to happen. Clint replaced him with Lester Salkow, an agent with a strong relationship to Universal, where Clint hoped eventually to move back into feature films.

But Salkow quickly proved to be more a figurehead than a power agent. Clint soon discovered where the real power lay in Hollywood's emerging post-studio era: the entertainment lawyers, who were increasingly playing the role of both manager and agent for their clients. Soon enough Clint attached Frank Wells to his expanding team of representatives. Both Leonard and Wells were up-and-coming Hollywood-based lawyers, and as soon as they connected with Clint, they edged out Salkow and took over virtually every aspect of his career. They financially restructured his income so that he could legally keep considerably more money for himself and pay less in taxes. They arranged salary deferments and the purchase of extensive and still relatively cheap land in Northern California, mostly in Monterey County, including land in Carmel, a still underpopulated area that Clint especially liked.

Leonard was primarily the moneyman, while Wells handled career decisions. Leonard arranged to have all of Clint's income sent directly to him; he then dispensed what was needed for expenses, mostly to Maggie, who had taken over full-time management of the Eastwood household. Having retired from her "career," such as it was, and having to deal with Clint's increasingly long absences, it was a bit of a relief for her. She also developed an intense interest in tennis. To accommodate Clint, Leonard reportedly kept two sets of books, one for the IRS and one for Maggie, so she would remain unaware of how much money Clint spent pursuing other women.

Meanwhile Clint's fame was growing. He appeared on the cover of *TV Guide* several times, a sure sign of his entrance into the pantheon of TV royalty, sometimes alone and sometimes with Eric Fleming. Clint was always happy when he didn't have to share the cover with Fleming, with whom it was widely believed he did not get along particularly well. They were never close, never buddies, did not travel in the same social circles, and did not share the same off-screen interests. Moreover, Fleming was fighting his career's downward slope, even as its highlight was *Rawhide*. Clint, on the other hand, was on the way up, which did not sit well with Fleming.

Adding to their strained relationship, series television then, as now, was and is a grind, rather like baseball's endless summers. No matter how much money he made, or how much extracurricular freedom it allowed him, Clint was still tied to a long workweek. Each season's production schedule commenced in late July and did not finish until April, with frequent location trips. And playing the same character week after week, season after season, year after year, was unavoidably tedious.

After a long run in a series, audiences, as well as performers, tend to get trapped in a syndrome of expectations difficult to break. Clint instinctively understood this trap and was constantly trying to stretch the relatively rigid parameters of the character of Rowdy Yates; at the same time Frank Wells was hard at work trying to convince Universal to let Clint appear in movies during the show's off-season. The network, however, continually turned all offers down, not wanting to have audiences see Clint Eastwood as anyone but Rowdy Yates.

The network was loath to tinker with the show's successful formula and kept its brand-name characters and the actors who played them on a tight rein. They also saw to it that no one director became too valuable to the series (meaning too expensive). So the producers regularly chose from an informal team of TV (and occasional movie) journeymen that they kept in a steady rotation. They believed this system further diminished the chance of any stylistic flourishes and therefore potentially damaging digressions. Each director was given a shooting script with pre-directions written into it—when to cut, when to pan, when to push in, when to pull out. Rather than creative directors, they were, in effect, formulaic technicians, required to closely follow the formula and the format.

The writing too was formulaic. Very little was ever revealed about the lead characters' backstories. Eventually it did come out that Rowdy had been in the Confederate army, spent time in a northern prison, and was starting a new life as a herder. But there was never a lot of information given about any of the characters because, the producers felt, it wasn't germane to the self-contained week-to-week story lines of the show.

While the network held firm and did not let Clint take any movie work (or appear on any other CBS shows as a guest in contemporary clothing, such as *The Jack Benny Show*), Universal did manage to hire him out to play live rodeos, along with Sheb Wooley (substituting for Fleming, who refused to do them), who had had some rodeo experience in his years before becoming an actor, and Paul Brinegar. Together they put on a little skit with some singing and dancing. Both Wooley and Clint could sing well enough to pull it off, and they were quickly able to master the dancing, mostly some fake rope twirling. Audiences, mostly kids, flocked to see Rowdy Yates (not Clint Eastwood) in person. Clint and Wooley each received $1,500 per show.*

The other thing Clint was allowed to do was to make a 45-rpm single recording. A lot of the stars of 1950s and 1960s shows made records, and perhaps the most successful was Edd "Kookie" Byrnes of *77 Sunset Strip*, who had an improbable hit with "Kookie, Kookie (Lend Me Your Comb)," at once the high-water mark and the drowning point of Byrnes's relatively short-lived stardom. In 1961 Clint recorded "Unknown Girl" (backed with a cover version of a 1950s pop tune, "For All We Know"). The recording did well enough to get Clint an album deal, *Rawhide's Clint Eastwood Sings Cowboy Favorites*. Recorded on the Cameo Records label, the album featured Clint in a cowboy outfit on the front and back, without identifying his character as Rowdy Yates. The breathless back liner notes read in part:

*Reports vary as to the actual amount. Schickel, who presumably heard it directly from Clint, reported it as $1,500. Patrick McGilligan said $15,000. Considering that rodeo money has always been notoriously modest to performers, Schickel's figure is more likely the correct one.

The folk song that truly represents a branch of American culture is the western cowboy song. Ever since courageous Americans crossed the prairies, western songs have been popular. And there is no better pro- totype of that "cowboy" than Cameo/Parkway's recording artist, Clint Eastwood, a "native" westerner and a "natural" performer.

This album represents a collection of songs closely identified with the spirit of America. Here, then, Cameo/Parkway's talented vocalist Clint Eastwood, and America's most popular "cowboy favorites" . . . an unsurpassed combination that spells "entertainment."*

Audiences bought it in fairly good numbers, a testament to Clint's popularity rather than to his singing. Most of the money went to Uni- versal and Cameo, but Clint was less concerned about the profits than about what the gimmick might mean to his career. He wasn't a pop country tune singer and didn't want to be—his musical interests remained firmly rooted in jazz. When Cameo, with Universal's enthu- siastic approval, wanted to follow it up, Byrnes-style, Clint flatly rejected the notion. To avoid becoming the next "Kookie," he brought his potential teen idol career to a screeching halt.

In February 1962 the show's by-now-worldwide popularity led to a personal PR tour of Japan that featured Fleming and Clint in full- dress cowboy outfits. They were mobbed everywhere they went. Mag- gie did not accompany Clint on the tour, and many suspected that he simply did not want to take her, preferring to enjoy the fruits of his stardom unencumbered by a wife.

So Maggie stayed home, either oblivious to or unconcerned by Clint's philandering, playing tennis with her new upscale friends that included William Wellman's daughter, Cissy Wellman (whom she had met and become close to when Clint appeared in *Lafayette Escadrille*), Bob Daley, and other neighbors and acquaintances.

More offers for starring roles in films came from both England and Rome; Clint wanted to take them but had to turn them down. In April 1963, his fourth year on the show, CBS sensed they needed to loosen

---

*The tracks are: "Bouquet of Roses," "Sierra Nevada," "Don't Fence Me In," "Are You Satisfied," "Santa Fe Trail," "Last Roundup," "Mexicali Rose," "Tumblin' Tumble- weed," "Twilight on the Trail," "Searchin' for Somewhere," "I Love You More," and "San Antonio Rose."

the reins just a bit and allowed Clint to make an appearance on another network TV hit series. One reason may have been that, for the first time, *Rawhide* had dropped in the ratings against some new and formidable competition. *International Showtime* on NBC managed to knock *Rawhide* out of the top twenty-five. Believing the show needed some fresh publicity, the network asked Clint to guest-star on an episode of its highly rated hit sitcom, Arthur Lubin's *Mr. Ed*, based on a short story, "Ed Takes the Pledge," by Walter Brooks.

Although it wasn't exactly the type of stretch Clint was looking for, he agreed to do it as long as he did not have to appear as Rowdy Yates or wear cowboy clothing. The network readily acquiesced.

One of that show's writers was his friend Sonia Chernus, who had helped arrange the meeting with Warren that led to his being cast on *Rawhide*. For this episode she wrote "Clint Eastwood Meets Mr. Ed." The episode's plot was as idiotic as the talking-horse premise of the sitcom: Mr. Ed is jealous of Clint's horse on *Rawhide*, Midnight, because she's been having affairs with other horses in the neighborhood. Clint remained above it all, did the episode dressed in the contemporary So-Cal style of sweater and slacks, smiled amiably, collected his fee, and went on his way. Nonetheless, by playing himself he had officially earned the status of "big television star." Only upper-echelon celebrities such as Bob Hope, Jimmy Stewart, John Wayne, and Frank Sinatra could regularly make appearances on programs as themselves. Clint may not have particularly enjoyed the experience, playing, in effect, a horse's ass, but that week's numbers for *Mr. Ed* were huge, and afterward *Rawhide*'s ratings ticked up—but not enough to return it to the top twenty, a ranking it would never again attain.

Clint's troubled marriage took a potentially disastrous turn when he became involved with a twenty-nine-year-old statuesque brunette by the name of Roxanne Tunis. A stuntwoman, dancer, and occasional actress, Tunis had appeared in Robert Wise and Jerome Robbins's 1961 *West Side Story* and as an extra in Alfred Hitchcock's 1963 horror film *The Birds*. She now showed up fairly regularly on *Rawhide*, where she met Clint. Separated from her husband, she and Clint began an intense and highly sexual affair. Tunis was openly affectionate to Clint on the set, as if she wanted the world to know what was going on. She cared for him constantly, openly massaging his neck, listening to his problems, and putting absolutely no pressure on him for anything more than what she already had.

Often in the evenings, when shooting was through, he would go with Tunis to her place, stay awhile, and then leave for his home. No matter how late he arrived, Maggie never said anything and never complained. That he often may have smelled of another woman was something she tried to avoid dealing with, even though *Rawhide* had very little romance in its script and virtually none for Rowdy Yates. Everyone on the show knew about the affair, and if it bothered Clint or made any difference to him, he didn't seem to care. If everyone knew, everyone knew.

Then one day Tunis was noticeably absent from the set. No one knew why; they may have just assumed that Clint had decided she was becoming too much of a distraction. That was not the case. Tunis was pregnant with Clint's child, and they both decided it might be better if she stayed out of sight for the duration of her pregnancy.

A more immediate problem for Clint was Fleming's increasing absences. Fleming was worried that he was becoming too typecast in his role and that as he got older, fewer and fewer parts would be offered to him once the series ended. He was unable to come to terms with the network about other offers he wanted to take and was looking for a hefty increase in salary. In 1964, as in almost every season of *Rawhide*, he dramatically walked off the show.* This time Charles Gray, who had been on the show since 1961, compensated for Fleming's absence and was now elevated to the larger role as the primary scout. Guest stars became increasingly prominent in the show's plot lines. Both actions infuriated the always short-fused Fleming.

Then late in 1964 Fleming was offered a starring role in a Mexican-based western to be shot in Italy called *El magnifico stragnero (The Magnificent Stranger)*. Henry Fonda, Rory Calhoun, Charles Bronson, James Coburn, Henry Silva, Steve Reeves, and Richard Harrison had all previously turned it down because of director Sergio Leone's lowball offer of $15,000. Fleming thought about it for a while but ultimately said no.

---

*Fleming's first walk-off happened during the second season, when he was unhappy with Warren's having been replaced by Endre Bohem. This was the first season that entire episodes appeared without Fleming, but it wouldn't be the last.

Clint was now represented by the venerable and powerful William Morris Agency (but he still retained the financial management and industry clout of Irving Leonard for some deals, including anything that came out of *Rawhide* and anything else Leonard found on his own. Leonard was one of Clint's most trusted associates; in the vernacular of *The Godfather*, his "consigliere"). One of its agents stationed in the Rome office, Claudia Sartori, had the idea of offering the Leone film to Clint. She screened an episode of *Rawhide* for Leone and his producers, Jolly Films, which was financing the movie.* Miffed that Fleming had turned him down and increasingly desperate to find an American actor, Leone was pleasantly surprised at Clint's ability to take the focus off of Fleming in virtually every scene they were in together. By the end of the screening, Leone was interested in Clint.

Sartori then took the script of *The Magnificent Stranger* back to America, to give to Clint, via Irving Leonard, to make sure all proprietary representation claims were honored. Leonard assigned a recent young protégé, Sandy Bressler, to personally deliver the script to Clint and gently urge him to take it. This was no easy task, as Clint, like Fleming and all the others, was firmly against appearing in something that sounded as absurd as a European-made western.

"I knew I wasn't a cowboy," Clint said later on. "But if you portray a cowboy and people think you're a cowboy, that's fine. . . . I was asked if I was afraid of being typed when I started *Rawhide* . . . but in reality everyone is typed for something."

Clint offered little resistance to Bressler's arguments because, as he discovered, the script wasn't all that bad. It was, in fact, reminiscent of the great samurai films of Kurosawa and other classic Japanese filmmakers (whose movies, in turn, had been inspired by American westerns of the 1930s and 1940s). Clint was familiar with Kurosawa's films because he had often shown them during his projectionist stint at Fort Ord. Besides, he'd never been to Italy before, and he could pick up a quick $15,000 (plus all expenses for the eleven-week shoot, including a round-trip coach ticket for one) for the few weeks' work during

---

*She watched Episode 91, "Incident of the Black Sheep," which originally ran November 10, 1961. (Up to and including the show's sixth season, when new producers were brought in, all episodes of *Rawhide* had "Incident" in their title.) In it battling herders settle a dispute with a knife-fight between Rowdy and hostile sheepherder Tod Stone (Richard Basehart). Stone "falls" on his knife, and the dispute ends.

Rawhide's hiatus. He told Leonard he would take the deal if CBS allowed it. Leonard told him not to worry—pending Leone's approval, he would convince the network to agree.

According to Clint, "Sergio Leone had only directed one other picture, but they told me he had a good sense of humor . . . [Besides] I had the series to go back to as soon as the hiatus was over. So I felt, 'Why not?' I'd never seen Europe. That was reason enough to go."

At least that was what he told the public. Privately, he may have had an even more urgent reason for wanting to make the movie. He was about to become a father for the first time. Tunis was scheduled to deliver while he was in Spain, and that was one climactic event he wanted to be as far away from as possible.

FIVE

What struck me most about Clint was his indolent way of moving. It seemed to me Clint closely resembled a cat.

—Sergio Leone

Clint left for Rome the first week of May, the day after *Rawhide*'s 1964 hiatus began, without Maggie but with his one-time neighbor and friend Bill Thompkins. Clint had helped Thompkins land the small part of Toothless on *Rawhide*, and he now hoped to pick up some work on Leone's film as Clint's stunt double and stand-in, something he also occasionally did on the show.

At the Leonardo da Vinci Airport they were met by a small entourage that consisted of the film's publicist, Geneviève Hersent; assistant director Mario Cavano; and dialogue director Tonino Valerii, who offered Clint Leone's apologies for not being there himself, saying he was unfortunately tied up with preproduction. In truth, Leone did not speak a word of English and did not want to be embarrassed by it in public, especially since a handful of dependable paparazzi were sure to be there to photograph the arrival of the famous American TV cowboy.

Leone was thrilled that Clint had agreed to be in the film. Leone loved Hollywood films and actors. In his early, struggling years he had worked as an assistant to various American directors who occasionally shot abroad and needed some native help. Among those Leone had worked for were Raoul Walsh, William Wyler, Robert Aldrich, and Fred Zinnemann, mostly for their sandals-and-robes ventures such as Wyler's 1959 production of *Ben-Hur*.* Wyler, like the others, had used Leone to help organize and stage the big outdoor scenes, such as the famed chariot race.

When he finally got the chance to direct his own movie, it was *Il Colosso di Rodi* in 1961 (released in the United States as *The Colossus of Rhodes*), with American actor Rory Calhoun in the lead. The film did surprisingly well internationally as well as in Italy, briefly resurrected

---

*Aka *Ben-Hur, a Tale of the Christ.*

Calhoun's Hollywood career, and put Leone in a position to choose his own next project.

He had had it in mind as early as 1959, when he was still a screenwriter on Mario Bonnard's 1959 *Gli ultimi giorni di Pompei (The Last Days of Pompeii)*, filmed on location in Pompeii and Naples and starring Steve Reeves, of *Hercules* fame. (Reeves seriously dislocated his shoulder during the film; the injury eventually forced his acting career to end prematurely.) Bonnard had fallen ill the first day of shooting, and with no one else available, Leone stepped in and "finished" it, directing all but the first day's footage. Working closely with Duccio Tessari, his co-writer, Leone managed to turn out a respectable film that made money. He was determined now to direct his own films.

In between working on other directors' movies, he and Tessari went to see as many as they could. One day in 1961 they saw *Yojimbo*, and Leone was blown away as much by Kurosawa's directing style as by the film's story. (Kurosawa had co-written *Yojimbo* with Hideo Oguni and Ryuzo Kikushima.) Leone contacted Kurosawa and asked for permission to adapt *Yojimbo* as an American-style Italian-made western. He already had a title that was in itself an homage to another favorite film, if not an outright steal: *The Magnificent Stranger* was a play on *The Magnificent Seven*, John Sturges's smash 1960 western adapted from Kurosawa's 1954 classic *Seven Samurai (Shichinin no samurai)*, the film that had made Kurosawa's reputation in the United States.

However, Kurosawa, perhaps weary of his films being "borrowed" by other directors, asked for an upfront $10,000 rights fee. Leone was confident he could get the money from Jolly Films, the production company that had agreed to back the first acceptable script he brought them; but to his surprise and dismay, Jolly said no, even though the entire proposed budget for the film, including Kurosawa's fee, was only $200,000. When it appeared that no deal could be reached, Jolly Films producers Harry Colombo and George Papi managed to work out a tentative deal with Kurosawa that bypassed the upfront $10,000 in exchange for 100 percent of the film's gross profits in Japan. Colombo and Papi thought it was a good deal for Kurosawa because *Rawhide* was a big hit on Japanese TV and Clint Eastwood was considered a major star. But in the end Kurosawa said no, a decision that would later come back to haunt Leone.

Nonetheless, early that June location shooting began in Spain, before moving on to Rome for interiors at the famed but underused and relatively inexpensive Italian studio Cinecittà.

Within days of his being on the set, Clint realized that the film Leone was making was far different from the more conventional script he'd read back in the States. The story was familiar enough—a stranger comes to town, watches bad guys bully good people, is reluctant to take sides, gets drawn in to it, is nearly killed and left for dead, and then comes back and takes revenge against impossible odds to emerge victorious. Westerns in every decade of Hollywood filmmaking had elements of this scenario, including John Ford's *My Darling Clementine* (1946) and his *The Man Who Shot Liberty Valance* (1962), Howard Hawks's *Rio Bravo* (1959), Raoul Walsh's *The Lawless Breed* (1953), Fred Zinnemann's *High Noon* (1952), and George Stevens's *Shane* (1953), to which Leone's film also bears an especially strong resemblance in plot and visual stylistic touches; the Man with No Name, in poncho and sheepskin vest, vividly echoes Alan Ladd's mysterious stranger, gloriously costumed in buckskins.

Though it owes much to *Yojimbo* and *Shane*, however, *A Fistful of Dollars** also owes a great deal to the great pulp and genre writers of the first half of the twentieth century. The British critic and film historian Christopher Frayling has traced all these films' common plot line and characters to Dashiell Hammett's 1929 novel *Red Harvest* (the Continental Op is, significantly, a man without a name) and even further back to Carlo Goldoni's eighteenth-century play *Servant of Two Masters*. Leone himself often said that *Red Harvest* was a primary source of his script.[†]

What impressed Clint, and first clued him in to the fact that something might be going on other than just another European ripoff of American genres, was the stylistic flourish Leone used to shoot the film. Clint had become interested in directing well before he showed up in Italy, especially in the stylistics of directors that made their films personal. As he told it, during one episode of *Rawhide:*

We were shooting some vast cattle scenes—about two thousand head of cattle. We were doing some really exciting stampede stuff. I was

*Aka *Fistful of Dollars*.
†Kurosawa insisted that the primary source of his script was always and only *Yojimbo*.

65

riding along in the herd, there was dust rising up, and it was pretty wild really. But the shots were being taken from outside the herd, looking in, and you didn't see too much. I thought, we should get right in the middle of this damn stampede. I said to the director and producer, "I'd like to take an Arriflex [camera], run it on my horse and go right in the middle of this damn thing, even dismount, whatever— but get in there and really get some great shots, because there are some beautiful shots in there that we are missing." Well, they double-talked me. They said, "You can't get in there because of union rules." I could see they didn't want to upset a nice standard way of movie-making.

Even before he worked on *A Fistful of Dollars*, Clint had been thinking a lot about how familiar setups, camera angles, and methodology—establish the scene in a master shot, cut to over-the-shoulder one-shots for the dialogue, finish the scene with the master shot, dissolve into the next master—bred a uniformity in TV directors and made them all (directors and their shows) stylistically look the same. The day Clint wanted to shoot the cattle drive a little differently was the day the seeds of his future role as a director were planted.

Finally, I asked Eric Fleming, "Would you be averse to my directing?" He said, "Not at all, I'd be for it." So I went to the producer and he said great. Evidently he didn't say great behind my back; but he said great at the time. He said, "I'll tell you what, why don't you direct some trailers for us—coming attractions for next season's shows?" I said, "Terrific. I'll do it for nothing and then I'll do an episode." And I did the trailers. But they reneged on the episode because, at that time, several of their name actors on other television shows were directing episodes, not too successfully.

So about the time I was getting set to do it, CBS said no more series actors could direct their own shows . . . then I went to work with Sergio Leone.

Acting in the film proved difficult for Clint, primarily because Leone insisted on shooting in three languages simultaneously. Clint had to speak his lines in English while the other actors spoke in either Italian or Spanish. The result was a limited amount of dialogue that

Leone used to help create the strong silent mystique of the Man with No Name. Rather than having the character talk a lot, at Leone's insistence (Clint enthusiastically supported this decision and, with Leone's permission, cut much of his own dialogue out), he smoked cigarillos and used his big gun to do a lot of the talking for him. All of it allowed Clint to act with his face and his eyes rather than to talk as Rowdy Yates and almost every other character on *Rawhide* did, because on TV describing action is always a lot cheaper than actually showing it. ("You know those rustlers we rounded up yesterday?" "Yeah, I remember." "Well, two of them had a fight in their jail cell last night and we had to break it up." "Too bad I missed it." "One of them hit the other over the head with a bottle . . . and now the doc is with him. Let's go see how he's doing and maybe we can get some more information out of the varmint . . .")

Gradually, the slim backstory of the Man with No Name began to take shape. He was some kind of wandering knight in shining armor, which is revealed in a single sentence, after he helps a young couple escape the clutches of the evil Rojo, by explaining, "I knew someone like you once and there was no one there to help." That was all, and that was enough.

Clint found a wide hat he liked and wore it low to shade his eyes, giving him an even more menacing look while preserving a certain coolness—not an easy balance to maintain. And he wore a poncho, donned in the second half of the film, to hide his mangled hand from his opponents.* It became akin to Batman's cape. Finally, the metal shield he wore during the climactic shoot-out made him appear unearthly, as if he were an invincible alien from another world. Clint combined all these character accoutrements perfectly, throwing the cape back with a flourish in the film's final shoot-out, which Leone cut perfectly in sync to the extraordinary score by Ennio Morricone, the best film music for any western since Tiomkin's Academy Award–winning theme for *High Noon*.

Besides the stylized music-to-action and the low angles that Leone used to shoot the Man with No Name, he also cut close-ups of the characters' eyes in strong, rhythmic motions. As the action of the film

---

*Clint, like most actors, is superstitious. According to the Internet Movie Database, he used this poncho in all three Leone movies and insisted it never be washed or cleaned.

intensified, the close-ups got closer. And for the final, climactic shoot-out, Leone came up with one of the film's most unforgettable sequences; after a series of close-ups of eyes, a double-barreled shot-gun appears through a window, and the shot turns them into the perfect cold, unfeeling, unblinking steely eyes of evil incarnate. The moment never fails to evoke cheers and chills in audiences, and rightly so. It is the kind of effect no other form can achieve, not theater, not television, not the novel—a moment that is purely kinetic, a triumph of directing and editing that does not take away from the story but adds a dramatic flourish to it.

Leone's cinematic feel was not lost on Clint:

> An American would be afraid of approaching a western such as *Fistful of Dollars* with that kind of style. For instance, there were shots of a person being shot. In other words, you never shot a tie-up shot of a man shooting a gun and another person getting hit. It's a Hays Office rule from years ago, a censorship deal. You'd cut to the guy shooting, and then cut to a guy falling. That was all right—the same thing—the public isn't counting the cut. But you could never do a tie-up. We did because Sergio didn't know all that. He wasn't bothered by that. Neither was I. I knew about it but I couldn't care less. The whole object of doing a film with a European director was to put a new shade of light on it.*

With filming completed, Clint packed his things and boarded a plane for America. It would make a brief stopover in London, then continue to Los Angeles, just as filming on the seventh season of *Rawhide* was about to begin. Maggie met Clint in person at the airport. Roxanne Tunis called the next day and happily informed him that he was now the proud father of a baby daughter, Kimber Tunis, born June 17, 1964, at Cedars Sinai Hospital in Hollywood. Although the

---

*The Production Code (also known as the Hays Code) was the set of industry censorship guidelines governing the production of American motion pictures. The Motion Pictures Producers and Distributors Association (MPPDA), which later became the Motion Picture Association of America (MPAA), adopted the code in 1930, began effectively enforcing it in 1934, and abandoned it in 1968 in favor of the subsequent MPAA film rating system. The Production Code spelled out what was morally acceptable and unacceptable content for motion pictures produced for a public audience in the United States.

father is listed on the birth certificate as Clinton Eastwood Jr., Tunis publicly gave the baby her last name, protecting Clint. He promised to support the child and did, emotionally and financially, asking from Tunis only that, if possible, the baby's identity be kept secret.

Clint now had to negotiate a fine line to make sure his worlds (and women) didn't collide. Thompkins, his longtime friend, agreed with Tunis that Clint should at least tell Maggie about the baby. Clint immediately and permanently cut him off. Thompkins was summarily fired from *Rawhide* and permanently disappeared from Clint's life.*

As for Maggie, it is difficult to say for sure that she actually knew about the baby, although it would have been nearly impossible for her not to. Everyone on the set knew, many of Maggie and Clint's friends knew, and it is simply too difficult to keep a secret like that when the mother and the illegitimate child live in the same small town, especially when that small town is Hollywood.

Perhaps that was one reason Clint suddenly decided he and Maggie should move north, to the Monterey Peninsula. He found a small home for them in Pebble Beach, and a second getaway place in Carmel, and assigned Maggie the familiar job of making the two houses into homes, even if he was going to be away from them, and her, most of the time, working on the show.

Meanwhile *Rawhide* was continuing to have problems not just with ratings but with salaries. The standard seven-year contracts that both Fleming and Clint had signed, the maximum allowed under AFTRA (American Federation of Television and Radio Artists), were set to expire at the end of the season, and neither the network nor the stars were particularly eager to extend them. New contracts for Fleming and Clint, the network knew, would be expensive propositions, more now for Clint than for Fleming, whose fan mail had markedly decreased while Clint's had steadily grown.

Moreover, CBS had decided to job out the entire production. Bruce Geller and Bernard Kowalski, two aggressive young independent producers, had formed a company called Unit Productions and won the

---

*He later tried to reconcile with Clint, who eventually did get him a few days' work as stunt coordinator on *A Fistful of Dollars*. Despite that assignment and the subsequent success of the film, Thompkins was unable to regain a professional foothold in Hollywood. He died of injuries he sustained in a 1971 automobile accident.

assignment from the network to take over *Rawhide*. They hired Del Reisman as executive producer, or "show runner," and made themselves highly profitable middlemen. One of the first things Reisman did was to screen episodes from all six previous seasons. He immediately saw that thirty-four-year-old Clint Eastwood was no longer suited to play Rowdy Yates; nor was Fleming, about to turn forty, to play Favor.

Reisman's solution was to fire Fleming and focus on Clint, hoping that Clint's maturing character Yates would work better solo. But before he could actually do it, Fleming, sensing trouble coming his way, went directly to William Paley and complained that the new production team was going to ruin the show. Paley, a big fan, listened to Fleming and decided that CBS should not be jobbing out its shows. He fired Unit Productions, which meant that Reisman was gone as well, and he convinced Endre Bohem, one of the show's longtime line producers who had been let go when Unit was brought in, to come back.

But it did no good. By the end of the season, the show had slipped to number forty-four in the ratings. *Rawhide* had clearly turned into a tired replay of a good thing—the cattle could have reached the shores of China by now. "Every time they wanted a format change," Clint later recalled, "they'd drag in some other [producer] . . . they tried a lot of different approaches but Paley would tune in every now and then and get on the horn with 'What have you done with the show,' and they'd get back to basics."

In the spring of 1965, after one more season playing Rowdy, Clint jumped at the chance to return to Italy to star in Leone's planned sequel to *A Fistful of Dollars*, to be called *Per qualche dollaro in più (For a Few Dollars More)*.

By now, a mystique had grown around *A Fistful of Dollars* in America, where (in the days before video, cable, and the Internet) no one could actually see the film without traveling to Europe. Even so, it was talked about in magazines, on the radio, on television, and on college campuses all across the country. Tales of the film's "unbelievable" action sequences traveled in whispers, while *Variety*, the showbiz bible, printed story after story about the movie's phenomenal overseas boxoffice success.

Indeed, in Europe it had been a hit from the day of its release; in the November 18, 1964, issue of *Daily Variety*, the newspaper's Rome reporter kicked off the type of noncritical enthusiasm that would follow the film wherever it played: "Crackerjack western made in Italy and Spain by a group of Italians and an international cast with James Bondian vigor and tongue-in-cheek approach to capture both sophisticates and average cinema patrons. Early Italo figures indicate it's a major candidate to be sleeper of the year. Also that word-of-mouth, rather than cast strength or ad campaign, is a true selling point. As such it should make okay program fare abroad as well." Clint, who now was widely known throughout Europe as "Il Cigarillo," rightly figured that sooner or later the film would have to play in America, Hays Code or no Hays Code. When the offer came for him to make the sequel, he quickly accepted it.

But before Leone could actually start production, he had to settle the still-unresolved dispute between Jolly Films and Kurosawa over the division of profits from the first film. When the case went to formal litigation, Leone simply declared himself free from all future obligations to Jolly and signed a new deal with Produzioni Europee Associates, headed by Alberto Grimaldi, one of the better-known Italian producers, who had worked with many of Italy's greatest directors. Leone secured a $350,000 fee for himself, plus 60 percent of the profits for his proposed sequel to *A Fistful of Dollars*, if—and it was a big if—he could get Clint Eastwood to return as the star. Leone told Grimaldi not to worry and quickly found himself a new screenwriter, Luciano Vincenzoni, who, working together with the director, came up with a completed shooting script in nine days.

The character of Ramón Rojo, played by Italian actor Gian Maria Volontè, had been killed off in the first film, but this one would bring the actor back in a different (but essentially the same) character. Lee Marvin would play a rival bounty hunter to the Man with No Name, who is also hunting down Volontè. Marvin was all set to go until he asked for more money. Leone fired him and replaced him with Lee Van Cleef, a Hollywood character actor with a once-bright future who had fallen on hard times. He had made his debut in *High Noon* as one of Frank Miller's gang out to kill Will Kane. Van Cleef was originally cast in the far better role of Kane's deputy, but when he refused to get his big and hooked nose "fixed," the part went instead to Lloyd

Bridges, and it made him a star. Van Cleef, relegated to playing one of the Miller gang, was not given a single line of dialogue. Still, his debut was so powerful, he managed to get steady work as a bad guy throughout the 1950s, until his career finally petered out and he turned to painting. Starving in Europe and living on his oils, he leaped when Leone offered him Marvin's part for the $50,000 that Marvin had turned down.

Clint was also offered $50,000, plus a first-class round-trip plane ticket and top-of-the-line accommodations. Having accepted the terms, Il Cigarillo boarded a plane as soon as *Rawhide* went on hiatus, bound for Rome and Cinecittà studios, to begin filming.

This time Maggie accompanied him for the first ten days, then returned home and flew back again for the last ten days of filming in Spain. Clint's press agent played up the husband-and-wife angle for all it was worth, but as soon as Maggie left Italy, Clint was seen with some of the most beautiful actresses in Rome, and his villa was filled day and night with them, even as dozens of friends and co-workers came and went. Clint partied like a teenage boy with the keys to the liquor cabinet while his parents were away on a trip. He had become such a movie star in Europe that he could no longer walk down the street without hordes of people, mostly women, running after him, like something out of Richard Lester's satire on Beatlemania, *A Hard Day's Night*.

The film's three-way competition among gunfighters gave the film an added level of dramatic tension that the first film did not have, and Van Cleef especially, as he had been in *High Noon*, was superb in his role. When the completed film was released, it proved an even greater sensation than the original. This time, without Kurosawa to contend with, and with film censorship crumbling in America along with the entire studio system, Leone and Grimaldi were intent upon getting a distribution deal for this film for North America, where, they knew, the real money was. They approached Arthur Krim and Arnold Picker, the new heads of the reinvigorated United Artists looking to restore the studio's original vision as a distributor for the best works of other producers and directors. While in Europe looking for product, they were approached by Vincenzoni.

Grimaldi took Krim and Picker to a movie theater in Rome, rather than a private screening, so they could witness firsthand the attention and excitement the film created in audiences. Afterward in a hotel room, Grimaldi asked for a million dollars. Krim and Picker countered with $900,000—a phenomenal amount of money for a foreign-made American-style western. Grimaldi took the deal.

Papers were drawn up, and at the actual signing Picker asked Leone what his next film would be, adding that UA might be interested in bankrolling it in return for exclusive distribution rights. On the spot Leone improvised a story of three post–American Civil War losers scrounging for money. That was it, that was all he had, and a title he made up then and there—*Il buono, il brutto, il cattivo* (*The Good, the Bad and the Ugly*)*—that drew a laugh from Vincenzoni and broad grins when translated for Krim and Picker. Based on only that much, they agreed to put up between $1.2 million and $1.6 million to fund the making and to retain the North American rights.†

Back in the States, meanwhile, Clint reverted once more to playing Rowdy Yates on *Rawhide*, a show that by this time seemed like a cultural artifact from the past, a leftover from the days of *I Love Lucy*. Another nail in its coffin was the network's stubborn refusal to allow it to switch to color. James Aubrey, then the head of programming, turned thumbs down on the idea because of the expense; shooting in color would mean that more episodes would have to be shot to justify the cost, and there was very little stock footage of cattle drives. (The show had long ago switched to buying old footage from movies rather than staging its own, wildly expensive runs.)

The show was saved from cancellation only because Paley still loved it, and when Aubrey began talking about removing it from the schedule, Paley instructed CBS's executive vice-president Mike Dann to keep it on the air, no matter what Aubrey said. A new producer was

---

*Leone's original titles had been *The Magnificent Rogues*, and *The Two Magnificent Tramps*, which he spontaneously changed at the meeting.

†Grimaldi sold the world rights to UA for an additional million-dollar guarantee and 50 percent of the profits, excluding Italy, France, Germany, and Spain. Not long afterward the lawsuit with Kurosawa was settled and Krim and Picker purchased the rights to *Fistful of Dollars*, giving Krim and Picker North American rights and a percentage of world rights to the trilogy, as well as the right to decide the American release dates for all three. Not long after UA's settlement, Jolly Films, meanwhile, which had produced *Per un pugno di dollari* (1964), came out with a film called *The Magnificent Stranger*, which was actually two episodes of *Rawhide* (1959) edited together. Eastwood sued Jolly Films, and *The Magnificent Stranger* was quickly withdrawn.

brought in to try to spruce things up. Ben Brady, whose past hit show credits included *Perry Mason* and *Have Gun—Will Travel*, announced that for the new season the characters of James Murdock (Mushy) and Sheb Wooley (Pete) were to be eliminated from the cast, replaced by David Watson as an English drover; Raymond St. Jacques, an African-American actor with Shakespearean credits, as Simon Blake; and John Ireland, one of the stars of *Red River* and other gritty movie westerns, as Jed Colby. And there was one more change: Eric Fleming was out, and Rowdy Yates was promoted to trail boss (something Clint read about while in Rome, from a *Variety* clipping that Maggie sent him while he was finishing up *For a Few Dollars More*).

Clint's initial reaction was that they should have kept Favor and lost Rowdy. Shortly after the changes were announced, the *Los Angeles Times* dispatched Hal Humphrey to get Clint's reaction. He began by asking him if he was happy about becoming the top star of his show. "Why should I be pleased," Clint answered, not yet used to the fact that every word he said could and would be reprinted. "I used to carry half the shows. Now I carry them all. For the same money."

Clint was angry and had a right to be. Fleming's salary had been much higher than his ($220,000 per season, against Clint's $100,000 a season), and now he was expected to fill those big boots without a raise—a detail that CBS had significantly left out of its revamping of the show.

If the season began in turmoil, it descended rapidly from there. After only two episodes, the network announced that it was bringing back Sheb Wooley. Then it announced it wasn't. Both decisions had been made by Paley, without consulting Brady, who abruptly resigned. CBS then brought Bohem back, who said he wanted to relocate the show to Hawaii. He quickly retreated from that idea and resigned. Finally, in a last-ditch effort to save the show, CBS inexplicably moved *Rawhide* out of its regular Friday-night slot to Tuesday, opposite ABC's hotshot *Combat*, a hit World War II action series starring Vic Morrow, just as Vietnam was beginning to burn itself into the hearts and minds of the American public. After thirteen more episodes, *Rawhide* was canceled by CBS. The 217th and last first-run episode, "Crossing at White Feather," aired December 7, 1965, after which the series entered the ether of syndicated reruns.

Clint could not have been happier. Within days of shooting his final scene, he flew back to New York to meet with producer Dino De Laurentiis, who said he had a proposition for Clint, the starring role in a new, big-budget movie to be shot in Europe and intended mainly for European audiences. Disappointed but resigned, Clint took the job, believing that big-screen Hollywood stardom was out of his reach.

SIX

I came back and did a very small-budget picture, called Hang 'Em High . . . *the movie business . . . was still thinking of me as an Italian movie actor.*

—Clint Eastwood

De Laurentiis was on a mission to sign Clint, believing that, once the Leone westerns were released in the States, he would be box-office gold anywhere in the world there was a movie screen. De Laurentiis thought Clint could be his generation's Gary Cooper, and he wasn't shy about telling him so. Like any good hustler, he knew how to seduce to get what he wanted.

De Laurentiis had been in a successful film business partnership with Carlo Ponti, who in the mid-1950s had decided to turn his wife, Sophia Loren, into Italy's finest screen actress by having her play working-class Italian women and allowing her real-life glamour to peek out like expensive lingerie. She often starred opposite Marcello Mastroianni, who could effortlessly flip back and forth between glamour and working class, comedy and drama. Under Ponti's guidance, both Mastroianni and Loren became world famous and (along with Ponti) extremely wealthy.

De Laurentiis envisioned the same thing for himself and his new wife, Silvana Mangano. Another icon of postwar Italian cinema, she had gained international fame with her performance in *Bitter Rice* (1949), written and directed by Giuseppe De Santis and produced by De Laurentiis. At that time "anthology" films were the rage in Europe, so he decided to put together five of the best directors and have them each make a short film with Mangano. Each would reflect, like a highly polished diamond, a different facet of her ability.

And he didn't want any superstar like Mastroianni to steal his wife's thunder. After searching among suitable actors he could afford, De Laurentiis decided that Eastwood might be right. He knew he wasn't the best actor—a plus, to De Laurentiis—but he was one of the hottest faces in Europe. His popularity could only help his box office, but his acting, De Laurentiis was confident, could never overshadow Mangano's.

To entice Clint, De Laurentiis laid out the proverbial red carpet for his arrival in New York. He put Clint in a five-star hotel and drove him all around the city in a black stretch limousine, talking up the "great" script he had in mind. Then he closed in for the kill. De Laurentiis, who had done his homework, knew that Clint loved cars and so offered him his choice of two deals: $25,000 for one month's work, or $20,000 and a brand-new Ferrari. Clint grabbed the Ferrari deal (knowing he wouldn't have to pay an agency fee on it if it was listed as a gift).

That February 1966 Clint flew to Rome, a city that by now he knew quite well and had come to like a great deal, to appear in one episode of De Laurentiis's planned five-part epic, *Le streghe (The Witches)*. His episode was to be directed by Vittorio De Sica, who had made his name helming one of the defining films of postwar neorealism, *The Bicycle Thief* (1948).*

"A Night Like Any Other" (aka "An Evening Like the Others"), nineteen minutes long, featured Clint in modern dress, with button-down shirt and slicked-back hair, trapped inside a loveless, unfulfilling marriage to Silvana Mangano. Only when he is asleep does he "live," as the sex star of his wife's fantasies; the episode climaxes with a self-imagined suicide, while his wife "dances" for dozens of men in a flesh club. This description does too much justice to the actual piece of film.

The film's American rights were acquired by Krim and Picker's UA on the strength of Clint's appearance. They were hoping to cash in on their eventual release of the Leone trilogy, but it was not officially released in the United States until 1969.†

According to Clint: "The stories [of the five episodes] didn't mean a whole lot. They were just a lot of vignettes all shuffled together. I enjoyed them, they were fun to do. Escapism."

---

*The other four segments and their directors were: "The Witch Burned Alive" directed by Luchino Visconti; "Civic Sense" (aka "Community Spirit"), directed by Mauro Bolognini; "The Earth as Seen from the Moon" (aka "Earth Seen from the Moon"), directed by Pier Paolo Pasolini; and "The Girl from Sicily" (aka "The Sicilian"), directed by Franco Rossi.

†UA eventually dropped it into a few test markets in America in March 1969, as a courtesy to De Laurentiis. It managed to snag a couple of rightfully dreadful reviews. UA quickly pulled it, and it has not been seen commercially in the States since, making it one of the few films in the Eastwood canon that has been seen by almost no American audiences. Clint's segment occasionally shows up in its entirety on YouTube.

It wasn't a total loss, though. When the film premiered in Paris (dubbed inexplicably into English), Clint met and had a brief but passionate affair with Catherine Deneuve that both managed to keep from the public. And there was also the new Ferrari, which he shipped home to Carmel while he remained in Rome to begin production on *The Good, the Bad and the Ugly.* Filming began at Cinecittà in May 1966, after a short delay during which Clint refused to report for work because Leone had yet to agree to his demand for $250,000 and another new Ferrari. Soon enough Clint got everything he wanted, and with cigarillo in place and fake guns strapped to his body, he slid himself back into his European cinematic saddle.

Early into production of Leone's third spaghetti western, Clint began to feel the same vague discontent he'd experienced with *Rawhide:* that the film was bloated, rather than expansive; that the script was far too wordy (something he would clamp down on for virtually every film he would eventually produce); and that the only fully fleshed character was "the Ugly" (Eli Wallach), while "the Good" (himself) and "the Bad" (Lee Van Cleef) were more caricatures than characters, without enough satiric heft to make that approach workable. Leone still didn't (or perhaps preferred not to) speak a word of English, despite the fact that this film depended far more than the first two on the spoken word than on the visual image.

Clint's instincts as to the diminution of his character's stature were essentially correct. In the first film he had been a loner, a man with practically no past and no foreseeable future. His singular stature suggested isolation, cynicism wrapped in heroic determination, and a forcefulness that made him—even with all his glamorized imperfections—irresistible to the audience. In the second film the Man with No Name had been forced to deal with and ultimately share his screen space with Colonel Mortimer (played by Lee Van Cleef, whose successful appearance in *For a Few Dollars More* had not only resurrected his film career but guaranteed his return in the last film of the trilogy). Now Van Cleef was playing someone named Sentenza, along with movie veteran (and inveterate scene stealer) Wallach. "If it goes on that way," Clint grumbled to Leone, "in the next one I will be starring with the whole American cavalry."

Between takes Clint took to practicing his golf swing, a signal to Leone and everyone else that he was now so detached from the production that he no longer cared about his character, the other characters, the director, or the film itself. Later on, when Leone approached him about a fourth film, Clint would flatly reject the offer.

During the filming, Clint and Wallach had become good friends, and Clint, who had a long-standing aversion to flying in small planes, convinced Wallach to drive with him from Madrid to Almeria. As production dragged on, Clint helped guide Wallach through the script, emphasizing the importance of action over dialogue, acting as Wallach's personal director. Then, the week before filming finished, Clint and Wallach had dinner together. "This will be my last spaghetti western," he told Wallach. "I'm going back to California and I'll form my own company and I'll act and direct my own movies." *Oh sure, that'll be the day*, Wallach thought to himself.

Meanwhile Leone had visions of creating a second, more expansive trilogy. According to Leone,

> After *The Good, the Bad and the Ugly*, I didn't want to do any more westerns. I had totally done that kind of story and I wanted to do a picture called *Once Upon a Time in America*. But because people are not willing to forgive success, and to forgive failure, when I went to the States the first thing they said was do another western and we'll let you do *Once Upon a Time in America* . . . at that point I needed to make another movie that was completely different from the first three and I thought of starting a new trilogy which started with *Once Upon a Time in the West*, developed with *A Fistful of Dynamite* and ended with *Once Upon a Time in America*.*

While Clint knew this would be his last film for Leone, it was by no means his last western. He had had too much spaghetti and not

*The first film was made in 1968, *C'era una volta il West* (*Once Upon a Time in the West*), starring Henry Fonda, Jason Robards, and Claudia Cardinale. Charles Bronson played the role of Harmonica that Leone had originally offered to Clint. Leone often said that he had cast Clint in *A Fistful of Dollars* because he looked like Henry Fonda, then later cast Fonda because he looked like Clint Eastwood. *A Fistful of Dynamite*, starring Rod Steiger and James Coburn, was made in 1971. *Once Upon a Time in America*, starring Robert De Niro and James Woods, was completed in 1984.

enough hamburger; he was determined now to take the essential elements of the character of the Man with No Name, which had been so good to him in Europe, back to Hollywood, where it could be redeveloped and redefined.

Home by July, Clint quickly grew restless in Carmel and frequently hooked up with old friends, including David Janssen, who had finished production on his fourth and final season as Dr. Richard Kimble on the hit TV show *The Fugitive*. The series had perfectly touched the boomer zeitgeist of the 1960s, made a cultural hero out of Kimble, and (for a relatively brief time) a star out of Janssen.

Clint and Janssen got together often during these months, as Clint sought guidance from his friend, now a major TV star, for his own floundering career. (Clint had been offered, and accepted, the role of Two-Face on the campy *Batman* series, but it was canceled before he could do it.) Janssen, meanwhile, had just accepted an offer from John Wayne to appear in the upcoming Wayne-produced-and-directed *The Green Berets*, as a skeptical liberal newspaper reporter embedded with a unit of the Green Berets.

And then on September 30, 1966, Clint was shocked to learn that Eric Fleming, while on location in Peru filming an MGM movie for TV called *High Jungle*, had died. About halfway through the shoot, Fleming's canoe had capsized on the Huallaga River. With him was another actor, Nic Minardos, who managed to swim safely to shore. Fleming's body was found two days later.* Clint found out by reading it in the newspaper.

On January 18, 1967, *A Fistful of Dollars* finally opened in Los Angeles, followed by a national release a month later. The film's stylized violence (which viewed today is neither all that violent nor all that stylized) had prevented it from being shown in America for three years. In 1966 Mike Nichols's groundbreaking *Who's Afraid of Virginia Woolf?*, in which vulgar language was crucial to the film's story, had finally broken through the outdated restrictions of the Produc-

----

*Or so it was reported. The circumstances of his death and the fate of his remains are cloudy to this day. Unsubstantiated reports persist that he was eaten by a crocodile. He was to have been married two days after his death.

tion Code. Thereafter Krim and Picker thought the time was right to try an American release for their Leone film.*

And critics wasted no time in pouncing on it. Leading the parade of negative reaction was Bosley Crowther, the crusty film critic of the *New York Times*, who dismissed the film as "cowboy camp." Judith Crist, the main film reviewer for the *World Journal Tribune*, called it "perfectly awful . . . an ersatz western . . . [where] men and women [are] gouged, burned, beaten, stomped and shredded to death." Philip K. Scheuer wrote in the *Los Angeles Times:* "Like the villains, it was shot in Spain . . . pity it wasn't buried there." *Newsweek* called it "excruciatingly dopey." In almost every review, Clint received only casual mention, and Leone was barely mentioned at all.

Yet, to everyone's surprise, *A Fistful of Dollars* made money from its first day of release. If the critics didn't get it, audiences did. They could sense the power of Clint's character, the attraction of his strength and conviction, and the film's original viewpoint on brutality. Moreover, every campus town in America had a revival theater that regularly played *Yojimbo*, so college audiences—who made up a large number of the film's early faithful—were familiar with the tactics of the scenario. The artifacts of the Man with No Name's character—the cigarillo, the poncho, the wide-brimmed hat—all became elements of 1960s campus hip style.

Meanwhile, Clint was having trouble getting work, or at least the kind he wanted—an American western with a toned-down version of his nameless hero—even as that May, United Artists, encouraged by the box-office take of *A Fistful of Dollars*, released *For a Few Dollars More* as one of their big summer movies, while *A Fistful of Dollars* was still holding on to a sizable number of its first-run screens. It had already grossed a hefty $3.5 million, which was excellent for a 1960s studio film and extraordinary for any foreign independent released in America.

In between promotional interviews and extensive redubbing sessions for all three films, at UA's expense (rather than using the more conventional and less expensive subtitles), Clint continued to meet

---

*Shortly after the box-office success of *Who's Afraid of Virginia Woolf?*, the Production Code was replaced by Jack Valenti's ratings system. United Artists then agreed to distribute *A Fistful of Dollars* in America. Also, the Kurosawa-rights issue had finally been resolved.

with producers and directors and continued to be rejected by all of them. At best they considered his current movie success to be a fluke, the product of a novelty, and at worst they still thought of him as a TV actor, a ghetto from which few actors managed to escape.

As the months passed, Clint formulated an idea that had been cooking since the days of *Rawhide*, when he had wanted to film that cattle drive differently: to make a project of his own choosing, shot in the way he wanted it done. If American studios weren't falling over themselves to latch on to Clint Eastwood Movie Star, then he would produce a film that would not only equal but surpass Leone's achievement with the western genre.

The project he had in mind was a script called *Hang 'Em High*, an Americanized single-feature amalgam of the Leone trilogy. It had been written by Mel Goldberg in 1966, as a pilot for yet another western TV series. Clint thought it might be the right project to launch his Hollywood film career and approached producer Leonard Freeman, who had originally commissioned it as a pilot, about the possibility of turning it into a feature film. Freeman had already produced *Mr. Novak*, and co-created the idea for a new series, *Hawaii Five-O*, after which Freeman and Goldberg shelved *Hang 'Em High*.

The script had first come to Clint via Irving Leonard, who happened to be friends with Freeman's agent, George Litto. Over dinner one night Litto had told Leonard about *Hang 'Em High*. Leonard thought it might be what Clint was looking for and asked if he could send him a copy. Litto sent it over the next day. Clint, rather than going back to the well with Leone, wanted to do it. "When [Leone] talked to me about doing *Once Upon a Time in the West* and what later became *Duck, You Sucker*, they were just repeats of what I'd been doing," he said.*

I didn't want to play that character anymore. So I came back and did a very small-budget picture, called *Hang 'Em High*, which had a little more character. Maybe it was time, too, to do some American films, because even though these films were very successful, the movie business for

---

***Duck, You Sucker* (1971) was also known as *Giù la testa*, and *A Fistful of Dynamite*, and *Once Upon a Time . . . the Revolution*. James Coburn appeared in the role of John Mallory, originally intended by Leone for Eastwood.

some reason was still thinking of me as an Italian movie actor. I can remember the field guys at Paramount years ago said they'd talk about using me but all they got was, "He's just a TV actor." I wasn't marked to be accepted. There were a lot of other actors who were marked to succeed more than me.

The first thing Clint did was take the script to his more powerful agent at William Morris, Leonard Hirshan, who, like any good WMA rep, did not like projects coming to his clients from outside sources. It was a question less of ego than of packaging. Putting agency writers together with in-house actors gave the agency a voice in virtually every aspect of a production. Hirshan's first inclination was to pass on *Hang 'Em High*. He wanted Clint instead for a production called *Mackenna's Gold*, an ensemble action film whose cast would be headed by Gregory Peck and Omar Sharif. Clint read the script for *Mackenna's Gold*, and it left him cold. Being part of an ensemble, he felt, would be a step backward for him, a return to the ensemble style of *The Good, the Bad and the Ugly* or, worse, *Rawhide*.*

Clint insisted he was going ahead with *Hang 'Em High*. He believed the back-to-back financial successes of *A Fistful of Dollars* and *For a Few Dollars More*—the latter received even worse reviews than *Fistful* but so far grossed $4.3 million in its initial theatrical run, nearly a million dollars more than *Fistful*—could get the film funded by Krim and Picker at UA. He was right. Once the deal was set, he approached Ted Post, one of his favorite *Rawhide* directors, to make the film.

On December 29, 1967, production began on *Hang 'Em High*, Picker and Krim released *The Good, the Bad and the Ugly*; all three films in the trilogy had been released in the space of a year. It set off a tsunami of debate among the more esoteric critics, who either loved it or hated it but could not ignore it. Mainstream critics like Charles Champlin complained in the *Los Angeles Times* that "the temptation is hereby proved irresistible to call *The Good, the Bad and the Ugly*, now

---

*The screenplay was by Carl Foreman, based on a novel by Heck Allen. Foreman had been nominated for an Academy Award for his 1952 script for *High Noon*, then was blacklisted in the 1950s. One of Foreman's comeback films was *The Guns of Navarone* (1961), directed by J. Lee Thompson. So *Mackenna's Gold* was considered an important film, and Hirshan pressured Clint, unsuccessfully, to accept a role in it. The film was released in 1969, without Clint, directed by J. Lee Thompson.

playing citywide, *The Bad, the Dull, and the Interminable*, only because it is." Pauline Kael, the high priestess of film criticism writing from her perch at *The New Yorker* far above the world of the common man, pronounced the film "stupid" and "gruesome" and wondered why it was called a western at all. *Time* magazine sniffed its nose too, after minimally acknowledging Leone's stylistics, giving Leone a good spanking for daring to encroach on that most holy of American turf, the movie western.

The *New York Times*'s first-string film critic Renata Adler wrote in the newspaper's January 25 edition:

"The burn, the gouge, and the mangle" (its screen name is simply inappropriate) must be the most expensive, pious and repellent movie in the history of its peculiar genre. If 42nd Street is lined with little pushcarts of sadism, this film, which opened yesterday at the Trans-Lux 85th Street and the DeMille, is an entire supermarket . . . it lasts two and a half slow hours . . . there is a completely meaningless sequence with a bridge—as though it might pass for "San Luis Rey" or "Kwai." Sometimes, it all tries to pass for funny.

The film would fare no better in later years, after Adler's departure from the *Times* and a string of exceedingly esoteric film critics increasingly turned their noses up at Clint, until the arrival of Manohla Dargis in the first years of the new century, a film reviewer who did not automatically dismiss Clint by definition (of the times, of his genre, of the so-called fashions of the times). The *New York Times*, however, would continue to push its more standard party line. In its television section, whenever *The Good, the Bad and the Ugly* showed up, it ran the same one-line blurb year after year that, while acerbic and condescending, was, in truth, not that far from what Clint himself felt about the film: "Snarls, growls, and a smattering of words. Clint treading on water, on land."

Only Andrew Sarris, in the *Village Voice*, was willing to admit that there was something to Leone and his trilogy. Sarris, a forerunner of the "auteurist" movement in American film criticism, derived from the French Nouvelle Vague critics a highly controversial assessment of American movies; he was then considered a rebel (but ironically is rightly revered today as a reactionary). His auteur theory celebrated

genre films and the directors who made them as more purely cinematic and personal than the corporate, impersonal, and therefore
indifferent product of the old industrial studio system. Having seen the
trilogy before it opened, he wrote a two-part "think piece" that
appeared in the *Voice* on September 19 and 26, 1968, called "The
Spaghetti Westerns." It explained the Leone films' box-office success
in terms of their auteurist appeal—something to which the other critics were completely blind—and he allowed the trilogy, and Leone, to
enter the world of the hip (or the hipster), such as it was. If it still
wasn't okay to laud the films at cocktail parties on Fifth Avenue, after
Sarris it was the essential stuff of coffee shops and kitchen counters.

The New York cultural scene, Sarris wrote,

> remains basically hostile to westerns even as precincts of camp . . . The
> western, like water, gains flavor from its impurities, and westerns since
> 1945 have multiplied their options, obsessions and neuroses many times
> over . . . What Kurosawa and Leone share is a sentimental nihilism that
> ranks survival above honor and revenge above morality . . . Strangely,
> Leone has moved deeper into American history and politics in his sub-
> sequent [films following *Fistful of Dollars*]. I say strangely because an
> Italian director might be expected to stylize an alien genre with vague
> space-time coordinates, like the universal Mexico that can be filmed
> anywhere on the Mediterranean for any century from the sixteenth to
> the twentieth . . . The spaghetti western is ultimately a lower-class
> entertainment and, as such, functions as an epic of violent revenge.*

The Good, the Bad and the Ugly packed movie houses to the tune of
$6.3 million in its initial domestic release. With his star rising like a
rocket, Clint was finally able to put together the funding for *Hang
'Em High*. To ensure that it became the film he envisioned, he formed
his own production company, Malpaso (Spanish for "bad pass," or

---

*Clint was well aware of the critics and said in his February 1974 *Playboy* interview: "I've
been treated well—flatteringly so—by the better, more experienced reviewers, people
like Andrew Sarris, Jay Cocks, Vincent Canby and Bosley Crowther. Judith Crist, for
some reason, hasn't been knocked out over everything I've done—or *anything* I've
done, as a matter of fact. I think she liked [the porn film] *The Devil in Miss Jones*, but
she thought *Beguiled* was obscene . . . everybody's entitled to his opinion."

"bad step"), named after a creek on his own property in Monterey County, to function as his producing umbrella. "I own some property on a creek in the Big Sur country called Malpaso Creek," Clint told *Playboy* magazine:

> I guess it runs down a bad pass in the mountains . . . My theory was that I could foul up my career just as well as somebody else could foul it up for me, so why not try it? And I had this great urge to show the industry that it needs to be streamlined so it can make more films with smaller crews . . . What's the point of spending so much money producing a movie that you can't break even on it? So at Malpaso, we [won't] have a staff of 26 and a fancy office. I've got a six-pack of beer under my arm, and a few pieces of paper, and a couple of pencils, and I'm in business.*

With a staff consisting of himself, Robert Daley as the resident producer, Sonia Chernus as story editor, and one secretary, he felt ready to make the film he wanted, the way he wanted, and maybe even make some real money doing it. *Hang 'Em High* became Malpaso's first release.†

---

*According to Arthur Knight, who interviewed Clint for *Playboy* in February 1974, the walls of the Malpaso office were "decorated with posters; looming in one corner is a life-sized cardboard cutout of Eastwood—which, like his best-known screen characterizations, is curiously one-dimensional and strangely ominous. The most bizarre object in his private office, though, is a three-foot-high, balloon-shaped, shocking-pink, papier-mâché rabbit piggy bank."

†"The three [Leone] films were successful overseas," he said in the 1974 *Playboy* interview, "but I had a rough time cracking the Hollywood scene. Not only was there a movie prejudice against television actors but there was a feeling that an American actor making an Italian movie was sort of taking a step backward. But the film exchanges in France, Italy, Germany, Spain were asking the Hollywood producers when they were going to make a film starring Clint Eastwood. So finally I was offered a very modest film for United Artists—*Hang 'Em High* . . . I formed my own company, Malpaso, and we got a piece of it."

SEVEN

I think I learned more about direction from Don Siegel than from anybody else . . . he shoots lean, and he shoots what he wants. He knew when he had it, and he didn't need to cover his ass with a dozen different angles.

—Clint Eastwood

Clint's vision of Malpaso as a self-contained, in-house movie production company that he owned and operated in the service of his own career would take a little longer to realize than he had anticipated. Although his success in Hollywood via the Leone trilogy was impressive, he still did not have enough clout to be able to make his own movies independently, and he knew even less about running a company. For the time being, he would still have to rely totally upon studio financing and therefore remain in the service of others. He brought in Irving Leonard to be Malpaso's president and watch the books and act as Clint's personal business manager.

Clint used Leonard's business savvy to flex Malpaso's newborn muscles. The final decisions were mostly Clint's, but they were shaped, refined, and delivered by Leonard. UA had initially wanted a name director for *Hang 'Em High* to ensure that their investment would be well protected, shot in a commercial fashion, and kept within budget. Picker and Krim thought that either Robert Aldrich or John Sturges, both action directors, could do the job. Aldrich's *The Dirty Dozen* (1967), an ensemble war movie heavy on testosterone, made him a top choice, as did Sturges's *The Magnificent Seven* (1960).

Clint's choice, however, was Ted Post. Post had directed only two theatrical features, both quickies that created not so much as a ripple of interest (or revenue),* twenty-four *Rawhide* episodes, and dozens of other TV episodics and was, according to Clint's way of thinking, especially good with dialogue, which most episodic television is. The primary difference between film and TV in the 1960s was that film was about what the audience saw and TV was about what it heard. Having never had much dialogue to deliver on either *Rawhide* or the Leone

---

*They were *The Peacemaker* (1956) and *The Legend of Tom Dooley* (1959).

trilogy, Clint wanted someone who could help him handle the wordy *Hang 'Em High* script. The job went to Post.

Once Clint's choice of director was on board, casting for the rest of the picture went relatively quickly. Post hired veteran character actor Pat Hingle, twitchy bad boy Bruce Dern (whom Clint had befriended in the years when they were both knocking about in Hollywood trying to find work), Ed Begley, always dependable to play a dangerous old loony, and Charles McGraw. Not coincidentally, all had appeared in episodes of *Rawhide* that Post had directed.

For the female lead, Clint wanted Inger Stevens. Women had not been much of a factor in the Leone trilogy, except to act as symbolic Madonnas in the films' heavily suggestive faux religiosity. *Hang 'Em High* emphasizes the Madonna theme via Rachel (Stevens), a local businesswoman who nurses Jed Cooper (Clint) back to health after he is nearly hanged in the opening scenes, a violent graphic depiction that recalled Leone.* A good-time prostitute (played by Arlene Golonka) completes the triangle. According to Post, by the end of the film Golonka had become another notch on Clint's real-life sexual gun belt: "She [Golonka] began to like him very much . . . then, very *very* much, et cetera. When we got to the love scene, they had already found their way together. At the end of the picture she came over to me and said, 'Anytime you do a picture with Clint and there's a part in it, call me.' " On the other hand Stevens, a tall, statuesque blonde with a sophisticated air, was not all that eager to work with Clint, regarding him as something of a philistine.

The film was shot relatively quickly and under budget—something that would become one of Malpaso's trademarks inside the industry. It was filmed on location (something else that would also come to define a Malpaso picture) in the Las Cruces territory of New Mexico, with the interiors done at MGM studios in Culver City, California. The plot followed the Leone blueprint—for most of the film Clint pursues the men who tried to kill him and kills them instead in a spectacular shoot-out and, ironically, a suicide-by-hanging of the man who had tried to lynch Cooper, Captain Wilson (Begley).

---

*The character's name, Cooper, recalls Gary Cooper's tall, silent-type western heroes, most notably Will Kane in *High Noon*.

Released in the summer of 1968, following the assassinations of Dr. Martin Luther King Jr. and Robert F. Kennedy, and during the self-destructive Democratic National Convention in Chicago, *Hang 'Em High*'s star-powered, testosterone-driven blood and gore was a welcome dose of adolescent action escapism and cleaned up at the box office, grossing approximately $7 million in its initial domestic theatrical release, nearly a half-million more than *The Good, the Bad and the Ugly*. Unlike some films that have to find an audience, *Hang 'Em High*, made for approximately $1.5 million, took off from day one and became the biggest-grossing film in UA's storied history, a tribute to the times and to Hollywood's newest action star, Clint Eastwood. It went into profits almost immediately, and established both Clint and Malpaso as power players in the independent film scene of 1970s Hollywood.

Some critics bemoaned the fact that the Man with No Name had taken on a real identity, "Americanized" and softened for a broader appeal; but most believed that westerns were still best (meaning most popular) when made in Hollywood in English with gorgeous women and familiar-faced villains. Archer Winston, one of the more popular daily New York City print critics, called the film "a western of quality, courage, danger and excitement, which places itself squarely in the procession of old fashioned westerns made with the latest techniques." Even the *New York Times* (Howard Thompson this time, in place of Crowther, who was on the way out after his grossly negative reading of Arthur Penn's 1967 *Bonnie and Clyde*), which had had no use for the Leone-Eastwood movies, begrudgingly admitted that "*Hang 'Em High* has its moments." But the *Times* still didn't get Clint: "Most unfortunate of all, Mr. Eastwood, with his glum sincerity, isn't much of an actor."

But he was enough of a star to ensure that his films made money, and the bottom line was the only critique that mattered to Jennings Lang, the head of Universal. Following the completion of *Hang 'Em High*, Lang offered Clint a cool $1 million to star in his first "big" (i.e., fully studio-financed) American major studio film, the fish-out-of-water *Coogan's Bluff*, to be directed by Alex Segal, about an Arizona horseback deputy assigned to bring back a murderer hiding out in New York City.

Writer Herman Miller originally conceived the script as a two-hour pilot for Universal TV, but Lang ordered it revised for a big-screen feature and assigned the task to Jack Laird. As it happened, both Miller and Laird were *Rawhide* alumni.

Lang had convinced Hirshan that *Coogan's Bluff* was the perfect vehicle for Clint's next film, and when Clint signed on, pending script approval, Lang took Miller and Laird off the project—reportedly Clint did not like their version. They were replaced by a succession of writers assigned to tailor the script to Clint's satisfaction.* Once the script met with Clint's approval, director Alex Segal was the next to go, replaced, at Clint's insistence, by Don Siegel. How that happened is a story only Clint should tell:

> I had signed with Universal Pictures to do a film called *Coogan's Bluff*. That was to be my second American film after coming in off the plains of Spain. The studio had recommended a director by the name of Alex Segal, who had come from back east and had several plays, television shows, and movies to his credit. Segal had some personal problem which precluded him from doing this film and he withdrew. Then the studio came up with the suggestion, "How about Don Siegel?" Now, in a business in which nepotism runs rampant, I began to think, "Hold on just a minute, what relationship do these two have and how many more Siegels are we going to go through before we get this picture on the road?"

More than a little skeptical, Clint agreed to screen a couple of Siegel's films before setting about to find a real director. But Siegel's *Invasion of the Body Snatchers* (1956) made him sit up and take notice. It was, as he later recalled, "one of the two or three finest B movies ever made and I realized that this was a man who could do an awful lot with very little. *Coogan's Bluff* was a [relatively] modest-budget picture, but perhaps we could get a lot more on the screen for the dollar

---

*The concept for the film survived later on as a TV show called *McCloud*, starring Dennis Weaver (Chester of *Gunsmoke* fame), created by and credited to Miller. The screenplay underwent at least seven full revisions, and final on-screen writing credits went to Herman Miller, Dean Riesner, and Howard Rodman, story by Herman Miller.

and push the film on to a higher echelon of 'look.' So I said, 'Yes, let's go with Don Siegel.' "*

Siegel was something of an oddity in Hollywood. He had worked at Warner Bros. in the 1930s making shorts, and on dozens of hit movies in various subdirectorial roles. After bouncing around from studio to studio, he landed at Universal, where he directed *Invasion of the Body Snatchers*, one of the most spectacular and disturbing films of the 1950s, a classic sci-fi horror crossed with political paranoia that did to falling asleep what Hitchcock's *Psycho* (1960) did to taking showers. Based on a novel by Jack Finney, it had perfectly captured the fear and loathing of an America that believed communism was to individuality what the pods were to human beings—irretrievably stealing one's individuality. (Its stylistic use of stairs and heights, and the climactic relentless pursuit through the streets and into the hills, would be echoed in *Dirty Harry*.) Siegel's next assignment at Universal was to direct *Baby Face Nelson*, which received terrific reviews but went nowhere. A series of ho-hum jobs followed, including *Spanish Affair* (1957), *The Line-Up* (1958; adapted from the hit TV series, its stark semidocumentary view of San Francisco police work and the pursuit of maniacal killer Eli Wallach foreshadow the action, mood, and pace of *Dirty Harry*), *The Gun Runners* (1958), *Hound-Dog Man* (1959), *Edge of Eternity* (1959), *Flaming Star* (1960), *Hell Is for Heroes* (1962), *Stranger on the Run* (1967—TV), and *Madigan* (1968). The thirty-eighth film (out of the fifty he would eventually make) was *Coogan's Bluff*, the smash he had been looking for to return him to the spotlight. It was the first of a series of films that Clint and Siegel would make together.

Clint, the temperamental don't-tell-me-what-to-do-unless-you-

---

*Siegel remembered it a little differently: "There was a mix-up at Universal. Clint Eastwood, whom I not only did not know but had never seen in person or on film, was considering two directors for his first starring feature at Universal. Their names were Alex Segal and Don Taylor . . . In the basement of the Black Tower [Universal Studios corporate headquarters] there existed proudly a brand-new computer. Two names were fed into it—Alex Segal and Don Taylor . . . the name that appeared was Don Siegel. Clint asked the executive producer, Dick Lyons, 'Who the hell is Don Siegel?' . . . when I found out he had screened three of my pictures and wanted to know if I was interested in directing *Coogan's Bluff*, I responded that I'd like to see the three Sergio Leone pictures." Don Siegel, *A Siegel Film: An Autobiography* (London: Faber and Faber, 1993), p. 294.

know-what-you're-doing star, and Don Siegel, the just-do-what-I-tell-you authoritarian, each marked his turf, and neither would let the other upset the power balance necessary to get this movie made.

Many on the set were surprised by how well they did get along, after a couple of early and minor bumps in the road. The key was mutual respect; Clint had been looking for someone (who spoke English) to show him how a movie was put together, and Siegel was more than happy to show Clint how the tricks were done.

Early on in the shoot, according to Clint,

> I learned a lot from [Siegel] in the sense that he's a man who does a lot with a little—so therefore our philosophies are pretty much akin . . . he's a very lean kind of director . . . *Coogan's Bluff* was the first picture we did together. It was a fun film to do in the sense that it started out with another director, and Don and I didn't know each other. We started out butting heads together a little, and as it turned out, we ended up with a great working relationship.

Siegel agreed: "I thought we did very well."

One aspect of the film that seems unmistakably Siegel is its heavy, at times obvious, metaphorical overlay. In the turbulent 1960s, when the country was divided by the unpopular and ultimately unwinnable war in Vietnam, uncomplicated heroes in popular movies were hard to find. *Coogan's Bluff* works precisely because it depicts New York City as an urban, lawless "jungle," commandeered by a tough yet ineffective cop. Detective Lieutenant McElroy was played by the always powerful Lee J. Cobb, an actor who couldn't be more different on-screen from Clint. Cobb, heavyset, rough, sneering, and street-smart, was the polar opposite of the tall, lean country boy Clint. If the American psyche was desperate for someone to come in and end the Vietnam nightmare, it found its savior in the movies. Cobb is reminiscent of General Westmoreland, while Clint is the heroic rebel who comes in, cleans up the situation, and removes the bad guy. As Coogan, he was a Central Casting American hero who single-handedly captures the villain by waging a guerrilla-type war on "foreign" turf.

The sub-rosa Vietnam symbolism, overlaid with a good-guy-gets-bad-guy formula that is as old as film itself, was right in Siegel's wheelhouse. The alien fighting the bad guy was a kind of inversion of the plot structure of *Invasion of the Body Snatchers* and became the cinematic glue that held the film's spine in place.

Coogan's Bluff, which stretched Clint beyond his Man with No Name, was highly anticipated by audiences and critics alike. But reviews for the film were mixed at best; critics either loved or hated it. Judith Crist called the film, in *New York* magazine, "the worst happening of the year." But Vincent Canby, the *New York Times*'s newest and most astute film critic (and its best overall writer yet about film), in a combination review and think piece, enthusiastically compared Clint to screen icon James Dean. Archer Winston, writing in the *New York Post*, noted Don Siegel's directorial contribution but more or less ignored Clint, as did the weekly edition of *Variety*.

Kitty Jones, an agent during the late 1960s, was someone Clint had befriended in his early TV days and had remained a member of his inner circle of friends. She regularly held social salons in her apartment on Cahuenga Boulevard, which Clint often attended with a couple of his friends from the old studio days. A young starlet by the name of Jill Banner remembered those afternoons and, in particular, Clint's presence at them:

> He and his buddies were like a pack of wild college comedians, always horsing around, cracking jokes, telling risqué jokes, rough-housing and teasing the girls . . . his chums were guys he'd known a long time, one was Bill, another George, and he got them regular work on the *Rawhide* series. Another was Chill Wills, who was Francis the Talking Mule's speaking voice in Clint's first two films.
>
> Clint didn't give a shit about the la-de-da Hollywood crowd, or the traditional stylish symbols. He drove an old pickup truck [despite having two Ferraris], and I never saw him wear anything but Levi's, T-shirt, windbreaker jacket, and tennis shoes. He was a health nut. He didn't smoke but he could stow away plenty of beer, which he said was a health tonic.
>
> Kitty's girlfriends were crazy about him, not because he was so young and good-looking or a star but because he was kind, intelligent, and such a fun guy.

Maggie, firmly planted up in Carmel, never attended any of these salons.

Two days after the completion of *Coogan's Bluff*, he left for Europe; Brian G. Hutton's *Where Eagles Dare* was to be shot on location in England and Austria for MGM. In this World War II action drama a British officer is given a top-secret assignment to parachute behind enemy lines, somewhere in the Bavarian Alps, to rescue a captured American general before the latter can be tortured into revealing the details of the impending D-Day invasion at Normandy. He is accompanied by five commandos, one of whom is an American lieutenant, played by Clint Eastwood.

Where Eagles Dare was a big-budget action film starring one of the world's most famous actors, Richard Burton, at the peak of his fame but also on the brink of financial collapse. Burton was forced to accept movie work like *Where Eagles Dare* that didn't necessarily fit his needs or desires as an actor but earned him millions. Burton agreed to star in *Where Eagles Dare*, he told the insatiable coterie of press that followed him everywhere, because he wanted to make a movie that he could watch with his two daughters; his most recent films, he said, were not especially well suited for that. Behind the scenes, though, it was widely believed that he took it solely for the money.*

Costarring with Burton would bring Clint international attention for something other than a spaghetti western. And European audiences would get to see him again in a noncowboy role. *Where Eagles Dare* was sure to push his steadily growing salary toward his goal of a million dollars a movie.

To write the script, Burton approached his friend and colleague Elliott Kastner, who in turn recruited the well-known adventure novelist Alistair MacLean. MacLean had achieved a fair measure of film credibility from the adaptation of his novel (done by Carl Foreman) for J. Lee Thompson's World War II adventure *The Guns of Navarone* (1961). Burton particularly liked that film and wanted a script for *Where Eagles Dare* that would match it. MacLean had never written an original screenplay, but as all of his novels had already been made into movies or remained under option, he tried his hand with *Where Eagles Dare*, which he banged out in six weeks.

---

*The daughters, Kate and Jessica, were from his first marriage, to actress Sybil Williams.

Even as MacLean was putting the finishing touches on it, Clint held firm for $800,000 up front, a percentage of the profits, and equal-size name-above-the-title billing with Burton to compensate for his de facto second billing. He got almost everything he asked for: the $800,000 up front, the percentage, and the equal size, but without Burton's name-above-the-title credit.

After a few days in London he flew to Salzburg to begin the shoot, still wearing faded jeans and carrying a single torn canvas bag. His style was markedly different from that of the Burtons (Elizabeth Taylor accompanied her husband on the flight to Salzburg), who flew in formal attire via private jet amid the rush and glare of European-style paparazzi. No sooner had Clint settled into his hotel, the same one where the Burtons were staying, than he received a call from the actor to join him in the lounge for drinks.

For the rest of that day and into the night the two drank—or rather Burton drank and Clint observed, and what he saw was not pleasant. Here was Burton, conceivably the biggest movie star in the world, a hopeless drunk, self-justifying and self-pitying, with one eye on his whiskey and the other on the waitress who kept bringing it. He had made a fortune in film but was still strapped for cash—something incomprehensible to Clint. And while Burton could still pass as a leading man, he looked at least a dozen years older than he had five years earlier, when he shot to international stardom and scandal in *Cleopatra*. What's more, he was puffy and out of shape and smoking up to sixty cigarettes a day despite his needing to be fit for a film that would tax all his physical abilities.

According to Ingrid Pitt, who played a minor role in the film (Heidi), Burton's fragile condition was apparent to everyone on set: "Clint and Richard Burton were so different. Clint was looking forward to the rest of his career. He was watching everything . . . Richard Burton was just drinking and spouting Shakespeare. He was unhappy. He drank . . . he was just tired of living." It was a powerful cautionary tale for the always-careful Clint.

Elizabeth Taylor—Liz, as everyone who knew her called her—was another story. She stayed only briefly in Salzburg, leaving shortly before the filming of the most difficult physical scenes—she could not stand to watch them because the untimely death of her third husband, producer Mike Todd, in a plane crash still haunted her dreams. While in Salzburg, she formed an easy, informal friendship with Clint.* Often while Burton was off doing a scene, Liz and Clint would sit and talk—about their careers, their lives, their loves, their dreams. Early on Taylor knew she wanted to work with Clint. She received dozens of scripts every day from producers and studios hoping to work with her and had recently come across one she liked. It was about a nun caught in the crossfire of a Mexican insurgency and an American mercenary who rescues her from being raped and murdered and helps to bring her to safety. The plot had a few clever twists—the mercenary at first doesn't know the woman is a nun, and she winds up at one point rescuing him. Whatever her motives—friendship, mutual attraction, rivalry (on both their parts) with Burton—Taylor thought the script was perfect for herself and Clint, he in the role that would naturally have gone to Burton if he had been in better shape and if he had had any interest in that type of film, which he didn't. Not even opposite her. Or *especially* not opposite her.

By now Burton had—inevitably, perhaps—begun to feel negatively about sharing the stage with his wife's all-encompassing persona. The problem was, she was a far more limited actor (as far as he was concerned), and their films together were the least worthy—if, ironically, most successful—of his career. Clint, who lacked any classical training or pretenses to greatness, had no such concerns.

But their talks of working together went nowhere. As Clint later explained, "The script was given to me by Elizabeth Taylor when I was doing *When Eagles Dare* with her husband. We wanted to do it together, and the studio approved of the combination [of stars], but [as it turned out] she was going through some deal where she didn't want to work [alone] unless it coincided with Richard's working, so we had it set up to do in Mexico while Richard was working there on something else,† but then there were other problems." Whatever those problems may have been, the imagined Taylor-Eastwood collaboration never happened.

Before any of his *Eagles* scenes were shot, Clint had taken to alter-

---

*Burton was Taylor's fifth and sixth husband (she married him twice), following her brief marriage to singer Eddie Fisher.
†Probably *The Assassination of Trotsky* (1972), directed by Joseph Losey.

ing his dialogue. For the most part he disregarded Hutton, the director, whom Kastner had hired despite a notable lack of credentials. Hutton had directed only three films before *Where Eagles Dare*: *Wild Seed* (1965, aka *Fargo*), *The Pad and How to Use It* (1966), and *Sol Madrid* (1968), a detective story also known as *The Heroin Gang*. Before that he had worked occasionally as an actor, mostly in TV episodics. Kastner, with his partner Jerry Gershwin, had produced *Sol Madrid* and was impressed by Hutton's abilities. The film's financial success also helped Kastner to decide to go with Hutton on *Eagles*, even though it would be considerably more difficult and expensive to make. Because Burton's fee took a lion's share of the film's budget, with Clint's right behind, Kastner needed to keep the rest of his production costs down while maintaining an acceptable level of quality. Hutton may have been talented, but his best asset for this film was that he came cheap.

Burton did not waste much time studying his part in MacLean's screenplay. To him, these films were all the same; he had a job to do, and he wanted to get through it as quickly and painlessly as possible. Clint, on the other hand, went through the script page by page. He was confused by the inconsistencies in his character's dialogue, which made little sense. As he had for *A Fistful of Dollars*, and as he would do with every script henceforth, he went through it and slashed every unnecessary line of his own dialogue, leaving himself relatively little to say while he performs his character's impressive physical feats, for which he was doubled most of the time. After the film was released, he joked to friends that it should have been called *When Doubles Dare*.*

The production encountered innumerable problems, including blizzards, four-foot snowdrifts, and avalanches; outbreaks of altitude sickness and frostbite; fistfights on a moving cable car (Burton); and a high-speed motorcycle ride through a fierce snowstorm on a winding mountain road (Clint). But when the film was finally finished and rushed into production, it received surprisingly good reviews. *Variety* said it was "so good for its genre that one must go back to [John Sturges's 1963] *The Great Escape* for a worthy comparison." Rex Reed,

---

*Clint's stunt-heavy action scenes were done by veteran stuntman and second-unit director Yakima Canutt, best known for creating the chariot-race sequence in William Wyler's *Ben-Hur* (1959).

then writing film reviews for *Women's Wear Daily*, told his readers, "If you stop being so serious and sophisticated . . . you can have a wonderful time at *Where Eagles Dare.*" Andrew Sarris also liked it. "Richard Burton and Clint Eastwood," he wrote, "balance out the savage and sardonic elements of the movie into an inconsistent but generally engrossing entertainment."

Whether its audiences came to see Burton or Clint or both, the film grossed more than $15 million in its initial domestic theatrical release, enough to make it MGM's top earner of 1969. A million more was tacked on when the film was released worldwide.

At home things were changing as well. In May 1968, after fifteen years of marriage, Maggie gave birth to a baby boy whom she and Clint named Kyle Clinton Eastwood. The baby's arrival was a mixed blessing. For Maggie, Kyle was an undeniable reaffirmation of her unusual marriage. In a rare interview the two gave shortly afterward, Maggie explained that the secret to their long and successful marriage (as she described it) was "We don't believe in togetherness!" Clint echoed that emotion, although he put a slightly different slant on it: "By [the time we had our child], I knew we could get along well enough to last . . . that we'd stay together."

Amid all the change and accolades, Clint went straight off to make yet another movie; but this one would come to be universally regarded as one of his worst. *Paint Your Wagon* was a big-screen version of a relatively obscure 1951 Broadway musical that had yielded only one semi-hit song, "They Call the Wind Maria." It was a collaboration of Alan J. Lerner and Frederick Loewe, who had also done several other musicals, most notably *Brigadoon* (1947), *My Fair Lady* (1956), and *Camelot* (1960). All of these Broadway shows had been made into hit movies, leading the way to the film version of *Paint Your Wagon*.

Movie musicals were a huge gamble in the late 1960s as the song-and-dance era of Fred Astaire and Gene Kelly was long over; still, *My Fair Lady* (1964), directed by George Cukor, won eight Oscars, including Best Picture, and was nominated for four more; its star, Rex Harrison, won Best Actor. But only three years later Harrison nearly single-handedly destroyed the genre and his own career (and along the way 20th Century–Fox, still reeling from the debacle of *Cleopatra*, in which he costarred) in Richard Fleischer's ill-conceived, poorly executed, and publicly ignored *Doctor Dolittle*, which inexplicably received an Oscar nomination for Best Picture. The film's poor showing appeared to have once and for all put an end to big-budget musicals—until Paramount decided to try to turn *Paint Your Wagon* into a $14 million cinematic musical extravaganza.

Since the end of Hollywood's studio era, a new logic had taken over the industry. *Paint Your Wagon* was (at least ostensibly) a "western"—another troubled genre, thanks mostly to the proliferation of westerns on TV. So the studio wanted the last big Hollywood "cowboy" star around, Clint Eastwood, to help revive both genres. To get him, they created a role, Pardner, that had not existed in the original Broadway version. Pardner was a curious mixture of the "good" Rowdy from *Rawhide* and the "bad" Man with No Name from the spaghetti westerns. The producers paired Clint with Lee Marvin, who had played "grizzled" to Oscar-winning perfection in Elliot Silverstein's *Cat Ballou* (1965). In Hollywood terms, it was "can't miss" casting. Added to the mix was Pulitzer Prize–winning director Joshua Logan,* whose film versions of several other Broadway musicals, including the moneymaking *Camelot* (1967), seemed like the financial icing on the cake.

Clint very much wanted to be a part of this project. He had always liked Joshua Logan's films, believing he was an actor's director, and felt he needed to work with someone like that after Brian Hutton's mechanical directing on *Where Eagles Dare*. He also very much looked forward to working with screenwriter Paddy Chayefsky, who promised a radical rethinking of the original Broadway book that would make it infinitely more screen-friendly. And finally Clint liked Andre Previn's easygoing musical style; Previn had been hired to write several new songs specifically for Clint, and he promised to make them close to the quiet, jazzy style Clint favored and that was easy for him to sing.

Irving Leonard managed to get $500,000 up front for Clint, a figure still considerably below his sought-after million, but Leonard had so constructed the deal that much of Clint's salary would be deferred for tax advantages and he would have a hefty participation in the

---

*Logan shared the Pulitzer Prize awarded for helping to bring Rodgers and Hammerstein's *South Pacific* to the Broadway stage in 1949.

expected profits. Leonard also managed to get Clint cast-approval, which was how actress Jean Seberg managed to land the role of the Mormon wife Pardner decides to buy, and who subsequently becomes part of a three-way relationship. Lerner had created this character to juice up the film a bit for younger audiences, and Clint insisted that it be played by Seberg.

The actress was widely believed to be French because of her roles in Otto Preminger's *Saint Joan* (1957), his in-French production of *Bonjour Tristesse* (1958, aka *Hello, Sadness* in English), and especially Jean-Luc Godard's groundbreaking French *Breathless* (1960, *À Bout de Souffle*), one of the jewels of the French Nouvelle Vague that became an international sensation and inspired the post–*Bonnie and Clyde* generation of independent American filmmakers. In fact, Seberg was born in Iowa and had moved to Paris during her appearances in *Saint Joan* and *Bonjour Tristesse* and lived there for a while after *Breathless*. By the time she agreed to appear in *Paint Your Wagon*, her career was on the decline due mostly to her active involvement with various leftist radical organizations and her outspoken support of the widely feared American Black Panther Party. That support caught the attention of J. Edgar Hoover, who many believed used the Bureau to hound her until she committed suicide in 1979 at the age of forty-one from an overdose of sleeping pills.

But at thirty-one she was still a ravishing beauty, with big eyes, high cheekbones, and a European-acquired air of sophistication that, when he first met her during the casting, nearly drove Clint wild. At his insistence she was hired, and the two immediately began an on-set affair that they hid from no one. They carried on even as the film itself escalated out of control under the direction of Logan, whose manic-depression went wildly unchecked. The result was a budget that escalated to $30 million, to produce a film that had as much life as an embalmed body.

Seberg and Clint stopped carrying on only when Maggie showed up to pay a visit at the Oregon location shoot, infant in tow. As soon as she left, the entire cast and crew let out a collective sigh and the affair resumed—until the film ran out of location money amid script differences between Logan, Chayefsky, and Clint, and the cast had to return to the soundstages of Hollywood to finish the shoot. At that point, perhaps feeling he was too close to home, and also near the end of the shoot, Clint dropped Seberg. Already in a troubled marriage to Romain Gary, Seberg's heart was broken.

After five grueling months of work it became clear that Logan had no idea what to do with the growing financial monster that was *Paint Your Wagon*. The film was unofficially finished by assistant director Tom Shaw. By now Paramount, the studio financing the film, just wanted it to end, believing, as did everyone involved, that it was going to be one of the most expensive Christmas turkeys ever given to the filmgoing public. Although it grossed a respectable $14.5 million in its first full year of domestic release—helped by charitable reviews and Clint's undeniable box-office pull—it came nowhere near its break-even point, which, because of all the cost overruns, was somewhere close to $60 million.* In the years to come the film's critical response would not improve. (The *Times* always runs the same blurb about it whenever it shows up in its TV listing: "California gold rush musical. Elaborate but squatty, and Clint sings like a moose.")

Paint Your Wagon, while not an out-and-out disaster, was undoubtedly a downward turn in the otherwise steadily rising arc of Clint's career. Now, as the 1960s cross-faded into the 1970s, and as independent film was gaining its strongest foothold in Hollywood since the beginning of the studio-dominated century, Clint decided to make a giant leap forward. A studio effort like *Paint Your Wagon* was, he felt, now a dinosaur from an industry that had long ago lost its hold on fresh and independent moviemaking. He was sure he could do better.

In other words, he wanted to direct.

But to do so he would have to also produce, as no one was about to hire him despite his star-status, and with no previous directing credits, to helm a movie with a budget of several million dollars. He would have to find the money himself and use it to deep-seed Malpaso. In

---

*In many overseas markets, the film was released with all its songs removed, in the hope it might attract loyal Clint Eastwood western fans. Clint later tried to defend the decision: "In Italy they did that on the first release. That's common practice. Musicals have been terrible flops in Europe, with the exception of *West Side Story*. Most times, they omit all the music." Quoted by Dick Lochte in *Los Angeles Free Press*, April 20, 1973.

the interim he would watch, listen, produce, and star in the films of other directors from whom he thought he could learn something.

Which is why, having decided to move out of the Hollywood mainstream, he figured the quickest and most expedient way to get what he wanted was to dive even deeper into it.

EIGHT

I feel Don Siegel is an enormously talented guy who has been deprived of the notoriety he probably should have had much earlier because Hollywood was going through a stage where the awards went to the big pictures and the guys who knew how to spend a lot of money. As a result, guys who got a lot of pictures with a lot of effort and a little money weren't glorified. So Don had to wait many years until he could get to do films with fairly good budgets. He's the kind of director there's not enough of. If things don't go as planned, he doesn't sit down and cry and consider everything lost, as some directors do.

—Clint Eastwood

Seeking to capitalize on his growing popularity and steadily growing box-office clout, Clint wanted to make pictures that showed off his best qualities without turning him into a perpetual cartoon version of the Man with No Name. While others in Clint's position might have happily accepted simple, popular, gritty western after gritty western and enjoyed a single-persona run (as Arnold Schwarzenegger did until the novelty wore off and his film career ended), Clint was after something different, even if he wasn't sure yet exactly what that was. Having attained the level of a legitimate Hollywood star, he would surely remain there—going back to pumping gas held no allure at all.

As an actor, Clint knew that the Man with No Name held audiences' interest because of his unique imperfections (no family, no woman, no past, and no future) rather than the standard-issue imperfections (heartbreak, separation, and desperation). He understood that it was their fascination with this unique character that had ignited his rising star.

But as a filmmaker, Clint had no interest in perpetuating that character until it became a caricature. Instead, he wanted to get behind and inside of the image he projected onto the screen. To do so, he needed to generate work that not only suited this goal but was within his grasp.

Despite his surprise success with the spaghetti westerns, his journey of cinematic self-exploration had thus far been neither quick, nor easy, nor smooth. Now the well-intentioned misadventure of *Paint Your Wagon* had nearly wrecked all that he had previously achieved. The artistic failure of that film, even more than the financial one, convinced him once and for all that no one in Hollywood knew anything, certainly no more than he did and probably a lot less, about how to make a good film that could earn a decent profit.

Still, he had a lot to learn about putting what was in his head onto the screen, and he had five years to learn it. His nonexclusive 1968 contract at Universal (Lang had gotten him to sign it by doubling his salary for *Coogan's Bluff* to $1 million) would expire in 1975 at the earliest, depending upon how many pictures he made for them during that time. It would not be easy to make the films he wanted. Disappointments came early, as the projects he brought to the studio were met with little or no support. To make matters worse, in December 1969 Irving Leonard—Clint's longtime business manager, the president and primary of Malpaso, and a true friend—died suddenly of a heart attack at the age of fifty-three. Few events outwardly affected cool-customer Clint, but the loss of Leonard visibly shook him up.

Leonard was irreplaceable in his uniquely combined roles as father-figure and mentor and pervasive guiding light. But to try, Clint chose entertainment lawyer and now his resident producer, Bob Daley, whom he had known since *Rawhide* days, when Daley was a cost analyst at the studio, working his way up to unit manager. His job had been to control the flow of money during productions, including *Rawhide*. Clint had always liked Daley's business style and acumen, keeping costs low and cutting out the usual ego-stroking expenditures like providing limos for stars and other perks. Daley's job now at Malpaso would be to continue to help Clint find great projects he could star in and produce and help him handle his daily finances and act as go-between with Malpaso's accounting firm, Kaufman and Bernstein.*

The first film that Clint decided to pursue after Leonard's passing was the one Elizabeth Taylor had brought to him, *Two Mules for Sister Sara*. He had run it by Leonard, who approved of the idea shortly before he died. Clint wanted to make it because he felt the character was a more humanized, in-depth version of the Man with No Name. The film's producer was Marty Rackin, a screenwriter who had enjoyed a fair measure of success in the 1950s before turning to full-time producing—he held the option on the original script, written by veteran writer-director Budd Boetticher. Clint and Taylor were his first choice to star in the film.

Then Taylor informed Rackin that she wanted the production transferred from Mexico to Spain, but Rackin insisted on keeping the

---

*Roy Kaufman and Howard Bernstein had been brought together to form their accounting firm by Leonard. Their first client was Clint Eastwood.

location in Mexico, to be faithful to the script and to keep production costs down. Taylor was also experiencing some of the recurring "health problems" that had plagued her throughout her career. When the insurance for her alone proved beyond the film's budget, Rackin and Universal decided to cut her loose.* Clint agreed to stay on, as long as he could have a say in who would direct. Rackin had no objections to bringing in Clint's first choice, Don Siegel.

To replace Taylor, Universal chose Shirley MacLaine, a Broadway dancer who had become a glittering movie star after her performance in Alfred Hitchcock's *The Trouble with Harry* (1955). Now that she had just finished making *Sweet Charity* at Universal for Bob Fosse, the studio, believing that was going to be huge, pushed for her to be in the picture. Clint, Rackin, and Siegel all agreed, and MacLaine was in.

"There was no question that Shirley was a fine actress with a great sense of humor," Siegel later recalled.

> But her skin was fair, her face—the map of Ireland. She most likely would look ridiculous if she played a Mexican nun. Nevertheless, Shirley was assigned to the picture . . . naturally the script had to be rewritten to fit her appearance . . . After working with Marty and Clint on the script, I made a startling discovery. Budd Boetticher, in addition to writing the story, had also written the script. He was a well-known director and a good friend of mine . . . I asked him why he wasn't considered to be the director, and he claimed that Marty never gave him a straight answer. He needed money, so he sold his story and script to Marty, who took the property to Universal, got their okay, and hired Albert Maltz to write another script. I felt funny about being his director. Budd laughed and told me that everything was settled with Marty long before I appeared on the scene. We remained good friends.

As shot by Siegel, the film resembled nothing so much as the Man with No Name trilogy cut with the moral high ground of *Coogan's Bluff*. Siegel deepened Clint's familiar cigar-chomping character (here

---

*Universal may have balked at the idea after Taylor's previous film, Joseph Losey's *Boom!*, costarring Richard Burton, bombed at the box office and she refused to reduce her seven-figure asking price to appear in *Two Mules for Sister Sara*.

called Hogan), contemporized and Americanized his feelings toward women, expanding his need for self-redemption by rescuing them. What had been a one-line backstory in the Leone films now became the main plot in *Two Mules for Sister Sara*, which couldn't have pleased Clint more.

The setting of the film is mid-nineteenth-century Mexico, during the Juarista rebellion to oust Napoleon's occupying French army. A plan is in the works to attack a French army post in Chihuahua. Hogan (Clint) is an American mercenary (as was the Man with No Name) who comes upon a group of outlaws about to rape a woman (MacLaine). In a quick but fierce gun battle (like the opening sequence in *A Fistful of Dollars*) an unshaven Hogan, smoking a cigar butt and wearing an approximation of the Man with No Name's iconic poncho, kills the men and agrees to help the woman to safety after he discovers she is a nun trying to escape the French who want to kill her for having aided the Juaristas. Along the way he discovers she is no ordinary nun. She swears, she drinks, she seems comfortable with her womanliness, and she uses all of her considerable charm to get him to help her sabotage a French supply train. Hogan is wounded during the attack, and Sara nurses him back to health. Then he discovers Sara is really a prostitute disguised as a nun. They fall in love, and when the mission is completed, this curious and mysterious couple ride off together, disappearing into the beautiful Mexican terrain.

The film was scored by Ennio Morricone, who had written the unforgettable scores for the Leone trilogy, further linking Hogan to the Man with No Name and making the film an informal kind of Americanized sequel. Said Clint:

> I think [the Leone films] changed the style, the approach to Westerns [in Hollywood]. They "operacized" them, if there's such a word. They made the violence and the shooting aspect a little more larger than life, and they had great music and new types of scores. I wasn't involved in the music, but we used the same composer, Ennio Morricone, in *Sister Sara* . . . They were stories that hadn't been used in other Westerns. They just had a look and a style that was a little different at the time: I don't think any of them was a classic story—like [John Ford's 1956] *The Searchers* or something like that—they were more fragmented,

episodic, following the central character through various little episodes . . . Sergio Leone felt that sound was very important, that a film has to have its own sound as well as its own look.

Clint's intention was to develop the Siegel-Eastwood connection as an extension of the Leone-Eastwood one, to Americanize the spaghetti westerns and hopefully duplicate their phenomenal commercial success and restore Eastwood's prime film persona as a soft-spoken, charming killer with a redemptive soul. Clint later claimed to have done his best acting to date in the film, especially in the scene where Sara removes the arrow from his shoulder. The sequence is done in medium close-up, and Clint had to play "drunk," which Sara has gotten him, in order to extract the arrow, an unmistakably evocative scene. During it he softly sings a song, an unexpected choice that both quiets and deepens his character. Here the film defines itself as something other than a retroactively slick sequel; it reveals itself for what it really is, a love story. For Clint, this was a crucial step forward in his development as a romantic leading man whose box-office reach would take him beyond fans of action films and dopey musicals to include a wider audience.

Women.

Once *Two Mules for Sister Sara* was completed, Clint returned to Carmel and Maggie only long enough to repack his bags and take off again, this time to London and Yugoslavia. For the next eight months he would serve as one of the stars of MGM's *The Warriors*, a film Clint was allowed to do because of his nonexclusive contract with Universal. The title was later changed to *Kelly's Heroes*, and it was a satire protesting the Vietnam War. Robert Altman's *M*A*S*H* (1970) had been the first anti-Vietnam film, set in Korea to ease the pain. *Kelly's Heroes* was set even farther back, during World War II, making its satire even more striking (and safer), set against the most hallowed, uncriticized war in American history.

Clint agreed to make the movie for a number of reasons. Although he was a Nixon man, having voted for him in the explosive year of 1968, he rejected the president's constant bombing of Vietnam as unnecessary, both politically and morally. In no way could Clint ever be described as a liberal, but neither was he ever a proselytizing

Republican. The best way of describing his politics would be "prag-matic independence." By 1970, after seven years of a blistering war that was going nowhere, he, like many Americans on both sides of the political fence, was simply fed up with it. The script of *Kelly's Heroes* (in which he plays the title role) brought just the right amount of cyn-icism to the whole affair.

Supporting him on-screen were Telly Savalas, who had made an impact a few years earlier as fellow inmate Feto Gomez in Burt Lan-caster's star-turning prison biopic, John Frankenheimer's *Birdman of Alcatraz* (1962); insult-comic-with-a-heart-of-gold Don Rickles, who had appeared in Robert Wise's *Run Silent Run Deep* (1958, in support of Clark Gable), Robert Mulligan's *The Rat Race* (1960), and a host of less memorable TV appearances before breaking into live late-night television on Johnny Carson's *Tonight Show* in the vicious but lovable stand-up-comic persona that finally made him a star; Donald Suther-land, coming off his portrayal of Hawkeye in *M*A*S*H;* and Carroll O'Connor, who later that year would find his best role as the bigoted but somehow lovable Archie Bunker in TV's *All in the Family.* All these supporting players here planted the seeds of their coming personae (and Rickles the elements of the "wise guy" that he never fully real-ized on film) that helped focus the attention on Clint's lead.

He really wanted Don Siegel to direct, so much so that he had signed on to the film because Siegel had agreed to do it. But at the last minute Siegel had to pull out because of postproduction editing prob-lems with *Two Mules for Sister Sara*—he and Rackin clashed over the editing. The picture was offered instead to Brian Hutton, with whom Clint had last worked on *Where Eagles Dare.* Although his aesthetic side may have hesitated to go with him, Clint's practical side knew that Hutton's films made money, and he approved his being assigned to the picture.

But the addition of Hutton and the subtraction of Siegel upset the directorial skill needed to maintain the balance between satire and "clever caper." Under Hutton, the film focused far more on the blocks of gold bullion than on the bombs and bureaucracy.

In the end, *Kelly's Heroes* looked more bloated than big, more bulky than expansive; the complicated location shoot went on for what felt like forever to Clint, although by all accounts the on-set chemistry was great. According to Rickles, Clint was easy and fun to work with:

I worked on *Kelly's Heroes*, with Clint Eastwood. They told me the shoot would take three weeks. It took six months. I also had a problem with the food. Everything was swimming in oil. Some of us became track stars as we broke the sound barrier to the bathroom. Bottom line, though, was that the cast and I became buddies. "You'd be great, Clint," I told Eastwood, "if you'd ever learned to talk normal and stop whispering." Clint gave me that Eastwood look and whispered something I couldn't understand.

After nearly eight months of shooting and postproduction in London, Clint was obliged to do some additional promotion for *Paint Your Wagon* and to log some pieces for the still-unreleased (and still unfinished) *Two Mules for Sister Sara*. When he saw the final cut of *Kelly's Heroes*, he was particularly unhappy with something he had missed, a late-in-the-film parody of the climax of *The Good, the Bad and the Ugly*, reprised here with Clint, Savalas, and Sutherland. It confirmed for Clint how far off the film had gone, and he attributed it to the loss of Siegel as its director: "It was [originally] a very fine anti-militaristic script, one that said some important things about the war," Clint said later, "about this propensity that man has to destroy himself."

In the editing, the scenes that put the debate in philosophical terms were cut and they kept adding action scenes. When it was finished, the picture had lost its soul. If action and reflection had been better balanced, it would have reached a much broader audience. I don't know if the studio exercised pressure on the director or if it was the director who lost his vision along the way, but I know that the picture would have been far superior if there hadn't been this attempt to satisfy action fans at any cost. And it would have been just as spectacular and attractive. It's not an accident that some action movies work and others don't.

Kelly's Heroes actually opened June 23, 1970, just one week after *Two Mules for Sister Sara*, which got much better reviews. None was more laudatory than the *Los Angeles Herald-Examiner*'s, which declared that *"Two Mules for Sister Sara* is a solidly entertaining film that provides Clint Eastwood with his best, most substantial role to date; in it he is far better than he has ever been. In director Don Siegel,

Eastwood has found what John Wayne found in John Ford and what Gary Cooper found in Frank Capra."

Both films ran simultaneously during the summer, something Clint wasn't happy about. He felt he was competing with himself and he wasn't entirely wrong. "Why should I open across the street from myself?" he complained to Jim Aubrey, the head of MGM, with whom Clint had butted heads before, at CBS. Nonetheless, both films proved successful at the box office, and with *Paint Your Wagon* still in theaters, three Clint Eastwood films were playing at the same time. Ironically, *Paint Your Wagon* proved the biggest hit of the three, its $7 million initial gross nearly doubling *Two Mules for Sister Sara*'s $4.7 million and well ahead of *Kelly's Heroes*'s $5.2 million. (*Two Mules* was ultimately more successful than *Kelly's*, as its ratio of cost-to-gross was much less.)

Clint should have been thrilled by his triple-header summer, with across-the-board hits and theaters all over the world filled with his image, but none of the three even came close to what he wanted to do in pictures, what he thought he could be, and what he thought he could earn. Instead, each had moved him closer to the ordinary mainstream and the bottom line of popular movie appeal—and taken his edge away.

He was still looking for the film that could cut him loose. He thought he found such a project in a script that Jennings Lang had sent to him during the making of *Kelly's Heroes*. Based on a novel by Thomas Cullinan and adapted into a screenplay by Albert Maltz (the onetime blacklisted, reformed alcoholic writer who had done the same for *Two Mules for Sister Sara*), the script for *The Beguiled* was impossible for Clint to forget. He read it in a single night and had anticipated yet another grizzled-hero western, but early in realized that it was much more. Perplexed, he asked Don Siegel to read it and give him his opinion. Siegel said he loved it, and on that assessment Clint decided to do it.

The story tells of John McBurney (Clint), a badly wounded Union soldier who is discovered by a ten-year-old girl named Amy (Pamelyn Ferdin) while she is picking mushrooms near the broken-down schoolhouse where she lives. She brings him back to the house, where headmistress Martha Farnsworth (Geraldine Page) offers him shelter. Eventually several students, including Amy and Edwina (Elizabeth Hartman), realize that if they let him go, he will certainly be captured and killed by the Rebel army. So to save his life, they make him a prisoner, confining him to the schoolhouse. At first McBurney does not realize what is happening, distracted by the apparently easy seductive powers he enjoys over many of the seemingly willing schoolgirls and their sexually repressed headmistress.

All of this takes a (literal) bad turn when Edwina sees him making love to one of the girls and vengefully pushes him down a long flight of stairs. The fall reinjures his bad leg, and the headmistress decides it must be amputated. When McBurney awakens and realizes his leg is missing, he angrily accuses all the girls of doing it to keep him their prisoner. Eventually, though, he becomes the sexual master of them all, picking and choosing each of the girls as he pleases, using and abusing them until they plot to kill him with poison mushrooms.

But before they can, McBurney dies of a heart attack (although they think at first they have indeed killed him). Afterward they erect a shrine to him to acknowledge how he has changed all of their lives forever.

The film's metaphor for devilish (or Christian) imperfection, McBurney's broken leg, is double-edged, symbolizing at once the inability (or unwillingness) to be free, physical injury (crucifixion), and moral defection (less than whole). The film's very loose retelling of the Christ tale—a man walks among us, is killed, is worshipped and immortalized by the very group that planned to kill him—is also one of the devil, of sexual passion, physical imprisonment, and moral domination.

However one chooses to read this unusual and absorbing film, *The Beguiled* is about a social rebel and an unrepentant ladies' man who becomes both a hero and a burden to those who care most for him. In that sense the film was his most autobiographical to date.

Even before Clint returned from Yugoslavia, the studio had assigned Julian Blaustein to produce, a decision that Clint, through Malpaso, meant to do something about. He had had enough of assigned studio "help," and just before production began on *The Beguiled*, Malpaso boldly dismissed Blaustein. Clint went to Don Siegel to convince him to direct, and Maltz to work on the script. Universal did nothing to stop any of these moves.

But, despite several rewrites, Maltz could not get down on paper what Clint was looking for. He wanted, more than anything, to have

McBurney's dark side emphasized and, in turn, the girls' as well. He was interested in shadows, not in sunlight, a choice that would make an even stronger contrast between the Sex Machine with No Name and the women who are both enthralled by and eventually driven to kill him. He envisioned the school as a metaphor for the dark chambers of the soul.

When Clint and Siegel could not make Maltz go as dark or as deep as they wanted, they enlisted the services of Irene Kamp, who had helped create the moody, jazz-framed script for Martin Ritt's 1961 *Paris Blues*, a film that held strong appeal for Clint. He loved the subtle way the script moved, and the open and frank adult sexuality among its four leads.

Kamp worked closely with Clint, adding nuance upon nuance to the script to make it more adult, more complex, and ultimately more personal. Still not completely satisfied, however, Clint turned to Claude Traverse, one of Siegel's longtime associates. In the end, Clint may have felt a man had to do the final draft. Maltz, meanwhile, so objected to anyone else working over his script that he took his name off it, using "John B. Sherry" as his on-screen credit (Irene Camp, as "Grimes Grice," shared the official on-screen credit).

Shooting on *The Beguiled* began in early April 1971, on location on a plantation in Baton Rouge, where the original novel was set. Among Clint's hand-chosen cast of female schoolgirls was JoAnn Harris, who quickly became his newest on-set romance. Neither one made any secret of their affair (which would burn brightly and then die out by the last day of production), and filming progressed smoothly and without incident. Then Lang, who had not seen the finished script before the film started production, loudly protested that he hated the ending. For the first time Clint Eastwood would die on-screen, an ending that was radically different from the novel and that made an already dark film that much darker. But, Clint (via Malpaso) by contract had the last word, and the ending stayed the way he wanted it.

The film opened late spring and bombed at the box office, grossing less than $1 million in its initial domestic release. Journalist James Bacon complained that Universal's advertising campaign had totally missed the meaning of the film, promoting it "as another spaghetti Western." In the few interviews he gave to promote it, Clint mused that his character's death was the problem, or that blind faith was a subject too dark for most audiences.

Reflecting on the film's failure, Don Siegel had this to say:

> Eastwood films are almost always released like a scatter-gun: play as many theaters as possible and the money pours in. Great. But it should have been recognized that a picture like *The Beguiled* needed to be handled differently. After winning a number of film festivals and acquiring some great quotes, it should have opened in a small theater in New York . . . It would have played for months, maybe a year . . . it would have grown slowly by word of mouth from a small start into a very successful film. [Releasing] the film [the way they did] was a brilliant way of ensuring its failure.

Clint's intention to make more personal movies that somehow also appealed to the mainstream was proving harder than he had thought. To interviewer Stuart M. Kaminsky, Clint explained why he had wanted to make the movie and to shape it the way he had:

> Don Siegel told me you can always be in a Western or adventure, but you may never get a chance to do this type of film again . . . it wasn't a typical commercial film, but we thought it could be a very good film, and that was important . . . I think it's a very well-executed film, the best-directed film Don's ever done, a very exciting film. Whether it's appealing to large masses or not, I don't know . . . [The studio] tried to sell it as if it were another western. People who go in expecting to see a western are disappointed and people who don't like westerns—but who might like *Beguiled*—don't go because of the ad. [They claimed that] the only way the film could do really well is if we could draw on those people who don't ordinarily like "Clint Eastwood" as well as those who do. People who like Clint Eastwood won't like *Beguiled* because I get offed.

There was some talk of submitting *The Beguiled* to Cannes, but Lang objected, and the film disappeared quietly and has been seen only rarely ever since. If it really was a career misstep for Clint, it was a good one, at least as far as he was concerned.

Although about to turn forty-one, an age considered "old" for a leading man, or at least "older" by Hollywood's standards, Clint felt younger than ever. With this, his first big-time flop coming as it did so soon after the death of Irving Leonard, he decided the time was finally right to take complete creative control of his career. He intended to direct the next film himself, to ensure that anything that went up on the screen looked exactly the way it did in his head.

NINE

After seventeen years of bouncing my head against the wall, hanging around sets, maybe influencing certain camera set-ups with my own opinions, watching actors go through all kinds of hell without any help, and working with both good directors and bad ones, I'm at the point where I'm ready to make my own pictures. I stored away all the mistakes I made and saved up all the good things I learned, and now I know enough to control my own projects and get what I want out of actors.

—Clint Eastwood

PREVIOUS PAGE: Dirty Harry, *1971*

Lhe last deal Irving Leonard put together before he died was the one that meant the most to Clint. Leonard had set up *Play Misty for Me* so that Clint would be able, for the first time, to direct as well as star in and produce the film, all under the auspices of Malpaso.* Timing has a way of accentuating changes—in this instance the departure of Don Siegel, who had become his unofficial creative partner and, more than Sergio Leone, his directorial mentor. It may be seen as the teacher giving way to the student, or the father stepping back to allow the son to take over the family business. The father-son aspect had a deep resonance, as Clint lost not only both Leonard and Siegel but his real father as well.

After moving from the Container Corporation to Georgia-Pacific, Clinton Eastwood Sr. had retired from the box and paper business and moved to Pebble Beach. While getting dressed for a day on the golf course, he dropped dead of a heart attack in July 1970. He was sixty-four years old.

Clint was, of course, shaken up by the death, but after a short and intense period of private mourning, he resumed preproduction on his new film. Familiarly reticent, Clint would be able to talk easily about the loss of his father only years later, expressing both regret and caution: "My father died very suddenly at sixty-three [*sic*]. Just dropped dead. For a long time afterward, I'd ask myself, why didn't I ask him to play golf more? Why didn't I spend more time with him? But when

---

*Clint may have wanted to only produce and direct, but at Lang's and Lew Wasserman's insistence, Universal demanded he star in the film as well. Because Clint was untested as a director but one of their biggest box-office stars, Lang saw his on-screen appearance as an insurance policy on the film's success. To seal the deal, Clint, via Leonard, agreed to give up his usual acting salary in return for a percentage of the profits.

you're off trying to get the brass ring, you forget and overlook those little things. It gives you a certain amount of regret later on, but there's nothing you can do about it, so you just forge on."

He told himself that if he didn't want to wind up like his father, he had better start cleaning up his own act—give up the smoking and cut back on the drinking. Exercise and health food were already part of his daily regimen, but several cold beers interspersed throughout the day remained and still are an essential part of his daily intake.

At the same time he promoted Bob Daley to full producer for Malpaso. One of Daley's first assignments under his expanded duties was to pull together the rest of the preproduction of *Play Misty for Me.*

The original screenplay had been written by Jo Heims, another longtime female friend of Clint's from his days as a contract player at Universal, when she was one of the studio's many legal secretaries. Like everyone else in Hollywood, she really had two professions, her own and the movies. All the while she was working her day job, she spent her nights writing screenplays. When she finally had what she considered a strong sixty-page treatment for a film, she took it to everyone she knew who might be able to help get it made. She got it into Clint's hands while he was still shooting *The Beguiled.* He promised Heims he would read it. He did and liked the story about a disk jockey who has a one-night stand with a caller to his late-night radio request show, who turns violent when she refuses to accept that it's over between them.

Clint turned the sixty pages over to Dean Riesner and asked him to work his magic and turn them into a shooting script that, since Malpaso was producing, could be made quickly and cheaply. As he later recalled, "It was just an ideal little project. The only downside to it, it wasn't an action-adventure film in the true sense of the word . . . but you have to keep breaking barriers."

Under the provisions of the deal he had made with Universal, Malpaso was going to have to underwrite the film. That meant a lot of nearby location shooting, so Clint chose to film it in Carmel, closer to home than any previous movie he had made; it meant few if any special effects or outdoor setups, and no large and expensive cast.

None of that especially mattered to Clint. The only thing that did now was the chance to direct. As Clint would later remember,

I started getting interested in directing back when I was still doing *Rawhide*. I directed a few trailers and [the producers] were going to let me do an episode until CBS kind of reneged. Somebody sent down an edict that said no more actors from the series could direct so they dropped me from that. I forgot about it for a while. Then I worked with Leone in Italy, and Don Siegel close together on several films. Don was very encouraging. "Why don't you direct, why don't you try it," he kept saying to me. It took a while for me, because I'd come in as sort of an outsider, through three European films, and now here I was, after hanging around for five or six years, suddenly here's this guy who wants to direct. I think there was a certain [industry] negativity toward it in the beginning. But I learned the most from Don Siegel and Sergio. They were such completely different people. Sergio was very humorous, and working on shoestring budgets, especially the first two, it was a little bit of chaos all the time. Everything was very loose, to say the least. But we were making a film for $200,000. With Don Siegel, he was very efficient and printed [used] only what he wanted.

The key to making the film work, Clint felt, was the casting of Evelyn, the murderously obsessed fan. The actress would have to make him believable as the victim of her sexual advances and violent abuse—not an easy thing to do. He saw and tested numerous actresses before catching Jessica Walter's performance in a screening of Sidney Lumet's 1966 film version of Mary McCarthy's controversial novel, *The Group*. Despite the studio's stubborn insistence that he cast a star in the role, something he never liked to do—Clint was not a big sharer in that way, as the roster of his costars reveals—he felt Walter was a perfect Evelyn and gave the part to her. She was attractive without being "bombshell," good-looking enough to do the nude-scene montage but not overly voluptuous (which would get in the way of her neediness), yet explosive and capable of projecting the kind of craziness the script required.

To play Dave's (Clint's) "normal" girlfriend, Tobie, he cast TV soap opera actress Donna Mills, who Burt Reynolds suggested might be good for the part. Walter, Clint felt, would be particularly good in the early part of the film, before her craziness becomes both apparent and shocking. Here was yet another film where women—Evelyn and Tobie—willingly fall to their knees and roll backward for Clint's character. More to the point, his emotional attachment to either is, for all intents and purposes, nonexistent. If Evelyn is a casual one-night stand, Tobie is the saner equivalent—a woman without a deeper connection to his soul. If one even existed.

This was the essential character Clint was looking for: the loner. Not the romantic loner of most films, redeemed by the love of a good woman, but the one who functioned best alone, unencumbered. In that sense Dave was a modern version of the Man with No Name.

Clint worked on the shooting script for several weeks before he felt he was ready. The night before filming began, he later recalled, "I was lying in bed, going over the shots in my mind. I had them all planned out. I turned out the light, thought 'Jesus! I've [also] gotta be in this thing!' I turned on the light and started approaching the scenes all over again, from the actor's point of view. Needless to say, I didn't get much sleep."

On set, not too far away, just in case Clint lost control of the ship and needed some dependable directorial backup, was Don Siegel, present for most of the shoot and visible in the movie playing the small part of a bartender. Later on Siegel, who had signed Clint's director's card (signifying Clint's debut behind the camera), would jokingly refer to his role as "a good-luck charm, my best piece of acting."

Even with that buffer, Clint ran into trouble early on with Universal, which wanted to make sure the film did not veer too far from its commercial center. For instance, he wanted to use Erroll Garner's jazzy original song "Misty" for the film's ironic title track, which Universal adamantly opposed. It preferred something that had more potential hit appeal and suggested "Strangers in the Night," recorded by Frank Sinatra, for which it happened to own the rights. Clint rejected that idea out of hand and instead added a second song to the film that he had heard on a local jazz station while driving to Universal one morning early in production. "I was absolutely knocked out by it," Clint later recalled, and drove directly into Hollywood to find a copy of it. None of the record stores in town had it as a single, but he finally found it on an album—*First Take*—in a supermarket bin marked down to $1.38. It was Roberta Flack's 1969 darkly intense version of Ewan MacColl's "The First Time Ever I Saw Your Face." Clint felt it was perfect to set the mood for Dave's romance with Tobie.* In an age when rock and roll was the current style in movie sound tracks, ignited by Simon and Garfunkel's remarkable one for *The Graduate* and the far more intense Dylan/Steppenwolf/Jimi Hendrix Experience one for *Easy Rider*; Clint's choice of the bluesy "First Time" and the jazz-infused "Misty" seemed a throwback to the 1950s.

The whole film, for that matter, had a dated feel to it, invoking a time when stalkers and violence were the stuff of drive-ins and midnight showings. Many reviewers were quick to compare Clint's debut to Hitchcock's ultimate 1950s B-movie *Psycho*, which was actually released in the summer of 1960 and whose artistic merits were initially overlooked by the impact of its shocking story.

Clint finished the shoot in just four and a half weeks, in October 1970, five days early and $50,000 under its original $1 million budget. Amid the big movies of 1971, the year of its release, *Play Misty for Me* seemed to most critics more reactionary than revolutionary, especially compared to the five strong films nominated for Best Picture that year: William Friedkin's tough and supercharged New York police drama, *The French Connection*, which won Best Picture and Best Director; Stanley Kubrick's striking *A Clockwork Orange*; Norman Jewison's paean to Hollywood's ethnic soul, *Fiddler on the Roof*; Peter Bogdanovich's extraordinary Texas-based sleeper *The Last Picture Show*; and Franklin Schaffner's turgid but nonetheless popular *Nicholas and Alexandra*, an instant relic about the Russian Revolution's most celebrated victims.

In that company *Play Misty for Me* didn't stand a chance even for a disapproving Academy sniff. It was neither big enough to merit attention, nor small enough to seem independent-film revelatory, as did Bogdanovich's movie. But what *Play Misty for Me* did have was a bottom line that showed a profit, and for the moment, not having his film laughed out of the movie theaters was all that really mattered to Clint.

And if the Academy had overlooked him, others did not. Selected scenes from *Play Misty for Me* served as the centerpiece for a January

---

*The album was released by Atlantic Records, and Clint reportedly paid a "modest fee" for its usage. The single then became a hit all over again after its use in the film.

1971 "mini-retrospective" of Clint's films at the San Francisco Film Festival, the first time he had been celebrated in that fashion.* That same month Clint and actress Ali MacGraw (who had become a sensation after her star turn in Arthur Hiller's 1970 adaptation of Erich Segal's novel *Love Story*) were selected "Stars of the Year" by the National Association of Theater Owners (NATO) for their respective box-office appeals. Even fiercely independent filmmaker John Cassavetes, who had financed his own independent directorial efforts by acting in mainstream ones, thought the film was good, if a bit derivative of Hitchcock's *Psycho*. "There's only one problem with this film," he later remarked. "It doesn't have Hitchcock's name on it."

The film turned a fairly decent profit, earning more than $5 million in rentals in its initial theatrical release, five times its negative (finished film) cost. For the moment both Clint and the studio were satisfied, if neither was completely happy with the other. Universal did not like Clint's offbeat style of moviemaking and his lack-of-conventional-love-story style; Jennings Lang and even Lew Wasserman believed the film had strayed too far from Universal's mainstream standard, while Clint felt the studio did not sufficiently or effectively promote the film, especially on television, the new favored medium for film. Each site was ready to sever ties, with both waiting for the right moment, one that would not publicly embarrass either the studio or the star.

Play Misty for Me may not have been the blockbuster the studio had wanted, or the completely personal statement Clint was looking to make, but it left him a millionaire. Shortly after the film opened, he bought twelve acres of pristine property within the highly coveted stretch of Pebble Beach, where many of California's wealthiest lived, alongside celebrities such as Kim Novak, cartoonist Jimmy Hatlo, Merv Griffin, and novelist John Steinbeck. Clint built a house with a gym above the garage and a large steam room.†

---

*The three spaghetti westerns—*A Fistful of Dollars, For a Few Dollars More,* and *The Good, the Bad and the Ugly*—were the centerpiece of the schedule. In fact, they had never gone out of commercial exhibition and were often shown together on a triple bill with the advertising slug: "How would you like to spend eight hours with Clint Eastwood?" Prior to this showing, the three films as a unit had already had a total of fifteen major U.S. "revivals" since 1968.

†He was prevented from building on the site that had once been an Indian reservation until he reached an agreement with the Regional Coastal Zone Conservation Commission to hire a professional archaeologist to gather and classify any Indian antiquities found on the land. *Los Angeles Herald-Examiner,* May 24, 1973.

Having by now become an avid golfer with a sixteen handicap, he wanted to be as close as possible to Pebble Beach's acclaimed golf course. He was also an accomplished helicopter pilot and loved to fly back and forth from Hollywood to Carmel, cutting short several hours–long commutes.

"I've traveled all over the world—beautiful places like Italy, Spain, France and so forth," Clint said shortly after he bought the new property. "But there is not another place in the world I'd prefer to live than the Monterey Peninsula. I plan on staying here forever."

Moving up, however, did not mean moving out. Clint held on to the house in Orange County, for those times when his Hollywood schedule would not permit him to drive back and forth to Pebble, and he made it a point to keep intact his small circle of friends that included Ken Green, whom he'd known since high school, his close friend Paul Lippman, a journalist whom Clint had met at the Carmel Valley Racquet Club, and the local tennis pro Don Hamilton. (Clint used Hamilton in one of the bar scenes in *Play Misty for Me*.)

About the same time Clint opened his first retail establishment, a local bar in Monterey, where he and his buddies could hang out away from their wives, their jobs, and the public. Meanwhile Maggie, whose profession was now listed by several magazines as "former model and painter," was given the job of designing and supervising the construction of their new home, something she delighted in doing. Clint continued to see Roxanne Tunis, as he had since they'd met, getting her small parts in his movies, even though—their child that he supported notwithstanding—she still could not officially exist in Clint's world.

And he continued to bed as many women as he wanted, including Beverly Walker, a struggling writer and actress who was also working on certain films as a publicist to pay her rent. While involved with screenwriter Paul Schrader, in the years before he hit it big, she had what journalist Peter Biskind described as a "desultory romance" with Clint. The reason they got involved with each other, according to Walker, was because Clint could take women as easily as picking fruit from an overripe tree for his own pleasure, and for him, women were about as hard to resist as a piece of that luscious fruit: "In Hollywood, men put enormous pressure on women to fuck them, even if it's only once. It's like the dog that pisses on the lamppost. They want that kind of connection to you, and then maybe they can relax." Walker claims she and Clint remained friends, although she never shows up in any of his movies.

As for his loner character in *Play Misty for Me*, Clint, in one of his infrequent interviews, explained his portrayal of this type of man as part of his own special brand of Method acting:

There are a million Mr. Perfects. The nice guys come and go, but the Bogarts, the Cagneys, the Gables, John Wayne and up through Mitchum—they're all a bit of . . . they really could treat women like dirt. I think women like to see other women put down when they're out of line. They have a dream of the guy who won't let them get away with anything . . . and the man in the audience is thinking, "That's how I'd like to handle it—cool and assured . . . knowing all the answers." He wants to be a superhero . . . Some people have a need to discuss deep, intimate things about themselves, discuss and analyze. I don't feel that need. Maybe it's a strength and maybe it's a weakness. Once I went to a psychiatrist. I did it as a favor to some-one else who was having a problem, and after we'd talked the guy said to me, "You seem to have things in hand." I think I do . . . to me love for a person is respect for individual feelings—respecting pri-vacy and accepting faults.

So that was it: he wasn't perfect, and he was proud of it, even if he had lately seen a psychiatrist "as a favor to someone else." These were remarkably revealing comments from a man whose public off-screen persona was depicted as the happily married man, good father, and easygoing suburban weekend golfer. To his friend and journalist Earl Leaf, Clint's life was tinted a slightly different shade of rose:

Clint lives a double life—not surprising, he being born under the sign of the twins. Though he never ceased loving and caring for Maggie, he hasn't made a secret of the free-living sexy side of his life around other women, especially young free-thinking chicks . . . Maggie doesn't question or nag her husband about his excursions to the Hol-lywood fun arena. Clint has described himself as a "married bache-lor." The meaning is clear to those who know him well.

If *Play Misty for Me* had any major flaw, it was Dave's lack of self-recognition. Although Evelyn is obviously crazy, and Dave may at first be perceived as an innocent, what made the film far different from (and weaker than) *Psycho* was the absence of any hint at the darker, deeper side of Dave, a man who hides behind the persona of a smooth voice, who is sexually indiscriminate, and who engages in violence as a solution.

Still, audiences stood up and took notice of Clint and the "something new" he had brought to the screen, even if his film characters did not connect all the dots between his private reality and his public image. All that was about to change with his next movie, about a detective who not only breaks all the rules but takes extreme (and extremely dark) pleasure in doing so.

Dirty Harry would allow Clint to let out the shadow side of his on-screen persona and have it happily shake hands with the light one. That extraordinary feat thrilled audiences around the world even as (or because) it scared the shit out of them. In that sense, *Dirty Harry* was even more personal than *The Beguiled*—a remarkable achievement indeed.

And one that almost didn't happen.

After coming across Harry Julian Fink and his wife R. M. Fink's script for *Dirty Harry*, Jennings Lang had taken an option flier and offered it to Paul Newman, thinking the film perfect for him. But after reading the script Newman turned it down cold because he felt the character was too right-wing for him.

Lang then thought of Sinatra, because he had previously appeared in a couple of successful detective movies. The character he'd played, Tony Rome, was also tough, but Sinatra had given him enough ring-a-ding-ding to give him some charm. Lang hoped he would do the same with Callahan. Sinatra initially showed some interest, but once he realized how unsympathetic Callahan really was, he passed on it, fearing audiences would turn on him for playing such a low-life character. He begged off, claiming a hand injury would prevent him from doing justice to the role.*

---

*Clint never believed Sinatra's story about his hand injury. "Probably just bullshit," he told Jeff Dawson of the *Guardian*, June 6, 2008.

With Clint still tied up with *Misty*, a film in which Lang had little confidence, Lang was unable to find any star to play the role, so he sold the rights to ABC Television. ABC intended to make it into a TV movie but then realized the excessive violence would be unsuitable for television audiences. So they, in turn, sold it to Warner.

Warner Bros.–Seven Arts, as the studio was then called, had been in turmoil, in danger of going under, when it was acquired in 1969 by Kinney National Company, a car rental, parking lot, and funeral services company owned by Steve Ross, who leveraged Kinney's assets to gain entry into the film business. While he worked to straighten out the studio's seemingly hopeless finances, Ross hired a triple-threat team: Ted Ashley, one of the most powerful agents in the business; former Filmways producer John Calley, who had made many successful films, including Jules Dassin's *Topkapi* (1964); and Frank Wells, the attorney, to head business affairs.

Ross's short-term goal was to build up a roster of box-office talent, and the first star he wanted to bring over was Clint Eastwood, whose nonexclusive deal at Universal was not only ending but, according to Frank Wells, gone sour. Wells was one of the few industry people Clint trusted and with whom he shared his frustrations. When Wells found out about *Dirty Harry*, the script Lang had hesitated to give Clint, he jumped at it.

The same character traits that had turned off Newman and scared Sinatra attracted Clint, as they would give him the chance to display the element missing from *Misty*, the sense of inspired rage. Dirty Harry Callahan was ragingly antiauthoritarian, particularly in his relationship to the chief of police and the mayor of the city of New York, where the story was originally set.

In addition, the script contained a fair amount of violence that would allow Callahan to flex some familiar muscles and show he was still a macho tough guy who didn't take shit from anybody—no man, no woman, and no criminal he considered a subspecies of the human race. Here, though, the script took on a deeper and more interesting twist. Unlike other villains Clint had faced down, especially in the spaghetti westerns, the psychotic killer Callahan sets out to track down is obviously linked to him. Clearly the sadistic woman-and-child-killer Scorpio (Andy Robinson) is, in some ways, a personification of the dark (or darker) side of Callahan himself, the murderous deep end he may have stuck his toe in but never actually jumped into. As film critic and historian Lawrence Knapp put it, "Harry's pursuit of Scorpio is so intense, it becomes an aberration in itself, a sickness as profound as Scorpio's. Scorpio is Harry's doppelgänger." Scorpio likes to leave cryptic notes and send the authorities on wild-goose chases, enjoying such games in the fever of his own sadistic madness. Callahan likes to play a life-or-death how-many-bullets-left-in-the-chamber-of-my-.44 game, a peculiar and no less sadistic one. Done once, Callahan's game seems like a product of chance-and-capture as he corners a bank robber who momentarily thinks about reaching for his gun. It is an enjoyable sequence that allows the audience, at least for this moment, to identify with the hero's unwavering strength, a modern-day Man with No Name. However, played a second time at the climax of the movie, with Scorpio himself on the receiving end, it becomes a psychotic ritual, an almost hypnotic reaction to his own sadistic lunacy, with his wounded prey helpless to do anything but play along until Callahan definitively blows him away.

This crazy cat-and-mouse game the two play ultimately decides whether Callahan's "good" side will defeat the "bad." (The outcome is something of a draw.) The film's terrific and unexpected plot twists deepen Callahan's character. Scorpio has kidnapped and murdered yet another victim, this one a young girl. Callahan tracks him to an empty stadium and traps him there (a neat metaphor for both the missing conscience in Scorpio's head and the gladiatorial aspect to their titanic battle). Later Callahan is shocked to find out that the cold-blooded killer has been set free because his rights had been violated. His disbelief is cut with fury, and he begins to stalk Scorpio, confident the killer cannot stop himself from killing again. Predictably Scorpio (whose linear psychology brings his character and the film dangerously close to parody) goes on another murderous rampage, this time kidnapping a busful of innocent children. That gives Callahan the opportunity to corner and kill him once and for all, before he can be released by the law to kill again. The beauty (and the horror) of this aspect of the story is that the next time, Callahan becomes judge, jury, and executioner. Scorpio has taken a boy hostage, holding him at gunpoint. Callahan kills him, shooting just above the boy's head; the force of the second shot from the .44 blows Scorpio into the swampy bay. Then Callahan shockingly hurls his badge into the swamp as well, and walks away, as the final credits begin to roll.

If Clint identified with the Callahans of the world, he also identified with the Scorpios, or at least with every Callahan's fear that a Scorpio was lying in wait. That was, at last, the character he wanted to play. But not direct.

When Wells first floated the possibility of doing *Dirty Harry* and Clint expressed interest, Wells asked him what it would take to make it happen. Understanding that, after *Play Misty for Me*, he was not ready to direct a film this complicated and star in it as well, Clint replied without hesitation: Don Siegel. "I was the one who hired [Siegel] . . . When I came over to Warner, [the movie] . . . I got Siegel involved. My agreement with Warner Bros. was, 'I'll do it if you let me hire a director like Don Siegel and we'll take this story back to its original concept.' "*

Although Clint could certainly have directed *Dirty Harry*, he had found the experience of *Play Misty for Me* both "exhausting and detrimental" to his acting. For now, at least, he preferred the next-best thing, his off-screen alter ego, Don Siegel. "Directing is hard work," he told one interviewer. "You have to stay on top of everything all day long, and it can be tiring. I learned to pace myself. It's not like acting, where you can stay up till one o'clock the night before work. As a director, I had to crash before eleven."

Siegel was under contract to Universal, but Lang was all too happy to loan him out—he wanted to keep Clint happy (and get rid of the project) so that if the right property should come along, they could work together again. The deal was in place by that spring. The script had gone through numerous rewrites, including one by John Milius, but it was decided that the Finks' version was still the best. It was the only one that included the " 'Do I feel lucky?' Well, do ya, punk?" sequence that would become one of Clint's signature lines.

The brilliant cinematographer Bruce Surtees, whom Clint had per-

---

*Interestingly, one of the film's most memorable scenes, looking like none of the others, is a suicide-intervention sequence early on, wherein Callahan rescues a lunatic perched on the edge of a building ready to jump. Siegel fell ill on the day it was scheduled to be shot, and Clint directed it himself.

sonally requested, shot most of *Dirty Harry*'s exteriors at night,* accenting the movie's noirish feel. The drop-in and pull-back of the opening and closing overhead shots of the city suggest a godlike observational point of view to the proceedings while at the same time offering a sense of randomness, as if anywhere the camera falls, it will find a story. This neat stylistic touch would eventually help define the look and feel of a "Clint Eastwood film."

To be sure, the film also had a social and stylistic element, one that marked it at the time with political relevance. It was filmed at the height of the Vietnam War, nearly a decade after the Gulf of Tonkin incident. By then Americans had grown weary of the conflict and fearful that the lion's roar from their once-mighty place in the international psyche as the Cops of the World had turned into a frustrated, frightened yelp, the hollow sound of a paper tiger. The Vietnam War would not be portrayed directly by Hollywood until years later; Michael Cimino's *The Deer Hunter* (1978), Hal Ashby's *Coming Home* (1978), and Francis Ford Coppola's *Apocalypse Now* (1979) would all look back at it. But in 1971 *Dirty Harry* confronted the supercharged anti-civil-rights, pro-Vietnam instincts of a faction of Americans (and anti-Americans around the world). Its memorable " 'Do I feel lucky?' Well, do ya, punk?" sequence put Callahan's outsize, phallic .44 Magnum into the face of a black thief and dared him to test his luck and courage against the almighty white authority of justice, law, and order. The classic moment remains alive in the memory of anyone who has ever heard and seen it, even if it has lost its historical relevance. As an image of Callahan's (and America's perceived) dark sadism, it is cinematically timeless.

Echoing TV's Joe Friday (Jack Webb in *Dragnet*) and Gene Hackman's Jimmy Doyle in *The French Connection* (1971), Callahan took the character of the American police officer farther and lower than anyone previously had in American motion pictures. Friday, as portrayed by Webb, was robotic in his joyless enforcement of the law, while Hackman's Doyle was societally embittered and equally joyless. Callahan, however, was more frightening than either because of the pleasure he got from torturing his "opponents." In Sidney Lumet's *Serpico* (1973)

---

*Surtees had been the cinematographer on *Coogan's Bluff* (uncredited), *Two Mules for Sister Sara* (uncredited), *The Beguiled*, and *Play Misty for Me*, and he would go on to direct the cinematography on several future Clint Eastwood films.

Al Pacino's antihero character, the little prince in jeans and long hair, takes on the establishment and (in a sense) wins; in *Dirty Harry*, Callahan *is* the establishment, and unless the means justify the ends (as went the big sell of Vietnam to the American public), then nobody really wins. Callahan's toss of his badge into the river at the end of the film echoes Will Kane's (Gary Cooper's) gesture at the end of *High Noon*, released at the height of the Korean War, representing a rejection of the corruption, hypocrisy, and fear of establishment law and order.

But for Callahan, the similar gesture means something even more personal, the interior battle against his own ever-present, ever-threatening darkness. He may have killed off Scorpio, but in a larger and truer sense, both in classic mythology and in biblical wisdom, in great literature and *especially* in Hollywood movies, evil never really dies. Callahan's toss of the badge is at best his declaration of the stand-off, at least for now (as well as a perfect setup for a sequel, of which there would be four).

The decision to toss the badge was not an easy one. Clint and Siegel went back and forth on it, with Clint initially rejecting it. Early on Clint told Siegel he couldn't do it because it would mean he was quitting the force. Siegel replied that it didn't mean that at all, that it was a rejection of police department bureaucracy and all its fixed rules and hierarchy of authority. But Clint didn't buy it. Instead he suggested that Callahan put his arm back as if to throw the badge away, hear the distant wail of approaching police sirens, put the badge back in his pocket, and head off. Siegel reluctantly agreed, and Clint, according to Siegel, mussed his director's hair in happiness.

The day of the shooting of the final scene, however, Clint had a change of heart and decided to throw the badge in the water after all. (Perhaps he realized that he could never get rid of his own dark side by killing Scorpio or by tossing away the symbol of legal righteousness.) Siegel then told him they only had one prop badge—they would have ordered more if he'd known they were going to film the toss. To be able to reuse the badge as needed, Siegel had a black cloth put in the bottom of the swamp. But it proved unnecessary—he got the shot in one clip, with Clint tossing it with his favored left hand.

Dirty Harry was released in December 1971, only two months after *Play Misty for Me* (which had been delayed in postproduction by

Clint's difficulties in editing). Christmas is traditionally a time for lighter, more uplifting fare, and critics were almost universally negative about the film, but it broke box-office records, hitting number one its opening week and earning more than $18 million in its initial domestic release (and eventually nearly $60 million worldwide). In the *New York Times,* Roger Greenspun wrote that "the honorably and slightly anachronistic enterprise of the Don Siegel cops-and-crooks action movies over the last few years *(Madigan, Coogan's Bluff)* takes a sad and perhaps inevitable step downward in *Dirty Harry* . . . Clint Eastwood's tough San Francisco plainclothesman [is] pushed beyond professionalism into a kind of iron-jawed self-parody." *Newsweek* dismissed it as a "right-wing fantasy," while *Time's* Richard Schickel praised Clint's performance as "his best to date." And *Daily Variety* condemned it as "a specious, phony glorification of police and criminal brutality."

Pauline Kael, who inexplicably prided herself on seeing a movie only once lest she be given a privileged viewpoint apart from the ordinary viewer, launched a vicious attack on *Dirty Harry,* in many ways rougher than anything in the film. That her review came between the covers of the otherwise sophisticated *New Yorker* gave it added gravitas. "The film," she insisted, "made the basic contest between good and evil . . . as simple as you can get . . . more archetypal than most movies, more primitive and dreamlike . . . with the fairy-tale appeal of *fascist medievalism* [italics added]." Whether pro or con, the film sparked reams of literature about whether Harry represented the best or the worst of early 1970s America, and as a consequence it became the must-see film of late 1971 and early 1972.

In August 1972 Clint and Maggie, along with John Wayne, Glenn Ford, and Charlton Heston, were invited to attend Richard Nixon's "Western White House" reception just prior to his anticipated renomination at the Republican National Convention. Nixon fawned over Clint as if the president were the fan and Clint were the president. Clint, soft-spoken and smiling like a Cheshire cat, knew that he had, for sure, inherited a new mantle. Wayne had, until now, been the official western (movies and world) tough guy, but he had grown old and fat and was something of a self-parody as well as the proud darling of the extreme right wing. Clint was the one whose screen persona played fastest and loosest with civil rights and the Constitution itself when it came to enforcing law and order and who preferred a pickup truck to his Ferrari (at least according to his press releases). Here he was, rubbing shoulders with the power elite. Not long afterward Nixon appointed Clint—along with Judith Jamison, Edward Villella, Rudolf Serkin, Eudora Welty, and Andrew Wyeth—to a governmental panel on the arts and a six-year term on the National Council on the Arts, an advisory group to the revered and influential National Endowment of the Arts.

Not a bad score for Clint who, on the strength of *Play Misty for Me* and *Dirty Harry*, had topped Wayne, McQueen, and Newman to become the top-grossing star in the world.*

---

*According to the forty-first annual poll of theater owners by Quigley Publications. Wayne had dropped to fourth place in this, his twenty-third appearance on the highly influential poll. Coming in second behind Clint was George C. Scott, then Gene Hackman, Wayne, Barbra Streisand, Marlon Brando, Paul Newman, Steve McQueen, Dustin Hoffman, and Goldie Hawn. After Clint's appearance on this list the Academy invited him to be a presenter of the Best Picture Oscar on its 1973 awards broadcast. Besides his appearance in second place in 1970 and 1971, Clint had appeared in fifth place in 1968 and 1969. Also in 1972 Clint had another, dubious honor when *Mad* magazine spoofed his spaghetti westerns as *Fistful of Lasagna* and *For a Few Ravioli More*.

TEN

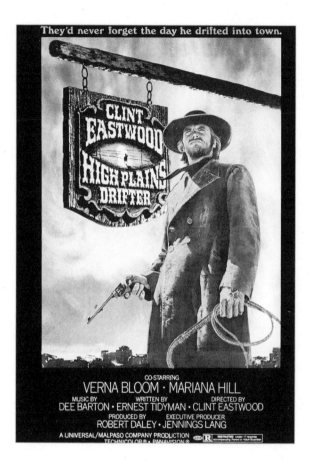

We live in more of a pussy generation now, where everybody's become used to saying, "Well, how do we handle it psychologically?" In [the old] days, you just punched the bully back and duked it out. Even if the guy was older and could push you around, at least you were respected for fighting back, and you'd be left alone from then on.

—Clint Eastwood

O n the heels of his fabulous success with *Dirty Harry*—without the sure hand of Leonard to guide him, and on the advice of the less visionary, more bottom-line-oriented Bob Daley—Clint signed on once more at Universal, via Malpaso, to star in a John Sturges film, *Joe Kidd*, a pale-faced imitation of the Leone westerns, with a script by Elmore Leonard. Sturges was a journeyman director who had had a string of early successes: *Bad Day at Black Rock* (1955), *Gunfight at the O.K. Corral* (1957), and most notably *The Great Escape* (1963). *Joe Kidd* was made amid the groundswell of controversy created by *Dirty Harry* and slipped in and out of theaters early in 1972 without stirring much interest in either audiences or critics. It was perhaps just as well; the film didn't work on any level and remains one of Clint's least-remembered movies, but the money was good, and it did give him a chance to work with one of his old army buddies, John Saxon, whose screen career had never blossomed into anything memorable or lasting.

High Plains Drifter was something else again. It too came via Universal, in the form of a nine-page treatment written by Ernest Tidyman. Tidyman, a pro, had written both the original novel and the screen adaptation for Gordon Parks's 1971 seminal *Shaft*, and the Academy Award–winning adapted screenplay of *The French Connection*, for which the previous year he had won an Oscar, the Writers' Guild Award, and the Mystery Writers Edgar. He wrote *High Plains Drifter* specifically with Clint Eastwood in mind, certain he would not be able to resist the temptation to both star in and direct the script.

At least part of what made Tidyman so sure was his familiarity with the so-called Gold Rush Syndrome that sooner or later afflicts every star in Hollywood—the desire for official anointment by the faceless little statue called Oscar. Clint had every reason to believe his performance as Harry Callahan had a shot at the big trophy in 1971;

it was, after all, one of the biggest box-office movies of the year and had screwed Clint into the consciousness of its viewers. It was therefore something of a letdown, if not a total surprise—so-called pure action films are rarely considered "important" enough by the elitist Academy—that he wasn't even nominated.*

After his disappointing stint with Sturges, Clint believed more than ever that no one could direct him like Don Siegel, and should never even try. But it seemed too soon to work with Siegel again—some of the critical fallout from *Dirty Harry* had to fade—so he decided once more to try to direct himself.

For budgetary reasons, Universal wanted *High Plains Drifter* to be shot on their expansive western backlot, but Clint preferred something more original and, for him, director-friendly. He managed to convince Lang (credited as the executive producer on the film) to green-light the building of an entire western-town set, in the desert near Lake Mono in the California Sierras. It took eighteen days to build. (Film critics and historians Richard Thompson and Tim Hunter would later describe its main street as "looking more like a new condominium in Northern California than a Western town of the past.") Clint shot the entire film in sequence, which was unusual and usually more costly due to the extra setups, but the film came in early and under budget.†

Clint played his familiar role of a Man with No Name—called the Stranger this time. His costars were featured players (but not stars) Verna Bloom, Mariana Hill, and Mitch Ryan, and the film held unmistakable echoes of the Leone trilogy. (Typical of its reviews, *Box Office Magazine* described it as having a "dog-eared plot-line of a mysterious stranger who shoots up a town.") What is notable about this film is the introduction of an "otherworldliness" (already seen in *The Beguiled*) that would reappear in several of Clint's later films.

High Plains Drifter's script strongly suggests that the Stranger is

----

*Best Actor that year went to Gene Hackman for *The French Connection*, a character-driven *policier* with an East Coast, ultrarealistic style and timely theme based on the Academy-loving "true story." The other nominees were Peter Finch in John Schlesinger's *Sunday Bloody Sunday*; George C. Scott in Arthur Hiller's *The Hospital*; Walter Matthau in Jack Lemmon's *Kotch*; and Topol in Norman Jewison's *Fiddler on the Roof.*

†Bob Daley, who had executive-produced *Joe Kidd*, was moved down a notch by Clint to the position of hands-on producer.

actually the ghost of the sheriff killed by the gang that controls the town; now the Stranger kills them off, one by one, before disappearing into the sunset.* With touches of *High Noon, Shane,* and Leone's trilogy, the film contained a menu of surefire story ingredients; Bruce Surtees's unusually wide lenses intensified the brightness of the landscape and added a hellish look to the film.

This was a Clint Eastwood cowboy audiences wanted to see, the cold-blooded, infallible, noble killer—not the imperfect ex-con *Joe Kidd. High Plains Drifter* was a huge hit at the box office, grossing nearly $16 million in its initial domestic release. It appeared to have everything the early Eastwood westerns had had, but its success was uneasy: the film was derivative and less than authentic, and its faux mysticism was a facile substitute for the real mystery of the Man with No Name. Clint felt to some a little like post-army Elvis—he still looked and sounded like the performer who had so recently exploded onto the cultural scene, but was instantly and obviously not the same thing. There was something too safe, too slick, and too comfortable about *High Plains Drifter.*

While the film proved to be a cash cow, audiences were not really interested in it. This time there was no talk of awards for either the film or Clint Eastwood's performance. It was, however, for Clint the director, a start.

On May 22, 1972, Maggie Eastwood gave birth to her second child, Alison, who weighed in at a manageable seven pounds, four ounces. In fact, she arrived fifteen days premature, just after Maggie had flown down to Los Angeles to see Clint. Barely a month later Maggie was with Clint at the opening ceremonies of the three-day Pebble Beach Celebrity Tennis Tournament, hosting such legendary participants as the John Waynes and the Charlton Hestons.

By now virtually anybody who spent time with Clint on a set or at Malpaso knew that the Eastwood marriage was, at the very least, a bit unorthodox. But no one in his circle, or hers, seemed particularly

---

*Clint has always denied any supernatural affect to the film, stating on more than one occasion that his intention was to insinuate that the mysterious drifter is the murdered sheriff's brother. See Boris Zmijewsky and Lee Pfeiffer, *The Films of Clint Eastwood* (New York: Citadel Press, 1993), 152. But multiple viewings reveal little, if any, evidence of such a link.

bothered by it, least of all the Eastwoods themselves. And while he was still involved with Roxanne Tunis, contributing money to help to raise their child, he and Tunis had cooled off when she turned to Eastern spiritual practices and took their daughter to Denver so she could devote herself to full-time study. Roxanne and Clint still saw each other, but not as often nor as intensely as before, and almost never anymore when he was making a movie.

In October 1972, two years after Clint's father's death, his mother, Ruth, quietly remarried. The Hawaii-themed ceremony was held in Pebble Beach, and the groom was John Belden Wood, a wealthy widower who had made a fortune from his Piedmont-based lumber business. Clint happily escorted his mother down the aisle, relieved that she would no longer have to be alone.

Clint then turned his attention back to directing, but this time he wanted to see if he could sell a film, both to the studio and to audiences, in which he wasn't also acting. The project he chose must have resonated quite loudly with him: it was the Lolita-like story of a middle-aged salesman, Frank Harmon (William Holden), and his relationship with a teenage hippie type, Breezy (Kay Lenz).

In some ways *Breezy* signaled a shift in Clint's focus, away from the violent and (so-called) socially relevant action picture to a small-scale love story. Romance had been missing in previous Eastwood films; even *Play Misty for Me* belongs solidly in the horror category. The shift was a retreat from the social clamor that had surrounded *Dirty Harry*, although the story of a middle-aged man in a sexual relationship with a teenager also was potentially controversial.

Partly because he wasn't in it and partly because the subject veered too close to breaking a taboo, Universal was inclined to turn it down, despite Clint the actor's current number one standing at the box office. They finally green-lighted it on condition Clint brought it in for under $1 million (meaning they would put up the million, and the revenues from ticket sales would reimburse the studio until break-even, after which Malpaso would take a healthy cut of the gross).

To play the part of the older man, Clint chose William Holden, a handsome, soft-spoken actor who was equally at home in westerns, love stories, and war pictures. Always manly, he was in many ways a 1950s version of Clint Eastwood. But he also represented the repressed American male lover, constricted by social mores from getting down and dirty with costars such as straitlaced and demure Grace Kelly in Mark Robson's *The Bridges at Toko-Ri* (1954), in George Seaton's *The Country Girl* (1954), and with Jennifer Jones in Henry King's *Love Is a Many-Splendored Thing* (1955). With all three films a kiss is the only physical contact (we see) between proper lovers. Such repression, in a way, helps explain Holden's misplaced passions in such rage-fests as Billy Wilder's *Stalag 17* (1953), with its prisoner-of-war setting, and David Lean's *The Bridge on the River Kwai* (1957), in which noble sacrifice redeems Holden's unbridled passions.

Clint did not have to operate under Holden's characters' social and sexual restrictions, but he nonetheless shared a manly resistance to portraying lust in his own movies. And he had yet to show a simple, open, happy, loving side to any of his male characters, without the woman being a murderer, witch, prostitute, deceiver, or helpless victim.

The part of the young girl Breezy was much harder to cast. Among the many hopefuls he saw was a cute, southern born and bred, twenty-five-year-old blond actress by the name of Sondra Locke. Locke had gained some notice in Hollywood for her Oscar-nominated performance in Robert Ellis Miller's 1968 adaptation of Carson McCullers's *The Heart Is a Lonely Hunter*, but afterward her career had experienced a slight stall. Jo Heims, the screenwriter for *Breezy*, suggested her to Clint, saying she thought Locke was exactly right for the role. Locke never made it to a screen test, however, because after looking at some eight-by-tens and a few minutes of *The Heart Is a Lonely Hunter*, Clint felt she was too old for the role. In his film he wanted to emphasize the age difference between the two lead characters. He eventually chose the very young and coquettish Kay Lenz, who looked exactly right to him but had almost no film experience.

Production began in November 1972, and almost immediately it was apparent to everyone on set that Clint had a very special attraction to her. Clint, interestingly, was pulling back from his screen image as a law-and-order warrior while drawing closer to his real-life character as an aging Lothario. This was heady stuff, doubling the intensity of Clint's relationship to Breezy as a director and as an authority figure to a younger woman.

But whatever electricity flowed between Lenz and Clint off-screen, it failed to ignite between her and Holden on-screen. Audiences turned away from this May-December romance. Holden just looked too tired and too old for audiences to believe he could be attractive to Breezy. The movie had no romantic chemistry. It was an out-and-out failure at the box office, not just for its unbelievability but because, simply put, no one was particularly interested in seeing a so-called Clint Eastwood film that did not star Clint Eastwood. Several reviewers sharpened their pencils and had a critical field day. Judith Crist's reaction was typical: writing in *New York* magazine, she chuckled condescendingly that *Breezy* was "so perfectly awful that it's almost good enough for laughs." Only auteurist critics like Molly Haskell, writing in the *Village Voice*, took the film seriously: "Clint Eastwood's most accomplished directorial job so far . . . a love story in which almost everything works." A then-fringe auteurist critic like Haskell, however, had neither the readership nor the clout to make a commercial difference, while Crist had a huge following, especially in box-office-rich New York City.

By and large, critics like Crist got it right, but an oversensitive Clint was quick to blame Universal's promotion, rather than his own direction, for *Breezy*'s failure to float: "This was a small film—it was just the story of the rejuvenation of a cynic. I thought that was an interesting subject, especially nowadays in the era of cynicism . . . it was a disaster at the box office, very poorly distributed and very poorly advertised . . . that's Universal. They have a terrible advertising department, they're not smart. I tried to keep an eye on it but [at Universal] it was a harder thing to do."

The abject failure of *Breezy* drove Clint back into the warm and waiting (and wealthy) arms of Warner, which was eager to green-light a sequel to *Dirty Harry*. Enough with the silly romances, they both agreed. Let's get back to good old blood-guts-and-gore.

Clint would not make another romantic "love story" for twenty-two years.

One thing Clint agreed to was the subtle softening, if not exactly mellowing, of Harry Callahan. It was not wholly Clint's choice; rather, a combination of talented writers working in collaboration with him and Robert Daley, all of whom believed the character and therefore the film would be much more appealing if Callahan were more accessible to and easier on women, as a way to boost the date-movie weekend audience. Of course, Callahan couldn't become a pussycat, but they felt that a slight declawing wouldn't hurt the franchise.

The inspiration for the story—whose working title was *Vigilance*, later changed to *Magnum Force*, named after Callahan's weapon of choice and the elite enforcement squad of the San Francisco police force—came from screenwriter John Milius, who had done some uncredited partial revisions on the original *Dirty Harry* and had since written the screenplays for Sydney Pollack's *Jeremiah Johnson* (1972) and John Huston's *The Life and Times of Judge Roy Bean* (1972) and was on track to write and direct *Dillinger* later that year. This time, however, nothing came out of Milius's rewrites before he opted out of the project to work on *Dillinger.*

Clint then turned to a talented young newcomer offered to him by the William Morris Agency. Michael Cimino was charged with developing Milius's main contribution to the picture—the eventual showdown between Callahan and the secret and deadly Magnum Force unit rather than some crazed killer. This plot element was key. While it kept Callahan as violently antiauthoritarian as before, it also put his maverick behavior more clearly on the side of law and order, making him a hero while maintaining his rebel status. Cimino (who would go on to write and direct the phenomenally successful *The Deer Hunter* and win the Best Director Oscar for it,[*] then self-destruct with his 1980 remake of *Shane, Heaven's Gate*) prior to *Magnum Force*, had partially written only one screenplay. It was a collaborative effort with Deric Washburn of Douglas Trumbull's *Silent Running* (1971), not a big winner at the box office but good enough for William Morris to put him up for Clint's film.

To direct, Clint surprised everybody by going with Ted Post over Don Siegel, feeling either that his creative teaming with Siegel had run its course or that Siegel was not going to be able to ease up on the intensity of the Callahan character.

That may not have been the only problem. Clint, by now, had begun to feel restricted by Siegel, as much by his methods as by his style. Clint liked to move quickly, especially as Malpaso was now producing most of the films he worked on. Siegel was deliberate and liked

---

[*]He was also one of the producers and shared in the *Deer Hunter*'s Oscar for Best Picture.

to shoot scenes over and over again—which drove Clint to the brink of his patience. Finally, the aging Siegel's on-screen bluntness was losing some of its edge, where Clint was looking to go younger and sharper. He believed that speed and instinct were the ways to do it, and he wanted a director who was less committed to a set style of directing, less deliberate, and more willing to go with the moment.

Clint felt grateful to Post for the success of *Hang 'Em High*, and the studio liked him as well. Not long afterward the trades announced that Siegel was "unavailable," due to a prior commitment to direct a project in Europe tentatively called *Drazzle*, starring Michael Caine. (It was never made.)

However, things did not go as smoothly as Clint had hoped. On set Post, who had known Clint since *Rawhide*, wanted to expand on the notion of Harry as a dirty cop, while Clint wanted less, to bring more couples into the theaters. Most of all, he wanted to keep the movie in the entertainment sections and out of the general news pages of the newspapers. (He did allow a Japanese TV crew to follow him around for an episode of the popular Japanese series *Leading World Figures*, which had previously profiled Pope Paul VI, Pablo Picasso, Aristotle Onassis, Princess Margaret, Chou En-lai, Indira Gandhi, Princess Grace, and Henry Kissinger.)

One adjustment to the original *Dirty Harry* was the addition of a partner for Callahan called Early Smith, who was played by Felton Perry. The fact that Perry was black was a conscious attempt by Warner to ameliorate the outrage that the punk in the "'Do I feel lucky?'" scene had been black. Everyone, it seemed, had been upset that the figure cowering on the other side of Dirty Harry's gun was African-American, just when militant groups such as the Black Panthers were denouncing lethal police violence inflicted on Fred Hampton and George Jackson. (In 1987 the "buddy" teaming of a "crazed" white cop and his more sensible black partner would be reprised by Mel Gibson and Danny Glover, respectively, in Richard Donner's *Lethal Weapon*, a hugely popular film that would enjoy three sequels, all of which owed some measure of debt to *Dirty Harry*.)*

During preproduction, Clint was asked to present the Best Picture

---

*Even Mel Gibson's character's name, Sergeant Martin Riggs, is an echo of Lieutenant Neil Briggs, played in *Magnum Force* by Hal Holbrook.

Oscar at the Academy Awards ceremony on March 27, 1973. Although it was and still is considered an honor to present the most important award of the evening, Clint initially turned down the job, but because of pressure from the studio and from Maggie, he decided to accept the assignment. As long as his appearance was short and sweet, with one or two lines, he would be fine.

That night he showed up for the ceremony with Maggie and took his assigned place in the audience, smiling and waving to friends scattered about the Dorothy Chandler Pavilion. The telecast show was to have multiple hosts, as it had for the past several years. (Clint had previously presented the Best Foreign Language Film award, alongside Claudia Cardinale, to Costa-Gavras's *Z* in 1970.)

And then the roof fell in. One of the show's four "hosts," Charlton Heston, was scheduled to kick off the proceedings, but had not shown up for his half-hour call and was nowhere to be found.* His introduction, explaining the voting rules and regulations, had been tailored to Heston, as a parody of the gravitas he was known for from his biblical hero films.

Howard Koch, the show's producer, nervously signaled for Clint and Maggie to hurry backstage. They went, not knowing what was going on, and Koch asked Clint to fill in for Heston. He refused. That wasn't his thing, he told Koch. He wasn't prepared, and he just couldn't do it. Koch continued to plead as the audience began to murmur about the delayed start. Finally Maggie stepped in and told Clint he ought to help out. With nowhere to go and stuck between a begging producer and an urging wife, he silently nodded and walked out onto the stage. There he was greeted by thunderous applause and the occasional shrieks caused by his unexpected appearance.

In his gut, he felt a sense of panic. The teleprompter was filled with Heston-related movie jokes, written by screenwriter-novelist William Goldman. Clint stopped in the middle, looked out at the audience with a tight smile on his face, and said, "This was supposed to be Charlton Heston's part of the show, but somehow he hasn't shown up. So who did they pick? They pick the guy who has said but three lines in twelve movies to substitute for him."

Only mild laughter came back at him—the audience was as

---

*The other three were Carol Burnett, Michael Caine, and Rock Hudson.

confused as he was—so he read the prompter as best he could, making jokes about *The Ten Commandments* that nobody could possibly have found funny, especially coming from him. After several torturous minutes, sprinkled with the nervous laughter of an audience of nominees already on edge, Heston arrived backstage out of breath, claiming to have been the victim of a flat tire. Koch grabbed him and literally threw him onto the set. Now, the audience roared.

A much-relieved Clint quickly and gratefully handed the proceedings over to Heston, who began from the top as if nothing had happened. When he reread the same jokes Clint had done, the audience erupted, this time with good-natured laughter. Clint returned later that night to present the Best Picture Award, but by then the audience was reeling from Marlon Brando's personally chosen stand-in to accept his Best Actor Oscar for the title role of Francis Ford Coppola's *The Godfather.* Sacheen Littlefeather, a woman dressed as an Apache, had protested the treatment of American Indians in Hollywood movies and was received less than enthusiastically. Clint had to follow that. He took the opportunity to make what was for him a rare and witty, if sarcastic, ad-lib: "I don't know if I should present this award on behalf of all the cowboys shot in John Ford westerns over the years!"

He then presented the Oscar to Albert Ruddy, who won for *The Godfather.**

The next day Rex Reed commented, "Last night we learned Clint Eastwood can be funny!" It would be twenty-seven years before Clint consented to be a presenter for this or any other live event.†

Magnum Force opened in December 1973, and despite the lack of controversy surrounding the Callahan character, was the biggest hit of the year. Its only real negative criticism came again from Kael, who derided Clint's abilities as an actor and pompously held her nose throughout her review. But neither she nor any other critic could stop audiences from flocking to see this film, which outgrossed *Dirty Harry*

---

*Thirty-two years later, Clint and Ruddy (and co-producer Tom Rosenberg) would jointly accept the 2004 Best Picture Oscar for *Million Dollar Baby*.
†In 2000, he presented the Best Picture Oscar to the producers of *American Beauty* (1999).

by more than $2 million, to become Clint's highest-grossing film to date. During its initial domestic release, it broke through the $20 million ceiling, which at the time defined a "blockbuster," the next big step above "big hit." And, because it was a sequel, it broke another Hollywood rule of thumb—that a sequel is usually half as good as the original and earns about half as much.

So here was a film that may or may not have been half as good, that was made for little more than the original (minus the original director)—that actually managed to outgross the original. The reason was singular and definitive; Clint Eastwood's name above the title, in the role he had created two years earlier, was enough to draw audiences in huge numbers. More than any other achievement, *Magnum Force* removed any lingering doubts that he was a worldwide box-office sensation.

But something else was equally undeniable. For the first time, both in person and on screen, Clint looked old, or older—every day of his forty-three years. His thick, brown mane of hair had begun to thin and recede on both sides. His face had weathered, and lines were visible on his forehead and two short vertical ones, like quotation marks, on the bridge of his nose between his eyes. By Hollywood standards, he was no longer industrial-strength young.

And he knew it, which only added to his desire to shift from star to director. Could anything be more ludicrous than a middle-aged, huffing and puffing Harry Callahan? That was something he believed might happen if he worked with and trusted the wrong advisers. "People who go to the movies like me," he reminded one interviewer, explaining that he had never felt beholden to any one studio. "I haven't had a special push or a big studio buildup. I never get my picture taken kissing my dog when I get off a plane, that sort of thing. There are stars who are produced by the press. I'm not one of them. Bogart once said he owed it to the movie-going public—and to them alone—to do his best. I feel that way too."

For his next project, Leonard Hirshan had a project he thought Clint might like, which had come to him through Stan Kamen, the head of the William Morris Agency's motion picture department. Kamen was, at the time, helping propel the rising star of Michael Cimino, whose script-doctoring of *Magnum Force* had made him 100 percent bankable, with producers lining up to throw development money at him. Cimino had written a road movie script with Clint in mind. The genre had become popular in the new independent Hollywood following the extraordinary success of Dennis Hopper and Peter Fonda's *Easy Rider* (1969), one of the last, and perhaps the biggest, nail in the old studio system's coffin.

Everyone now wanted to do a road picture, including Clint. Or at least that was what he decided when he read Cimino's script, an unlikely pairing of a bank robber and a drifter. Kamen had already attached one of his biggest clients, Jeff Bridges, who was fresh from a Best Supporting Actor nomination for Peter Bogdanovich's *The Last Picture Show*, to the project (in the part that not too long ago would have gone to Clint). Kamen wanted Clint to play the bank robber, a Vietnam War veteran.

Cimino knew what Clint liked and made sure the script had plenty of it: foamy barroom philosophy and lots of dialogue about women's "tight asses," "cock-sucking," and other vainglories of the proverbial and never-ending (and ultimately existential) road. The film would have no shortage of women, all young, sexy, and willing, who came Thunderbolt's (Clint's) way.

Cimino also insisted that he had to direct his own script. Clint—sensing in this fellow traveler a fiercely independent young hothead who wanted to do things his own way—approved it, as long as Hirshan could make the film a Malpaso project. No problem, Kamen assured him, although Frank Wells at Warner had, prior to Clint's firm commitment, turned down the project, feeling it was too idiosyncratic and lacked blockbuster potential. When Clint found out about that, he was furious. According to Clint, "Lenny Hirshan took a script that I liked called *Thunderbolt and Lightfoot* to Frank [Wells] and John [Calley], and they said, no, not at that price, so twenty minutes later I had a deal at United Artists."

To sweeten the deal, UA—Clint's original American distributor for the spaghetti trilogy—offered Malpaso a nonexclusive two-picture deal, which he immediately accepted, the second picture to be decided at a later date. With Bob Daley in place as the film's line producer, filming *Thunderbolt and Lightfoot* began in July 1973, on location in Montana, and lasted until the end of September.

While he had loved the script, and Cimino's cockiness, Clint hadn't counted on the director's perfectionism. It closely resembled what Clint had experienced with Siegel, times ten (bordering on the obsessional, it would contribute to Cimino's later self-destruction with *Heaven's Gate*).

Clint was well known on his sets for preferring to do one take in the morning and spending the afternoons on the golf course. During *Play Misty for Me*, in which he wore three caps—as director, de facto producer, and star—he said, "I must confess I can't stand long locations or production schedules. Once you get moving, I don't see any reason to drag your feet. During production, I can function much more fully and efficiently if I move full blast. Maybe it's because I'm basically lazy."

Clint found Jeff Bridges easy to work with and his performance revelatory. When the film was released in 1974, Bridges was nominated for Best Supporting Actor.* But according to several sources, including (but not limited to) Steven Bach's *Final Cut*, Clint perceived himself as having been upstaged by Bridges. His disappointment and anger were palpable. And when the film proved a disappointment at the box office (settling in at about $9 million in its initial theatrical release, less than half of *Magnum Force*), according to Bach, Clint excused his unofficial and overly indulged protégé Cimino. Instead he pointed the finger at UA, which, Clint felt, had failed to adequately position or promote the film. Despite all they had done for him, going all the way back to the Leone westerns, he swore he would never work for the studio again. He remained true to his word and never made the second film of the two-picture deal or any other for UA.

Instead, Clint went back to Universal to make a more comfortable type of movie, and a more reliably profitable one—straight action, with no women, no matter how tight their asses were, to interfere and slow things down. He wanted to return to the safety of the kind of film where he had to hang by his fingertips for dear life, while the audiences eagerly lined up to see him do so.

Only this time, he nearly fell making it.

---

*Bridges lost to Robert De Niro in Francis Ford Coppola's *The Godfather Part II*. The other nominees were Fred Astaire in John Guillermin and Irwin Allen's *The Towering Inferno*, and Michael V. Gazzo and Lee Strasberg in *The Godfather Part II*.

ELEVEN

I went into The Outlaw Josey Wales *a little in awe of Clint Eastwood, top star. I finished it in awe of Clint Eastwood, the total talent.*

—Sondra Locke

The film was *The Eiger Sanction*, a James Bond–style movie in which Clint plays a government assassin on a mission to kill a renegade spy; in reality, the agency believes he is the renegade and wants *him* killed, or so he thinks. The politics of paranoia are insinuated in the backstory. It is the physical assault on Switzerland's Eiger mountain that dominates the screen.

Clint leaped at the chance to do another film that would emphasize his physical prowess, in a surrounding where he would not have to share the stage with other, perhaps more talented or more famous actors, be harried by a self-indulgent director, and for a script that was more colorful than the resulting movie. *The Eiger Sanction* was just the kind of picture he knew best how to do—its content and form melded into one continuous flow of action, so that its content *became* its form, like a film with no plot starring a Man with No Name.

Apparently, at the relatively late-for-Hollywood age of forty-four, Clint felt he still had something left to prove. The financial dip that *Thunderbolt and Lightfoot* had taken was enough for Clint to want to fall back on more familiar turf, preferably in an outdoor setting, playing a silent but deadly hero with death-defying physical skills. Jonathan Hemlock (Eastwood), the former assassin who has lately turned to the clergy (of all things), is once again summoned by a "secret (i.e., CIA)" U.S. intelligence agency to return for one final assignment that will, upon its completion, enable him to make some new art purchases. As preposterous as it sounds, this plot offers the perfect setup for pure action, the essential ingredient of *The Eiger Sanction*. As he always liked to do, Clint personally went through the script with a thick blue pencil and slashed the dialogue as much as possible.

The Eiger Sanction property had been owned by the studio for quite some time. They had purchased the screen rights in 1972 to the first of what became a series of *Sanction* novels by Trevanian (*sanction* means "assassination" in the lingo of his books), its twisty hook being its intellectual hero who is all-too-easily able to become a man of action who thrives on danger.* The production team of Richard Zanuck and David Brown, sitting pretty with a strong development deal at Universal, had purchased *The Eiger Sanction* with Paul Newman in mind. (The next year they would score big with their filmed version of the novel *Jaws*, directed by Steven Spielberg.) Newman was red hot after George Roy Hill's *Butch Cassidy and the Sundance Kid* (1969) and *The Sting* (1973), but after expressing preliminary interest in the project, passed. Jennings Lang then suggested that Zanuck and Brown offer it to Clint (who had been Lang's first choice). He read it, loved it, and with Malpaso worked into the deal, signed on.

Once aboard, Clint assumed complete control of the project, becoming its nominal producer, although Zanuck, Brown, and (for Malpaso) Bob Daley got the on-screen credit. The first thing Clint did was toss the script and contact Warren Murphy, a novelist whose work he liked (Murphy's action-oriented *Destroyer* series would be the basis for at least one movie—Guy Hamilton's 1985 *Remo Williams: The Adventure Begins*; Murphy eventually provided the story for Richard Donner's *Lethal Weapon 2*). Clint liked Murphy's minimal style, and although he had as yet no background in scriptwriting, Clint convinced him to try one for *The Eiger Sanction*.

Working off what Murphy considered his first draft, Clint went into production with a cast that included costar George Kennedy as Big Ben Bowman, Hemlock's pal and also his secret enemy. Clint and Kennedy had gotten friendly during the making of *Thunderbolt and Lightfoot*, and as was Clint's way, he rewarded that friendship by making Kennedy a member of the Malpaso "family." Clint filled out the rest of the cast with Jack Cassidy and Vonetta McGee (playing the female spy Jemima Brown). McGee had made a couple of "blaxploitation" pictures and had the kind of "taut bottom" that Trevanian had given Brown in the book.

He wanted the film to look authentic, which not all his pictures did. This time, because he saw the film as essentially a great moun-

---

*The no-first-name Trevanian was the pen name of University of Texas professor Rod Whitaker.

tain climb with a little story and even less dialogue, he recruited Mike Hoover to serve as the film's technical adviser. The set was, in reality, the north face of the Eiger in the Swiss Alps, a mountain with a reputation of being nearly impossible to climb; the names of those who had died trying was a grim roster. Hoover had made a documentary called *Solo* that had been nominated for an Oscar for Best Short Subject—Clint had seen and admired it. For this film his assignment would be twofold—to teach Clint how to look professional while he climbed, and to serve as a cameraman on the more dangerous shoots. After several days rehearsing the action sequences at Yosemite Mountaineering School, Hoover and his handpicked team (which included at least one veteran of the north face), and the cast and crew all left for Switzerland, where they were booked into the Kleine Scheidegg Hotel, located at the base of the mountain.

One of Hoover's crew was David Knowles, a twenty-seven-year-old British climber who had been awarded the Royal Humane Society's highest honor for his part in the 1970 rescue of several stranded climbers in Glencoe, Scotland. His good looks made him a perfect double for Clint in some of the more difficult mountain shots. (Clint and the rest of the cast did very little actual climbing—helicopters transported them to and from the mountain.) The last shot of the first week of filming was a pickup of a mountain slide, re-created by using rubber rocks. Hoover and Knowles decided to shoot it themselves. They positioned on a lower ledge to get the angle they wanted, when suddenly the rubber rocks triggered real rocks, and they all started falling at the same time. Possibly the vibrations from the helicopters created the landslide. Hoover suffered a broken pelvis and clung to the side of the mountain until rescuers could get to him. Knowles wasn't so lucky. He was found dead, hanging upside down, dangling from one foot, his head crushed by a boulder that had killed him instantly.

Everyone was, naturally, upset, and for a while Clint considered canceling the production, but Clint's unofficial statement was this: let it continue.

It was a very difficult picture to make. A good thing our gadgets were limited in number; we were running the risk of heading in the direction of the James Bond movies. And especially the mountaineering sequences posed enormous problems. We had to shoot with two crews, one crew of technicians and one crew of mountain climbers. Every morning, we had to decide, according to the weather report, which one to send up the mountain. The three actors and myself had to undergo intensive training. On the seventh day of filming, we lost one of our mountaineers and, believe me, I asked myself repeatedly if it was worth it.

The unfortunate incident was used, rather coldly, to promote the film. In an interview entitled "Clint's Cliff Hanger," James Bacon described some of the footage (he'd had an advance look) as "white knuckle" material. He also said that "the only time [Clint] ever used a double was a dummy. One professional mountain climber hit on the head with a falling rock was killed in Switzerland. Clint had dropped from the same site only moments before." Bacon quoted Clint about it this way: "I just got myself involved deeper and deeper. There was no turning back. At first, I was going to use a double but a double can only think of the stunt. He can't think of the characterization. It just wouldn't have worked with a double." Bacon wound up his piece noting Clint's youthful looks: "Clint, at 44, is the world's greatest advertisement for health food . . . Even Clint's restaurant in Carmel—'Hog's Breath Inn'—features health food. He even serves organic booze—no preservatives added. The menu includes such goodies as 'The Dirty Harry' dinner, 'Fistful of T-Bone,' and a 'Coogan's Bluff' New York–cut steak. It seems that everything Clint touches makes money. His wife Maggie told me that the restaurant took off like Clint's box-office record."

The restaurant was in a former antiques shop and had become the prime social hangout for Clint and his local non-show-business friends, including Paul Lippman and Walter Becker, whom he knew from one of Carmel's more upscale restaurants, Le Marquis. According to Bacon, "The Hog's Breath's courtyard has an old-fashioned fireplace, and the entire place is surrounded by white picket fence and climbing ivy. The menu offers such basic food as Swiss cheese on rye with avocado and alfalfa sprouts, a char-broiled hamburger on organic bun with cheese or sliced tomatoes, a vegetarian salad bowl, fresh mushroom omelets and an assortment of Monterey Bay fish, including crisply sautéed filet of sole, squid sautéed in white wine and minced shallots, and a wide selection of teas."

"It's been a gold-mine," Maggie happily told Bacon.

Clint's rare inclusion of Maggie in an interview (probably in order to "humanize" him after the accident) prompted Bacon to portray her as Clint's partner in the fun-and-games pastime of running this other family business. In truth, she was increasingly frustrated by her continued marginalization in her marriage and in Clint's life. Clint brought her along to another interview to promote the film; she told Peter J. Oppenheimer in an off-the-cuff response how she handled Clint's propensity for "danger" in his moviemaking: "There's nothing I can do about it." It was a strikingly apt response as well as a reflection on her life with Clint—an innkeeper hostess while her husband costarred with nice asses. In the same interview Clint described his home life as sheer perfection. Asked why he shot some of the sequences for *The Eiger Sanction* back in Carmel, Clint replied, "Because I have a home in Carmel and this way I can stay home with my family and bounce my kids on my knees."

Lippman, who was also interviewed for the piece later on, claimed—doubtless in a joking manner that somehow did not come across—that Eastwood was a "romantic Casanova at the pub. He chats up all the girls. Especially the blondes. Clint likes small or slight women—he calls them 'squirts' or 'shrimps' and 'spinners.' " Lippman also claimed that he and Clint "often double-dated and compared notes the morning after, while watching cartoons."*

To Clint's great surprise and disappointment, *The Eiger Sanction* proved a dud at the box office, earning fully a third less than *Thunderbolt and Lightfoot*. After its initial domestic release, it settled in at a little more than $6.5 million in sales, to *Thunderbolt*'s already modest $9 million. Five years away from fifty, with his career on the decline, and a marriage that served only to scrub his public image, Clint allowed himself to be lured back to Warner by Frank Wells, who vowed to resurrect his fading star.

To do so, Wells insisted, Clint should revisit the money franchise, *Dirty Harry*, hoping that it would return him to the top of the box-office heap, flush with cash, fame, and all the eager young blondes he could handle.

Part of Clint's deal was a new suite of offices on the Warner lot, a re-creation of his old Malpaso offices at Universal, down to the same

---

*Clint later denied it, claiming that Lippman had exaggerated their friendship.

knickknacks dotting the place. Warner is only about a mile away from Universal in Burbank, California; he would remain in that office for the next quarter-century.

But before Clint could do another *Dirty Harry*, a suitable script had to be written and developed. Restlessly, he asked Wells if he had anything ready to go. When Wells said he didn't, Clint went in-house to Sonia Chernus, whom he had made head of Malpaso's story department as payback for her help in getting him the part of Rowdy Yates. As it happened, in keeping with Malpaso's bare-bones makeup, Chernus *was* the story department. She did have an outline and story treatment of a novel that had come in unsolicited—such over-the-transom submissions were usually rejected unread and returned. But Chernus had taken a quick look at this one, liked it, and now felt it might be of interest. The tentative title was *The Rebel Outlaw: Josey Wells.**

Chernus was proven correct when Clint had Malpaso take out an option on the rights to the unpublished book. Wells agreed to fund the movie if Clint could bring it in at $4 million. Once the money was in place, Clint went to the William Morris Agency in search of a writer and director to develop the project. They put Philip Kaufman up for the job, who in 1972 had written and directed *The Great Northfield Minnesota Raid*, a bank-robbery western drawing on the seemingly endless adventures of Jesse James.

Clint hired him with the expectation of a quick return, but Kaufman's deliberate preparations made Clint antsy. He was used to filming unpolished scripts, like *The Eiger Sanction*. But because of that film's failure, he was willing to give Kaufman a little more breathing room.

When he finished the script, wearing his director's cap, Kaufman boldly cast Chief Dan George in the key role of Lone Watie, the Chero-

---

*The novel had originally been self-published in 1972 as *Gone to Texas*. The author, Forrest Carter, was actually a (purported) half-Cherokee Native American, Asa Carter, a notorious racist who had been a public supporter of the Ku Klux Klan and a speechwriter for George Wallace. The novel glorified a Southern soldier, a Johnny Reb, who refuses to surrender after the end of the Civil War and goes on a bloody rampage while pursued by a Northern posse. The story appealed to Clint, who was always attracted to antisocial types. Carter's true identity was not discovered until after the film's release. To one reporter Clint declared, during preproduction, "It's a story written by an Indian about the period right after Reconstruction. The guy's a poet . . . wrote Indian poetry . . . and someone talked him into writing this book . . . and I just fell in love with it." Clint's quote is from Larry Cole's "Clint's Not Cute When He's Angry," *Village Voice*, May 24, 1976.

kee companion, and conscience, of Josey Wales. (The chief gave the film a bit of a wounded–Native American authenticity that would be echoed in Kevin Costner's 1990 *Dances with Wolves*, which owes more than a little of its physical look, directorial style, and thematic story line to *The Outlaw Josey Wales*.) As Wales's mission progresses, he and the chief pick up stragglers along the way, which gave the film a light coating of Christian allegory—unusual for a Clint Eastwood film, which usually emphasized physical revenge over moral redemption. In the end the film is less Jesus than journey, as the conquest of a mountain, à la *The Eiger Sanction*, leads to a greater understanding between the two.

To play the role of Laura Lee, another convert to Josey's bandwagon of soul-searching Civil War survivors, Clint wanted Sondra Locke, the actress he had once considered for *Breezy*. Her career had languished since her Oscar-nominated performance in *The Heart Is a Lonely Hunter*, but she had managed to hang on to the fringes of the business, and when Clint saw her, he immediately remembered her. Despite the seventeen-year difference between them (or because of it), he was strongly attracted to her, and she to him. He pushed Kaufman to green-light Locke, but it seemed the more he did, the more Kaufman resisted. So Clint went directly over his head and hired her anyway—which he had every right to do but was considered poor form.*

Locke remembers that moment of their connection this way: " 'So what have you been up to since I saw you last,' Clint asked as if it were just last week." Locke was given the part, and a few nights later Clint called to ask her out for dinner. " 'I gave the orders to hire you . . .' 'Really?' 'I never forgot meeting you for *Breezy*, Sondra.' 'But you didn't hire me for that film, did you,' I teased. 'No. I didn't. Big mistake . . . but I've hired you now.' 'I'm glad.' I genuinely blushed."

Shortly after Clint signed on Locke, Kaufman privately told a friend that Clint's going over his head was "the worst thing that anybody's ever done to me. He cut my balls off."

....

*In the hierarchy of Hollywood power, in the post-studio era of director-as-star/auteur, the producer was, and still is, the boss—for the simple reason that money always supersedes talent. Whoever writes the checks controls the production, no matter how creative or domineering a director appears. In this case, the man who was paying Kaufman's salary was Clint.

Production began in October 1975 on location in Arizona, Utah, and Wyoming. Clint was holding a script in one hand, so he could study his lines, a stopwatch in the other, so he could bring the film in on or under budget and thereby keep Wells to his financial commitment. But Clint fumed at Kaufman's snail-pace style of directing, considering it a sign of his lack of talent.

Some believe that what happened next was solely attributable to Kaufman's failure to assert his authority from day one, beginning with Clint's hiring of Locke. Passivity was a quality Clint had little use for in a director. Clint always preferred the shoot-the-film-now, ask-questions-later kind of moviemaking—not a style in which the director contemplated his ammunition.

The situation took a nuclear leap in the wrong direction when Kaufman (despite being married and having his wife along for the shoot) asked Locke out to dinner—on the same night Clint had. Locke, no fool she, turned down the director for the producer. Kaufman claimed he needed extra time to work with Locke on her characterization, but a testosterone-fueled battle had clearly erupted between Kaufman and Clint.

A few days after his faux pas with Locke, Kaufman, appearing timid and confused on set, totally messed up her rape scene by letting the camera roll too long and apparently confusing the word *cut* with the word *action*. Finally, his inability to catch a golden-hour sunset during another important scene proved the breaking point for Clint. Kaufman was nowhere to be found—he had apparently gone to another location—so an impatient Clint shot the scene himself. The next day he angrily handed Kaufman his walking papers.

Clint was furious about Kaufman's apparent bungling, but the Directors Guild of America (DGA) did not sanction the firing. All directors' contracts, they said, contain a clause that says if a director completes preproduction and has begun shooting, he or she cannot be fired at an actor's command. The fact that Clint was also the producer only made matters worse, and the film's production nearly came to a halt. Finally Wells frantically negotiated a buyout for Kaufman and accepted a DGA penalty for Clint of $50,000 (which Warner almost certainly paid).

Kaufman's firing angered some among the cast and crew and

frightened others. To many it looked as if Clint had had Kaufman do all the preparation work on the film—which was a lot—so he could then come in and get all the so-called glory. Although Kaufman to this day has never spoken about the incident, he did not direct another movie for nearly three years, and when he did it was, ironically, a 1978 remake of Don Siegel's *Invasion of the Body Snatchers.**

No matter who is right and who is wrong, when a director takes a case to the DGA, it is a serious act not soon forgotten by producers. The *Josey Wales* incident resulted in the Eastwood Rule—a DGA mandate that no current cast or crew member could replace the director of a production.

The Outlaw Josey Wales opened to mixed reviews but did phenomenal box office. (*Time* magazine called it one of the year's ten best.) Audiences thought the "old" Clint Eastwood had returned; the antisocial, violent, cynical antiromantic loner they had all missed so much. The rentals from the initial domestic release reached $14 million, good enough to reestablish Clint as a legitimate box-office power.[†] It also brought him once more to the attention of Pauline Kael, who complained that with *Josey Wales*, Clint had established himself as the "reductio ad absurdum of macho today." Kael's continual attack-dog reviews disturbed Clint greatly.

With his career back on the winning track, Clint shifted his concentration to the building of his Carmel dream house, now in its seventh year of construction. Between sessions of Transcendental Meditation (to which he had recently become devoted) and Malpaso business, he had been increasingly absent from the homestead.

---

*After a series of so-so films, Kaufman went on to direct *The Right Stuff* in 1983, which definitely established him as a major Hollywood director.

†That same year, 1976, Clint remained in the top-ten list of Quigley Publications box-office champs, while John Wayne fell off, never to return. It is believed that Wayne sent Clint a letter highly critical of his revisionist view of the American West (some would put that onus on Wayne himself) and that Clint was upset by it. However, the contents of that letter, if it existed, were never released, and neither Wayne nor Clint ever discussed it on the record. Clint that year came in at number five. Number one was Robert Redford, followed by Al Pacino, Charles Bronson, Paul Newman, Clint, Burt Reynolds.

He spent some time, too, in Las Vegas, anonymously. But it wasn't all fun and games. Up in San Francisco he began to see a psychiatrist, Dr. Ronald Lowell, who, regarding Kael's reviews, told Eastwood, "What Kael says is actually 180 degrees the opposite of what she says, and . . . often a man or woman obsessed with preaching great morality is more interested in amorality." A bit later at a speaking appearance, Clint pointed out to the audience that while Kael hated his movies for their maleness, she had adored Bernardo Bertolucci's *Last Tango in Paris*, wherein Paul (Marlon Brando, a Kael darling) has anal intercourse with Jeanne (Maria Schneider), in a relationship dictated by Paul to be based only on (debasing) sex. So much for her neofeminist tirades, Clint said, chuckling. The audience chuckled with him.

Clint was forty-six now and feeling every second of it. A preoccupation with age, or more precisely aging, is a universal occupational hazard for performers in Hollywood, and it became one of his most favored subjects whenever he did grant the occasional interview. "I don't have any new properties on my mind right now," he told one writer. "One thing about getting old is that I've developed patience over the years."

Patience with everything and everyone, perhaps, except his desire for Sondra Locke, whom he was now seeing as often as he could. It was a relationship that he could not resist, and it was about to effect an extraordinary shift in the dynamics of his work and his life. It would change forever the lives of all three of its principal players—Clint, Locke, and Maggie—casting them in a real-life melodrama that would make *Breezy* seem wistful by comparison.

TWELVE

*People thought I was a right-wing fanatic . . . all Harry was
doing was obeying a higher moral law . . . people even said I was
a racist because I shot Black bank robbers. Well, shit, Blacks rob
banks, too. That film gave four Black stuntmen work. Nobody
talked about that.*

—Clint Eastwood

Mid-1975, several months before *The Outlaw Josey Wales* went into production, a script called *Moving Target* had come to Clint directly, via the Hog's Breath Inn, written by two Oakland High School graduates. Clint read it, liked it, and turned it over to Bob Daley, to see if it was worth dipping into Malpaso's discretionary fund to attach a professional screenwriter to develop it. Daley liked it as well and put in a call to Stirling Silliphant, an established Hollywood writer who in his salad days had written an episode of *Rawhide*, then moved up to the big screen with his script for Don Siegel's 1958 post-noir big-screen *policier, The Lineup,* based on a popular TV show. A decade later he won an Oscar for the screenplay of Norman Jewison's *In the Heat of the Night* (1967). Clint had always liked Silliphant personally as well as his abilities and agreed with Daley that *Moving Target* could be the next Dirty Harry film.

They sent Silliphant the script, then met to discuss it. Silliphant all but dismissed the writing, but liked the film's central notion that Dirty Harry takes on a politically subversive terrorist organization, with an added twist that his partner is a woman. Clint liked what Silliphant had to say and green-lighted money to develop a script.

Not long after *Josey Wales* was released, Silliphant completed a first draft. Clint read it and wasn't thrilled with it. It didn't have the necessary delicate balance to keep Dirty Harry's antisocial character intact while softening him enough to allow for a woman to "get" to him. Clint turned it over to Dean Riesner. Meanwhile Silliphant had suggested young and up-and-coming (and decidedly non-leading-lady-like) Tyne Daly for the partner role. She read it and turned it down, not once, not twice, but three times. Changes were made with each revision, but she felt that playing off a hard-ass like Harry would make her sympathetic character look like a total ditz, too laughable to be believable. Clint ordered several more rewrites, which he hated to do because of the delays and the added expense and because he had always preferred first instincts over studied deliberation as the best method to make a Clint Eastwood movie. But this time the waiting paid off, and when Daly read a version of the screenplay that was acceptable to her, she agreed to play the role.

Still not ready to pick up the reins of directing again while producing and starring in the same film, Clint looked for someone who would not challenge his opinion, would not screw with themes, and would get the film done quickly and within budget. Looking to avoid a repetition of the Kaufman fiasco, Clint turned to James Fargo, his longtime assistant director, to helm what was now called *The Enforcer*.*

When Daly suggested the basic story line be changed so that her character and Harry did not have a romantic involvement, he quickly agreed. Clint never wanted romance in his films. He didn't see himself as a leading man and believed his audiences would stay away from anything that even resembled a love story between the great loner and some moony costar. Dirty Harry in love? That would be like having a love interest in a film about the invasion of Normandy. It was an insane notion, and Clint was grateful that Daly recognized that.

Production began on the streets of San Francisco during the summer of 1976. Until then Clint had been relatively absent from the proceedings. The reason was simple: he was by now hot and heavy with Sondra Locke, a fact later confirmed by several people who knew and/or worked with Clint at the time, including James Fargo.

The affair continued throughout the shooting of *The Enforcer*. Several times he stayed overnight at one of the several apartments he kept in San Francisco and Sausalito. So frequently was he away that his usual tight control and supervision were missing when it came time to edit the film. Two scenes simply didn't match, no matter how cleverly Ferris Webster, who had a reputation for being able to fix anything, tried to put them together.

Fortunately for this action film, imperfect scene-matches did not matter all that much. In *The Enforcer* Callahan battles a group of ter-

*Fargo had served as AD on *Joe Kidd, High Plains Drifter, Breezy, The Eiger Sanction*, and *The Outlaw Josey Wales*.

rorists (who were not explicitly political; in 1970s action movies a *terrorist* was a conveniently generic "bad guy" more interested in getting an enormous amount of money than in overthrowing a government), with a female newbie of whom he reluctantly becomes fond. She is (naturally) killed, prompting Callahan, angrier than usual, to dispose of the terrorist group with a single blast from his giant bazooka, a phallic symbol that made Callahan's hitherto-famous Magnum seem like a cap gun.

Although the film had some good moments—Tyne Daly would use it as a springboard for her own cops-and-robbers TV series, *Cagney & Lacey*—critics excoriated it. Not surprisingly, Kael with heightened glee noted that "Eastwood's holy cool seems more aberrant than ever."

Kael may have actually picked up on the one thing that other critics had chosen to ignore: Clint had grown weary of the role and perhaps of moviemaking in general. In retrospect, passing off directorial duties to Fargo may have been less an act of insecurity than of indifference. During the filming of *The Enforcer* the real action for Clint was more likely with Locke than on the set. The film looks more complacent than violent, more repetitious than revelatory, more tired than tough, and poorly edited, with a story that was strictly formulaic. Clint's performance borders on the somnambulistic.

Typical of most critics was the always-too-easily-offended-by-genre-films Rex Reed. Writing in the *New York Daily News*, Reed said, "*The Enforcer* is the third or fourth Dirty Harry movie with Clint Eastwood blowing people's heads off and creating the kind of havoc Batman would find juvenile . . . it all went out of style years ago with Clint Eastwood's mumbling . . . save your money, it'll be on TV by Easter."

None of the film's criticism was very objective, and none of it mattered. Audiences still couldn't get enough of Clint as Dirty Harry. The movie grossed a phenomenal $60 million in its initial domestic release and doubled that overseas, making it Clint's biggest moneymaker to date.

At Warner's urging, a commercially reinvigorated Clint soon began thinking about his next movie, which the studio hoped would be ready in time as its big Christmas 1977 release.* Both the studio and the star

---

Dirty Harry, Magnum Force, and *The Enforcer* had all been huge-grossing Warner/Malpaso Christmas-holiday-release pictures.

wanted a follow-up blockbuster that would capitalize on the momentum of *The Enforcer* and equal or surpass its box-office take. *The Gauntlet* was the film they chose, in which Clint is a policeman, not Callahan, charged with delivering a prisoner from Los Angeles to Arizona. The prisoner is a prostitute, and a virtual gauntlet of "bad guys" wants to kill them both: Clint because, presumably, he is, well, *Clint*, the ultimate enforcer who will deliver her no matter what, and the prostitute because she is the key witness to a politically charged sex scandal and her arrival will bring down the corrupt forces in the Arizona police.

Clint's character, Ben Shockley, is actually an inverted Callahan, a shaky cop trying to get over his problems with alcohol when Phoenix police commissioner Blakelock (William Prince) assigns him to extradite the prostitute, Gus Mally (Sondra Locke). When Shockley realizes the trail of incrimination leads directly back to Phoenix, and that neither he nor his prisoner is meant to live, he becomes especially enraged and plots a spectacular revenge-fueled scheme that takes him through the final police gauntlet and results in Blakelock's death instead of his own.

For the part of Mally, Warner had wanted Barbra Streisand, but Clint, who as always had the final say in casting, said no; his films were usually filled with lesser names than himself. He told the studio that he felt Streisand was too old to play opposite him (she was thirty-five, he was forty-seven). Instead, he insisted that Locke play the part. Casting his new girlfriend put her once more into Clint's dark spotlight; she had already been sexually assaulted in *The Outlaw Josey Wales* before being rescued by Clint, and now in *The Gauntlet* she was to undergo a brutal near-rape, only to be rescued again by her knight in tarnished armor.

Warner, to say the least, was not thrilled. The studio had earmarked $5 million for production, making it a very expensive project, and it wanted a double-barreled, name-above-the-title star to decorate marquees across the country. It had already paid $200,000 for the script by Dennis Shryack and Michael Butler—they were very hot due to their much-buzzed-about script for Elliot Silverstein's as-yet-unreleased *The Car*. And it had paid fifteen points of the net and another $100,000 for the future novelization rights (something that was then a very popular source of ancillary income). When Clint was informed of the terms Warner had agreed to get Shryack and Butler, he was not happy.* Clint, who through Malpaso was a partner in the deal, never paid much for scripts and *never* offered points as an inducement. Besides, he was always more interested in story than in dialogue, preferring to formulate a movie off a general plot idea and filling it in with as few words as possible.

Feeling perhaps that he had made enough of a concession by approving the writers, he stood firm on his decision to cast Locke instead of Streisand. Once Warner caved, principal shooting began in April 1977 on location in Nevada and Arizona.

The plot of *The Gauntlet* was leaner and more singular than usual. Neither Shryack nor Butler conceived its thundering, explosive violence—Clint had inserted it, and Warner happily encouraged it. As far as the studio was concerned, a Clint Eastwood movie could never have enough violence, sexual abuse of women, or raw brutality.

The resulting film was *Coogan's Bluff* meets *Magnum Force*, minus the West Coast/East Coast trickery and the character of Dirty Harry. Ben Shockley's frailty makes the story even more compelling, at least in theory, as he is sent, without knowing it, on a suicide mission. The set-piece of the film is the physical gauntlet that Shockley and Mally must pass through while driving a bus, attended by the entire Phoenix police force. At this point the film turns surreal but gains no potentially redemptive transcendence. The attack on the bus loses all sense of drama once it becomes obvious that shooting out its tires would stop it dead in its tracks. And the ending is even more absurd; once Shockley has delivered his prisoner and killed all his attackers, no one wants her or knows what to do with her. Presumably the two of them take another bus out of town and live happily ever after.

Despite its ridiculous plot and cartoonish denouement, Clint's genre-driven star power was enough to make the film a bona fide box-office hit. As always, the negative criticism did not matter. Judith Crist, writing in the *New York Post*, summed up her opinion in five words:

---

*The deal for *The Car* had made the duo "hot" in the industry, not the actual script or the film that was made from it. As ever in Hollywood, money talked, and more money meant more power, one of the reasons Clint never liked to pay that much to writers. He had formed Malpaso to ensure his own autonomous power base (and financial stronghold) and did not like to give up a great deal of money, because that meant, to him at least, surrendering authority, or power, to underlings.

"*The Gauntlet* is the pits." Vincent Canby, in the *Times*, didn't like it either but at least acknowledged the film's "Eastwood" touch.

> Clint Eastwood . . . plays a character role. *The Gauntlet* has nothing
> to do with reality and everything to do with Clint Eastwood fiction,
> which is always about a force (Mr. Eastwood) that sets things straight
> in a crooked world. A movie without a single thought in its head, but
> the action scenes are so ferociously staged that it's impossible not to
> pay attention most of the time. Mr. Eastwood's talent is in his style—
> unhurried and self-assured.

The Gauntlet grossed more than $54 million in its initial domestic Christmastime release and would top the $100 million mark by the time it finished its worldwide theatrical run.

As if to somehow compensate for all the private time he was spending with Locke, Clint made his home life with Maggie unusually public. For the first time in years he invited reporters to Carmel to witness for themselves how happy he was, what a normal married man he was, away from Hollywood.

Every magazine jumped at the chance to interview the elusive Clint, but if they were looking for anything candid or spontaneous, they didn't get it. Then in the midst of all this publicity-spinning, the February 13, 1978, issue of *People* magazine "scooped" everyone with a cover shot of Clint and—*Sondra Locke*. No one missed it, including Maggie, who was rightly infuriated.

Maggie had tolerated a lot during their long marriage. She had looked the other way during all of Clint's extramarital affairs. She had even strained her neck looking to the opposite side of the room when Locke showed up at several parties that the Eastwoods had recently attended. But the cover of *People* was too much, even for her. Public flaunting was the one thing Clint had never before done, allowing Maggie to maintain her public dignity. The week the cover story appeared in *People*, Maggie hired a lawyer and sought a legal separation. After much discussion, Clint persuaded her to take a Hawaiian vacation with him to see if there was any way they could save their marriage.

During the vacation Clint admitted to Maggie that he was in love with Sondra.

When they returned, Maggie filed for the separation.

Sondra too was upset. Certainly Clint's marriage looked like it was going to end, but for her the notion of Clint being a single man was a bit too complicated.

Because she too was married and had no intention of getting a divorce.

Locke had married Gordon Anderson, her childhood sweetheart from Shelbyville, Tennessee, where they had spent their days imagining what the rest of the world must be like. Locke's family disapproved of Anderson and what they claimed was his impure "hold" on her. The night following their high school graduation they eloped. Anderson moved to New York City to pursue a career in acting, while Locke stayed behind, picking up the occasional local job modeling and acting in commercials. Then Anderson read about a nationwide talent hunt for a teenage girl to play the lead in an upcoming movie of *The Heart Is a Lonely Hunter.*

He immediately returned to Tennessee, picked up Locke, and took her to Nashville, where the preliminary interviews were taking place. Anderson worked on her to prepare her, spending a lot of time detailing her face and appearance. He scruffed her up, redid her hair, taped down her ample breasts to make them less prominent, and clothed her in the style of the novel. They agreed to lie about her age—she was twenty-one, but the part called for a teenager. After her successful interview, they drove to Birmingham, Alabama, for the first major eliminations. A thousand young girls auditioned, and about a hundred passed, including Locke. The next stop was New Orleans, where the finalists were to meet with the film's director, Robert Ellis Miller.

A week after meeting Miller, the girls were called to Warner Bros.' New York offices, all expenses paid, for the last round of auditions. Fine-tuned by Anderson, Locke was confident as she went before the producers and director and won the role. In 1968, the same year Clint appeared in his seventeenth feature, *Coogan's Bluff,* in her first, Locke was nominated for an Oscar for Best Supporting Actress.*

---

*She lost to Ruth Gordon in Roman Polanski's *Rosemary's Baby.* The other nominees were Lynn Carlin in John Cassavetes's *Faces,* Kay Medford in William Wyler's *Funny Girl,* and Estelle Parsons in Paul Newman's *Rachel, Rachel.*

Even before the film was released, Locke and Anderson had moved to Hollywood—or rather to West Hollywood, the predominantly gay neighborhood between Beverly Hills and Hollywood proper, where Anderson set them up in a spacious town house. He wanted to live in West Hollywood for a reason—he was gay. He had been in the closet most of his life; Locke first found out before the marriage, but she said it didn't bother her. He was who he was, and she loved him. They were friends first, and lovers without physical sex, which did not prove a problem because they were both able to get what they wanted elsewhere. West Hollywood gave Anderson the chance to come out, and he did so with a vengeance. By the time Locke met Clint and appeared with him in *The Outlaw Josey Wales*, Anderson was seriously involved in a relationship with another man.

The fact that Locke was married had not bothered Clint at all; in fact, it initially held great appeal. *Married* translated into *safe*, as in his own marriage. Now, the more he got to know Locke and found out about her unorthodox marriage to Anderson, the more he recognized in her a kindred soul, a talented loner with a marriage that was convenient and even advantageous, but unsatisfying.

A month before Clint and Locke appeared on the cover of *People*, he had appeared with Burt Reynolds on the January 9 cover of *Time* magazine. Inside the eight-page spread covered a lot about Clint's official (i.e., studio-sanctioned public) life but said relatively little, comparing him to his old friend Reynolds, who was still a bankable star after his impressive performance in John Boorman's *Deliverance* (1972). That performance had had Oscar written all over it—until Reynolds self-destructed by posing as the seminude centerfold for *Cosmopolitan* magazine. The gesture relieved his career of any remaining pretense of seriousness. The movies he made after *Deliverance* failed to ignite the public, until he returned to southern-redneck form in Hal Needham's *Smokey and the Bandit* (1977), which was a huge box-office success but which the Academy universally avoided. The *Time* piece, written by Richard Schickel, lauded Clint and Reynolds as the only two actors in sync with the popular tastes of moviegoing America, audaciously awarding them the mantle of Everyman once held by James Stewart and Henry Fonda and favorably comparing them to such tough-guy screen stalwarts as John Wayne, Marlon Brando, and Paul Newman (while all but ignoring Al Pacino and Robert De Niro). He concluded, "In today's climate it may actually take more courage and more imagination to become an Eastwood or a Reynolds than it does to be a Nicholson or a Redford." Lurking just behind them, given the separate "box" treatment, was, according to Schickel, the "third great action star" of his generation, Charles Bronson.

The Eastwood-Bronson comparison was a common one; publications like the *Hollywood Studio* magazine said,

> In a modern society bristling with violence and pervaded by an ever increasing air of helplessness, Clint Eastwood and Charles Bronson fulfill a burning psychological need on the part of filmgoers the world over by exemplifying western heroes capable of overpowering hostile forces and proving that one individual can make a difference in a restless and turbulent world . . . these two images from the western culture surface when referring to the laconic loner syndrome.

Both Reynolds and Bronson bought into the idea that they were iconic, but Clint ran from it. If Reynolds allowed himself to be stroked by Schickel's overblown *Time* piece, Clint kept his distance from it.

Instead, he turned to Locke for his creative validation. Of all the women he had dated, she stood out in one crucial aspect. She was young, blond, largely inexperienced (he believed), and perhaps even a bit malleable, but she gave off an air of cool, of hip understanding that belied her rural southern roots. She dripped "artist" from every pore, and as critics were, for the most part, still trying to figure out Clint Eastwood and the meaning of his personal appeal, hitting 180 degrees wide of the mark, the only one who really "got" him was Locke.

If some wanted to anoint Clint as the reincarnation of the Great American Hero (the original having been lost in the country's ignominious defeat in Vietnam), Clint was more than happy to let them, leaving the glorification of his screen heroics to self-appointed critical know-it-alls like Schickel. Clint was too busy trying to balance his private life between what he thought he needed (a home, a wife like Maggie, kids, a big house in Carmel) and what he thought he wanted: a woman like Locke who could run with him, who understood him, and who could take him where no other woman had. For the first time since he had gotten married, he didn't hit hard and then run home to his wife.

It was she, according to Locke, who convinced Clint to follow *The Gauntlet* with a complete turnaround, the off-the-wall *Every Which Way but Loose*. To her (and then to Clint), it was the perfect response to all those who insisted he was the primal American cinematic hero. One thing that she pointed out to him was that he had thus far (excepting the occasional paychecks like *Where Eagles Dare*, *Kelly's Heroes*, and *The Eiger Sanction*) created essentially two iconic characters that reappeared again and again in his movies. The Man with No Name had appeared in the three Leone spaghetti westerns and was echoed in one way or another in most of the later westerns including *Hang 'Em High*, *Two Mules for Sister Sara*, *Joe Kidd*, *High Plains Drifter*, and *The Outlaw Josey Wales*. All these characters, including the original Man with No Name, were Vietnam-era antiheroes, men who went against the establishment mostly because the establishment was itself controlled by outlaws, thereby making the outsiders heroes. Clint's other great screen persona was Dirty Harry, in some ways a modern-dress version of the Man with No Name. These characters (and their other variations) are not knights in tarnished armor, they are just tarnished, and that's what made them unique. Doing *Every Which Way but Loose*, Locke suggested, would expand Clint's realm and suit the shift in the postwar cultural zeitgeist.

She was right on the money, and he knew it. Pushing ever closer to fifty, he was more than ready to trade in his John Wayne mantle for a little bit of what Burt Reynolds had going for him. (Since 1972 Reynolds had ranked higher in the popularity polls than even the Duke and was now threatening to pass even Clint.)*

The outsize success of Reynolds's *Smokey and the Bandit* the year before told him two things: first, he didn't have to knock himself out with big, brawling action films; and second, the public might be shifting toward (or back to) working-class, southern-based humor, something he felt he could play in a walk. In an interview he gave around

---

*The primary difference between Wayne and Clint was that Wayne's movies deliberately proselytized *über*-patriotism, roughly from David Miller's *Flying Tigers* (1942) through Wayne's self-directed Vietnam War opus, *The Green Berets* (1968). Clint preferred to explore the flaws of individual characters in his films rather than deliver an explicit message. Both actors (and directors) may have achieved similar results—some might say *Dirty Harry* is more political than *The Green Berets*, but as artistic statements, the films, taken out of their social context, reflect far different creative approaches and artistic results.

this time, the influence of Locke on his thinking comes through: the sudden references to Capra and Sturges, the rejection of his established image, and his abilities as a filmmaker, particularly in terms of story, even if the allusions here are a bit of a stretch:

> The script [for *Every Which Way but Loose*] had been around for a long time, rejected by everyone. The script itself was dog-eared and food-stained. Most sane men were skeptical about it; there were conflicts about it in my own group. They said it was dangerous. They said it's not *you*. I said, it *is* me . . . Here was a guy who was a loser but who wouldn't acknowledge it and who was a holdout against cynicism. It wasn't old-fashioned but in a way it was. The guy was fun to play because he had to be stripped bare of all his dignity . . . I didn't have to prove my commercial value at this point in my career. I didn't play off the bad sheriff. I suppose a "normal" Clint Eastwood picture might have.

Instead he played off an orangutan.*

Jeremy Joe Kronsberg's screenplay concerns a two-fisted truck driver who travels from town to town making money in bare-handed pickup prizefights; he is accompanied by, of all things, an orangutan he has won in a previous fight. He falls in love with a country-western singer, loses her, wins her, and loses her again. Clint may have first come across the script from a secretary who was a friend of Kronsberg's wife. Everyone at Malpaso was against the project except Clint, and Locke had liked it as well. He took it to Warner to find the funding for it.

Warner, eager to get another Eastwood film in theaters, was nonetheless split on this one. The new head of production, John Calley, wanted to pass, but Frank Wells, Clint's steadfast ally at the studio, thought it might be a good commercial departure for him. After a lot of back-and-forth, Warner finally said yes and put up the production money. Shooting began shortly thereafter, in April 1978, in Albuquerque, Santa Fe, Taos, and Denver—the stops along the trucker route in the film. The film's production caravan eventually

---

*Clint's character, Philo Beddoe, was twenty-nine years old in the original script. During production, writer Jeremy Joe Kronsberg teased Clint that the script would have to be revised to make Philo older so that he could be believable as a Clint Eastwood character. When Clint asked how much older, Kronsberg replied, "About thirty-five."

wound up in Los Angeles, both for additional locations and the sound-stages of Warner.

To direct, Clint brought back James Fargo, who had last worked with him on *The Enforcer*—someone who, essentially, wouldn't get in the way. Wanting country music to be played throughout, he hired Snuff Garrett from the old *Rawhide* days to write some tunes, and chose the title of one, "Every Which Way but Loose," as the title of the film (originally called *The Coming of Philo Beddoe*). He then cut a publishing deal with Warner and used all of their artists on the sound-track album. The title track, by Eddie Rabbitt, was released as a sin-gle a month before the film came out, became an unlikely cross-over hit, and provided free promotion every time it was played on the radio. In the film Locke's character, Lynn Halsey-Taylor, sings two songs, something she didn't particularly want to do nor was especially good at, but Clint hired a singing coach, in this case Phil Everly of the famed Everly Brothers, to work with her until Clint thought the songs, and the scenes, were good enough.

Although Sondra Locke was cast as the female country-singer-love-interest, as usual in an Eastwood film, the woman was part of the back-story rather than the major plot line, dominated here by the orangutan. Working with animals is always iffy, and Clint knew it. He had worked with animals before, as far back as his all-but-invisible part in the *Francis the Talking Mule* series, but felt he could pull it off. His costar was an orangutan called Clyde in the movie (three orang-utans were used in the production, but one, whose real name was Manis, was on-screen most of the time), a Las Vegas–trained per-former with whom audiences immediately fell in love.

Clint, with perfectly understated comic timing, played to the film's lowbrow mentality, up to and including the simplified moral—what life lessons man learns from an orangutan. The set piece that every-one remembers most happens when Clint points his fingers like a gun at Clyde and yells *bang*, to which Clyde responds by pretending to fall down dead. That bit of comedy, plus tough-guy motorcycle gangs, bare-chested fistfights, insincere women, and a buddy-buddy "'tan more faithful than even Tonto was to the Lone Ranger," added up to an improbable hit but a box-office sensation. Women, who ordinar-ily stayed away from the harder Clint movies (unless dragged to them by their husbands or boyfriends) loved this one and helped drive the movie's take into the stratosphere.

But the reviews were almost universally awful: "The film is way off the mark" *(Variety)*. "This is a redneck comedy with no stops pulled. If I could persuade my friends to see it, they would probably detest me" (Stuart Byron, *Village Voice*). "A Clint Eastwood comedy that could not possibly have been created by human hands . . . One can forgive the orangutan's participation but what is Eastwood's excuse" (David Ansen, *Newsweek*). "The latest Clint Eastwood disgrace" (Rex Reed, *New York Daily News*). Nonetheless, *Every Which Way but Loose* grossed an astonishing $124 million in its initial domestic release, about eight times what *The Gauntlet* had done, making it the second-biggest Warner film of the year, behind Richard Donner's *Superman*, whose title character Clint had seriously considered playing.*

Early in 1979, after a year of negotiations, Clint thought he was ready to agree to a divorce settlement. He would pay Maggie a lump sum of $25 million and allow her to keep the big house in Carmel and have the kids live with her; Clint would be able to freely come and go with them, something he insisted on. While he was never around all that much, he still loved and felt close to them. He kept his brand-new $100,000 Ferrari Boxer. He then assigned Locke the job of finding a new house for them, promising her that "it would be theirs forever, together in retirement." There was, reportedly, no anger or viciousness between Clint and Maggie. A coolness coated the wall between them, but for the sake of himself as much as (he claimed) the kids, and to keep the prying press off both his and Maggie's necks, he was determined to melt it.

For that reason, and because Maggie's lawyer was demanding 50 percent of everything Clint had earned while they were together, he suddenly reversed his stand and no longer pressed for a final divorce. Instead, he felt a longer separation was needed so that both could have time to think, giving an ironic meaning to the newest Clint Eastwood–inspired catchphrase, "every which way but loose."

---

*Every Which Way but Loose earned more than $200 million in its first year of international release.

PART II

FROM ACTOR TO AUTEUR

THIRTEEN

I've been advised against nearly everything I've ever done.

—Clint Eastwood

There was no part for Sondra Locke in Clint's next movie, *Escape from Alcatraz*, his thirty-fourth feature film in twenty-five years. The virtually all-male adventure was based on the true story of Frank Lee Morris and John and Clarence Anglin's 1962 escape from the notorious island prison located in San Francisco Bay. While Clint was in production, Locke looked for a new house where they could live together. She did not say what if anything she intended to do about her husband, although he was, at this time, living with another man.

The film was based on J. Campbell Bruce's 1963 nonfiction book *Escape from Alcatraz: A Farewell to the Rock*. Richard Tuggle, the editor of a small magazine devoted to health, had initially bought it to break into the movie business. Tuggle wrote his own screen adaptation and, when he was satisfied it was good enough, sent it to the one director he thought might like it enough to make it.

Tuggle had a lifelong fascination with prison stories, both true and fictionalized, and considered Don Siegel's *Riot in Cell Block 11* (1954) the best of the genre; film producer Walter Wanger had conceived it after being released from prison for shooting a man he suspected was having an affair with his wife. While incarcerated, Wanger found the living conditions so appalling, he wanted to expose them to the public. The result was one of the toughest and most brutally realistic prison dramas ever filmed.

Late in February 1978, when Tuggle sent the script to Siegel via his agent, Leonard Hirshan, at William Morris (also Clint's agent), Hirshan sent it on to Siegel, who liked it but was tied up on another project, *Das Boot*, and had to pass. Then a severe illness struck one of the top executives at Bavaria Studios, in Germany, and *Das Boot*, already in production, had to be halted. Early in March Hirshan went back to Siegel and asked him to reconsider the project. Siegel told Hirshan he thought it would be perfect for Clint. Hirshan did and then sent it to Daley (annoying Siegel, who felt his relationship was strong and personal enough that the script should have gone directly to Clint). Clint read, loved it, and wanted Siegel to direct; he wanted to star in and produce it through Malpaso.

But Siegel, rather than taking an option on the script, had bought it outright for a cool $100,000 with the irreversible proviso that he would direct. He made an offer to Clint and Malpaso (and presumably Warner). Clint balked over the issue of who would have the final cut. Siegel (still miffed at Hirshan for not sending the script directly to Clint, or for not completely understanding the deal) heard nothing from either Clint or Hirshan about the terms he wanted. He then angrily took his offer off the table and moved the project to Paramount. The joint heads of that studio, Michael Eisner and Jeffrey Katzenberg, had saved Paramount from going under by developing a highly successful TV unit and a series of in-house sitcoms. Now they were looking for the right project to restore the studio's big-screen glory. They thought *Escape from Alcatraz* was the perfect choice. They made the deal and looked for a star in their own stable to play the lead.

None proved either interested or available. (Paramount especially wanted Richard Gere but he was not excited by the project.) Eisner then urged Siegel to reconcile with Clint and try to bring him to Paramount. Siegel was reluctant, but he had felt underappreciated at Warner: like Clint, he blamed the studio's lack of a sufficient pre-awards-industry campaign for his not even being nominated for *Dirty Harry*. He bit the bullet, visited Clint at his Malpaso office for sandwiches and beers, and mea culpa'd his way into signing a joint venture between Malpaso, Siegel Film, and Paramount, with options for all parties to join in future projects together.

Moving to Paramount, even just for this picture, was a big deal for Clint. For the first time in nearly a decade his big summer 1979 release would carry Paramount's name and its familiar circle and mountain logo. It was not only a victory for Paramount but also a slap in the face to Warner, which had enjoyed a steady stream of Eastwood holiday fare every year since *Dirty Harry*.

Clint had stayed away from Paramount for so long because of his grudge over the production delays and excess spending on *Paint Your Wagon*—two of the primary reasons he had formed Malpaso. He knew he was taking something of a risk returning to the studio, but this time he was at a far higher level of power in Hollywood, and his defection, as it were, from Warner might shake that studio up and remind them how valuable he really was to their bottom line.

Production on *Escape from Alcatraz* began in October 1978, and as Siegel had feared, the set turned into an ongoing battle between him and Clint for control over every aspect of filming. Clint apparently prevailed; Siegel left the production in anger before the completion of its all-important final cut. Clint, his longtime editors Ferris Webster and Joel Cox, and Jack Green, his cameraman, put it together.

Not surprisingly, the finished product looked less like a Siegel film than any of his four prior collaborations with Clint. In Siegel's projected final version, the film had ended inside the prison, giving it an air of grim reality. In Clint's a flower is left behind, indicating that the three escapees make it—the triumph of the outlaw over his society of imprisonment. This crucial change altered the entire meaning of the film. Both versions were dark: Siegel's reflected the inescapable reality of Alcatraz, while Clint's suggested the greater blackness of the escapees' lives on the run, suggested by the black, murky waters that surround and engulf the flower. In this as in all Clint films, survival is sometimes harder and therefore more dramatic than death. (Clint dies in only three films in his entire career: *The Beguiled, Honkytonk Man,* and *Gran Torino.*) Asked by *Time* magazine about the darkness and the mood of the film and if it had any personal relevance, Clint responded with a succinct, end-of-conversation "I don't know."

Although Clint did not officially direct the film (Siegel is credited as producer and director), its moody, grim level of intensity and the clear and imposing presence of his dark personality on-screen clearly identifies it as a Clint Eastwood film.

Upon its release in 1979, *Escape from Alcatraz* received mostly rave reviews, some of the best of Clint's career. Vincent Canby of *The New York Times* led the way, omitting any mention of Siegel while emphasizing the importance of Clint: "This is a first-rate action movie. Terrifically exciting. There is more evident knowledge of moviemaking in any one frame than there are in most other American films around at the moment. Mr. Eastwood fulfills the demands of the role and the film as probably no other actor could." Frank Rich, writing for *Time* magazine, called it "ingenious, precise and exciting."

Clearly Clint had hit a critical nerve with *Escape from Alcatraz,* although audiences proved less interested. The film's initial domestic gross was a relatively modest $34 million, about a third of what *Every Which Way but Loose* had taken in.* It also grossed less than one-fifth of that year's biggest film, Richard Donner's *Superman*, a Warner Bros. hit that made a star out of its title hero, Christopher Reeve, a role that Clint had repeatedly turned down. His disappointment at *Escape*'s soft box office, and his lingering ill feelings about how Siegel had put the deal together, especially buying the rights before coming to see him at Warner, made *Escape from Alcatraz* their last collaboration.†

If Clint as Frank Morris had to escape from an inescapable prison, Clint as Clint found real life even harder. Despite reported pressure from Locke for him to finalize his divorce from Maggie, Clint continued to drag his feet, perhaps ambivalent about ending his marriage to Maggie. Approaching fifty, Clint had found a new health regimen, and he was now said to be an enthusiastic devotee of the Life Extension program by Durk Pearson and Sandy Shaw, who theorized that human beings were capable of living to 150 years of age while retaining their physical and mental powers. The program required exercise and a regimen of pills and vitamins that the couple promoted.

"During [1978] Clint began a new obsession, to consume vast amounts of vitamins and amino acids," according to Locke.

> At first Clint explained his new "megavitamin" kick was part of getting beefed up and buffed out to play his character . . . He would keep large bowls of boiled potatoes in the fridge and eat them like popcorn throughout the day . . . he kept all the [rest of the] concoctions in enor-

---

*Clint's take was reportedly 15 percent of the gross of the film, in addition to his regular acting and producing fees. By contrast, Tuggle and Siegel received net points, payouts based on a film's profits after all expenses are deducted from the cost of prints, advertising, distribution, etc., for a total of less than $2 million each, according to the *Hollywood Reporter.*

†Neither Clint nor Siegel ever discussed their working relationship in any terms except the most positive. In his autobiography Siegel suggests ever so gently that there may have been some friction between them: "Clint is very loyal to his friends; in my opinion, sometimes too loyal . . . We've never had a quarrel. Disagreements, yes. Differences of opinion, yes. Perhaps that's because he might look up to me as a surrogate father." Siegel, *A Siegel Film*, 495.

mous glass jars on the kitchen cabinet shelves, and after carefully blending all the powders for our latest batch, we would sit on the living room sofa scooping and stuffing the miracle powder into these enormous clear gelatin capsules. Sometimes the two ends of the capsules would bend or refuse to fit back together and Clint would go ballistic . . . some of the mixtures that he consumed in such abundance began to worry me, like selenium and hydergine, L-arginine, Tryptophan, DMSO for bruises, so much carotene that his hands turned orange . . . and gone were the days of red meat and any fat—even the avocados with the dollop of mayonnaise that we'd always had for lunch.

It was also reported in the *Herald-Examiner*, but denied by Clint, that he had had a face-lift.

In the summer of 1978, shortly after they had completed work on *Every Which Way but Loose*, Locke became pregnant. The situation left Clint ice-cold. He had never wanted children, he told her, and had had them after more than a decade of marriage only because Maggie had insisted. (The child with Roxanne Tunis was a subject that apparently did not come up.) Now, he told her, fatherhood was out of the question, and he urged her to have an abortion. Although she did not want to do it, after considering all that it meant to Clint, she agreed. For a while afterward everything between them seemed all right again. Then shortly after production was completed on *Escape from Alcatraz*, she became pregnant again.

Once again Clint insisted she have an abortion, and once again she reluctantly did so. When she came out of the hospital, as if to reward her or compensate her for her loss, he bought her the new home in tony Bel-Air she wanted. And apparently feeling generous (and also not wanting him to be anywhere near the Bel-Air house), he threw in one for her husband as well, in less upscale West Hollywood. At the same time he bought another house for himself in Carmel, by the ocean, where he could stay by himself when Locke was stuck in Hollywood on business. If any of this sounds familiar, it's because it is; in his early years with Maggie, Clint kept various fortresses of solitude, in Hollywood and in Carmel, allowing him the freedom to spend time not just with himself but with other women, if he so chose.

His next film, *Bronco Billy*, began with a script that came to him after a casual conversation during an informal dinner with friends at Dan Tana, a popular film industry red-gravy hangout on the edge of Beverly Hills. "When I was sent the script by Dennis Hackin," Clint later recalled, "at first I thought it was about Bronco Billy Anderson, the silent movie star. I devoured it at one sitting and I immediately thought it was the kind of film [Frank] Capra would do today if he were still making movies."

When he finished reading it, he gave it to Locke, who shared his enthusiasm. Five and a half weeks later production began on *Bronco Billy* near Boise, Idaho. Clint starred as the down-and-out star and owner of a Wild West show that is as faded as the times it seeks to glorify, and the spoiled society girl he falls in love with along the way is played by Sondra Locke.

In *Bronco Billy* the central character is in show business, playing two-dimensional re-creations of western heroes, surrounded by a band of loyal players. He falls for Antoinette Lily, another in a long string of imperfect, socially outcast women. It turns out she is married to a man she does not really love, who has now abandoned her and apparently swindled her out of her fortune. Billy helps her by letting her join the show as the target for his sharpshooting and knife-throwing stunts. Eventually she straightens out her money and marital problems and returns to her life in New York City, only to realize she was really in love with Billy all along. Leaving everything behind, she rushes to rejoin him and the show.

If the movie also sounds like a lot of other Hollywood films, it's because it does resemble several of the great ones, including Clint's role model for it, Capra's *It Happened One Night* (1934), which featured a wealthy but unhappy woman on the run from her husband who is aided (rescued and ultimately redeemed) by a poor but honest workingman (a newspaper reporter). It also echoes Preston Sturges's 1941 on-the-run romantic comedy *Sullivan's Travels*. Clint's by-now-familiar cynical view of modern urban city life appears, cloaked here in the familiar poor-but-happy, rich-but-miserable themes that especially appealed to the working-class audiences at whom this film, like *Every Which Way but Loose*, was aimed.

By now, Clint once more felt strong and self-assured enough to direct himself. He bolstered the sound track with a lot of country music produced once more by Snuff Garrett, highlighted by a duet he sang with Merle Haggard that rose to number one on the country charts. Figured into the film's profits, it helped increase its bottom line. *Bronco Billy*, released in the spring of 1980, gained Clint some of the best reviews of his career. The critics liked this Clint more than the public did, but no one liked him more than Clint, who had found a comfort zone parodying the very western characters that had first brought him to the attention of the public.

On May 31, 1980, a few weeks before *Bronco Billy* opened and flopped at the box office, Clint began to make wholesale changes at Malpaso. Many of the original members of the production team were let go. Frank Wells, Malpaso's best ally at Warner, took off, he said, to fulfill his dream of climbing the highest mountains on each continent. Robert Daley's "voluntary" departure may have been due at least in part to his growing objection to Locke's presence and apparent influence on Clint. Some felt she had taken him away from his moneymaking tough-guy characters, softening him up and pushing away his core audience.

To mark Clint's birthday and the onset of the new decade, New York's Museum of Modern Art (MOMA) scheduled a one-day tribute to him with a marathon screening of four of his films, *A Fistful of Dollars*, *Escape from Alcatraz*, *Play Misty for Me*, and *Bronco Billy*. The museum was most likely celebrating Clint the populist actor, "who has given his personal imprint to a host of movie genres," as the program put it, and who earlier that year had been named by Quigley Publications as the number one box-office star of the 1970s. But the Clint who showed up for the tony audience's Q and A was not the hotheaded action hero but the self-styled auteurist.*

And he showed up alone.

---

*Coming in number two was Burt Reynolds, followed by Barbra Streisand, Robert Redford, Paul Newman, and Steve McQueen. Clint was also named the top box-office star of 1972 and 1973 by the *Motion Picture Herald*, based on the annual poll of exhibitors as to the drawing power of movie stars at the box office, conducted by Quigley Publications.

FOURTEEN

In the westerns, you'd ride in four horses, you have a camera right there and four horses that all have to be side by side, which is very difficult to get them into a close shot. Right away they zing a boom mike out there and the horses don't like that. They get edgy, and then some guy yells at the top of his lungs through a megaphone, "Action," and it drives the horses crazy. I prefer not to say action. Actors are not horses but they have a similar anxiety about the word "Action." I try to keep that level low. I start just by saying something like, "okay." And at the end I simply say, "That's enough of that."

—Clint Eastwood

PREVIOUS PAGE: *In* Honkytonk Man, *1982*

Even as Clint was being honored by MOMA, *Bronco Billy*, despite its good reviews, was bombing at the box office. It wound up grossing a little over $18 million, even with the profits from the hit song it produced factored in. To some, it signaled a backlash of sorts against Clint's image-shifting. The critical intelligentsia thought it a violation of some elemental truth that Clint was spoofing his own assumed redneck persona, a sure sign to them that neither the film nor the image was true. No less a cultural arbiter than Norman Mailer sniffed sarcastically at Clint's notable lack of heated hipness: "Eastwood is living proof of the maxim that the best way to get through life is cool." Even more biting were James Wolcott's cutting remarks in *Vanity Fair* about New York's newest cultural darling: "*Bronco Billy* was an awkward, bow-legged bit of Americana, with Eastwood's girlfriend, Sondra Locke, giving her usual shrill, nostrilly performance."

Clint was already in production on a sequel to *Every Which Way but Loose*, called *Any Which Way You Can*, despite Warner's loud disappointment that he was not instead making the next Dirty Harry movie. Some at the studio held fast to the idea that *Every Which Way*'s success had been a fluke, due more to the presence of a cute orangutan than anything else; they thought that if Clint continued down that road, as he had with *Bronco Billy* and now with *Any Which Way You Can*, it could very well mark the irreversible decline of one of its biggest franchise stars.

Clint, on the other hand, was convinced that he was on the right career track. He sent out missives of his own rumbling that he was thinking of severing all of Malpaso's remaining ties with Warner. The first official comment from Warner came by way of outgoing Malpaso producer Bob Daley, who struck a melancholic note in his defense of Clint's career: "Clint Eastwood brought in *Bronco Billy* 13 days ahead and $750,000 under budget of the $5,000,000 film, and it's not because we over-skedded [budgeted] it . . . I've known [Clint] for 25 years, since he was digging pools and I was in the budget department at Universal. We talked efficiency all the time. When he got on 'Rawhide,' he never went to his dressing room—but stayed on the set and observed."

Clint then stepped directly into the fray, such as it was. "We've done okay," he told one reporter. "Everyone expected [*Bronco Billy*] to be another *Every Which Way But Loose*, but what is? We've gotten a little different audience. I've branched out a bit. It's not going to lose any money—it only cost $5,200,000 . . . and I've never had better reviews. I think it worked out well." These comments triggered a corporate showdown between Warner and Malpaso, scheduled to take place at Jackson Hole, Wyoming. There Frank Wells was called in from his mountain-climbing midlife crisis to orchestrate a peace powwow between Clint and the studio.

Clint, meanwhile, continued to consolidate his power at Malpaso by shedding several more longtime employees. On the strength of *Every Which Way but Loose*, Clint had asked Jeremy Joe Kronsberg to write another script along the same lines, to be called *Going Ape*, which he intended to direct. Kronsberg, meanwhile, having no idea he was slated to do a sequel, had signed a deal with Paramount to develop a similar type of film, with the promise that he could produce as well as write it. When Clint found out about it, he severed all ties with Kronsberg and brought in first-time screenwriter Stanford Sherman to write the *Every Which Way but Loose* sequel. Sherman's previous credits were mostly for the small screen—four episodes of *The Man from U.N.C.L.E.*, one episode of *The Rat Patrol*, and eighteen episodes of *Batman*. Nonetheless Clint gave him the plum assignment to write *Any Which Way You Can*.

To direct, Clint chose Buddy Van Horn, primarily a stuntman whom Clint had known since the *Rawhide* years at Universal, and although he had virtually no experience as a director, Clint liked and trusted him. Besides, Clint would be the unofficial director of the film. If it scored, he could take the credit. If it didn't, the critical hammers would fall on Van Horn. Sondra Locke's character, Lynn Halsey-Taylor, was brought back from the first film to continue her on-again-off-again relationship with Philo, as were Ruth Gordon and Geoffrey Lewis. For the now-obligatory musical number, Clint hired Ray Charles and once more assigned music production to Snuff Garrett.

But as Warner had predicted, *Any Which Way You Can* performed like a typical sequel, costing twice as much and grossing less than the original. Despite having the coveted first-up Christmas-release position, it barely broke the $10 million mark at the box office. The small profit it showed had more to do with the film's low budget than with box-office activity. If Clint had had any plans for an *Any Which Way* franchise, they evaporated after the poor box-office showing. Warner now hoped that Clint would realize his mistake, return to form, and make another Dirty Harry movie.

However, a year and a half passed without a new Clint Eastwood film, while he waited for the perfect script to revive his career. During that time he dealt with several real-life issues he had previously relegated to the back burner, claiming his schedule left him little time to concentrate on them. Now he had to deal head-on with his relationship with Locke, or more accurately its downslide, and to face up to Maggie's much-publicized new romance.

According to Locke, in her memoir, her relationship with Clint never fully recovered from the abortions. For all of Clint's explanations about not wanting more children, she saw it as a clear signal that he had no intention of staying with her forever. Moreover, in 1980 he even told Locke about his daughter with Roxanne Tunis.

Not long afterward Locke was offered and accepted the lead role in a TV film, Jackie Cooper's *Rosie: The Rosemary Clooney Story*, a project that had nothing to do with Clint. Shortly into the filming of *Rosie*, *Us* magazine whispered to its readers that "reports are circulating that Clint Eastwood and Sondra Locke are no longer such good friends. Clint plans to make his next movie, *Honkytonk Man*, without her—and Sondra has already expressed a desire to establish her own solo career. So their [recent] Christmas release, *Any Which Way You Can*, seemingly ends a long and financially successful collaboration."

The whispers, which were by no means confined to one magazine, contained a kernel of truth. Clint, never a big sharer of anything— money, credits, stardom—was, according to Locke, thrown by her acceptance of the role in a movie he did not control, even if it was only for TV. In some ways, that made it worse, for it separated them even more, bringing her down to the level of the little screen, from which Clint had worked so hard to escape.

On top of all that, Maggie was now publicly flaunting her new "companion," the millionaire playboy Henry Wynberg, who at the age of forty-six had gained the dubious reputation as the man who had become involved with Elizabeth Taylor between her two marriages to Richard Burton. After Taylor and before Maggie, Wynberg had been briefly involved with Olivia Hussey, the estranged actress wife of Dino Martin, Dean Martin's son.

Despite the fact that Wynberg spent most of his time in Beverly Hills and Maggie lived in Carmel, they saw each other several times a month. According to Wynberg at the time, "We meet as often as we can . . . Maggie and I spend our time together skiing, swimming, playing tennis . . . and sometimes we just take long walks and do some talking. We also love to cook and have friends over for a dinner party. That's one reason she likes me. I'm a great cook. I don't know what the future holds. As for now, we have no plans to marry . . . Maggie never speaks of Clint."

Apparently Clint's answer to Wynberg's public boasting was to get away. He took off with Locke for Helsinki and Copenhagen, to scout future locations, according to reports in both *Daily Variety* and the *Hollywood Reporter.* After their brief stay in Europe, Clint took Locke to London to see Frank Sinatra perform in concert.

Upon their return to America, Locke began filming her TV film, and Clint continued to search for a script worthy of being the next in the Dirty Harry franchise. In his spare time, which was increasingly plentiful, he began visiting the new Hollywood-friendly Washington, D.C., of President Ronald Reagan. Clint was warmly accepted into the cinematic circle that Reagan surrounded himself with at the White House. Because of it, Clint had access to several of the international mercenaries who were conducting "secret" government missions in the name of democracy, many of which were sanctioned by the president.

Fritz Manes, one of the few long-term survivors of Clint's major clean-out of Malpaso's staff, is credited with arranging for Bob Denard, a French self-described soldier of fortune who had seen action in Africa during the 1970s, to be introduced to Clint. After that meeting Clint, impressed with Denard's tales of intrigue, had Malpaso option his life story for a biopic.

At the same time, along with several other Hollywood conservatives, Clint privately funded a mercenary expedition into Laos to search for missing and possibly captive American soldiers taken during the Vietnam War. That project ended in failure, and at least one mercenary was killed during it. Clint said little to the press about either the excursion or his own financial participation in it, but after it became public and was subjected to much negative publicity, he quietly dropped the Denard project. Instead he turned to an adaptation of Craig Thomas's 1977 bestselling novel, *Firefox*. That film would mark the fifty-two-year-old movie star's return to the big screen.

In some ways *Firefox* fits neatly into the Eastwood canon and was in some ways a fictionalized version of the film he had wanted to make about Denard. It is an action flick whose lead character, pilot Mitchell Gant, is also an international spy. Gant has a potentially fatal flaw that sends him squarely into the dark side—he suffers from mental disabilities that leave him unable to function well—but finds himself on a mission to save the world from the cold war Russians. He is assigned to steal their newest and potentially most dangerous plane, the Firefox, and deliver it to the NATO alliance.

Despite the film's timely subject matter, its James Bond gadgetry deprived it of any sense of realism. Perhaps to further distance himself from current headlines, Clint—who directed and produced as well as starred in the film—saw to it that Malpaso had no producing credit.

Shot on location in Austria, England, Greenland, and the United States, it had a hefty budget of $21 million (another reason he may not have wanted to make Malpaso a partner) and took nearly a year to complete. When it was finally released, the reviews were at best mixed. Sheila Benson, writing in the *Los Angeles Times*, called it "a sagging, overlong disappointment, talky and slow to ignite. It is the first time that Eastwood the director has served Eastwood the actor-icon so badly, and it is unnerving."

"*Firefox* is fun," Andrew Sarris wrote in the *Village Voice*, "little more and not appreciably less." For Sarris and other auteurists, where *Play Misty for Me* failed as faux Hitchcock, *Firefox* succeeded as neo-Bond.

And the film resonated with audiences longing to see Clint return to his steely-eyed-if-flawed-action-hero stance. It became one of his highest grossers and returned him to the top of the Hollywood heap.*

With his career back on the main track, Clint allowed Locke to talk him into moving into the new Bel-Air house that she had decorated—despite (as Locke later described it) Clint's domestic temperament of wild outbursts. Brief but extreme fits of anger punctured his otherwise cool facade, usually precipitated by the lighting of some short emotional fuse. Locke also described Clint's growing narcissism: "Rarely did Clint acknowledge any flaws of his own. I was really surprised when, sometime in the mid-eighties, he had hair transplants. He actually finally admitted that he was losing his hair, but like everything else he was unbelievably secretive about it . . . actually the whole situation was so ridiculous that it was all I could do to keep from laughing. I interpreted these quirks of Clint as either humorous eccentricity or simple human failing."

Maggie's ongoing relationship with Wynberg didn't help Clint's intense and lightning-quick mood swings. She was now talking about finalizing her divorce from Clint and marrying Wynberg, which would mean for Clint a payout in the neighborhood of $25 million and an asset split that he had tried to avoid for several years. As if in response, Clint, according to Locke, rather than moving closer to her, pulled away and talked less and less of their future together.

Perhaps even more telling, she had not appeared in *Firefox*, which might have been understandable in the light of its typically Clintonian lack of any substantial female role. But when he publicly announced his next movie, a somewhat inexplicable return to Redneckville and country music, *Honkytonk Man*, the female lead, into which Locke would have fit like fingers into gloves, went to a young and beautiful unknown, Alexa Kenin.

Honkytonk Man, based on a 1980 Clancy Carlile novel of the same name, is a fictional biography of a failed country singer, Red Stovall, whose only apparent goal is to make it to the Grand Ole Opry before

Firefox did nearly $25 million in rentals and was a major popular success, but its profit was not great, due to the huge budget necessitated by the film's special aerial effects. While Clint was the producer-director, he was not the executive producer. That slot was filled, ironically, by Fritz Manes.

he dies. Loosely based on the lives of Hank Williams and Jimmie Rodgers, the book ends with Stovall's death before he achieves his dream.

Carlile, as it happened, was a William Morris client, and the agency, as always, wanted to keep the project in-house. That was how the book came to Clint, who was looking for a project to introduce his son, Kyle, now fourteen, to feature films. Clint offered to buy it, star in it, direct it, and produce it through Malpaso, believing it had a good part for Kyle that would bring them together both professionally and personally.

Carlile, however, was reluctant to sell Clint the rights, thinking that at fifty-two he was too old to play the role of a country singer who dies at thirty-one. And while Clint had done some singing, his voice in no way matched the soaring beauty of either Williams or Rodgers, the models Carlile had used for Stovall.

Clint invited Carlile to his home and promised him that, if he sold Clint the rights to the book, he could write the screenplay adaptation of his novel without any interference. That was enough to get Carlile to agree to the deal.

Once Carlile finished the screenplay, Clint went to work adapting the story to his liking. He never wanted to die in his movies, so he had Carlile change the ending so that Stovall is inducted into the Country Music Hall of Fame for his hit song, "Honkytonk Man," as he lies dying, thereby letting the character "live on." Clint also enlisted the services of his favorite music producer, Snuff Garrett, and charged him with juicing up Carlile's screenplay with "classic" country hits, including songs by John Anderson, Porter Wagoner, and Ray Price, all of which would appear on the original sound-track album.

If Carlile objected to any of these changes, he had no real opportunity to express them. Once production began, he made repeated requests to become more involved, but Clint paid little attention. To be fair, this often happens to writers, because producers, stars, and directors—of which Clint was all three on this film—do not want them watching the script to make sure every word they've written gets onto the screen. In this case, however, the situation was more delicate, as Clint and Carlile were both William Morris clients, which made it impossible for the agency to take sides. Carlile was left out, and there was nothing he could do about it. In struggles like these, the writer always loses.

As Carlile had feared, the obviously middle-aged Clint was not remotely believable in the part (although he did bear some resemblance to Hank Williams, whose dissipated look shortly before his death made him seem far older than he was). The film opened poorly, quickly disappeared, and is rarely seen to this day.

Locke's final big-screen appearance with Clint was in his next film, a one-more-time, perhaps desperate resuscitation of Harry Callahan in *Sudden Impact*. After seven years away from the Dirty Harry franchise, this would be his fourth visitation to his most successful screen persona. And to everyone's surprise, including no doubt Clint's, it turned out to be by far the best. "It was like an homage to Don Siegel. I was the only one who hadn't directed one so I thought, well, why not?"

The project began, oddly enough, with a script sent to Locke. It was by Earl Smith, with whom she had worked on a small independent film in the early, pre-Oscar-nomination days of her career. She agreed to help develop it. But by now she knew the dangers of doing anything without Clint's approval, so she talked with him about the possibility of her being involved as a producer. "Naturally, I talked about it with Clint, hoping that he would have no objections. But before I knew it, Clint had bought the treatment outright from Earl, had hired a writer of his own choice, and begun to turn my story into a Dirty Harry film, without even so much as a courteous 'Do you mind, Sondra?' "

To make it easier for her to give up control of the film, Clint promised Locke the female lead and $350,000 (at the behest of Fritz Manes, who knew that the project had originated with her and that she fairly deserved that kind of money). Having settled that part of the deal, Clint brought in screenwriter Joseph Stinson to convert the script into *Sudden Impact*. (As always, Clint preferred young and inexperienced personnel to veterans, who not only came with a hefty price tag but were better able to challenge Clint's authority.)

In the spring of 1983, with Manes in place as the film's executive producer, Bruce Surtees behind the camera, and Clint ready to perform a triple-play as producer, director, and star, production began on *Sudden Impact*. The film would, with Dean Riesner's help, give Clint his career's signature line of dialogue: "Go ahead, make my day!" It was so succinct and powerful that later Ronald Reagan would borrow it to take on Congress.* "When you point a gun at someone's head and say 'Go ahead, make my day,' well, I knew the audiences were going to go for it in a big way." "It was just a whimsical thing," Clint later recalled. "I hadn't directed one, and I thought, why not do one before I hang that series up. It was based on an idea that wasn't intended to be a Dirty Harry picture, just a little synopsis. I put together a screenplay on it and said, okay, I'll do it."

In the story Callahan has been suspended from the police force for abusively threatening a Mafia don, who then dies of a heart attack. Clint, ever careful not to make Harry an out-and-out loser, treats his suspension as one more abuse—of Callahan—by an overly authoritarian police force that just doesn't get his righteous sense of mission and mercy (or lack of it) that passes for personal justice in 1980s San Francisco.

Sent off to a small town to serve out his suspension, Callahan is a warrior without a war, unappreciated and tossed aside. But he investigates a homicide there and discovers that a serial killer is at work. As usual, detecting the presence of evil provides him with energy and heroism: it turns out that the local police chief, Jannings (played by the always-effective Pat Hingle, who played a similar type in *The Gauntlet*), is aware of the killer's presence. And Jannings suspects the pretty young artist Jennifer Spencer (Locke) is committing the murders as an act of vengeance—she was gang-raped by a group of young toughs led by Jannings's own son, Mick (Paul Drake). Harry becomes romantically involved with Spencer and eventually rescues her from one final kidnapping by Mick, who also manages to kill his own father. Then Callahan spectacularly disposes of him and the rest of his gang. He not only rescues Spencer but redeems her by shifting the blame for all her serial murders onto Mick.

The tailoring of the story once again mirrors Clint and Callahan (whose very name is a partial anagram—both share the letters C, L, and N). In the film, Callahan lets Spencer go free—a technicality in his world, justified by his larger (rougher, and to audiences more satisfying) sense of law and order.

---

*Reagan's March 13, 1985, response to Congress's threat to raise taxes was to threaten them with a veto, using "Go ahead, and make my day" to underscore his resolve. The American public loved it.

Sudden Impact opened in December 1983 and proved to be the colossal comeback hit that Clint had been searching for, grossing a whopping $70 million in its initial domestic release. It also earned him great reviews, including another nod of approval from Sarris: "The staging of the violent set pieces is stylized, kinetic and visually inventive," he wrote in the *Village Voice*. "Eastwood, occasional *langueurs* and all, has less to worry about in this respect than other filmmakers. When he stands poised for his civically cleansing shoot-outs, no one in the theater is likely to be dozing. I like Eastwood, always have. But then I even have a soft spot in my heart for law and order."

David Denby wrote in *New York* magazine:

> Directing the material himself, Clint Eastwood has attempted to retell the Dirty Harry myth in the style of a forties film noir. Much of *Sudden Impact*, including all the scenes of violence, was actually shot at night. In a stiff, sensational, pulp-filmmaking way, the mayhem is impressive: As the camera glides through the dark, sinister thugs emerge from the shadows, or Sondra Locke, blond hair curtaining her face in the style of Veronica Lake, moves into the frame, and violence flashes out, lightning in the air.

Locke's reviews too were excellent, and her on-screen pairing with Clint was nothing less than electrifying. As a doppelgänger for him, she shared his murderous dark(er) side, this time cut with a feminine edge; more than one critic referred to her in this film as "Dirty Harriet."

Warner quickly offered them fortunes to do yet another Dirty Harry film. But as winning as they were on-screen Locke knew it was never going to happen. Clint's heated passion for her was gone, and there was nothing she could do about it except stand and watch it— and him—fade away.*

---

*Locke and Clint worked together one more time, on TV, in an episode of NBC's *Amazing Stories*, "Vanessa in the Garden," that Clint directed; it first aired on December 29, 1985. It was written by Steven Spielberg, who was also the series' executive producer. Interestingly, Clint also cast Jamie Rose, a woman he was said to be secretly involved with at the time, in the show. The episode costarred Harvey Keitel. According to the *Los Angeles Times*, the episode attracted the smallest audience for the (failing) NBC series. "Vanessa in the Garden" was the eighteenth of twenty-nine episodes that were made before the show left the air.

FIFTEEN

Not until Tightrope *do the Eastwood films deal with the fact that the voyeurism in* Dirty Harry *matters most as a warm-up for* Tightrope.

—Dennis Bingham

Sudden Impact had been critically lauded and a box-office smash. Having finally climbed back up the commercial mountain, Clint next decided to take a giant leap off it by making a buddy-buddy movie costarring Burt Reynolds, whose career was not what it had once been. Some saw this as charity-casting by Clint.

He also appeared to have permanently warehoused Sondra Locke, as he had already begun an affair with a beautiful young Warner Bros. story editor and analyst by the name of Megan Rose, whom he had met during the making of *Honkytonk Man*. This relationship would last nearly five years, until 1988. During that time, Clint paid regular visits to her nearby Warner Bros. office. According to Rose, they made love in her office at lunchtime, in the bedroom he kept behind his office, at her apartment.

Due to scheduling complications having to do with everyone being available at the same time, the Burt Reynolds project was delayed. Instead Clint rushed into production a new film, *Tightrope*, shot on location in New Orleans. Locke was neither in the film nor accompanied him; the part that might once have gone to her went instead to Geneviève Bujold, a forty-something Canadian-born actress who had struck gold in her portrayal of Anne Boleyn opposite Richard Burton in Charles Jarrott's *Anne of the Thousand Days* (1969). Afterward, her off-center looks, strong accent, and lack of bombshell vavoom kept her career on lateral hold. She was actually recommended for the part by the always-willing-to-help Sondra Locke.

Clint loved the idea of putting Bujold in the film, because to him everything in and about the film was off-kilter, and so should be the woman he cast as his costar. Her character was the head of a women's rape center who is tough, tender, and decidedly unglamorous, but sexy nonetheless.

Tightrope was an original Richard Tuggle script that, like his *Escape from Alcatraz,* was loosely based on a true story—in this case, a series of Bay Area serial sex-and-slash murders that had been covered in a local newspaper. Tuggle had written the film with Don Siegel in mind as the director and Clint as the star, but Siegel begged off, still not willing to work again with Clint. Tuggle then thought about directing it himself. According to sources at Malpaso, that deal was done in a single thirty-second phone conversation to Clint, who had read the script and wanted to be in it. Some believe he was so eager to star in it that it was the real reason he pushed the Reynolds picture back to make room on his schedule.

The story transferred well to New Orleans, whose night-side atmospherics perfectly expressed the noirish mood of the story—darkness and fog everywhere. His character, a law officer, was both attracted to and repelled by not just the victims (mostly New Orleans–style prostitutes and hookers, echoing the notorious Jack the Ripper) but also the murderer—perhaps the embodiment of his own darker side. This time the struggle would be between a law officer and his inner self, between desire and fear of giving in to the darker, rougher, sexual side that lurked within (a sense of self utterly missing from the character of Harry Callahan).

It was that internal moral tug-of-war (the "tightrope" of the title) that Clint's character, Wes Block, had to deal with, minus the Callahan .44 Magnum, plus two motherless girls who themselves become potential victims of the killer. In the midst of it all, Block is attracted to his fellow social servant Beryl Thibodeaux (Bujold), the head of a rape crisis center who neatly embodies the liberation of Block's more disturbed desires and is a stabilizing force as well. She represents the social ties that bind, a restriction Block both envies and fears.

Block fears he will not be able to keep his secrets buried for long, especially from Thibodeaux; he is attracted to submissive women who give in to his kinky desires and weaknesses. He likes oral sex using handcuffs, the tools of his professional trade—then makes love to them. And a scene that takes place inside an especially seedy gay bar suggests that the aptly named Block might have some not-so-latent homosexual tendencies. The gruesome sex-and-slash murders that escalate throughout the film become a vicarious thrill machine for him, even as they set off an increasingly wild pursuit that becomes, literally, one dark soul chasing an even darker soul. The movie also marked the screen debut of Clint's second child by Maggie. Twelve-year-old Alison Eastwood played the role of one of his two small daughters in the film.

This time even the harshest critics of the Eastwood oeuvre, except Kael, went out of their way to recognize the quality of the film and of Clint's acting. Even if they didn't particularly like its content, they had to admire the masterful stylistics of its contextual unspooling and the increasingly desperate yet tightly controlled unraveling of Clint's Block. Kathleen Cornell wrote in the *New York Daily News,* "Eastwood is simply terrific, his lean and hungry face revealing all the right emotions . . . thanks to the efforts of writer-director Richard Tuggle, it's a raunchy but surprisingly intelligent movie, which at times scares the viewer as much as one of Hitchcock's tension-filled thrillers." J. Hoberman of the *Village Voice* called it "one of Eastwood's finest, most reflexive and reflective films since *Bronco Billy*—and for my money the best Hollywood movie so far this year." But Kael remained unrepentant: "*Tightrope* is the opposite of sophisticated movie-making . . . Clint seems to be trying to blast through his own lack of courage as an actor." In a rare display of public emotion, in the May 1985 issue of *Video* magazine, Clint finally responded by dismissing Kael as a mere parasite, clinging to his career in order to make herself more important: "[Kael] found an avenue that was going to make her a star. I was just one of the subjects, among many, that helped her along the way." In truth, there was no shortage of actors, actresses, and directors who felt the same way.

Tightrope opened the 1984 Montreal Film Festival and grossed an impressive $60 million in its initial domestic release, a number that ballooned to over $100 million after its first foreign release and before TV and eventual video rights. That year, due mainly to the success of *Tightrope*, Clint was named the world's top box-office star by Quigley (for the second year in a row). It was his sixteenth appearance on the top-ten list, more times than any other living star.

On August 22, 1984, Clint was invited to place his hands and feet into cement at the fabled Grauman's (Mann's) Chinese Theatre in Hollywood, alongside the greatest film legends of all time. After casually conversing with the relatively small daytime crowd that had gathered—these events were never well publicized, to keep the crowds intentionally small and manageable—and with Kyle and Alison proudly looking on, Clint scrawled alongside his handprints, *"You've made my day."*

While *Tightrope* was still in theaters, Clint finally went into production on *City Heat* with Burt Reynolds. The difference in the two stars' individual salaries reflected the level of their current popularity: Clint was paid $5 million, while Burt received $4 million. Both stars appeared happy to be working together, even if their much-publicized redneck and roadster buddy-buddy camaraderie was a product of PR more than reality. In truth, they didn't hang out all that much together. In Reynolds's memoir, Clint is little more than a passing acquaintance.

Early on tensions rose between Clint, Reynolds, and the director, Blake Edwards, who had also written the script. The central issue was on casting, but the real problems ran much deeper. To begin with, Edwards had originally given the script to Locke, rather than Clint, in one of the typical sleights-of-hand that take place in Hollywood every day of the week. Edwards had asked her if she would read his script, suggesting that she would be perfect in the role of Caroline, Murphy's (Reynolds's) girlfriend. He said he had seen her performance in *Bronco Billy*, loved it, and wanted her to costar in his new film. To seal the deal, he suggested that her appearance would once and for all take her out of the giant shadow cast over her career by Clint's.

Not surprisingly, Locke jumped at the chance. That was when Edwards pulled the switch and asked Locke if she would mind passing the script along to Clint. "Before I knew it," Locke said later, "Blake and his wife, Julie Andrews, were having dinner with Clint and me. Then Burt Reynolds was suddenly brought in, and within a few weeks I was simply out of the mix and forgotten."

Edwards had, apparently, used Locke as a way to get to Clint, to secure a deal with Malpaso, which in turn would secure the funding, and along with it a firm commitment from the two stars to appear in the movie that Edwards would direct.

Even before the film went into production, the triangle of Edwards, Eastwood, and Reynolds ran into a Cinemascope-size brick wall. Both Clint and Reynolds had script approval, and each was interested in making sure he came out looking and sounding better than the other. Reynolds's changes stretched into months of delays that drove Clint crazy, but allowed him to spend ample chunks of time on the nearest golf course. Reynolds continued to suggest changes. The two men fought indirectly over every nuance in the script, using Edwards as their reluctant intermediary.

Edwards had directed Reynolds in a movie the year before, *The Man Who Loved Women*, and so had experienced the difficulties and learned how to deal with his short fuse. But he didn't know how to handle Clint and may have assumed he had to wear the same kid gloves.

The problem was that Clint, always impatient with weakness, interpreted Edwards's running everything by him as just that. Once Clint green-lighted a production, he liked to go out and make it. The more Edwards equivocated, the less Clint believed he could get the job done. Then just before shooting was finally about to begin, Edwards, having had all he could take of Reynolds's ego and Clint's impatience, quit the film. "Creative differences" was the official reason given for his departure, but unofficially insiders talked of one final blowup with Clint that resulted in Edwards either being asked to leave the film or simply walking out on it.

According to Reynolds, in his memoir, Clint actually orchestrated the removal of Blake by goading him into quitting, in favor of Richard Benjamin, a less intense, more likable, and less expensive director. The original title, *Kansas City Heat*, was now changed at Clint's directive to the simpler and more marquee-friendly *City Heat*. The ever-reliable Fritz Manes replaced Edwards as the line producer, and Edwards's screenplay was credited to Sam O. Brown, a Screen Writers Guild–approved pseudonym.*

Naturally, Reynolds saw all this as nothing less than a takeover of the project by Clint, which upset the delicate balance of power between the two superstars. In addition, during the long preproduction, actors and actresses with other commitments waiting for them came and went like bowling pins on a Saturday night. The final

---

*Other factors may have contributed to the departure. At one point Edwards wanted to cast his wife in the film, but Clint vehemently objected, noting that he hadn't put Locke in the film. Edwards had also made some requests that Clint, as executive producer, did not appreciate, like a car and driver to get him from Beverly Hills to Burbank; according to one source, that sent Clint through the ceiling. "Let him walk," Clint was supposed to have said, "or get a horse."

supporting-roles cast was set only days before filming began: Madeline Kahn, Jane Alexander, Rip Torn, Irene Cara, Richard Roundtree, and Tony Lo Bianco.

The plot was as leaden as it was pedestrian—a Depression-era detective, Mike Murphy (Reynolds), discovers that his partner, Dehl Swift (Roundtree), wants to buy some ledgers from the bookkeeper of a gangster "godfather," to sell to his rival gang leader. That leads to Swift's swift demise. Soon enough Murphy gets the ledgers, and with them a death sentence from the godfather (Lo Bianco). He kidnaps Murphy's girlfriend (Kahn) and enlists the help of his former police force partner, Lieutenant Speer, played by a dark-fedoraed Clint, who managed to keep his eyes shaded for almost the entire film, as if he didn't want anyone to recognize him in it. The film ends with an explosion that explains nothing and only provides a way to halt, if not end, these confused, unfunny, and uninvolving events.

The on-screen chemistry between Reynolds and Clint was, not surprisingly, zero-minus-a-hundred, which may help to explain the nearly career-ending accident that occurred while they were filming a bar scene in which Speer punches Murphy in the face. During the fight a stuntman mistakenly used a real chair instead of a fake, "breakaway" chair to hit Reynolds. It badly broke Reynolds's jaw and developed into temporomandibular joint disorder (TMJ), which affects both balance and sensory perceptions. Reynolds's physical health deteriorated after that, and rumors ran rampant in the press that he had developed AIDS, a supposition supercharged by his dramatic loss of weight. (He was unable to eat solid food through his damaged jaw.)

It was, for all intents and purposes, the end of Reynolds's run as a major Hollywood movie star. Eventually he would recover and work, most notably in Paul Thomas Anderson's *Boogie Nights* (1997), for which he received an Oscar nomination for Best Supporting Actor, and in a couple of TV series, but he never again placed on a national film-star ranking. A lot of people believed that Clint had delivered the punch that did Reynolds in, that he had punched him out of commission for good.*

---

*It remains unclear who threw the actual punch, if it was Clint or a stuntman, or even what caused the accident, the punch, or the fall. As for Edwards, his next theatrical feature that he both wrote and directed, the satirical *A Fine Mess* (1986), included a brief but scathing send-up of Clint as the Man with No Name.

Meanwhile Locke, left out of both *Tightrope* and *City Heat*, went by herself to the William Morris office in search of a project she might be able to direct. (Clint would later claim that he had suggested she move into directing, but according to Locke, she came up with the idea first and Clint encouraged her.) At the agency she came across a script that had been lying around in development hell for years, something called *Ratboy*, by Rob Thompson, which was about just what the title suggests, a boy who is half-rat, half-human. Nikki, a small-time promoter, comes across Ratboy and decides to promote him into a big star. Along the way she falls in love with Ratboy and is then redeemed for her exploitative desires. The script was *Beauty and the Beast* crossed with *King Kong*.

Locke quickly made a deal to take over the rights and then brought the script to Terry Semel, at Warner. Semel gave it a green light, as long as she would agree to two conditions. First, Locke had to appear in the picture as well as direct it. She had no problem with that—she would play Nikki.

The second, that Clint would produce.

This condition made nobody happy. Clint did not want to work with Locke anymore, and Locke felt that as soon as Clint's name was attached to *Ratboy*, her project would turn into "A Clint Eastwood Picture" and defeat her attempt to emerge from his giant shadow. Clint's solution was simple; he would put his name on the picture but actually assign the line-producing chores to Fritz Manes. But Malpaso would not be involved: Clint, wanting to put physical and professional distance between himself and Locke, decided to create a new production company within Malpaso for this one picture.

Then, likely putting the final nail in the coffin of her relationship with Clint, Locke cast her husband, Gordon, to play Nikki's brother.

Predictably, Clint was vehemently opposed. An angry back-and-forth ensued: Clint accused Locke of nepotism. Locke reminded Clint that he had used his son and his daughter in two of his films. Clint insisted that he hadn't used either in his *first* film. Locke countered that her film wasn't really intended for the mainstream so it didn't matter. Clint said he didn't want Gordon in the film and halted all further development of the script until Locke agreed.

Having come to an impasse, Locke dropped her next bombshell: she had cast Sharon Baird (S. L. Baird in the credits), one of the original

Mouseketeers, in the title role. Clint couldn't believe it. He quietly reminded her that the film was called rat*boy*, not rat*girl.*

On it went, with Clint trying to maintain absolute control of every aspect of the film. By the time it was finished, Locke felt that her creative input had been totally buried. Being invited to the Deauville Film Festival in France, where the film received good notices, did nothing to soothe her.*

For its commercial release in 1986, Warner Bros. chose to open *Ratboy* in only one theater in Los Angeles and one in New York City and the top development executives at Warner—who included Semel, Lucy Fisher, and Mark Canton—agreed to a first-look, first-refusal deal for anything else Locke brought them.

From the beginning of the project, in 1984, Clint had not been easy for Locke to work with, but the deterioration of their relationship may not have been the only reason. Just as Clint had gotten involved with the film, Maggie officially filed for divorce and publicly announced her intention to marry Wynberg. Estimates ran the value of the original 1979 settlement agreement up to around $28 million in cash, plus property and child support.†

By the time Clint was ready to make his next movie, he had become involved with a new woman, Jacelyn Reeves, who was to become the mother of his next child. The film was called *Pale Rider.* The state of affairs was chaos.

So naturally Clint decided to run for mayor of Carmel.

---

*The brother was played by Louie Anderson; Gordon became the voice of Ratboy. Gerrit Graham played Nikki's other brother. Despite Clint's strong objections, Baird appeared in the title role.

†After a long and at times contentious battle, they finally divorced in May 1984. The monetary award was, reportedly, calculated on the basis of a million dollars for every year they were married, plus previously agreed-upon property divisions. Child custody was joint, with Maggie awarded physical custody. In an article in *People* magazine published shortly after the divorce was finalized, Maggie blamed Locke for her final breakup with Clint. But the divorce was reported as "friendly," and she and Clint continued as partners in various business interests they shared. Maggie married Wynberg in 1984. They were divorced in 1989.

SIXTEEN

I've always considered myself too individualistic to be either right wing or left wing.

—Clint Eastwood

The mayoral adventure began because of ice cream cones, or more accurately, their unavailability on summer afternoons, because the city fathers of Carmel-by-the-Sea (the town's legal name) had passed an ordinance prohibiting the storefront sale of ice cream cones because they felt that eating them in the street was "undignified." To Carmel's most celebrated citizen, who happened to like eating ice cream cones in the summertime, this was one civil outrage too many, and no matter what, he was not going to let it stand.

He had had his troubles with the town council before. In June 1983 he had applied for permission to build a two-story freestanding addition to the Hog's Breath—and been denied. The council cited problems with the design and the materials. Moreover, it said, San Carlos Street, where the Hog's Breath was located, already had too many glass and concrete structures and not enough wood. In the early spring of 1984, shortly after the completion of *City Heat* and a series of back-and-forth maneuvers, Clint made a final, personal appeal to the council, which promptly rejected it. Angry and frustrated, he threatened to file suit against the city council of Carmel, claiming the regulations the council used as the basis for its decision were "vague and subjective."

Not long after the start of the ice cream battle, with his Hog's Breath Inn situation also still unresolved, Clint was sitting around the inn with some friends when someone suggested he ought to run for mayor. Once he got elected, they said, he could change the rules. It may have been a joke, but no one was laughing, least of all Clint.

But he had more pressing, if not bigger, things (to him) to deal with at the moment. That spring he was being honored at the prestigious Paris-based Cinémathèque Française, which was to culminate in a special European preview screening of *Tightrope*. This invitation was especially important because he was going to be decorated as a

Knight in the French Order of Arts and Letters, an honor that he had won only with much outside support.*

His film career meant a lot to him. Even if some critics still didn't take his movies seriously, or the subjects were socially distasteful, he was very proud of them. As he told one interviewer during this period, "Maybe there were certain prejudices in the times of *Dirty Harry* in 1971 that don't exist now, or are changing now, or times are changing. Maybe I'm older, more mature, maybe the audiences are changing and I'm changing. It's just circumstances . . . I've never begged for respectability."

Respectability was the heart of the matter, and it no longer seemed out of reach. Most of the critics, who had been far behind audiences in recognizing Clint's movies as terrific entertainments, were beginning to "get" that he was more than just a genre moviemaker, and that his films were about something, even if it wasn't the usual boy-meets-girl love story.

As one critic wrote during this period in the *New York Times*, where its mere inclusion was a benediction: "The Eastwood persona caught a blue-collar discontent with a country portrayed as being run by bleeding hearts." In other words, Harry Callahan the immoral fascist had now turned into Harry Callahan the law-and-order hero.

Even the *über*-liberal Norman Mailer had changed his opinion. "Clint Eastwood is an artist," he said, and "he has a presidential face." In fact, he said, "maybe there is no one more American than Clint."

After his triumphal visit to Paris, Clint returned home and went directly into pre-general-release work on *Pale Rider*, his first western since *The Outlaw Josey Wales*, nine years earlier. Meanwhile a new script came his way via Megan Rose, *The William Munny Killings*; she had read it and thought it perfect for Clint. Francis Ford Coppola had

---

*The award was made by Pierre Viot, the former boss of the National Cinema Center and newly appointed president of the Cannes Film Festival, instead of Culture Minister Jack Lang, who excused himself due to a prior commitment. It was widely believed in France that Lang, who was a Socialist, did not want to honor an American star whose films frequently promoted a right-wing-leaning law-and-order view of society. In support of Clint were Terry Semel, Richard Fox (newly appointed head of WB International), and Steve Ross of Warner Bros. Their show of support for their star further affirmed that their past troubles were, at least for the time being, set aside.

an option on it; when Rose showed it to Lucy Fisher, a head of production and development at Warner, she agreed that it was a good choice for Clint. But he would never consent to being directed by Coppola, Fisher said. Their styles—Coppola's painstakingly slow brand of perfectionism, Clint's fast, instinctive method—were incompatible. Eventually Coppola let his option lapse, and as a 1984 Christmas gift to Clint, Rose put a copy of the script into his Christmas stocking. He liked it, bought it, and then put it away until he felt the time was right to make it. That time would come in 1992, when it was retitled *Unforgiven*.

This time out, with his confidence bubbling like chilled champagne, he assured himself he would have no more problems with temperamental or inexperienced directors (or girlfriends with excessive proprietary claims). As his affair with Rose was ending, Clint made sure to keep sufficient distance from her. With *Pale Rider* he was going to produce, star in, and direct the whole picture; Manes would have the nominal role of Malpaso's executive producer.

To some, Clint's choice to return to westerns (especially one tinged with a mysterious and elegant unearthliness) seemed odd, as the genre had been pronounced dead in the mud since *Heaven's Gate*. Moreover, *Pale Rider* was in many ways yet another version of the true events that that film, and *Shane*, had been based on, the Johnson County War. Following his success with *Tightrope* (and forgetting his failure with *City Heat*), *Pale Rider* seemed, at best, an offbeat choice.

Clint shifted the locale to Gold Rush California, where would-be instant millionaires are being terrorized by a ship-mining corporation led by Coy LaHood (Richard Dysart). His conglomerate needs the land in order to survive. (In previous versions, including *Shane* and *Heaven's Gate*, the battle pitted land-settlers against cattle-breeders.)

On the miners' side is Hull Barret (Michael Moriarty), a homesteader, who has a new girlfriend (Carrie Snodgress) and a daughter from his first marriage, Megan (Sydney Penny). Out of the mist comes a man known only as the Preacher (Eastwood), who succeeds in uniting the miners in a successful showdown with LaHood and his men, including on LaHood's side an evil marshal (John Russell), all of whom the Preacher battled sometime in the past. In a series of strange and violent confrontations, the Preacher helps the homesteaders achieve peace. Despite Megan's adoration of him, he rides off by himself into the sunset, a ghostly eminence who uses the violent ways of the lawless Old West.

Like Shane, the Preacher seems to come out of the past to confront the evil cattlemen before he heads out, presumably to Boot Hill, the inevitable destiny of all gunfighters, even the Old West itself. In *Pale Rider* (as in *High Plains Drifter*), the Preacher is less a former gunfighter than the ghost of a former gunfighter—perhaps, in the film's pseudo-religious overlay, a descendant of one of the Four Horsemen of the Apocalypse. (The Preacher is seen riding past a window as Megan reads that passage aloud from the Bible.)

A sense of the dramatic if ethereal power of the unexplainable, mystical, and supernatural pervades this film as it did *The Beguiled,* although here much more affectingly. Obvious earlier Eastwood-film allusions abound, from the vague history of the Man with No Name, to the brutal tactics of Harry Callahan and the aforementioned ambience of *The Beguiled.* The difference in *Pale Rider* is that the character is not merely out of the mainstream, he seems out of the stream of life itself.

In addition, a sense of political and social resurrection floats like a mist throughout the film, suggesting a post-Vietnam metaphor: the ghosts of the American war dead seem to live on, performing heroic deeds for the landowners, the South Vietnamese people, caught in a battle with the North not just over land rights but over the definition of what the law of the land will be. On that zeitgeist level, in its belief in the spiritual power of the defenders of the land, the film is pure Reagan-era fantasy.

Heady stuff, to be sure, but also the makings of a terrifically entertaining movie, which *Pale Rider* turned out to be. While they were making it in Sun Valley, the cast and crew felt that Clint was in a great groove, undergoing a resurrection of his own with this return to his most familiar genre and role, the western tough guy.

When he was invited to go to Cannes that spring to show *Pale Rider,* prior to its official commercial release, he took up the offer. "I enjoyed going there because I was taking a western. No one ever takes an American western. It was kind of fun and the film was received rather well. They gave me a thing called The Chevalier of Arts and Letters, and later on The Commander of the Arts and Letters."*

---

*The French version of British knighthood.

Pale Rider opened in June 1985 to raves. Vincent Canby went all out in his praise:

> An entertaining, mystical new western . . . played absolutely straight, but it's also very funny in a dryly sophisticated way that—it's only now apparent—has been true of Mr. Eastwood's self-directed films and of the Eastwood films directed by Don Siegel . . . like all Eastwood productions, *Pale Rider* is extremely well cast beginning with the star. Mr. Eastwood has continued to refine the identity of his western hero by eliminating virtually every superfluous gesture. He's a master of minimalism. The camera does not reflect vanity. It discovers the character within. *Pale Rider* is the first decent western in a very long time.

And Andrew Sarris in the *Village Voice:*

> On the whole Eastwood's instincts as an artist are well-nigh inspiring in the context of the temptations he must face all the time to play it completely safe. Consequently, even his mistakes contribute to his mystique . . . Eastwood has managed to keep the genre alive . . . through the ghostly intervention of his heroic persona.

But as always with Clint's movies, it was the audience that spoke the loudest. *Pale Rider,* which cost less than $4 million to make, was the top-grossing release its first week, raking in an amazing (for 1985) $9 million, and it brought in $21.5 million in its first ten days. It would go on to gross more than $60 million in its initial domestic release, a figure that would more than triple by the time it played on screens worldwide, everywhere to wildly enthusiastic reviews.

Typical of the international adulation was a piece in a French magazine that declared, *"Clint Eastwood, depuis 15 ans, la star de cinéma le plus populaire du monde!"**

Clint had made a spectacular return to form, and in more ways than one. On location in Sun Valley it was an open secret on set that there was a new "main squeeze" in Clint's life, a pretty young woman

---

*"For the past fifteen years, Clint Eastwood has been the most popular film star in the world!"

he had met at the Hog's Breath by the name of Jacelyn Reeves, an air-line stewardess whose home base was Carmel.

And he kept at least one other woman (as he had kept Tunis, Rose, Reeves, and even Locke for a while) in a "regular rotation." Jane Brolin, an actress who had married James Brolin in 1966, had known Clint since his Universal contract-player days, when they had first met on the grounds of the studio. After the breakup with Brolin, Jane had run into Clint, and before long they had become romantically involved.

Around this same time Clint began receiving anonymous "hate mail" regarding Sondra Locke. Some close to the situation suspected the letters were coming from Jane, despite the fact that Locke was on shaky terms with a fast-cooling Clint. He refused to believe it, and the matter was never satisfactorily resolved.*

On March 21, 1986, Jacelyn Reeves, who had become pregnant by Clint, gave birth to a son she named Scott. The registered birth cer-tificate shows the baby was delivered at Monterey Community Hos-pital. The name of the father is omitted.

In the midst of all this, Clint decided to do something about both the ice cream ordinance and the one that was preventing him from expanding the Hog's Breath: he threw his hat into the ring for mayor. Almost immediately campaign posters with his picture that looked like a cross between Ronald Reagan and Dirty Harry began to appear on the sides of buildings and streetlamps. Bumper stickers bore the slogan "Go ahead, make me mayor!" With Ronald Reagan's improb-able leap from movies to the White House still fresh in everyone's minds, the news that Clint had "entered politics" filled the front pages of newspapers around the world. (He ran as a nonpartisan, as the office of mayor does not require a political affiliation.)

On the morning of January 30, 1986, after completing his round at the Pebble Beach National Pro-Am golf tournament and just hours before the deadline, Clint dropped off his petition of thirty signa-tures (ten more than the minimum required), and his name was put into official nomination. In his first interview after declaring himself a candidate, Clint told the local Carmel newspaper why he had decided to run:

---

*Jane Agee Brolin died in a car accident in 1995.

I don't need to bring attention to myself. I'm doing this as a resident. This is where I live; this is where I intend to live the rest of my life. I have a great affinity with the community. There used to be a great deal of camaraderie, a great spirit in this community. Now there is such negativity. I'd like to see the old spirit come back here, that kind of *esprit de corps* . . . I can recall a time when you could walk down the street in Carmel and pick up an ice-cream cone at a shop—now you'd be fined . . . the city will be my absolute priority. I'll be a lot less active in films than I have in the past.

It was a startling statement. That he would put the brakes on his more-successful-than-ever film career in favor of small-town politics sounded like a reverse *It's a Wonderful Life*. The lines between his roles and his real life were blurring. In his films Clint was, in one way or another, always the defender of the people. Now he wanted to defend them in real life. At nearly fifty-six, when most men started to at least think about retirement, Clint was proudly and publicly opening up a new avenue and going so far as to suggest it meant a major career change.

Change was indeed in the air for Clint that year, although not entirely the change he had in mind.

On April 8, 1986, he won the $200-a-week mayoral post handily, spending more than $40,000 on his campaign; his opponent, incumbent Charlotte Townsend, spent $300. Clint got 2,166 votes, or 72 percent of the total cast. Townsend got 799. Clint voted before breakfast, after driving in a beat-up yellow Volkswagen convertible through a massive press gauntlet.

The next day he received a call from President Reagan, who congratulated him by asking, tongue firmly planted in cheek, "What's an actor who once appeared with a monkey in a movie doing in politics?" The not-so-inside joke was, of course, that Reagan had made *Bedtime for Bonzo*. Jimmy Stewart, the star of *It's a Wonderful Life*, who wasn't in politics but, true to his image, was the best friend of the president, also called to congratulate Clint.

At his swearing-in for his two-year term, his mother, his sister Jeanne, more than a thousand townsfolk, and at least that many paparazzi showed up to watch Charlotte Townsend hand over the symbolic gavel of power.

Even before he dealt with the ice cream crisis, one of the first things the 1985 box-office champion did as mayor was to fire the heads of the four planning commissions that had turned down his proposal to build the office addition next to the Hog's Breath.* The reversal of the anti-ice-cream ordinance followed, sparking a noticeable rise in sidewalk cone sales.

Soon after the election, Clint turned his day-to-day mayoral responsibilities over to Sue Hutchinson, a sixty-something consultant he had hired to organize his campaign. Her strong organizational skills were ideal for the job. She wasn't someone with whom he could possibly become involved, but she knew how to run a screw-tight ship. With Hutchinson firmly in place, he increasingly boarded the Warner corporate jet that was always available to him and flew to his Malpaso offices in Burbank, to turn his full-time attention back to filmmaking.

The first post–*Pale Rider* project he liked (one of the two feature films he would make while ostensibly serving as the mayor of Carmel) was a military-themed script called *Heartbreak Ridge*. Warner had sent him the script, written by James Carabatsos, a Vietnam veteran who had drawn upon his own experiences once before in a 1977 movie called *Heroes*, directed by Jeremy Kagan.† Distributed by Universal, *Heroes* had caught the eyes of the Warner executives who were interested in producing Kagan's next film, especially after the success of *Apocalypse Now* and *The Deer Hunter* made Vietnam a hot-button topic for mainstream films.

Nonetheless, Warner had problems getting a "name" interested to star in *Heartbreak Ridge*, a problem that often arose when a project was purchased without a star already attached; the reasons usually quickly became apparent. In the case of *Heartbreak Ridge*, very few actors wanted to play age against youth, presenting their own aging

---

*The ordinance itself had actually been partially reversed the previous November. It had required the new addition be set back farther from the street, with less exterior glass and mostly wooden exterior. Clint rejected that offer, and even after his full tenure as mayor, the problem went unresolved until the mid-1990s, when it was finally built, mostly to the specs of the original compromised plans, "only uglier," as one close to the project said.

†*Heroes* was a vehicle for Henry Winkler, best known as "Fonzie" from television's *Happy Days*.

facade against a bunch of scene-stealing newcomers. Clint, however, was not afraid to age on-screen and did not make conventional love stories; he was looking for just such a script, and as always one by a writer with little or no clout to challenge him.

After a couple of rewrites with specific verbal suggestions from Clint, an exasperated Carabatsos begged off any further work on *Heartbreak Ridge*, claiming other commitments. Clint promptly enlisted Dennis Hackin, who had written *Bronco Billy*, to punch up the action and the comedy. Still not satisfied, Clint next brought in Joseph Stinson, who had written *Sudden Impact*. Finally Clint and Megan Rose laid out pages from all the versions and cobbled together something they felt was at least filmable. Clint then brought back Hackin and Stinson and asked them to work on the script together. That marked the end of Rose's involvement with Clint, and the start of an ongoing dispute over who was responsible for the final shooting version.*

One reason the script may have been so hard to tailor to Clint's satisfaction was that few, if any, of the writers understood how personal, rather than genre-driven, the film actually was. Clint's days as a leading man were all but over, and even the facade of his long-standing relationship with Sondra Locke was gone. According to Clint:

----

*The Rose affair began and ended in typical Clint fashion: it was heat-fueled, ran its course, and ended rather coldly, when Clint wanted it to end. When *Unforgiven* was finally made, nearly a decade later, Rose received no on-screen credit or compensation (no co-producer or finder's fee). Meanwhile, she had moved on, left Warner Bros. after a brief but serious illness, then found a western vehicle for TV actor Tom Selleck, who was looking to move to the big screen. The script she found was *Quigley Down Under* (1990, Simon Wincer). She received co-producer credit. After *Unforgiven* was nominated for Best Picture, she hired a lawyer and asked for both the finder's fee and the production credit. To avoid the lawsuit, Clint offered her instead $10,000 to serve as story editor on his next film *(A Perfect World)*. On March 8, 1993, the story hit the gossip pages, beginning with the *New York Post*'s Page Six, and made its way through the snake-tunnel of gossip-and-whisper rags. Perhaps feeling the damage was done, Clint withdrew his offer. Eventually, Rose dropped her lawsuit and left Clint's life and world for good. Rose's contribution to the final script has been publicly questioned by the film's executive producer, Fritz Manes. In the end, Carabatsos received sole screen credit, after objecting to Clint's wanting to give Stinson a co-writer credit. The dispute went to SWG arbitration, which Carabatsos won. After the film opened, Clint continually referred to the contributions of Stinson, prompting an SWG official to advise Clint to refrain from any further public comments on the issue or face sanctions from the guild.

Heartbreak Ridge [is about] what warriors do when they haven't got a war. That's always interested me. And I thought, here's a character, let's see how he interacts with people, especially with women. It was an interesting story, also about a solider who hasn't ever done anything but fight wars, and he discovers that he's reached the end of his career, and he has nothing to look back on and nothing at all he can concentrate on now.

In its final form, an aging drill sergeant has separated from his wife and fears his time is just about up. He won the Medal of Honor at the battle of Heartbreak Ridge during the Korean War but has now been reduced to training new recruits, transforming boys still wet behind the ears into combat-ready Marines (for the invasion of Granada that took place in 1983). If any of this sounds familiar, it's because a similar story had been made in 1982 by Taylor Hackford, *An Officer and a Gentleman,* that starred Richard Gere as a punk runaway who is turned into a "real man" by his discovery of true love (via Debra Winger) and a tough-guy gunnery sergeant played by Louis Gossett Jr. It was Gere's picture, but Gossett Jr. took home a Best Supporting Oscar for his performance.* Perhaps ego, and Clint's long-simmering anger at the Academy for failing to recognize his achievements, were what really attracted him to a role very close to the one that had brought the elusive statuette to Gossett.

Besides the heavily doctored script, and Clint's clenched-teeth style of acting that made him seem now more doddering than daring, the production ran into trouble with the U.S. Defense Department. They had at first agreed to cooperate with the film but withdrew after seeing the final cut because of the excessive use of profanity and unfair combat tactics. (*An Officer and a Gentleman*'s below-the-belt training methods were unhampered by the military, as it was made without their cooperation.) One thing the DOD most objected to was Sergeant Highway (Clint) pumping an extra bullet into the back of an enemy soldier who had already been shot. Another was the fact that the Marines, in the real-life invasion, got to Grenada via Beirut, which

---

*Gere wasn't nominated. Winger was, for Best Actress, but lost to Meryl Streep in Alan J. Pakula's *Sophie's Choice.*

Clint eliminated from the film. Soon enough Clint grew tired of the military's constant bickering. When they pointed out that the army, not the Marines, had rescued the medical students in Grenada, he drew the line. He actually threatened to call Ronald Reagan and have him intervene if the military did not get off his back, and most of the military's requests were quietly agreed to.*

When the film finally did open, for the 1986 holiday season, it did surprisingly well, although more than one critic questioned that someone of Clint's age (which he had done nothing to disguise) would be involved in the film's action sequences. *Heartbreak Ridge* wound up doing almost as well as *Tightrope*, grossing over $70 million in its initial domestic release and double that overseas, where no one cared how old Clint looked or how accurate the film's depiction of the military. All foreign audiences wanted was to see their hero, Clint Eastwood, in action, and that's what they got.

Warner mounted a heavy and expensive campaign to promote *Heartbreak Ridge* for Oscar consideration, but all the heat that year went to Oliver Stone's *Platoon*: it won four Oscars, including one for Stone as Best Director and one for Best Picture, and it was nominated for four more. *Heartbreak Ridge* managed only one nomination, for Best Sound, which it lost to *Platoon*.

According to sources, Clint was angered all over again by what he considered to be this latest snubbing by the Academy and looked for someone besides himself to blame. He pointed his finger indirectly at the Department of Defense and directly at Fritz Manes, whose job as executive producer, Clint insisted, was to "handle" these kinds of situations. Manes had been on the outs with Clint since he had enthusiastically supported Locke and her *Ratboy* film. After that debacle everyone at Malpaso thought Manes, one of Clint's oldest and closest friends and one of his most trusted employees, became a scapegoat for everything that had gone wrong with *Heartbreak Ridge*.

Locke says that as her relationship with Clint broke down, so did Manes's:

---

*Some thought that Clint's noticeably lower and rougher voice in the film was his homage/impersonation of Ronald Reagan. Clint denied it, claiming it was actually his impression of an uncle who had damaged his vocal cords and had to talk that way.

I had known Fritz as long as I had known Clint, and Fritz and Clint had been close friends since junior high days; it seemed a shame for things to deteriorate [between them] that way. Clint only replied, "Stay out of this. This has nothing to do with you! I don't like the way he's running my company. *He's* not Malpaso. I am, nobody else."

Clint then began a campaign of collecting petty details to discredit Fritz . . . and then he learned that Fritz had let Judi, Clint's own secretary, occasionally use the company gas credit card, and had let the accountant, Mike Maurer, and his wife make occasional long-distance phone calls that got charged to the company . . .

Clint did not actually confront Fritz. He played cat and mouse. Once Fritz was safely fired, Clint . . . wanted Fritz's car phone returned; he didn't care that it was the old-fashioned kind that had been bolted down, he wanted it . . . He even concocted a scheme in which he wanted [my husband] to break into Fritz's home and make a sample of the type on Fritz's typewriter so that he could see if it matched that on the anonymous hate-filled letters he'd been receiving for several years.

Not long after *Heartbreak Ridge* failed to make a dent with Oscar, the long and fruitful professional and personal relationship between Fritz Manes and Clint came to a permanent end.

SEVENTEEN

I went to a jazz concert one time at the Oakland Philharmonic. This guy comes out in a pinstripe suit, standing off to one side, the joint is jumping, and then all of a sudden he steps up and starts playing and everything is doubled up. I'm thinking, "How the hell does he do that?" . . . It was a great acting lesson—the amount of confidence [Parker] exuded. I've never seen an artist, an actor, a painter, any artist have that kind of confidence.

—Clint Eastwood

PREVIOUS PAGE: *Clint, with Liam Neeson in the fifth and final Dirty Harry film,* The Dead Pool *(1988), hangs up his Magnum for good.*

That March, after the 1987 Academy Awards ceremonies, Clint reimmersed himself in the business of running Carmel. One of his first chores was to oversee an ongoing conflict over Carmel's Mission Ranch, a large wetland just south of the city limit that had been purchased by a private consortium that wanted to develop it into a modern housing project, with expensive town houses and maybe even a self-contained modern mall with ample parking facilities. The town council was opposed to the development, preferring to keep the land preserved in the image of Carmel, a beautiful, natural seaside village. To prevent the development from advancing any further, the city offered $3.75 million for the land, about half of what the owners said they would take to settle. The situation remained deadlocked until Clint decided to put up $5.5 million of his own money to help Carmel acquire the land. Having completed the sale, he took it out of the hands of any and all developers and vowed to keep it as it was. The elders of the township hailed the move, and the national press as well looked upon it favorably.

With that victory under his belt, Clint dove deeper into Carmel's municipal activities. He actively pursued projects meant to improve pedestrian access to beaches, adding public toilets, walking trails, and also a new library for the town. He began writing a column in the local paper, the *Pine Cone*, his personal forum to discuss and respond to issues of the day, especially those that generated the most mail to his office. And he even put a bit of the old-style, back-door politics of vengeance into play when he made it difficult for former councilman David Maradei to get a variance to put a gable on his roof. Maradei had been one of the people who had made it difficult for Clint to build his Hog's Breath Inn annex. Even though Clint officially abstained from voting on the issue, he made sure everyone knew he did not support it.

And when Jimmy Stewart was scheduled to be feted by the local film festival, the town council turned down permits for temporary high-stacked lighting, citing the garish, Hollywood-like atmosphere that it was sure to create. Clint, miffed at what he felt, probably rightly, was a veiled reference to his being a movie star mayor, made sure those lights got hung. He also saw to it that Pope John Paul II was able to make a stop in Carmel in 1987, which boosted tourism and filled the city's coffers. If Clint was the celebrity mayor, Carmel was becoming a place where tourists liked to come, hoping to catch a glimpse of him strolling around town, always ready, willing, and able to keep the peace.

Sondra Locke, meanwhile, was trying to move her stalled career forward. Occasionally she still made the drive up the coast to visit Clint in his Carmel enclave. Locke knew that if she wanted to see him, she would have to go up there; otherwise (and Clint had done nothing to hide it from her) a steady stream of other female visitors would come to his home. He was continuing to see, among others, Jacelyn Reeves, who gave birth to their second child, a daughter, in February 1988.

Locke's place in L.A., on Stradella Road, was becoming less and less hers and more and more Kyle Eastwood's. Clint's son, at Clint's directive, had moved in, according to Locke, even as he was struggling at the University of Southern California. Kyle brought home his pack, musicians and actors, most of whom Locke did not know. When she raised a red flag to Clint, he supported Kyle, seeing it, in his way, as taking Kyle in, even though Clint was rarely at that house. As much as Locke wanted to protest, Clint still owned the place, and she had no legal right to prevent the sudden influx of "family" and friends. "So this had become my life with him," she wrote,

> Clint being distant, rarely at home and Kyle and his friends playing their instruments into the wee hours, sneaking girls in and out for overnight stays. It was humiliating to feel that I had nothing to say about circumstances in my own home. The final straw for me was the night I woke up and saw someone staring down at me. It was a friend of Kyle's. I threw him out and locked my bedroom door from that day forward.

Nonetheless at times Locke felt that she and Clint were making progress, getting closer, having fun when they saw each other. For a while she became his official escort, even at home, where he entertained the usual round of obligatory celebrities in Carmel, including Merv Griffin, whose advancing age and mania for "old" Hollywood held little social interest for Locke (or ultimately for Clint). Cary Grant and Lucille Ball were also regulars, although again, the age differences and levels of sophistication proved difficult for Locke to handle.

Gradually, though, Clint's social circle changed as the older members disappeared or died off, and it updated itself with the likes of TV producer Bud Yorkin and his wife, Arnold Schwarzenegger and Maria Shriver, Al Ruddy (the producer of *The Godfather*), and Richard Zanuck and his wife, Lili. Most of these were friends from Clint's vacation home in Sun Valley, a place Locke always enjoyed. This circle was closer in age, temperament, and love for physical sports like skiing, which made her feel more a part of Clint's life. And of course, they were all active filmmakers.

But really it was all over between them. It had always been Clint's style to act passively when a relationship was ending. He had kept Roxanne Tunis and their child on a back burner (of sorts), while his marriage to Maggie slowly flickered out. If Locke was going to put up with all of Clint's ways, Clint was not predisposed to do anything more than hope she would just go away.

Toward the end of his term, papal visits notwithstanding, Clint's restlessness with local politics finally led him to think about making a new movie, one that he had actually signed on to before he put his film career on voluntary hold.

The project was a biography of alto saxophonist Charlie "Bird" Parker that had been around for years in what is disaffectionately known in Hollywood as "development hell." He couldn't possibly play the lead, because Parker was African-American, but he could produce and direct without starring in the film. That prospect excited him but sent automatic shivers up the spine of Warner Bros.

While Clint was perhaps the most valuable single commodity Warner had in the post-studio era, much of his value came from his on-screen appearances. To date, he had directed only one other movie that he had not starred in, the problematic 1973 all-but-forgotten *Breezy*, which did not even register in the top thirty of the forty-three films that he had appeared in (some of which he had also directed).

Probably no other actor-director at the time could have gotten *Bird* made the way he wanted to do it *except* Clint, who in 1988 accounted for a full 18 percent, nearly one fifth, of Warner's domestic revenues from films, plus an additional $1.5 million *per week* his movies generated internationally. A biography of a jazz musician, Charlie "Bird" Parker, who drank and drugged himself to death in the 1950s, filled with failure, despair, and death, was unlikely to find an audience with any kind of box-office pulse, especially with the all-important 18-to-25 rock-and-roll set who bought the majority of all theater tickets.

Like nearly every Clint Eastwood film, *Bird* was produced by Malpaso as a stand-alone project, which allowed Clint to rattle his saber and threaten to do business with another studio when the executives did something he didn't like. Because Clint's passion for *Bird* was so high, Terry Semel, not wanting to incur his wrath or, worse, lose the Eastwood/Malpaso franchise, put up no resistance, even though no one at Warner thought the film stood any chance at all of making a dime. Few films about jazz (excluding *The Jazz Singer*, Alan Crosland's 1927 box-office-busting novelty—the first talkie—which had absolutely nothing to do with jazz) had ever gotten made, let alone shown a profit in America. The best the studio hoped for was that the losses wouldn't be too big.

Clint had been indirectly involved in a film about jazz once before, Bertrand Tavernier's 1986 *'Round Midnight*, which lovingly followed the lives of several Paris-based American jazz expats. It won an Oscar for Original Score, awarded to Herbie Hancock, and gained a nomination for its star, Dexter Gordon. When that film's producer, Irwin Winkler, had shopped it, he had met a stone wall at the studios except at Warner, where Mark Rosenberg, then head of production, teetered on the fence. Clint exerted his influence to get the film green-lighted. Not long afterward Fox offered $3 million for the foreign rights. Winkler made the film with that foreign money, and it became one of the sleeper hits of 1986.

The script for *Bird* first came to Clint via a long and circuitous route, not unusual for projects the studios considered too fringe. Its writer, Joel Oliansky (also the originator of the project), had previously

written a mildly entertaining movie about a classical music competition (classical music was another studio no-no) that he also directed,
The Competition (1980). The film did well enough to get him a plum
assignment: writing an eight-hour historical miniseries for ABC,
Masada (1981), for which he was nominated for an Emmy and got a
contract from Columbia. They soon green-lighted *Bird*, his proposed
feature film bio of Charlie Parker. Although he had been promised he
could direct it, the studio eventually gave the project to Bob Fosse,
who had been nominated for Best Director for his autobiographical
All That Jazz (1979), a Broadway-based biopic.* *All That Jazz* had
nothing to do with jazz, but the title was enough for Columbia to con-
clude that he was the perfect director for the film. But Fosse passed,
and it came back to Oliansky.

Columbia's initial interest in the project was based on its belief that
Richard Pryor would play the title role. But after Pryor nearly burned
himself to death in 1980 in his infamous drug-related "accident," the
studio put the project on the back burner. Five years later Warner
revived interest in it as a possible vehicle for Prince, who had had an
unexpected outsize hit with his semiautobiographical *Purple Rain*
(1984, directed by Albert Magnoli). To get the Oliansky project, called
at the time *Yardbird Suite*, from Columbia, Warner traded a script it
had, called *Revenge*, to Ray Stark's Rastar, the longtime producer's
company under exclusive contract to Columbia.†

When Prince's involvement ended, the script once more lay idle—
until someone thought to send it to Clint. By now both Manes and
Chernus were gone (Chernus had been Manes's assistant, and when
Manes went, so did she), so Clint took to searching for projects on his
own. When he found out that Semel had *Yardbird Suite* and nowhere to
go with it, he requested a copy, read it, and decided he wanted to make
the movie. He called Oliansky, and they met, but despite their shared
interest in Parker, they failed to hit it off. Reportedly they fell out over
the development part of the deal: Clint wanted Oliansky to do a rewrite,
and Oliansky asked for rewrite money. Clint, perhaps feeling the writer
should have been a little more grateful and cooperative for a project

---

*Fosse had earlier won the Oscar for Best Director in 1972 for *Cabaret*.

†*Revenge* was released in 1990, directed by Tony Scott, starring Kevin Costner and
Anthony Quinn.

that had been sitting around for years, fixed the script himself, mostly cutting down on the dialogue. Clint kept Oliansky at arm's length for the rest of the movie.

Forest Whitaker was cast in the title role. Whitaker had made a name for himself in a trifecta of Scorsese's *The Color of Money* (1986), Oliver Stone's *Platoon* (1986), and Barry Levinson's *Good Morning, Vietnam* (1987). Production on *Bird* went smoothly, and Whitaker's performance was so strong that in the spring of 1988, when Clint took the film to Cannes, Whitaker walked off with the Best Actor vote. Unfortunately for Clint, it lost the Golden Palm to Argentinean Fernando Solanas for *Sur*. That loss put a drag on the film's momentum and slowed Warner's plan of release.

Disappointed at Cannes, Clint returned to the States and his mayoral duties. He quickly made two public announcements.

The first was that he was not going to run for a second two-year term as mayor of Carmel, putting an end to the collective fantasy that he would one day follow in Ronald Reagan's footsteps and make a successful run for the presidency. In truth, Clint had become disillusioned with local politics, finding most of it boring and mundane, and he had failed to bring a successful, definitive resolution to his Hog's Breath Inn battle with the city council that had made him run for the office in the first place. Eating ice cream in public somehow wasn't enough of a victory to motivate him to continue. Nor did the obligatory scrutiny that accompanied anything higher than small-town politics appeal to him. Exposure of the facts of his private life—rife with lovers and out-of-wedlock children before, during, and after his only marriage—would not only eliminate him from any serious run for larger office, but could conceivably damage his public image and, even possibly, his acting career. As he told the *Los Angeles Times* seven years later, "I would never have been able to pass the Bill Clinton–Gary Hart test . . . no one short of Mother Teresa could pass."

The second was that he was going to return to the well one more time to make another Dirty Harry film, the fifth, this one to be called *The Dead Pool*.

The screenplay came from the unlikeliest of sources, a pair of nutritionists whom Clint had known since at least the late 1970s. Durk Pearson and Sandy Shaw had a program they called Life Extension that promised, among other things, improved personal appearance, reduced anxiety, and of course long life. Pearson was a graduate of MIT who had majored in physics; afterward he had devoted his life to searching for a way for a human being to live to 150 years without any appreciable loss of physical prowess or mental awareness—in effect, to double the human life expectancy. Pearson's method was built around large doses of vitamins and minerals and other assorted nutrients. Along the way he met and teamed with Sandy Shaw, a UCLA graduate with a degree in biochemistry who had studied the aging process extensively.

Clint first met Pearson and Shaw at a dinner arranged by Merv Griffin, who was already a devotee of the pair and wanted to turn Clint on to them. In 1981 Pearson and Shaw wrote a bestselling book called *Life Extension*, based on their theories and their applications. There they recounted a meeting with Griffin and "Mr. Smith," who was in fact Clint Eastwood; he had tried the megadosing and extreme exercise system and found it to be an extraordinary help to his overall health and his allergies. It even improved his ability to talk to interviewers, which in the past had always caused a bit of anxiety, reflected in uneasy word flow. In 1984, after years of evasions and denials, Clint finally admitted that he was "Mr. Smith."* His daily regimen included three-mile jogs, two hours in the gym, and two sessions of meditation; a low-fat, high-vegetable, meatless diet (save an occasional cheeseburger); and doses of choline, selenium, deanol, L-arginine, and L-dopa. He later claimed not to have needed reading glasses until he turned fifty-eight.

To many who knew the story, his purchase of the screenplay seemed something of a payback to Pearson and Shaw for having helped keep him fit enough to be able to make another Dirty Harry film. In fact, Pearson and Shaw had worked on a previous film of Clint's, serving as "consultants" on *Foxfire*, but they had been left uncredited to keep Clint's deeper involvement with them confidential.

Now Clint was willing to give them a full story credit. This new Dirty Harry project had the familiar story trope of the tracking of a serial killer. *The Dead Pool* (not to be confused with Stuart Rosenberg's 1975 Paul Newman vehicle, *The Drowning Pool*) involves a game of betting on how long a celebrity will live. (He or she has to die a natural

---

*"Mrs. Smith" was Sondra Locke.

death for the winner to collect.) Unfortunately the film had few of the psychological overtones or dramatic elements of *Tightrope*, and on-screen Clint appeared weary and uninvolved. He seems to be simply going through the motions.

With a script heavily rewritten by Steve Sharon, and with Buddy Van Horn directing (Horn was the stuntman who had directed Clint's comic turn in *Any Which Way You Can*), the film did not have much going for it. It did take a clever jab at a female film critic, unmistakably Pauline Kael (who, reviewing *Bird*, had wondered if Clint had paid the electric bill, meaning the film looked too dark to her). In a very early screen appearance Jim Carrey (billed as James Carrey) acted a deadly unfunny parody of a doomed rock star. *The Dead Pool* grossed about $59 million in its initial domestic release, which would have been good for most films but was disappointing for a Dirty Harry movie. It did nothing so much as signal that the franchise was finally and forever dead.*

By the end of 1988, the arc of Clint's career appeared finally to have curved downward. The drop was neither fast nor sharp enough to cause alarm, but the glory days seemed to have faded into the sunset. To be fair, only a few actors from the 1960s were still box-office draws—among them Paul Newman and Dustin Hoffman—but even their movies were nothing like the ones that had brought them to prominence earlier in their careers.

Clint decided the time had come to take a good, long, hard, and realistic look at his career and his life. And to once and for all get rid of Sondra Locke.

He had continually tried to widen the growing distance between them, accelerating it after the box-office failure of *Ratboy*. He knew it wasn't going to be easy, but it made no difference; the time had come to remove himself from her life, and she from his.

What he didn't anticipate was how difficult, ugly, embarrassing, and costly that was going to be.

The Dead Pool was released before *Bird*. Both Warner and Clint agreed that *The Dead Pool* was a better summer film, while *Bird* might have a chance in early September. *The Dead Pool* received a national release in several hundred theaters; *Bird* was released in only a few cities and less than a dozen theaters.

EIGHTEEN

There is only one way to have a happy marriage, and as soon as I learn what it is I'll get married again.

—Clint Eastwood

Approaching his sixtieth birthday, Clint Eastwood wanted to clean house, literally and figuratively. The only property he actually owned in Los Angeles was the house he was leasing to Locke. She had to go, and there was no point in putting it off any longer, but California law had an especially sticky issue called palimony. The word had come into the popular lexicon in the late 1970s, after Lee Marvin's live-in girlfriend successfully sued for support when they broke up. That court decision sent a chill down the spines of the Hollywood social set, where it had once been business as usual for a star or an upper executive, married or single, to keep a girlfriend, maybe a pretty starlet, stashed in an apartment, with a car and a credit card, until the heat cooled, at which point the gal-pal had to give up everything and leave.

Clint, like most stars, enjoyed a lot of different women, and his privileged life allowed him to live by his own social (or antisocial) rules. By now his pattern had long been set. He had liked being married, or at least the appearance of it. Unquestionably it had been good for his image in his *Rawhide* days, when moral clauses hung on actors' backs wherever they went, and their personal indiscretions, real or suspected, were discussed in the powerful and feared *Confidential Magazine*, the forerunner of today's celebrity gossip megaindustry. Marriage to Maggie, even with all its restrictions and compromises, had given his life some structure and his image some sanitation. And to ensure that his real-life image did not clash too much with the righteous character of Rowdy Yates, he made sure that Roxanne Tunis was content to live separately, raised their child as a single mother, and stayed far away from Clint's public persona. Locke, however, had not been as cooperative or as willingly conforming; in fact, she had committed a couple of unforgivable sins, for which he was now going to make her pay.

The first was that she had never divorced her husband, Gordon Anderson. Now Clint was, more or less, supporting him by allowing him to stay in the house he had bought in Hollywood; as for the house on Stradella Road that he had bought for Locke, Clint had kept it in his name and set up a lease arrangement that gave him all the control and all the power. He had moved Kyle in, but Locke had dug in her heels and apparently was as ready as Clint for the coming slugfest.

It's difficult to pinpoint exactly when the fading blossom finally fell from the tree, but sometime in the middle of 1988 the tensions between Clint and Locke visibly escalated over, of all things, a relatively minor pickup accident Locke may (or may not) have had while driving one of Clint's trucks outside Tower Records on Sunset Boulevard, at the time the most popular music megastore in L.A. A motorcyclist claimed he had been hit by the pickup in Tower's parking lot.

The incident made Clint furious when the motorcyclist sued his auto insurance company. When Clint confronted Locke about it, she claimed she couldn't remember having had an accident in his pickup at Tower or anywhere else. Clint did not believe her. He took away her driving privileges and told her that from now on she was to drive her own car—not his pickup, not his blue Mercedes, just her own vehicle. And, he added, with emphasis, that went for Gordon as well.

When Locke took the bait and defended Gordon, Clint's response was "Well, I've divorced Maggie, but you haven't divorced Gordon." To Locke, he seemed to be invoking their not being married as one more reason why he was angry. Understandably, this made no sense to Locke, who called him on it. "Do you want us to get married now, Clint?"

"That's not the point," he barked. "You should do it without my asking you; you should make yourself available. I can't ask if you're not available."

It sounded right, but Locke wasn't buying any of it. She believed that it was just one of Clint's ploys to get Gordon out of his life as well as hers. Then two seemingly unrelated incidents cut Clint's slow-burning fuse down to ignition.

The first was a new film and a directing deal that Locke had managed to secure from Warner, green-lighted by Terry Semel and producer Lucy Fisher. The project was originally called *Sudden Impulse*, a psychological thriller with a female lead that Semel thought, based on the original *Ratboy*, Locke would be perfect for. She wanted to find a new name for it, though, lest Clint think it too close to *Sudden Impact*, in which she had starred with him a few years back.

According to Locke, however, even before she could make that change, Clint began doing everything he could to make the project difficult for her. "Suddenly, he'd want me to travel with him only when he *knew* I had an important meeting. When we were at the ranch, each time [producer] Al Ruddy would phone me, Clint would sit down at the piano and immediately start banging out Scott Joplin tunes as loudly as he could."

The second incident was the annual Christmas vacation that Locke and Clint had taken ever since they had known each other; Christmas Eve had been reserved for just the two of them, no matter how many other people were in their lives. But in 1988, just weeks before the holidays, Clint casually informed her that he was going to be spending them by himself, in Carmel, playing golf. Locke then spent Christmas with Gordon. Then, as she prepared for her annual New Year's Eve ski trip with Clint, she received a call from Jane Brolin. Brolin invited her to come to Sun Valley—where Locke was planning to go anyway— and told her that Kyle and Alison were coming too. Locke, fearing the worst, flew to Sun Valley on a private Warner plane with Brolin and Clint's two children.

The next morning, in Sun Valley, Brolin confronted Locke, telling her that she was really not wanted in the group. It was a bizarre confrontation, and the first thing Locke thought was that Clint was making Jane do his dirty work for him. Words were exchanged between the two women that quickly escalated into a screaming match. Just as it reached the neck-vein-popping state, Clint walked in, listened to the two of them, and told both of them to take the Warner jet and go home.

Locke tearfully packed and left. Brolin stayed with Clint.

As soon as the holidays were over, Locke went to see a lawyer, Norman Oberstein, who suggested that this was perhaps not the right time to start a legal proceeding.

Clint, meanwhile, was spending much of his free time with actress Frances Fisher, with whom he was quite taken. On the morning of April 4, 1990, he dropped by the house on Stradella Road and waited in the living room until Locke came down the stairs. His presence startled her. He was there, he said, to tell her he wanted her to leave the house. Locke, who was preparing to direct her film, was shocked into silence. With nothing left to say, Clint simply turned and walked out the door.

On April 10, while Locke was at Warner, Clint personally came by the house again and this time changed the locks. That same day he had Locke served with a hand-delivered written notice, on set, that she was no longer welcome at Stradella and no longer had any legal access to it. All her belongings had been taken to Gordon's house on Crescent Heights, the one Clint had bought for him. When Locke read the notice, she fainted.

Meanwhile, Clint had been busy working on a new movie, *Pink Cadillac.* Three years had passed since his last legitimate box-office success, *Heartbreak Ridge,* and he hoped this new film would finally turn things around for him. It was a working-class country cowboy film with a slightly harder edge, even a few echoes of Dirty Harry; a noticeable absence of singing and simians; the addition of the lovely Bernadette Peters; and an appearance by still relatively unknown Jim Carrey (billed as "James"), his second Clint movie.

In it, Clint plays Tommy Nowak, a tough skip-tracer assigned to find Lou Ann McGuinn (Peters, in a nonsinging, against-type role), an equally tough young mama who has taken off with her baby after being indicted for possession of counterfeit money. McGuinn's oppressive husband Roy (Timothy Carhart) has of late been hanging out with the toughest guys of all, a gang of white supremacists, the Birthright, who are the real counterfeiters. Lou Ann's method of escape turns out to be her husband's pink Cadillac. Somewhere along the way she finds some funny money in the car, drops off the baby with her sister, and heads for the nearest casino, where Nowak catches up with her. In a reversal (the script had more twists than a corkscrew), the money in the car turns out to be real. Even as Nowak and McGuinn are discovering this fact, the Birthright had sent a team of killers to kill McGuinn to recapture the money. Eventually, there is a confrontation, a shoot-out, and guess what, Nowak and McGuinn beat the bad guys, realize they are in love, and live happily ever after, or something approximating that within the confines of their colorless and uninspired lives. The film is meant to be a comedy with dramatic overtones, or a drama with comic overtones—it's difficult to tell which.

To direct, Clint called in his former stuntman Buddy Van Horn, who had helmed two previous Clint movies (*Any Which Way You Can* and *The Dead Pool*), while he, Clint, pulled his performance out of his back pocket.

Peters was more familiar to Broadway audiences than to filmgoers; Clint had hired her, it appeared to several witnesses on the set, simply because he was attracted to her. Clint's interior logic may have been that if he were attracted to his costar, his audiences would be too. Peters and Clint had good chemistry on-screen, but she showed no real-life romantic interest in Clint. At that point Clint turned his attention back to Frances Fisher, who was playing the small part of Dinah, Peters's sister.

Locke, still busy making her movie, kept hearing that Clint was running around town with Fisher, and in a fit of pique she went back to see Oberstein. This time he agreed the time had come to take action. The first thing he wanted was for Locke and Gordon to sign a severance agreement. In effect, this meant that while they were still married, Gordon voluntarily surrendered his access to any and all of Locke's property. The purpose was to remove Clint's possible defense that Locke's relationship with Gordon had a financial motive or that she was still beholden to him in any way.

Once they signed it, Oberstein (at Locke's insistence) met with Clint's attorney, Bruce Ramer, to see if any kind of informal resolution between the two was possible. Ramer said the only thing Clint would agree to was that Gordon could keep his house, but Locke had to remain out of Stradella. When Oberstein relayed Clint's conditions, Locke knew she had no choice but to go ahead and sue.

The story of the impending lawsuit hit the national press with all the force of a Hollywood hurricane. In the tabloids it wiped everything else off their front pages for weeks, echoing the highly volatile (and endlessly entertaining) ten-year-old palimony case between Lee Marvin and Michelle Triola that had all but ended Marvin's career.

Clint did not want to be part of anything like that, especially at a time when his career seemed in decline. *Pink Cadillac* had opened on Memorial Day weekend, the traditional start of the big-money, big-production summertime run of movies. But it disappeared quickly in the wake of mostly negative reviews (Richard Freedman, writing for the Newhouse News Services syndicate, called it "a 122 minute dozer") and the cinematic tsunami that was Steven Spielberg's *Indiana Jones and the Last Crusade*. In its first ten days, *Pink Cadillac* did about $6 million against *Indiana*'s $38 million, making *Pink Cadillac* one of the biggest flops in Clint's and Malpaso's history. (And it all but ended Peters's film career.) Whether or not the negative publicity surrounding the emerging legal slugfest between him and Locke had anything to do with it, the film simply did not draw the usual Clint crowd.

Even as *Pink Cadillac* was opening and closing, Clint was already planning his next film, *White Hunter Black Heart*, to be shot on location near Lake Kariba in Zimbabwe, an attractive place even more attractive to Clint because it was so far away. Fisher was not invited and, reportedly, did not even receive a good-bye phone call from Clint before he left.

But before he could leave, he received notice that Locke had gone ahead and filed a $70 million "palimony" lawsuit against him. Locke's revelations of Clint's philandering, and her two abortions—now a matter of public record—proved irresistible reading. The public consensus was surprisingly in Clint's favor, however, as it appeared to most that Locke was putting a noose around his neck in order to save her own pretty face.

If Hollywood was biased in Clint's favor as it hadn't been in Marvin's, the reason was not hard to understand. Despite his last few failures, Clint remained one of the most powerful, if not *the* most powerful, actor-producer-directors in post-studio-era Hollywood. He had built a human tower of strength on the back of Malpaso, and his thirty-five-year, forty-seven-film career had generated billions of dollars for the industry and untold jobs for actors, directors, screenwriters, and set designers, all the way down to the weekend popcorn vendors in the neighborhood movies.

Moreover, everyone in Hollywood who didn't work with him loved him, which meant they hoped one day to work with him. He had a reputation for being fast and easy, liked to be hitting the links by early afternoon, and generally let the actors play their roles the way they wanted to. The studio suits may not have liked his way of doing business, but they lived in fear—Hollywood's only known true emotion—

that if they somehow offended Clint, they might not be able to continue to pay the second mortgage on their beach houses. Marvin had
been nothing more than a fading actor, and Locke had appeared in one
noteworthy movie and six Clint films and had thus far directed one
unsuccessful movie.*

Locke's legal team pressed for immediate depositions to prevent
Clint from being able to leave for Africa without giving them. According to Locke, "My [oral] deposition was nothing short of hell." Clint's
litigator for the depositions, Howard King, led a fierce attack on
Locke's character and motivations. She loved fairy tales, as she had
told Clint many times, and King tried to somehow establish that she
was living in one in her own mind, casting Clint as her rescuer, her savior, her knight in shining armor. He pressed her on her longtime marriage to Gordon and why she had never divorced him. He wanted to
know if she had had other sexual relations while living with Clint. He
condemned her for "stealing" another woman's husband.

The deposition drove her to see a psychiatrist.

Then it was Oberstein's turn to put Clint on the grill. For six hours
Oberstein focused on Clint's "real" intentions with the house on
Stradella, pointing out that Clint had originally intended, via his will
(which he had since had rewritten several times), to leave it to Locke.
In response to a question regarding the nature of their relationship,
Clint suggested they had only gone steady but had not lived together
on a formal basis, because Locke was married to Gordon. A "part-time
roommate" was how Clint characterized Locke. Pressed to explain that
definition, Clint said that "anytime a person spends one night it's part-
time." Oberstein confronted Clint with the fact that he had wiretapped
Stradella's phone; he responded that he had been the victim of a stalker
and had been simply trying to gather evidence to build a case against
him—or her. On more than one occasion, he said, Locke had threatened to kill him. Later, in her autobiography, Locke described these
accusations as "ridiculous, preposterous and a slanderous lie."

A week later a closed-door preliminary hearing was held, to deter-
mine if Locke should be allowed back into Stradella. A variety of

---

*The six Clint films were *The Outlaw Josey Wales*, *The Gauntlet*, *Every Which Way but
Loose*, *Bronco Billy*, *Any Which Way You Can*, and *Sudden Impact*.

players, pro and con, mostly friends and relatives, testified in support of their respective sides. Jane Brolin testified that whenever she stayed with Clint at Stradella, which she often had, she couldn't help but notice how much of Locke's clothing and personal items were there. And she was testifying for Clint. It was, to say the least, a strange strategy on Clint's part; it made him look more like a playboy than he might have wanted; Brolin's interest in Locke's belongings may have seemed like snooping.

It came out, under cross, that Brolin had been the "unnamed source" for many of those *National Enquirer* "exclusive" stories about the deteriorating relationship between Locke and Clint and also the likely source of those poison-pen letters. Kyle testified that he was the primary tenant at Stradella Road. And Clint revealed here for the first time that he had had two children with Jacelyn Reeves, a girl, Kathryn, and a boy, Scott. Until then no one had known for sure who was the father of her children, as the birth certificate for both had read, "Father declined." The existence of these children came as a complete shock to Locke, who had had no idea Clint had begun yet another family, with another woman, during their time together.

Locke was granted interim support but was denied palimony, the judge ruled, because she had been married to another man while she was involved with Clint. But because the case was in arbitration, the decision was not binding. Locke declined to accept the ruling and pressed for a full hearing in Los Angeles Superior Court. That June, while she continued her case, Locke rented a relatively modest apartment for the duration on Fountain Avenue, in West Hollywood, and resumed postproduction on her project, now called *Impulse*.

While the hearing moved to the next court, Clint left it to his lawyers to fight it out and finally took off for Africa, accompanied by Jane Brolin.

White Hunter Black Heart was another of Clint's personal anti-genre films on the order of *Bird*. It was a thinly disguised biographical portrait of John Huston, one of the most respected directors in Hollywood. Novelist Peter Viertel had written a stunning roman à clef about Huston's experiences on location in the Congo while filming his award-winning *The African Queen* (1951). The novel revealed

Huston's on-location obsession with drinking and bagging an elephant on safari.

It seemed an odd choice for Clint. Why did he make it? He said, in his own words:

> A fellow by the name of Stanley Rubin, who I'd met a long time ago at the beginning of the fifties when he was a producer at Universal, was working for Ray Stark, and he asked me whether I'd be interested in reading a script that had been hanging around in Columbia's offices for quite a while along with some others . . . I met Peter Viertel and found out the whole story of the novel, how he began to write it and the adventures of the pre-production period for *The African Queen*. It fascinated me, as obsessive behavior always does . . . It was a very interesting character to explore.

In *White Hunter Black Heart* John Wilson (Clint) is about to kill an elephant when he has a sudden change of heart that instead causes the death of his native guide, Kivu (Boy Mathias Chuma), a Gunga Din type, the only person in the film Wilson cares about. Branded by the villagers as a white hunter with a black heart, Wilson returns to his only real love, making movies, in this case to finish the film he has ostensibly come to make. Art endures over life, as in the last shot of the film, Wilson shouts, "Action!"

It was as near a statement of self-definition as the tight-lipped Clint would ever give. Huston was someone he could identify with both as a filmmaker and as a contradictory personality; his flamboyance was both extravagant and selective, generous and thrifty, kindhearted and mean-spirited. And as both actor and director, often for the same project, Huston had made mostly genre films (like *The Maltese Falcon* and *The African Queen*, both of which he had only directed) that were also personal statements, and offbeat, quirky films that were still meant to be "big" (like *Freud*, for which he was both director and narrator) but never attained the kind of attention or box office he felt they deserved.

With *Bird* and now *White Hunter Black Heart*, Clint was steadily moving toward films that were, in many ways, thinly veiled autobiographies: Charlie Parker, the musical genius who went against the prevalent tide, only to leave a tidal wave in his wake; Huston, the physically daunting director-actor whose films did not always fit into a commercial category but nevertheless left an afterburn in the mind. Most interestingly, Huston was given to excess and lacked self-discipline. In other words, he was the exact opposite of Clint, whose self-discipline—both in filmmaking and in personal health regimens—was well known to anyone who had ever worked with him. As an all-warts homage, the film was Clint's way of humanizing and idolizing Huston (and himself) at the same time.

When filming was completed late in August, Clint returned to the States via London, where he met up with Maggie. Her marriage to Wynberg was on the rocks, and she wanted to see how Clint was handling the devolution of his own relationship with Locke into legal and emotional acrimony. It mattered to her if Clint was over Locke. Of all his indiscretions, she was the one whom Maggie had always blamed for the breakup of her marriage to Clint. Moreover, she and Clint were still business partners in a number of enterprises, the result of their complex divorce settlement, and the parents of two children. Maggie also told Clint that he had to try to play a stronger, more influential role in Kyle's and Alison's life.

And there was something else, Maggie told him. In the wake of his sensational palimony trial, she had learned along with everyone else that Clint was the father of a daughter, Kimber, who had been born to Roxanne Tunis, while Maggie and Clint were still married. Presumably Maggie had a few things to tell Clint about that. He listened to all she wanted or needed to say and did not argue or disagree.

Upon his return to L.A., Clint quietly resumed his relationship with Frances Fisher, and while the palimony case dragged on, he began postproduction work on *White Hunter Black Heart*. In May 1990 he took the finished version to Cannes where, inexplicably, he denied to the press that he had based his performance on John Huston. The cineast-heavy audiences and highly literate critics, well aware of the history of *The African Queen*, were puzzled as to what the film could otherwise possibly be about.

That September Clint showed it at the Telluride Film Festival in Colorado, where it was given a less-than-spectacular reception.

White Hunter Black Heart opened in the fall of 1990, and earned less than $8 million in its initial domestic release, one of the worst-grossing films of his career.

Entering his fifth decade of moviemaking, with three film failures in a row, and mired in a very public palimony trial, he went directly into production on a straight genre *policier*, albeit with a slight twist. Rather than playing his trademark loner, he would try to lure more youthful audiences by sharing the screen with a much younger and extremely popular male costar, Charlie Sheen. A rookie (Sheen) comes under Officer Nick Pulovski's (Clint's) wing, after Pulovski's last partner was killed by a stolen-car gang run by ruthless Latin murderers. The film, called *The Rookie*, had a script by Boaz Yakin and Scott Spiegel that seemed a pale imitation—some critics thought it an out-and-out spoof—of the Dirty Harry films, minus the dirt and minus Harry. Not that the film lacked appeal. Sonia Braga, playing a sadomasochistic murderess named Liesl, handcuffs and ties Clint to a chair, rapes him rather graphically, then comes this close to killing him until he miraculously escapes. It was an explosive sequence, and the only one in the film that people talked about. As obviously provocative and exploitative as it was, *ars gratia artis*, the scene may also be read as conveying Clint's feeling victimized at the hands of a beautiful but bad woman. In the scene, Liesl has him handcuffed, sexually tortured, and imprisoned and wants to kill him even as she is making love to him. And she is, in the end, killed by Clint's big gun.

The film received mixed-to-negative reviews but did better at the box office than any of his recent films, prompting Vincent Canby in the *New York Times* to wonder how Clint could reach so high and fail with *White Hunter Black Heart* and reach so low and succeed with *The Rookie*. Rushed into Christmas 1990 release, it grossed $43 million in its initial domestic release. It was good enough to stop the slide, but by no means a great film or even a very good one.

Two more years would pass before Clint made another movie.

PART III

FROM AUTEUR TO OSCAR

NINETEEN

Unforgiven *ends the trajectory begun in* Fistful of Dollars. *Instead of having no family, or just starting a family, this time East-wood's character has a family—again, with no woman in the picture, at least not a living one.*

—Brett Westbrook

In April 1990 Locke's movie, *Impulse,* opened to fairly decent reviews, including a coveted thumbs-up from the influential TV and print critics Siskel and Ebert, which usually helped boost a film's box office. Nevertheless, according to Locke, "Warner barely released the film. And on opening weekend in the few theaters in Los Angeles, the ad in the newspaper didn't even use the Siskel and Ebert review." Even worse for Locke, a few weeks after the movie's spring release, Lucy Fisher told her that, regrettably, Warner was dropping the other three projects she had in various stages of development with them.

As emotionally undone as Locke was during this time, and as fiercely as she pointed the finger at Clint for everything that had gone wrong in her life, she had no legitimate reason to believe that he had had anything to do with Warner's decision. Perhaps Warner dumped Locke because she had violated the industry-wide dictum against washing dirty laundry in public; if so, it was presumably a business decision, pure and simple. Business in Hollywood is a constant tightrope walk, attempting to balance art and commerce. In the years between her Academy Award nomination and *Impulse,* Locke's career had gone nowhere. She had not become a big star, and her films were never going to produce the kind of revenue Clint Eastwood's films had. In other words, she was expendable.

But, according to Locke, all of it was personal and connected, and all of it was due to Clint's furious need for vengeance. In her memoir she quotes Clint telling a friend, "Does she want to become a director or become Michelle Marvin? I'll drag her ass through court, until there's nothing left. I'll never settle with her; I paid her for jobs in movies, now she wants to be paid for love too?"

The postdeposition litigation was going nowhere, and meanwhile, Locke was racking up huge bills. Hoping to cut through it all, she simply picked up the phone and called Clint, asking if they could meet. Clint agreed, and the next day she came over to his office. She insists that Clint then started to flirt with her. In response, she asked him to drop his lawsuit. He exploded, insisting that she had started it, that if now she was desperate or broke, she should get a job as a waitress, and that he would accept a rapprochement, in which she also accepted returning to him as his lover, only "with no strings attached."*

Locke then wrote to Clint, hoping that the printed word would prevent his emotions from interfering with her attempt to settle. Clint's written reply to Locke was short and impersonal: "I owe you nothing."

Hoping to get a new start in Hollywood, Locke left the William Morris Agency and signed with agent David Gersh, who quickly got her a new deal at Orion Pictures for *Oh Baby*, a romantic comedy that she could easily direct.

She was all set to begin casting when she noticed a lump on her right breast. It proved malignant. That September of 1990, instead of beginning work on the new film, she entered the hospital for a double mastectomy.

In November, while she was still in the early stages of recuperation, producer Al Ruddy told her that he was willing to act as a go-between, to try to settle things between her and Clint before the start of the trial, scheduled for March 1991. Ruddy told her that Clint was willing to drop his lawsuit if she would drop hers; that Gordon could keep the house on Crescent Heights; and he would see to it that she got her development deals back at Warner. She would also receive $450,000 in cash if she gave up all future claims to Stradella Road and agreed never to sue him for anything again.

Locke was weary from her battles with Clint and her recent surgery; and her medical bills were piling up. Without thinking about why Clint would suddenly change his position and try to make peace, Locke accepted the offer.

---

*Clint has never commented on the meeting or even acknowledged that it took place.

It had taken two years to settle with Locke (and to settle another unrelated but nagging lawsuit that had erupted with a civilian over a car accident). Now Clint felt he was finally ready to make another movie, and he chose a western to do it with. It was a wise choice; westerns had always been good to him. He had, after all, begun his career with TV westerns and had made his big-screen breakthrough with westerns; now he would make his comeback in one, something called *Unforgiven*.

Clint had had the script under option for several years. Written by a relatively unknown screenwriter, it had stayed on the back burner until Clint could find someone other than himself who could better play the lead role (unlikely, as the part was perfectly suited for Clint), or (as he sometimes told interviewers after it opened, and which was far more likely) he felt he was old enough to credibly play the lead role. Even more revealing, perhaps, was what he told *Cahiers du cinéma* just before its European run:

Why a western? That seemed to be the only possible genre the story was calling for, because in fact everything grew out of the story. In any case, I've never thought of doing anything because it's *in fashion*, on the contrary I've always felt a need to go against it . . . as for what makes this Western different from the others, it seems to me that the film deals with violence and its consequences a lot more than those I've done before. In the past, there were a lot of people killed gratuitously in my pictures, and what I liked about this story was that people aren't killed, and acts of violence aren't perpetrated, without there being certain consequences. That's a problem I thought it was important to talk about today; it takes on proportions it didn't have in the past, even if it's always been present through the ages.

Unforgiven was the kind of story Clint could film in his sleep. Even before a single shot was filmed, he knew exactly how he wanted it to look.

Originally called *The Cut-Whore Killings*, the film's name was later changed to *The William Munny Killings*. Neither title Clint especially liked. *Unforgiven* was the brainchild of David Webb Peoples, a Berkeley English major who upon graduation worked as an editor in TV news, then moved on to documentary films. In 1981, with his wife, Janet, and Jon Else, he wrote and edited the documentary *The Day After Trinity*, about the development of the atomic bomb. Directed by Else, it was good enough to be nominated for an Academy Award for Best Documentary.

The film's success sent Peoples searching his desk drawers for anything he had that was immediately salable. There he found the screenplay he had written five years before *The Day After Trinity*, *The Cut-Whore Killings*. At the time it had gone nowhere, but now he was able to get it optioned.

Each time the film's option ran out, it got passed around for renewal. Eventually, via Megan Rose, it came to Clint, who read the script, liked it, and when it became available, bought it outright, and then put it in *his* drawer, waiting until the time felt right to make it.

It might very well have gotten made in 1985, as his elegiac summation and farewell to the genre that had launched his career, but then *Pale Rider* had come along and became that movie. Now, in search of something to push back the ever-louder industry rumors that he was washed up, Clint once more reached for his most dependable genre, the western, and produced, directed, and starred in *Unforgiven*. To ensure that the film was a big enough hit to return him to glory, he pulled out all the stops (or as many as he could bear without sending the budget skyrocketing).

In typical Clint fashion, the film was shot quickly and inexpensively, with very little done to the original script. According to Clint, "I started rewriting it and talked to David about it. I said I would like to do this, do that, write a couple of scenes . . . but the more I started fiddling with it, [the more I] realized I was disassembling a lot of blocks that were holding it together. I finally called him up one night and said, 'Forget about all those rewrites I was talking about. I like it just the way it is.' "

Set in fictitious Big Whiskey, Wyoming, the film was shot in Calgary, Alberta, using the best talent in the business to bring the town and the movie to life. At the head of this list was Henry Bumstead, who had last worked for Clint twenty years earlier on *High Plains Drifter* and who was still one of Hollywood's most sought-after production designers and art directors. Bumstead was probably best known to the public for his work on Robert Mulligan's *To Kill a Mockingbird* (1962), for which he won an Oscar,* and on Alfred Hitchcock's *The Man Who Knew Too Much* (1956) and *Vertigo* (1957).†

Mood was essential to *Unforgiven*, and Bumstead's work proved a key ingredient to help visualize the feeling that the vengeful living walk among the living dead, waiting for their turn at mythic immortality. It took Bumstead only a month and a day to build the entire set, on which Clint wanted every scene filmed, including interiors, to give the film a stylistic cohesion no ordinary soundstage could match.

Also for *Unforgiven*, Clint chose to work with other big-name stars, something he rarely did on Malpaso films. Morgan Freeman played Ned Logan, Munny's (Clint's) former partner in crime who joins him one last time to collect the reward money posted by the town prostitutes, led by Strawberry Alice (Frances Fisher, another real-life girlfriend of Clint's cast as a prostitute) for the capture of the men responsible for mutilation and murder of one of their own (Delilah, played by Anna Thomson), after Big Whiskey's corrupt and bullying sheriff, the fascistic Little Bill Daggett (Gene Hackman), let them go free. Several bounty-hunters are drawn to Big Whiskey hoping to collect the reward, including English Bob (Richard Harris) and his "biographer," W. W. Beauchamp (Saul Rubinek). The only lesser-known principal member of this cast besides Fisher was Jaimz Woolvett, who plays the Schofield Kid, a young gunslinger wannabe who longs to become the legend that Munny once was.

Several unexpected plot reversals give the film more irony and depth than any previous Clint Eastwood movie, while referencing many of them. Munny is a gunslinger of legendary proportions, who has renounced his murderous past and tried to make amends by going straight, marrying, having children, and raising pigs on a farm. Much of Munny's character and action has been developed and performed before the film begins (not unlike Shane, the cinematic model for *Pale Rider*'s Preacher). Munny sets out to collect the reward with the same sense of mission that was suggested in the Leone trilogy. In *Unforgiven*

---

*For Best Black and White Art Direction. He also won for Art Direction for George Roy Hill's *The Sting* (1973) and was nominated but did not win for *Vertigo*.

†Bumstead's career began in the 1940s. He died in 2006, following work on Clint's *Flags of Our Fathers* and *Letters from Iwo Jima*.

it is as if the Man with No Name has returned to gunfighting, older, weary, and repentant, because he needs the money to raise his children after his wife has died, but also because that's who he is, a gunfighter, a man whose destiny must be fulfilled. In that sense, the inevitable violent and horrific climax of *Unforgiven*, during which Munny avenges not just the murdered prostitute but also Ned Logan, killed by Daggett, is an elegant evocation of Heraclitus' well-known dictum about character and fate being one and the same. It is Munny's fate to kill Daggett because that is his character (much as it is Daggett's fate to be killed because that is his). In *Unforgiven*, as in several of the Dirty Harry movies (perhaps most vividly *Magnum Force*), justice may be evil but evil may be just.

And finally English Bob's biographer, W. W. Beauchamp, as played by Saul Rubinek, is so corrupt, cowardly, self-promoting, and unconcerned about truth (and unable to stand up for it) that history itself becomes suspect. Legend blends into fact when, in a coda, the audience is left to wonder what really happened to Munny. In a sense, Beauchamp represents for Clint all writers (biographers included) and probably none more so than film critics, who too often play loose and easy with movies and set up straw heroes and villains to knock down in the name of their own brilliance.

Other strings that run through the film are racism, sexism, and vainglory, all of which come together to one incredible climax that resolves, as do all the great westerns—and in a larger metaphorical sense, all great movies—in one of the most powerful gunfights ever filmed.

And it was all shot in less than a month.*

The pre-release buzz on this film was enormous from the start. The cast included two actors at the top of their respective games— Morgan Freeman, who had been nominated for Best Actor for Bruce Beresford's *Driving Miss Daisy* (1989), and Gene Hackman, who had won Best Actor for *The French Connection* (1972). Years before the script even came to Clint, Hackman had turned down the role of Munny. He'd also turned down the role of Daggett when Clint offered

---

*Ever actor-superstitious, Clint's talisman for this film was the boots he wore, the same ones he had worn for much of the making of *Rawhide*. In 2005 he loaned them to that year's Sergio Leone exhibit at the Gene Autry Museum of Western Heritage in Los Angeles, California.

it to him because he felt he was too violent and repulsive a character, until Clint somehow managed to convince him the film carried a strong antiviolence message. Richard Harris, an offbeat Irishman born in Limerick City, had hung around inside the Hollywood A-list long after his best movies were behind him; those who saw advance footage of his scenes said it was the performance of his career.

Because of all the good advance word, Warner volunteered to take over the film's promotion. Clint would normally have rejected the offer but this time readily agreed. Almost every previous Malpaso film had been promoted independently by Charles Gold and Kitty Dutton, whom Clint had hired, via Malpaso, during Warner's Frank Wells period, when he had little faith in the studio's ability to promote films. Now that Terry Semel and Bob Daley were in charge, the studio had become far more aggressive, and they convinced Clint they could do a better job than Malpaso on this one.

Several press junkets were arranged—Clint had been opposed to them before *Unforgiven*—and Richard Schickel, the film critic and documentary filmmaker, was allowed virtually unlimited access to produce a "making of the movie" promotional short. Jack Mathews of the *Los Angeles Times* was allowed aboard, as was Peter Biskind of the then relatively new and highly influential *Premiere* magazine, which had a *Rolling Stone* look and similarly hip style of reporting for movies. Numerous theatrical tie-ins and promotions, contests, and one-on-one interviews with Clint were arranged.* And something nobody thought they would ever see: Clint actually agreed to go on *The Tonight Show* to hawk the film.

The reason for all this atypical accessibility was not hard to understand. Clint still wanted to win an Academy Award. It was as simple as that. He would be sixty-two when the film came out, the fiftieth film that he had either appeared in, or directed, or both, and if it was ever going to happen, the time was now.

Unforgiven, dedicated to Sergio Leone and Don Siegel in its closing credits, opened August 7, 1992. August is a month where summer films that are not expected to do well are released; the best are given

---

*The interviews were nearly identical, and as always Clint's stock answers revealed little about himself. Questions were limited to the subject of the film.

the Memorial Day weekend slot, the next July Fourth, the also-rans after that. But with this film, the Daley-Semel strategy was to separate *Unforgiven* from the year's other big summer films that included Tim Burton's *Batman Returns* and Phillip Noyce's *Patriot Games* starring Harrison Ford, both of which opened before August.

The strategy paid off big time, with a $14 million opening weekend, Clint's best ever. Not only was his career resurrected, but suddenly he was the hottest actor *and* director in Hollywood. *Unforgiven* went on to gross $160 million in its initial domestic theatrical release and an additional $50 million overseas, placing it behind only Clint's two orangutan films as the highest grossers of his career to date.

That winter, when the Oscar nominations were announced, to no one's surprise, Clint and his film were prominent among them. *Unforgiven* was nominated for Best Picture, pitting Clint as producer against Neil Jordan's quirky, sexually ambiguous, highly original, and completely riveting *The Crying Game;* Rob Reiner's military courtroom drama *A Few Good Men,* which starred three of Hollywood's then-hottest stars, Jack Nicholson, Tom Cruise, and Demi Moore, and that carried the added imprimatur of having been a recent Broadway stage hit; James Ivory's *Howards End,* the obligatory prestige nomination that showed the world how literary Hollywood could be; and Martin Brest's bizarre *Scent of a Woman,* about a blind man who can really "see," starring Al Pacino as the "hoo-wa" man.

Clint was also nominated for Best Actor, a long-awaited first that put him up against Robert Downey Jr.'s facile Charlie in Richard Attenborough's windy biography *Chaplin;* Stephen Rea's affecting performance as an Irish subversive in *The Crying Game;* Denzel Washington in the title role of Spike Lee's *Malcolm X;* and Pacino.

He was also nominated for Best Director, against Robert Altman— for his inside-is-hell exposé of Hollywood amorality, *The Player*— Martin Brest, James Ivory, and Neil Jordan.

Other major nominations for *Unforgiven* included Best Supporting Actor for Gene Hackman, and Best Screenplay for Peoples.

On March 29, 1993, the night of the awards, a smiling, silver-haired Clint showed up resplendent in a tuxedo and tie, with a not-yet-showing pregnant Frances Fisher on his arm. The usual Academy dross that passes for humor and entertainment was kicked off by host

Billy Crystal being driven onstage in a chariot by Jack Palance, the unlikely winner of the previous year's Best Supporting Actor Oscar for Ron Underwood's *City Slickers*, thereby robbing himself and the ceremonies of any last shred of dignity.

The theme of the show was "Women in Film," and although memorable women's roles and performances were few that year, the appearance of Elizabeth Taylor and the presenting of a Jean Hersholt Award to the recently departed Audrey Hepburn sent an electric charge through the audience as the evening crawled toward the expected coronation of Clint Eastwood. One bump in the road came when the Best Actor Oscar went to Al Pacino, for one of the lesser performances of his career, not long after Gene Hackman had won for Best Supporting Actor. In a night that was a Vegas gambler's delight, always in danger of sidestepping the favorites, Clint braced himself.

Barbra Streisand, arguably the biggest female star in Hollywood, dressed resplendently in black, made the next presentation. "This award is for the Best Director," Streisand said, leaning slightly into the microphone, her bare shoulders glistening under the bright lights, "and it is my privilege to present it tonight." She dutifully read the names of the nominees and their films, while clips of them directing flashed across the screen. Clint's name was read last, and the visual showed him unshaven and looking into the viewfinder of a movie camera while slowly and steadily chewing gum. "And the Oscar goes to . . ." she said, opening the envelope, then breaking into a big smile as she nodded to Clint, sitting in the first row with Fisher, before saying, "Clint Eastwood!"

The audience erupted with its most enthusiastic response of the night, a rush of cheers and "yays" reaching above the happily clapping crowd. Just before he rose from his seat, Fisher gave Clint a quick kiss on the cheek. On the way to the stage, he stopped long enough to accept a handshake and congratulations from Attenborough. When he arrived at the podium and the cheering subsided, Clint made an off-the-cuff comment about his dry throat, the result of having to sit for so long waiting for the big moment. He wiped his lip and then began again. "I just want to . . . ," he said, then trailed off, looking at the Oscar in the tight grip of his right hand. "This is pretty good, this is all right." Then, laughing nervously, he continued his acceptance speech.

I've been, uh, I've been around for thirty-nine years and I've really enjoyed it. I've been very lucky . . . I heard Al [Pacino, winner of Best Actor] say he's lucky but everybody feels that way . . . when you're able to make a living in a profession that you really enjoy. That's an opportunity I think a lot of people don't have. I've got to thank the crew, and David Valdez [the film's executive producer], and Jack Green [director of photography], and all the camera crew . . . the trouble is with living this long you know so many people but you can't remember their names.

As Clint turned his head in mock confusion, good-natured titters rippled through the audience. Then he smiled.

You get a little flustered. So, but in the "Year of the Woman" I'd like to salute the women of Big Whiskey, that would be Anna Thomson, Frances Fisher, and Lisa and Tyra and Josie and Beverly and all the gals who really were the catalyst to getting this story off the ground, and David Peoples' fabulous script, the Warner Bros. for sticking with this film, the film critics for discovering this film—it wasn't a highly touted film when it came out—but they sort of stayed with it throughout the year, the French film critics who embraced some of my work very early in the game, the British Film Institute and the Museum of Modern Art, and some of the people who were there long before I became fashionable. Lenny Hirshan, my agent . . . I'm leaving out a whole bunch of people I'm going to regret when I sit down again, so, anyway, thank you very much.

With that, Clint raised the Oscar and waved it to the crowd, before leaving the stage to more thunderous applause.

Only to return a few moments later when a smirking Jack Nicholson read off the names of the nominees for Best Picture as if they were a private joke and then opened the envelope and calmly announced Clint's name. Once again enthusiastic applause filled the room, and this time Clint was ready with the names of those he'd failed to thank in his earlier speech, including Warner publicists Joe Hyams and Marco Barla, studio executives Terry Semel and Bob Daley, and "the whole executive strata" at Warner. He also paid special tribute to former Warner chief Steve Ross, who had died the previous year from prostate cancer, and who had been one of Clint's strongest supporters at the studio. And then, pausing and in a soft voice, Clint said, "In the Year of the Woman, the greatest woman on the planet is here tonight, and that's my mother, Ruth." The cameras quickly found her in the audience, eighty-four years old and looking quite robust, smiling with pride over her son's success.

It was a night of triumph for Clint and his film, which walked off with four Oscars, two for him, one for Hackman, and one for Joel Cox for Best Editor.

After dutifully, if briefly, attending all the official celebrations, including the obligatory Governor's Ball, Clint took a couple of close friends and Fisher to Nicky Blair's restaurant. Blair had been one of the Universal contract actors Clint had met during his early days who remained a friend and who also happened to be a talented chef. In those days he'd often made meals for all his out-of-work buddies, including Clint. He had since become a well-known restaurateur on Hollywood's Sunset Strip. Clint partied there with Fisher and his friends until dawn.

Asked by a reporter the next day how he felt, Clint replied, "Tired."

At sixty-two years of age, Clint had reached the peak of his career. A tottering John Wayne had been that old twenty-three years earlier when he won his only Oscar for his twilight-years performance in Henry Hathaway's *True Grit*. Clint felt not only redeemed but reinvigorated, and within days of his double Oscar win he was ready to begin work on a new film, *In the Line of Fire*. He was set to embrace the future, unencumbered at last by the limitations of his past, believing all the old scores in the game called Hollywood had finally been settled.

Until Sondra Locke reemerged, more determined than ever to settle her own score with him.

TWENTY

My feelings [about Sondra Locke] were the normal feelings you have when someone has been planning for many months to assault your children's inheritance.

—Clint Eastwood

$\blacktriangleright$ondra Locke's very existence was a recurring nightmare for Clint. Every time he thought she was out of his life, she returned, and every time the bad dream got a little worse.

In December 1990 Locke had finalized the details of her lawsuit against Clint, and before the start of the traditional Christmas break, when the entire industry disappears from town until after New Year's, she had moved into her new offices at Warner, per her settlement deal with Clint. She pored over scripts in search of a new project to develop, eager to get something going because *Oh Baby* had collapsed due to Orion's lapse into bankruptcy.

Knowing that Arnold Schwarzenegger had shown some interest in playing the lead, Locke figured it was a no-brainer to walk it over to Warner. She confidently pitched it to Terry Semel and Tom Lassally, together with a shooting script and Schwarzenegger's interest.

Semel and Lassally passed.*

Every day for the next three years Locke, with her $1.5 million development deal still in place, went to her office at Warner, searched for scripts, and tried to interest Terry Semel, Bob Daley, or Lucy Fisher in a project, or even to get the okay to direct one of the hundreds of scripts that were earmarked for future production by the studio. But there was nothing for her. Nothing. *Nada.*

Meanwhile Clint began work on his next film, *In the Line of Fire*, for Columbia. It was his first film for a studio other than Warner since 1979, when he had made *Escape from Alcatraz* at Paramount. Perhaps he felt that after all that had gone on, a change of corporate scenery might be good for both him and Warner Bros.

---

*According to Locke, in her memoir, once the deal was dead, Schwarzenegger took the concept to Ivan Reitman, who eventually made a reworked version of it without her into *Junior,* starring Schwarzenegger and Danny DeVito.

For this film Clint took a (relative) backseat to director Wolfgang Petersen (best known for *Das Boot* and personally chosen by Clint, who maintained directorial approval). Clint plays a retired Secret Service agent who was present at John F. Kennedy's assassination and is called back to duty to prevent an attempt on the new president's life. The film costars a slew of midlevel stars, including John Malkovich and Rene Russo.

One likely reason Clint wanted to take it easy was the outsize success of *Unforgiven*. More often than not in Hollywood, when a film wins that many Academy Awards, the director and the star do not immediately try to compete with their previous success. The next film they make is unlikely to be as successful, and they often prefer to do another film or two before their next "big" film.

Finally, if anyone deserved to take it a bit easier, it was Clint. At sixty-three years old, kicking back for one film and "only" acting in it was completely understandable.

So naturally *In the Line of Fire* became the highest-grossing film of Clint's career to date, taking in over $200 million in its initial domestic release and twice that overseas. Yet it was an ordinary film with a decidedly nonsuspenseful plot that some critics dubbed "Dirty Harry Goes to Washington," and the cast had no single star other than Clint who ever attracted anything near those kinds of numbers. The only logical explanation for the film's success was the tremendous drawing power of Clint Eastwood, once more the most popular movie star in the world.

In 1993, the third and final year of her contract at Warner, Locke was doing postproduction on a TV movie she had taken on, *Death in Small Doses*. She hoped it would be the icebreaker that would bring her back to features. While sitting in her office, she received a phone call from, of all people, Clint—she hadn't spoken to him or had any contact at all with him in years. This was just weeks before the big Academy Awards night, Clint and *Unforgiven* were the big favorites, and with all the promotion he was doing, his was about the last voice on earth she expected to hear in the receiver.

Their conversation was short and sweet and completely puzzling to Locke, even more so when Clint told her he was happy she had a movie and would love to see a rough-cut cassette when it was finished.

With Eric Fleming

With the cast of Rawhide, *left to right:*
Sheb Wooley, Paul Brinegar, Clint,
Eric Fleming

U.S. movie poster for For a Few Dollars More, *1965*

Italian movie poster for For a Few Dollars More, *1965*

The Witches, *1967*

Hang 'Em High, *1968*

Mexican movie poster for Hang 'Em High

Coogan's Bluff, *1968*

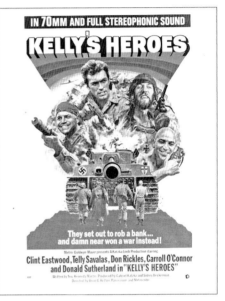

Kelly's Heroes, *1970*

The Beguiled, *1971*

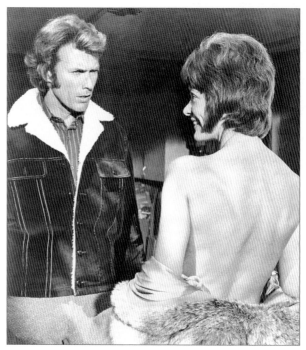

With Jessica Walter, Play Misty for Me, *1971*

With director Don Siegel on the set of Dirty Harry, *1971*

Dirty Harry, *1971*

In his iconic role as Inspector Harry Callahan

Magnum Force, *1973*

Where Eagles Dare, *1968*

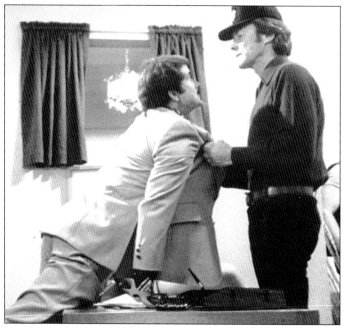

The Enforcer, *1976*

With Sondra Locke, The Gauntlet, *1977*

Every Which Way but Loose, *1978*

With his and Maggie's two children, Kyle and Alison, on the set of Star Trek, *late 1970s.*

Escape from Alcatraz, *1979*

With Sondra Locke,
Bronco Billy, *1980*

Clint bolstered the soundtrack of Bronco Billy *with country music produced by Snuff Garrett (right) and sang a duet with Merle Haggard (left) that hit number one on the country charts.*

Any Which Way You Can, *1980*

With Verna Bloom, Honkytonk Man, *1982*

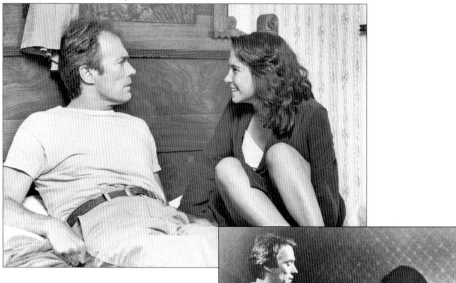

With Geneviève Bujold,
Tightrope, *1984*

Behind the camera in the mid-1980s

Heartbreak Ridge, *1986*

*Directing Forest Whitaker as Charlie Parker (left)
and Samuel E. Wright as Dizzy Gillespie (right)
on the set of* Bird, *1988*

White Hunter, Black Heart, *1990*

With Sonia Braga, The Rookie, *1990*

Unforgiven, *1992*

Celebrating his double Oscar win for Unforgiven *at the 1992 Academy Awards with Gene Hackman, who also won for Best Supporting Actor in the film.*

With Laura Dern, A Perfect World, *1993*

Firefox, *1982*

Gran Torino, *2008*

With that he hung up, leaving her bewildered. Kindness was not a part of Clint's personality she was that familiar with, especially after all the legal ugliness they had put each other through.*

Not long after Clint's grand night at the Oscars, Locke learned from mutual friends that Fisher was pregnant and had been for several months, although she had not been showing the night of the Awards telecast. Could that possibly have had anything to do with Clint's phone call? But trying to figure out his motivations, she knew, was like trying to solve Rubik's Cube.

Sensing something was not right but having no clue what it was, Locke tried to find out what was going on. In her office she reached for the phone and direct-dialed Clint's office. According to her, when Clint picked up, this was what she said: "I don't know what's going on, Clint, but something's not right with Warners and my deal. Nothing at all has come together here. I mean, I hope that they aren't still uncomfortable about our split-up. I would hate to think that's what's been going on." Not hearing anything on the other end, she continued: "Look, I have a script now which has a lot of potential. I've submitted it to one executive who likes it, but hasn't been able to get it past his boss, Bruce Berman. If you read it and like it, would you step in on my behalf? After all, the deal was I'd make some films here. And if you don't like it, I'd like to hear where you think I'm off-target."

Clint's response, according to Locke, was to quickly agree to look at the script and to remind her that he still wanted to see a cassette of her TV movie. That last suggestion sent up a flag for Locke. Clint seemed a little too interested in that movie. Was he afraid it was some kind of exposé, something personal and revealing about their time together? Three weeks later she called him again, and she brought up the script, and he promised to see if he could get Warner to green-light it.

Despite the two phone calls, nothing happened with the script, but

---

*Clint was no stranger to litigation. As early as 1984 he sued the *National Enquirer* over an article that had linked him romantically with Tanya Tucker. He asked for $10 million and settled out of court. He sued them again in 1994 over their publication of a so-called exclusive interview, and won $150,000 in 1995 that was held up on appeal in 1997. He donated it to a charity (which he did not name). His legal team was awarded $650,000 for legal fees.

weird things continued to happen with her other potential projects. Lance Young, a former Paramount producer who had moved to Warner, wanted to hire Locke to direct a movie there. A friend who knew Young from Paramount told Locke that he had been told Warner would not work with her because she was "Clint's deal."

"Clint's deal." What could that possibly mean? Exasperated and confused, Locke changed agents again, this time signing with International Creative Management (ICM) to try once more to jump-start her career. She brought up her Warner "deal" with them. They looked into the situation and reported back to her that Warner was simply not going to make a film with her. Any film.

Early in 1994 Locke retained counsel with the intent to sue Warner Bros. for breach of contract. Her hope was that Warner would extend her contract by one year and give her at least one film that would fulfill the conditions of her signing off on her lawsuit against Clint. One film, she felt, was all she needed to regain her career momentum.

The response from Warner to Locke's counsel was swift and direct. According to Locke, Terry Semel and Bob Daley made an insulting offer for her just to go away: "We have no interest in making any *real* deal with Sondra. We can give her a twenty-five-thousand-dollar settlement for her trouble, but that's it." Locke said no, moved out of her office at Warner, and necessarily changed lawyers because of her increasingly precarious financial condition. She acquired the services of Peggy Garrity, who, after reviewing all the facts involved, agreed to handle the case that Locke wanted to bring against both Clint and Warner on a contingency basis.

Winning a lawsuit against Warner was not going to be easy. Few witnesses would be willing to come forward and testify; for anyone looking ever to work again in Hollywood, it would be a career-ending move. Warner's initial reaction to the filing of Locke's suit was to shrug it off, claiming they simply had not been able to find anything for her; nor had she brought them anything that they felt was up to the studio's extremely high standards. But they *had* given her a parking spot on the studio and a free turkey every Thanksgiving, proof of their good intentions, they said.

For the rest of 1994 and 1995 and through the summer of 1996, Locke, via David-like Garrity, took on Warner's legal representation, the Goliath-like O'Melveny & Myers. Depositions were taken, during which Warner steadfastly maintained they had done nothing wrong. Not long afterward Garrity, sensing this was less a breach-of-contract case than one of actual fraud, a far more serious charge, urged Locke to add Clint to the lawsuit.* Locke agreed, Garrity filed, and in Locke's words from her memoir, Warner "went ballistic and mounted a massive campaign to keep Clint out of the lawsuit."

To Locke's shock and dismay, the motion to add Clint was denied.

Garrity then asked Warner Bros., as part of discovery, for a copy of the final cost runs for Locke's studio deal—everything that had been charged against her account in the entire three years. It was not an unusual request in these types of lawsuits. In order to find out how the studio would prepare its financial counterclaim, Locke needed to know how much money and service value Warner had advanced to her and her staff during that period.

Warner's documents revealed debits totaling $975,000, not all that unusual for a three-year period. But what surely wasn't normal operating procedure was that the entire amount had been transferred from Locke's account at Warner to Clint's, specifically folded into the overall budget and outlay production costs of *Unforgiven*. At first this was puzzling to Locke, as she had had absolutely nothing to do with any aspect of the production of that film. Then it hit her—Clint, she realized, was secretly paying the tab for her Warner deal. Only her Warner deal didn't really exist, at least not according to the papers Warner had given over to discovery. Locke now believed that Clint must have set up a secret, false, sham deal with Warner, where it would look like Locke had a deal there but really didn't. The whole thing was to be paid for by Clint, via *Unforgiven*, which meant that not a cent of the $975,000 actually came out of his own pockets. He had set it up in order to induce her to sign off on her original lawsuit for a relatively small amount, with the carrot-dangling promise of a deal at the studio to get her to settle.

The ramifications ran deep. If Clint had, in fact, charged that money to *Unforgiven*, then anyone else who had a profit-based deal connected to the film had also been defrauded by Clint and/or Malpaso, because the net profits of *Unforgiven* were based on all production costs and distribution and advertising expenses subtracted from the film's gross.

*This was a civil lawsuit. Only the state can bring criminal charges.

That could mean criminal charges somewhere down the line, and dozens of complicated and dangerous lawsuits both for the studio and for Clint.

Warner's first response was that that simply wasn't the case, because the money had come not from Warner or Malpaso but from his personal account. Garrity didn't think so, at least not according to the documents.

At that point, more depositions were scheduled, but Clint refused his subpoena and ordered Malpaso to also refuse any subpoenas Garrity tried to serve on him. Warner then asked the court for an immediate judgment to remove them from the case without a trial. Such summary judgments are usually requested when one side or the other believes the case has no merit, or the evidence is insufficient and doesn't merit a full trial. It is always a risk, because losing it usually indicates the judge believes the other side has a good enough case to bring. Asking for a summary judgment is like betting everything on red or black at a roulette table. This time the chips came down on Warner's side.

Devastated, Locke only had two choices left: to appeal the court's decision, which in a summary judgment is difficult, costly, time-consuming, and rarely successful; or to start a new lawsuit only against Clint for fraud. In other words, to start all over again, eliminating the studio from any further legal claims she had against them.

She did both.

This time Garrity filed the lawsuit in downtown Los Angeles, rather than in Burbank, where the first lawsuit had been filed. Burbank, she and Garrity felt, was just too close to Warner's power center. That would make it even more difficult to find an objective jury, as everyone in Burbank was connected one way or another to the film business, the primary reason people lived in this otherwise nondescript, hot, humid, and isolated community. Now, Garrity decided, distance was their best defense.

Without bothering to notify Garrity, Ray Fisher, Clint's attorney, responded by petitioning to have the case remain in Burbank. He succeeded and it was assigned to a different judge from the one who had heard and granted the summary judgment on the Warner case.

On the first day of trial, September 9, 1996, Fisher moved for dismissal for "nonsuit," which is similar to summary judgment; Fisher insisted Locke had no case and wanted the judge to concur. The judge took the motion under advisement and, for the moment at least, let the case continue.

After opening statements, Locke and Garrity starting putting their witnesses on the stand. The first was Terry Semel, who, under direct examination by Garrity, shaped his answers to suggest that Warner had indeed been willing to do business with Locke during the three years she was under contract, but that nothing she brought to them they considered filmable. Garrity then sharpened her focus and asked Semel if he was aware of Clint's "secret indemnity," as she put it. Semel agreed that "I would assume that at the end of the day that his intentions were to underwrite the losses." Garrity asked him when "the end of the day" was. Semel said that he guessed it was when the terms of the arrangement—the three-year contract—had ended.

No further questions.

The next day Locke took the stand, and Garrity led her through a detailed recapitulation of the terms of her original settlement and everything that had happened—or not happened—in the three years she was at Warner. That evening, as Locke left the courthouse, she was intercepted by Kevin Marks, Clint's full-time personal attorney, who had attended the trial. Earlier that day, on the way into the courthouse's parking lot, Locke had been in a car accident, smashing her front end. Marks just wanted to tell her that he had seen the whole thing and was willing to testify in her defense when she sued the other driver.

The next day Locke was cross-examined by Fisher, who went over the terms of the first lawsuit settlement, emphasizing along the way, no doubt for the jury's sake, the fact that all the while Locke was seeing Clint, she had been married to another man.

After a few more witnesses it was Garrity's time to put Clint on the stand. He was going to have to answer all of Garrity's questions under oath. She was swift and to the point, focusing in on what she thought was the most essential aspect of the case. Taking a deep breath and exhaling, she asked Clint if he had entered into an agreement with Locke in 1990 to settle her lawsuit against him.

In a soft and steady voice, he said he had. He then also admitted that he had made a separate agreement with Warner Bros. to indemnify them for all of Locke's expenses during the three years of her contract with them; that he had not told Locke of the arrangement; and that he had not offered Locke any type of similar deal during that period with Malpaso. That was it. Garrity was finished with him, and he was dismissed from the witness stand.

After a few more days and several other witnesses, Garrity rested and Clint's defense took over. Soon it was Clint's turn to take the stand in his own defense. He was upbeat and expansive as Fisher led him through his testimony. Then Fisher got to Clint's relationship with Locke.

FISHER: What was your opinion of Ms. Locke once the 1989 lawsuit was settled?

CLINT: My feelings were the normal feelings you have when someone has been planning for many months to assault your children's inheritance . . . Well, you know, I didn't feel very good about it, I must say . . .

Clint went on to express his dismay and his feeling that he was suffering from "social extortion."

After a few minor disruptions—a reporter had smuggled a camera into the courtroom—and several objections from Garrity, Fisher asked Clint if he had had any intention to commit fraud. Clint said no, adding that it would make no sense for him to use his influence to prevent Locke from getting work at Warner because, according to his deal, he would have to pay for her contract if she didn't earn any money. He then insisted that despite his best efforts, it was Warner, not he, that chose not to green-light Locke's various proposals.

During cross-examination Garrity tried to get Clint to admit that he had tapped Locke's phones, something Locke had long suspected, which Clint denied. She then went over the terms of his indemnification deal regarding Locke, which Clint corrected, reminding her and the court that his deal had been with Warner, to indemnify them, not with Locke.

When Garrity let Clint off the stand, Fisher, who had vehemently objected to several of Garrity's questions, moved for a mistrial. The jury was removed, and Fisher insisted the jury should not have heard any testimony about wiretaps. The motion was denied, and with the jury still out, the judge broke for lunch.

Among the defense's final witnesses was Tom Lassally, who admitted under cross-examination that Clint had never talked to him about any of Locke's proposed projects.

Final arguments began September 19, 1996. Garrity crisply summed up the case, as she saw it, finishing in less than a half hour. It was then Fisher's turn. He worked slowly and methodically, taking several hours to work his way through his version of the facts of the case and why it should be decided in Clint's favor. As he came to the conclusion of his summation, he made what sounded like a very solid point—the crux of his argument—that Clint had been under no legal obligation to tell Locke about his indemnification of Warner; that it was a completely separate deal totally unrelated to the terms of her settlement with him.

When Fisher finished, the judge instructed the jury and sent them out to decide the case. After three days of deliberation, the jury asked for a definition of "legal" as it pertained to whether Clint was under a "legal" obligation to inform Locke of his indemnification deal with Warner.

The next day, a Saturday, Garrity called Locke to tell her that she had just received a call from Fisher, who said he wanted to talk over the possibility of a settlement. At this point Locke was adamant; she didn't want to settle. This had been a long and difficult battle for her, and she was determined to see it through. When Garrity conveyed Locke's decision to Fisher, he pressed Garrity to prevail upon her client to reconsider. He stressed that a verdict was certain to damage at least one and possibly both of their clients' careers, and that no one can ever be sure what a jury will do.

Locke talked again with Garrity and took her suggestion to at least think it over. The next day Locke agreed to listen to Clint's offer. Fisher delivered it, and after deliberating once more with Garrity, she decided to accept. The only condition imposed by Clint was that the amount of money not be revealed to anyone. Locke agreed. The announcement that the case had settled brought a slew of reporters to the courthouse steps and interviews with several of the released jurors, all of whom claimed that they had already decided in favor of Locke, and that the penalty for Clint would have been in the millions.

A few days later Fisher first threatened to withhold the money and then wanted papers signed; Garrity ignored the first and refused the second. After much grumbling, Fisher personally handed over the check, and Clint's involvement with Locke was finally over, leaving Locke a little richer, Clint a little poorer. Both of them, after their fourteen-year romantic and six-year litigious relationship, appeared to be finally and forever free of each other.*

Although he almost never talked about his relationship with Locke after that, he did at least one time, to *Playboy*, during an interview he gave in 1997:

> I guess maybe I'm the only one who finds it weird that she's still obsessed with our relationship and putting out the same old rhetoric almost ten years later. There are two sides to this whole thing . . . she's been married for 29 years, but nobody puts that in their stories. As far as the legal action goes, it was my fault. I have to take full responsibility because I thought I was doing her a favor by helping her get a production arrangement with Warner Bros. I prevailed upon Warner Bros. to do it and it didn't work out. So she sued Warner and then she sued me and finally at some point I said, wait a second, I would have been better off if I hadn't done anything and had let her go ahead and file the palimony suit against me. I tried to help. I thought she would

---

*Several sources list the settlement of the fraud case against Clint—the second lawsuit—as 1999. In fact, it was settled in 1996. Locke's autobiography, which includes details of the settlement (but not the amount), was published in 1997. In it she discussed the case at length. Clint's only public comment was to *Playboy* in March 1997, when he told interviewer Bernard Weinraub that Locke played the victim very well. He indicated that he believed her history of cancer had made her more sympathetic to the jury. Although the terms of the settlement have never been disclosed, it was rumored to have been between $10 million and $30 million. (Some sources report the figure to be closer to $7 million.) After the settlement, Locke directed one more movie and appeared in two others. Her last known assignment in Hollywood was in 1999. She still lives there, for more than a decade now with Scott Cunneen, a director of surgery at Cedars Sinai Hospital in Los Angeles. Finally, in 1999, Locke sued Warner (but not Clint) yet again, this time for collusion, and won yet another out-of-court settlement with another undisclosed financial amount and a new production deal that has not yet resulted in any new films.

get directing assignments, but it didn't work out that way . . . I should have known that it would come back to haunt me . . . but you go on with your business. I'm going on with my life, and if other people can't get on with theirs, that's their problem.

Clint was not present for the handing over of his settlement check, leaving that to Fisher. Free at last from his tar-baby relationship with Locke, he took the next logical step in the never-ending drama of his own real life.

He became a father again, for the seventh time. And he got married again, for only the second time, to the baby's mother, who was thirty-five years his junior and three years younger than his firstborn, Kyle.

TWENTY-ONE

*If I start intruding and getting fancy and trying to dazzle people
with whatever tricks I may or may not have as a director, I'm
tampering with something . . . I revere the performances and I
don't want people to visualize a camera and a camera operator and
a guy with a focus-thing, and another person there . . . I just want
people to visualize the movie, so I keep things as subtle as I can, at
the same time punctuating the points I need to punctuate.*

—Clint Eastwood

On August 7, 1993, Clint quietly became a father for the sixth time when Frances Fisher gave birth to a baby girl they named Francesca Fisher. He had already begun to emotionally pull away from Frances. One reason may have been a souring on the notion of romance by his endless battles with former lover Locke. More likely, though, the cause was the arrival in his life of Dina Ruiz, who would eventually become the second Mrs. Eastwood.

Ruiz, born and raised in California of African-American and Japanese descent on her father's side and Irish, English, and German on her mother's, first crossed paths with Clint in April 1993, when she interviewed him about his recent Oscar triumph for KSBW, the NBC TV affiliate in Salinas. Having graduated from San Francisco State in 1989 and apprenticed with KNAZ, a small station in Flagstaff, Arizona, Ruiz had landed the job at KSBW, and one of her first assignments was to interview Clint Eastwood.

The first piece went so well, Ruiz asked Clint to answer more questions so she might expand it into two or three parts. The two met several times more, and the interviews show clearly that Ruiz, twenty-eight years old, and Clint, sixty-three, had very good chemistry. Ruiz readily admitted to Clint that she had seen few of his movies ("zero" was the number she used) and was in love with her boyfriend. However, even though Clint was about to become a father again, this time with Frances Fisher, the two agreed to stay in touch, which Clint normally did not do with reporters.

Ruiz and Clint met again in mid-1994, just after Clint finished *A Perfect World*, which starred Kevin Costner, who was still hot off the 1990 Academy Award–winning *Dances with Wolves*.* Costner had continued to appear in big, successful movies—Kevin Reynolds's *Robin*

---

*Costner also co-produced (with Jim Wilson) and directed *Dances with Wolves*. He took

Hood: Prince of Thieves (1991), Oliver Stone's *JFK* (1991), and Mick Jackson's *The Bodyguard* (1992)—that had made him one of the biggest stars in Hollywood for the first half of the 1990s. When Costner approached Clint about the possibility of directing *A Perfect World*, Clint read the script and was attracted to the plot's familiar escaped-convict tropes, especially the relationship between the pursued, Butch Haynes (Costner) and his pursuer, Red Garnett. Clint said yes, if he could play Garnett and, of course, produce it through Malpaso.

Filming on location in Martindale, Texas, proved more difficult than Clint had anticipated. His hurry-up directorial style clashed with Costner's snail's-pace multiple-take perfectionism. (During the making of *Dances with Wolves* more than one participant had complained, off the record, that the endless retakes had driven everyone crazy.) According to one story, Costner angrily walked off the set during a shoot, and Clint used Costner's stand-in to finish shooting. Afterward, when Costner complained, Clint told him that as far as he was concerned, he could take a walk off the set or off the film—either way was fine with him. Costner did no more complaining after that, and the film was finished without further incident. It opened on Thanksgiving weekend, becoming one of Warner's big fall releases of 1993; it grossed $30 million in its initial theatrical release and more than $100 million worldwide.

In 1994, after the arrival of little Francesca, Clint finished a showcase film for Fisher's talents that he had produced but not appeared in, for Malpaso (only the third time this had happened so far in Malpaso's twenty-seven-year career—*Ratboy* [from which he eventually detached himself] and *Bird* were the other two films). *The Stars Fell on Henrietta*, an early-America oil drama starring Robert Duvall, Aidan Quinn, and Fisher, would not get released until fall 1995. It came and went quickly and without much notice, or any special effort by Clint to promote it.

Before it even opened, Clint was off on another project, one that had been brewing for a long time and promised to be even bigger than *Unforgiven*, with a role that just might deliver to him the one

---

home Oscars both for Best Director and Best Picture. The film won seven out of the twelve Oscars for which it was nominated.

Oscar he still didn't have, and perhaps the one he wanted most, Best Actor.

As early as 1992, Steven Spielberg had approached Clint about starring in the film version of Robert James Waller's hugely popular 1992 novel *The Bridges of Madison County*, which Spielberg himself intended to produce and direct. At the time Clint was busy making *Unforgiven*, and Spielberg was fully and emotionally absorbed in his wrenching production of *Schindler's List*, but they agreed to talk again after their respective films had opened.

Spielberg and Clint were not strangers. They had met and worked together in 1985, when Clint directed that episode of Spielberg's TV series, *Amazing Stories*, called "Vanessa in the Garden," featuring Sondra Locke. While the series and Clint's episode were quickly forgotten, his friendship with Spielberg remained. The two had wanted to work together on a feature ever since, and six years later Spielberg's production company, Amblin, obtained the prepublication rights to Waller's novel, which would go on to sell ten million copies.

The Bridges of Madison County is essentially a modernized version of Noël Coward's one-act play *Still Life*, which he turned into a screenplay in 1945; it became David Lean's *Brief Encounter*, set in London, about the desperation, guilt, and temptations of two married people who meet, fall in love, commit adultery, and then separate forever. In *The Bridges of Madison County*, Robert Kincaid, a roaming, rootless photographer, passes through Madison County on a photographic assignment and has a brief but intense love affair with a lonely and unhappily married woman before traveling on. ("The bridges" refer both to the physical structures of the county and to the emotional bonds between the two.) Spielberg approached Clint about the possibility of playing Kincaid.

Clint, who saw in the role a chance to once more display his best persona, that of the quintessential loner, quickly agreed. But when *Schindler's List* proved a more difficult shoot than Spielberg had anticipated, he approached Sidney Pollack about directing *The Bridges of Madison County*. Pollack in turn wanted Robert Redford to play Kincaid. Both Pollack and Redford eventually fell away, after which several big names were considered. Finally, to direct it, Spielberg signed Bruce Beresford, best known for *Driving Miss Daisy*, which had won the Best Picture Oscar for 1989. Not long afterward Clint signed on to play Kincaid, but he wanted to co-produce it as well, with Spielberg, as an Amblin-Warner-Malpaso co-production.* Spielberg, who had always wanted Clint for the lead, following Clint's winning the Oscar for *Unforgiven*, quickly agreed, and production was set to begin late in the summer of 1994.

Clint, however, was still unsatisfied with the script, and, in an unusual move for him, not only wanted it rewritten, but wanted to do it himself with Spielberg, even though they were on opposite sides of the country and neither especially wanted to travel to work with the other.

> The three or four different versions of the screenplay they had were all over the place, and one or two of them changed the storyline completely. That didn't seem adequate so Steven and I rewrote it ourselves. He was back east at the time, in the Hamptons for the summer, and I was up in Northern California at Mount Shasta, so we wrote it by fax machine. I'd dictate some pages and then fax them to him, then he'd make some changes and fax them to me. We did this for about a week and then we agreed, this was the screenplay.

But even before the cameras were set to roll, Clint and Beresford clashed over the casting of the crucial female lead. Beresford, an Australian, had a vision of the film that directly conflicted with Clint's, over who should play the crucial role of the lonely, frustrated, and sexually available Francesca. Beresford had preferred two Swedish-born actresses for the role, Lena Olin, best known in America for her performance in Philip Kaufman's *The Unbearable Lightness of Being* (1988), and Pernilla August, a Swedish star virtually unknown in the States. Neither appealed to Clint, who had final say in casting, and insisted the role had to be played by an American—that was the whole point

---

*The film was a Warner-Malpaso-Amblin co-production, produced by Clint and distributed by Warner, whose book division had published the original novel and the paperback tie-in and was thrilled to have its biggest star, still hot from his double Oscar win, to helm the picture. Warner also released the film's sound track, which included several standard jazz compositions and the original theme song "Doe Eyes," aka the love theme from *The Bridges of Madison County.* The album remained at the top of the jazz charts for months and hovered near the top for years. During this time Clint formed Malpaso Records, which, like the film's sound-track album, would prove very profitable for both him and Warner. "Doe Eyes" was Clint's nickname for Ruiz.

of the movie as far as he was concerned (despite the fact that in the novel Francesca is Italian). Beresford offered up Isabella Rossellini as his compromise, Ingrid Berman's model-actress daughter, who was very popular in America but had a decidedly Swedish accent. Clint said no to her as well. Two weeks before the film's scheduled August 1994 start, Beresford was out and Clint took over as director, with Meryl Streep set to star opposite him. (Fisher had pressured Clint unsuccessfully to cast her in the role.)

Clint was adamant about casting Streep, although at first she turned the role down, saying she didn't like the book. According to sources, she was offended that Beresford had not first offered her the role. Everyone who read the book assumed she was going to play Francesca Johnson, rather like the national mandate that erupted, demanding that Clark Gable play Rhett Butler, when Margaret Mitchell's *Gone with the Wind* was first published. She demanded $4 million and a percentage of the profits, something that was normally anathema to producer Clint; but he wanted her so badly that he, Spielberg, and Warner all agreed to her terms, and she came aboard. Clint had wanted Streep for several reasons, not the least being the age factor. He thought Francesca should be a few years older than she was in the book, so the age discrepancy between her and Clint's Kincaid wouldn't be as noticeable on-screen. Meryl Streep was forty-five years old; Clint was sixty-four.

Production started the second week of August, on location in Des Moines, amid unfounded rumors that Streep and Clint were having an affair; the speculation was fueled when Clint discouraged Fisher from coming to visit him on location. But to Streep, it was all business. She had an interesting take on Clint's abilities as a director: "The reason he can direct himself and a film and take himself outside of it and put himself inside is I think he views himself at a distance." The notion of separating one from one's self was a variation on the loner concept and also a convenient way of excusing one's own behavior by blaming the other self for anything that shouldn't have happened.

Those on set may have correctly sensed that Clint and Fisher were over, but it wasn't Streep Clint was now interested in. It was Ruiz. By the time the film opened, Fisher had moved out of Clint's house on Stradella—the same one that Locke had lived in for so many years— and Clint was openly dating Dina Ruiz.

Just as the film was wrapping, Warner began a massive PR campaign to get Clint named as the recipient of the 1995 Irving J. Thalberg Award, given out annually at the Oscars ceremony to honor a producer's overall body of work. The award is named after the legendary 1930s MGM producer who is credited with elevating that studio's artistic level and Hollywood films as a whole. Thalberg was unusually modest—he never took an on-screen credit, which is one reason producing is said to be the least visual aspect of modern filmmaking. To Warner, the announcement by the Academy shortly before the annual gala that Clint was to be that year's recipient provided the perfect synergistic run-up to *The Bridges of Madison County*. Planned for release in June 1995, it would surely be one of that summer's biggest movies.

The Academy Awards ceremony took place on March 27 at the Shrine Auditorium in Los Angeles. For the glittering occasion Clint was accompanied only by his eighty-six-year-old mother—in Hollywood, a clear signal that his relationship with Frances Fisher was over. When it came time for the Thalberg Award presentation, Clint was introduced with a compilation of scenes from his movies put together by Richard Schickel, and then, when the lights came up, Arnold Schwarzenegger brought him onto the stage. After a solid ovation, Clint acknowledged the fabulous history of the Academy Awards and thanked Darryl F. Zanuck, Hal Wallis, William Wyler, Billy Wilder, and Alfred Hitchcock, "the people I grew up idolizing." The tribute was brief, respectful, and well received. As the audience applauded, he strode off the stage holding his first noncompetitive Academy Award, hoping he would be back on the same stage a year later for his performance in, and direction of, *The Bridges of Madison County*.

The film opened on June 2 to less than rave reviews. The *New York Times* liked it, as did *Newsweek*, although both had reservations, and the rest of the critics gave it the same half-cocked thumb-up. It stayed in theaters through Labor Day, grossing $70 million in its initial domestic theatrical release, and it would go on to do another $200 million overseas. Those were impressive numbers for a film that was unlike anything Clint had done before—a soft, gentle romantic love story between an older man and a "younger woman," with not so much as a single punch thrown or a single gun fired in angry vengeance.

That September Clint did a monthlong promotional tour for *The Bridges of Madison County*'s overseas debut, which took him through England, France, and Italy. Ruiz and two other couples, longtime friends from Carmel, accompanied him. When the tour ended and everybody had returned home, Clint took Ruiz to his winter retreat in Hailey, Idaho, near Sun Valley, for the holidays. On December 29 he proposed marriage to her with a diamond and ruby ring.

The next day they went to the county courthouse to apply for a marriage license. Everyone there was good-naturedly sworn to secrecy until the formal wedding, which was set for the following March, after Clint received the American Film Institute Achievement Award.

On March 31, 1996, Clint and Ruiz exchanged vows in Las Vegas, on the patio of Steve Wynn's home. Clint's mother was there, and his son Kyle was his best man. Ruiz was escorted down the aisle by her father, while the band played "Doe Eyes" and "Unforgettable."

Later, the happy bride said of the momentous occasion, "The fact that I am only the second woman he has married really touches me."

As for Clint, he had no problem being nearly sixty-six and marrying a thirty-year-old woman:

I don't think about it. You're as old as you feel, and I feel great. Certainly if you're a man there are advantages to being older . . . none of us knows how long fate gives you on the planet. People get so concerned about age, about the future, they don't live out their moment today. Moment to moment. I'm immensely happy with Dina, and I feel I've finally found a person I want to be with . . . This is it, win, lose or draw.

A few weeks later, back in L.A. after honeymooning in Hawaii, Dina was riding in a car with Clint when suddenly she asked him to pull over. "She was feeling a little nausea and asked me to stop at a gas station so she could buy one of those sticks," Clint later recalled. "She came back and said, 'We're pregnant.' " It would be Clint's seventh child by five different women, and her first.

That spring Clint went off to make his next movie, *Absolute Power*, to be filmed on location in Baltimore and Washington, D.C. Like *The Bridges of Madison County*, *Absolute Power* was adapted from a powerhouse bestseller, by David Baldacci. It was a curious amalgam of several genres—jewel heist, assassination thriller, and family conflict melodrama—that reteamed Clint with his Oscar-winning *Unforgiven* costar, Gene Hackman. Also included in the stellar cast were Ed Harris, Scott Glenn, Judy Davis, and E. G. Marshall. Two of Clint's children, Alison and Kimber, appeared in minor roles.

Clint was intrigued by the problem of transferring such a complicated plot-driven piece to the screen: "With *Absolute Power*, I liked the whole setup and I liked the characters, but the problem was that all those great characters were killed in the book, so my question was, how can we make a screenplay where everyone that the audience likes doesn't get killed off?"

To solve that problem, Clint—serving as director, producer, and star for Malpaso, which made the film in partnership with Castle Rock Entertainment (who owned the rights to the novel)—turned to William Goldman, the best screenwriter of his generation. Goldman decided to emphasize jewel thief Luther Whitney's (Clint's) relationship with his daughter (Laura Linney). He built the rest of the screenplay around the president (Hackman), who is having an affair with a young woman. In a fit of rage, she tries to stab him with a letter opener (recalling Hackman's great turn in Roger Donaldson's 1987 *No Way Out*, as Defense Secretary David Brice, who murders *his* mistress). The Secret Service kills her, and Luther, during his last great heist, happens to witness the scene, and takes the letter opener as a form of life insurance. Once the president becomes aware there is a witness, he orders the Secret Service to track him down and kill him too. Meanwhile, Luther decides to reconcile with his daughter, who happens to be the district attorney. Eventually the real killers—including, improbably, the president—are brought to justice, Eastwood-style.

The story combines too many different genres and certainly presented its share of problems to Goldman—in his first draft, which was faithful to the novel, he had Luther killed off halfway through. Clint liked everything about it but that. He told Goldman that a Clint Eastwood character should never die in his films and then ordered the script rewritten so that Luther not only lives but plays a key role in solving the murder. Goldman worked at a furious pace to get the revisions done on schedule.

Absolute Power opened on February 14, 1997, and grossed $50 million in its initial domestic theatrical release and nearly double that overseas. That was okay for most films but disappointing for a Clint Eastwood movie—about half what *The Bridges of Madison County* had done. Critics were not overly receptive to the film—most agreed that despite the theme of reconciliation that permeated it, the film was basically an action genre picture that, following *The Bridges of Madison County*, seemed like something of a throwback. It was given the prestigious closing-night slot at the Cannes Film Festival, but in light of the blasé reviews, Clint canceled his much-hyped scheduled personal appearance.

The film had another problem as well, one the critics danced around but that the public could not help but notice. For the first time, Clint simply looked too old for the part.

Clint celebrated his sixty-seventh birthday making two more films. The first was yet another bestseller adaptation, *Midnight in the Garden of Good and Evil*. John Berendt's novelistic, antebellum tale of murder and intrigue in Savannah was based on a true story involving art dealer Jim Williams and hustler Danny Hansford (called Billy Hanson in the movie). The book had been optioned early on by Arnold Stiefel, an agent-manager who in turn sold the rights to Warner Bros., where it eventually came to Clint and Malpaso from Semel and Daley. The script was by John Lee Hancock, who had also written *A Perfect World*. Hancock turned the book's author into one of the on-screen characters and eliminated many of Berendt's enjoyable meanderings.

One gothic element of the story that lent itself particularly well to film was its main setting, the Mercer House, built by Johnny Mercer's grandfather. Johnny Mercer was one of Savannah's most celebrated songwriters—and one of Clint's longtime favorites. He is remembered for, among others, the lyrics to "Laura," the theme song to Otto Preminger's 1941 film noir about a ghostly woman at the center of a murder mystery. When Clint read the script, he knew immediately he wanted to direct but not star, preferring to promote his daughter's stalled career. Alison was cast in the role of Mandy, the on-screen author's flirty girlfriend, a part greatly expanded from the novel.

Despite Clint's aging visage, Warner wasn't especially happy about his decision not to appear in the film—the last two he had directed without also starring in, *Breezy* and *Bird*, had not done nearly as well as the ones he had been in. When asked why he wanted to make the film at all, Clint said:

> The characters, who are interesting just because they're so diverse, and then Savannah, a very unusual city, which we wanted to make into a character in its own right. This isn't the South the way it's portrayed most of the time, with an overabundance of clichés. [We wanted to show a South that is] sophisticated, cultured, intelligent, very much in the public view, people no one would ever think could be interested in sorcery.

The all-star cast included Kevin Spacey—red-hot after his upset 1996 Best Supporting Actor win for his performance in Bryan Singer's sleeper hit *The Usual Suspects*—John Cusack, Jude Law, and veteran actress Kim Hunter. An outsize publicity campaign led up to its big Thanksgiving-weekend release: Clint agreed to a first-time appearance on *60 Minutes* but dodged some unexpectedly pointed questions by Steve Kroft about how many children Clint had by how many different women, and (by implication) why, and a far less intense double appearance on *The Oprah Winfrey Show*. Even after all these years, Clint had difficulty appearing relaxed on any stage that required spontaneous responses.

Despite all the buildup, the film did not even earn back its $30 million negative cost* in the States; it brought in only about $25 million in its initial theatrical release, making it one of the biggest flops of Clint's career. It did nothing for Alison's career and it resurrected the ever-louder whispers that Clint Eastwood's career as a Hollywood director was finished.

Almost immediately, as if on cue, rumors began to circulate that Clint was going to make another Dirty Harry movie, the sixth in the series. After all, Malpaso had optioned bestselling West Coast detec-

---

Negative cost is the cost of completing the film; it refers to the finished negative from which all the prints are struck.

tive novelist Michael Connelly's *Blood Work*.* Word was, Clint was thinking about bringing Harry out of retirement to solve one last crime, putting his own life at stake. But instead Clint announced that his next starring role and directing assignment would be *True Crime*, from the Andrew Klavan bestseller about a reporter who tries to stop an execution. Steve Everett (Clint) has to race against time to find the real killers before the wrong man is put to death. Nothing about the film really worked, and most people in Hollywood found its real mystery in its casting: Clint gave Frances Fisher the relatively small role of District Attorney Cecilia Nussbaum.

True Crime, released in the spring of 1999, did very poorly at the box office, barely grossing $7 million. Shortly after its disastrous release, Bob Daley and Terry Semel resigned from Warner Bros., ending their long association with the studio and with Clint. Controversy swirled around the double resignation, but both executives steadfastly maintained that they simply felt it was time to move on and that their decision had nothing to do with the success or failure of Clint Eastwood's latest movies.

Shortly thereafter, in January 2000, Time-Warner merged with AOL, a move that shook up the company and the film industry as it appeared to signal a major shift in the delivery of entertainment. The studio was turning away from the business of making motion pictures. Whether Semel and Daley had been forced out, were gently pushed, or chose to leave on their own accord, their departure underscored the fact that Clint Eastwood would no longer be as powerful as he once was. If ever there was a good time for Clint to be able to step down gracefully, this would have been it.

But Clint refused to believe that turning seventy—and looking every day of it, down to his well-worn face heavily wrinkled from a lifetime of living and acting outdoors and a bit of a turkey neck developing under his chin—meant his professional time was up. He still had something to prove, and he intended to do it with style, grace, big box office, and perhaps most of all, a Best Actor Oscar in his fist.

---

*Connelly was a William Morris client, published by Warner Books. (Little, Brown was then a subsidiary of the conglomerate.)

TWENTY-TWO

Dina keeps me on my toes, let's put it that way. We both enjoy family a lot, we both enjoy pets and we love to play golf. To me, as I said, life is like the back nine in golf. Sometimes you play better on the back nine. You may not be stronger, but hopefully you're wiser.

—Clint Eastwood

As the last night of the old century dissolved into the first day of the new one, Clint Eastwood was living the life of a man half his biological age. He was slim, trim, healthy, and handsome, married to a thirty-four-year-old woman, and the proud father of a three-year-old toddler he could happily bounce on his bony knee.

He was also the head of a business empire and one of the most enduring actors of his generation, still making mainstream commercial movies long after his contemporaries had either died, or retired, or like his friend Jack Nicholson turned to self-parody in the face of diminishing box-office returns. Clint had wealth beyond all expectation and lasting world fame. He had made or appeared in fifty-six features and directed twenty-one of them; he had been acknowledged by the Academy of Motion Pictures with two competitive and one honorary Oscar for his efforts; and he had been feted by the most prestigious museums and grandest film festivals around the world. And yet the need to keep working still stirred within him, as if he still had something that needed to be said, or some accomplishment still to be won. Only months into the new century, he had finished the twenty-second feature that he had directed, the fifty-sixth role he had played on the big screen.

It wasn't the Dirty Harry film everyone thought they were still waiting for. It was, instead, *Space Cowboys*, a space adventure comedy, starring what one producer referred to as the "geezer squad"—Clint, Tommy Lee Jones (the baby of the set), Donald Sutherland (whom Clint had last worked with in *Kelly's Heroes*), and James Garner (whom Clint had known since his *Rawhide* years, when Garner was starring next door in *Maverick*). The film was Philip Kaufman's *The Right Stuff* (1983) meets Ron Howard's *Cocoon* (1985)—Geritol laced with Viagra, with a can't-miss live monkey thrown in for good measure.

The new regime at Warner had no faith in the film and released—

or dumped—it in August 2000, hoping it wouldn't do too much damage to its bottom line. It didn't. *Space Cowboys* went on to be one of the biggest hits of the year, grossing more than $100 million in its initial domestic theatrical release and almost twice that in foreign and ancillary sales (including rental and purchase DVDs and pay-per-view, which had by now added significant profits to virtually all films, past and present).

Clint especially enjoyed the success of this film, literally laughing at the corporate towheads who scratched their scalps as he drove his pickup to the bank. But he had never been anyone's fool. He had to know that this movie really was a step backward, if not straight down. It put him on the same page with Garner, who had long ago stopped making anything like "big" films, and for whom *Space Cowboys* was a late-in-the-day bonus.

Without taking so much as a deep breath, he went straight into production on *Blood Work*. As FBI profiler Terry McCaleb (in whom one might see the vestiges of good old Dirty Harry), Clint suffers the onset of mortality (or acknowledges it) when a massive heart attack nearly kills him, even as he is hot on the trail of a dirty killer. As he told one interviewer, "At this particular stage in my maturity, I felt it was time to take on characters that have different obstacles to face than they would if I were playing a younger man of 30 or 40."

Despite the star power of Anjelica Huston and Jeff Daniels, the film failed to catch fire and grossed only $27 million during its initial domestic theatrical run, reaching no higher than tenth place with a paltry $3 million gross on its all-important opening weekend in 2002. Even Al Pacino was able to outdraw Clint at the box office, with *S1m0ne*, directed by Andrew Niccol, an unpronounceable sci-fi mishmash that nevertheless managed to come in ahead of *Blood Work*. No Pacino film had outgrossed an Eastwood film, when both were released at the same time, since *The Godfather* (1 and 2) in the early 1970s,

Clint blamed the film's failure on the new administration at Warner Bros.: they had dumped the film into the soft third week of August. Semel and Daley were clearly no longer there to promote his work. He was especially angry that the studio had not given the film a New York red-carpet premiere, or scheduled any pre-opening screening for the critics, giving them the unmistakable sense that the studio wanted to keep them from seeing it.

After the film opened in the States and quickly disappeared, Clint strongly hinted to the studio that he was thinking of giving up acting altogether. That was big, and not good, news for Warner, as the movies Clint acted in still far outgrossed the ones he only directed. In London for the overseas opening, he sent a message to the new power elite at Warner when he told the *Daily Telegraph*, "I've wanted to phase out of acting and into directing. I'll do it when the day comes when you look up at the screen and say, 'That's enough of that guy.' *And that day gets closer all the time*" (emphasis added).

After the relative failure of *Blood Work*, Clint made good on his threat not to act anymore, at least for his next film. He found a project whose grim story, with dark, mystic overtones, defined destiny as one's random placement in a world filled with misplaced desires, where vengeance is the only acceptable penance. Clint loved the nihilistic script that forty-two-year-old Brian Helgeland had adapted from the celebrated Dennis Lehane novel, *Mystic River*, which celebrated the effect and consequences of a higher-than-legal, if not traditionally religious, code of ethics.*

As he later told Charlie Rose, he wanted to do the project without acting in it, and it took a bit of haggling to get Warner interested:

> I knew of Dennis Lehane, I read a synopsis of the book in a newspaper and I said to myself, "I've got to have this, I think I can make an interesting movie out of it" . . . Warner has always been very good at leaving me alone and letting me operate as a sort of independent production house. I took the script to them and they liked it, but they knew it was unrelenting. At the time, this was the studio that was doing *The Matrix*, *Lord of the Rings*, and *Harry Potter*, all these films with high concepts and lots of action. Excite me some more, they said, and I knew I couldn't excite them any less. They said they'd do it, but at a certain price [$25 million for the negative] and I agreed, and took DGA [Directors Guild] minimum to get it made. I'd done a few complex stories before, but the

---

*Helgeland had written the script for *Blood Work*. In 1997 he co-wrote *L.A. Confidential* with the film's director, Curtis Hanson. They shared an Oscar for Best Screenplay.

fact that it was the unraveling of a mystery that went back a few generations, and when a tragedy reunites [a group of childhood friends] you see what their lives are like, what they've become and what effect an abduction that happened thirty years ago still had on them.

The acts of vengeance that follow were what made the film prime Clint material; in his movies, when vengeance is above the law, heroism takes on mystic (and at times mythic) proportion. It was a favorite theme that reached all the way back to the Man with No Name, through the Dirty Harrys, *Tightrope*, and all the way forward to *Blood Work*.

Mystic River is about Boston's working-class society, which cannot withstand the social and emotional eruption that follows a violent murder and whose ultimate consequence is the moral breakdown of its social order. The breakdown can be only restored (and further broken—one of the film's brilliant ambivalences) by an equally violent act of retribution, even when the target of that retribution is at least partially innocent. That act, rather than any moral force that may be behind it, delivers a measure of relief for the characters involved, as well as the audience. But the relief that defines and drives this dark and vicious movie is incomplete and ultimately unsatisfying.

Darkness and death pervade *Mystic River* as they do in no other Clint Eastwood movie. Here death is the ultimate force that drives both good and evil, searching around corners and seeping into souls, like water seeking its own level. The river, one of the first geographical boundaries we discover from Clint's signature skyview opening, also serves throughout as the metaphorical river of life—the flowing lifeblood of the people who live by it. As critic Dennis Rothermel points out, it "absorbs the past, without forgiving and without healing."

Clint cast an offbeat, eclectic, and intense cast of actors and actresses who would help make the film mesh as an ensemble presentation. He felt they were the best ensemble he had ever put together, even though his leads had never attracted the kind of box office that he had drawn for most of his career; none had ever been in a true blockbuster. The peripatetic Sean Penn, whom Clint cast first—"for his edge," he said—set the tone for the rest; he was a hardened, muscled-and-tattooed ex-con to whom fate deals a horrifying blow, driven to respond by dealing life an equally horrifying one. Penn was backed up by Tim Robbins, whose life was ruined by a childhood abduction that comes back to haunt him as an adult; by Kevin Bacon as a tough, clever, but ultimately ineffective detective; by Laurence Fishburne, as his no-nonsense partner; by newcomer Emmy Rossum as Penn's young, beautiful, but ill-fated daughter; by Laura Linney as Penn's wretched wife; and by Marcia Gay Harden as Robbins's wife.

The $30 million film was shot quickly and efficiently in Clint's familiar one-or-two-take method—catching the normally slow, methodical, and Method-intense Penn a little off guard:

I think the most takes I ever did on Clint's movie was three, and that was rare. A lot of one-takes . . . In the script it was written that six guys are stopping me. I thought maybe two of them could take me. But if it's only six of them, someone might get hurt if I really let myself go, so I don't know what to do. I don't want a really fake fight, and I don't want to hurt anybody. Clint said, "I'll figure it out," and that's all he said. When I came back to the set, he had about 15 guys jump on me, and I was locked down—I was literally able to try to head-butt people, I was able to try to bite people, I was able to try to kick them. I didn't have to hold back at all, and it fixed me to do anything. This is Clint thinking.

Mystic River opened on October 15, 2003, and took the normally Clint-cool critics totally by surprise—it looked, sounded, and felt like no other Clint Eastwood movie. The reviews were universally terrific— easily the best that Clint had ever received as a director. *Newsweek* called it "a masterpiece." Dana Stevens, writing in the *New York Times*, declared that "*Mystic River* is the rare American movie that aspires to— and achieves—the full weight and darkness of tragedy." *Rolling Stone*, where Clint, with his anti-rock, pro-jazz preferences, was rarely at the top of the editorial favorites, raved about the film. Said Peter Travers: "Clint Eastwood pours everything he knows about directing into *Mystic River*. His film sneaks up, messes with your head, and then floors you. You can't shake it. It's that haunting, that hypnotic." David Denby, one of Pauline Kael's successors at *The New Yorker* (after her 2001 passing), gave Clint one of the magazine's best reviews of him ever, saying the movie was "as close as we are likely to come on the screen to the spirit of Greek tragedy (and closer, I think, than Arthur Miller has come on the stage). The crime of child abuse becomes a curse that determines the pattern of events in the next generation."

In the *New York Observer*, Andrew Sarris praised both the film and Clint:

> *Mystic River* must be considered a decisive advance for the director toward complete artistic mastery of his narrative material . . . Like most of the more interesting films this year, *Mystic River* displays a darker view of our existence in the new millennium than was the norm in the old Hollywood dream factories. Mr. Eastwood is to be commended for reportedly insisting that the film be shot in its natural Boston habitat rather than in a cheaper approximation of Boston, such as bargain-basement Toronto. This emphasis on geographical authenticity helps make this film a masterpiece of the first order.

The film had a carefully planned limited-release opening—Warner hoped that word of mouth would help build an audience. The plan worked. *Mystic River* went on to gross just under $100 million in its initial domestic theatrical release and more than doubled that internationally. Perhaps even more important, the film won every important pre-Oscar award and led in the run-up to that year's Academy Awards.

As expected, *Mystic River* did well in the nominations, two for Clint Eastwood (Best Picture, along with co-producers Judie Hoyt and Robert Lorenz, and Best Director). Sean Penn was nominated for Best Actor, Tim Robbins for Best Supporting Actor. Marcia Gay Harden was nominated for Best Supporting Actress, and Brian Helgeland for his screenplay.*

The ceremonies were held at the Kodak Theater, on February 29, 2004, hosted by the actor and comedian Billy Crystal. By then the battle for Best Picture had shaped up as Clint had predicted when he

---

*Penn had been nominated three previous times, in 1996 for Robbins's *Dead Man Walking*, in 1999 for Woody Allen's *Sweet and Lowdown*, and in 2001 for Jessie Nelson's *I Am Sam*. Robbins's only other nomination had been for Best Director, *Dead Man Walking*. Harden had won Best Supporting Actress for Ed Harris's 2000 *Pollock*.

first encountered the noticeable lack of enthusiasm for it from the Warner executives. They had put all their PR muscle behind Peter Jackson's *Lord of the Rings: The Return of the King,* the result being eleven Academy nominations for a film that was also one of the highest-grossing in Warner's history. Penn and Robbins won in their categories, but *Lord of the Rings* won all eleven awards for which it was nominated, tying William Wyler's *Ben-Hur* (1959) and James Cameron's *Titanic* (1997) for the most Oscars ever won.

Nonetheless, Clint had made a strong statement to the studio about his abilities as a director. Among the most important was that he wasn't a one-shot Oscar wonder, that he could contend year after year and be taken seriously as a popular filmmaker. And he set the stage for his next movie, the somewhat misleadingly titled *Million Dollar Baby,* which sounded like nothing so much as a 1930s-era musical.

It wasn't.

The script for *Million Dollar Baby* had been around for years, an adaptation of several short stories by F.X. Toole, who was a legendary "cut man" in the fight business—the one who stays in the corner of his fighter and must stop the bleeding on his fighter's face between rounds. Paul Haggis had read the stories and tried to put them into a single overview in order to make them into a movie.

The script came to Clint, after several other studios rejected it, but even after he agreed to be in it, Warner refused to okay the film's $30 million budget, despite Clint's success the year before with a similarly difficult, between-the-cracks *Mystic River.* Clint then took the project to Tom Rosenberg, an independent producer at Lakeshore Entertainment, who agreed to put up half if Warner would match it. With the deal finally in place, Clint shot the film in thirty-seven days.

From the beginning, Clint had it in mind to play the trainer, Frankie Dunn, who has seen better days, not just in the ring but in virtually every aspect of his life. His daughter won't talk to him. He cannot get a major talent to train. He has little money, and he simply hangs on the sweaty periphery of the fight world.

One of the more interesting aspects of *Million Dollar Baby* is how smartly it works into a metaphor of Hollywood. Dunn could just as well be a down-and-out director (or producer) looking for the next big thing to teach and to train into a winner so he can return to his past glory. In other words, he is looking for a star to bring him back to his own former glory.

Into his life comes thirty-one-year-old Maggie Fitzgerald (Hilary Swank), who has very little going for her. She's too old, Dunn thinks, and not especially good, and of course, a woman. Undaunted, she convinces him to work with her. We watch her progress with a narration provided by Dunn's friend, ex-boxer Eddie "Scrap Iron" Dupris, played by Morgan Freeman, here reteamed with Clint after their memorable pairing in *Unforgiven*.

To this point, the film is a rather conventionally uplifting *Rocky*-type boxing film. But then all hell breaks loose: during a match, Dunn's female great white hope is injured in the ring and paralyzed from the neck down. Unable to move and wanting to die, she finally convinces Dunn to mercy-kill her. He does, as Dupris's narration tells us, and disappears.

The film unexpectedly changes course in the middle, going from *Rocky* to *Camille*, from a so-called man's picture with the novelty of a woman in the lead to a so-called woman's picture with a man as the reluctant father-figure hero. It is saved from the melodramatics of soap opera by the superb performances of Clint, Freeman, and especially Swank.

Clint liked the film's sense of balance, liked that Dunn's failure with his own daughter could somehow be atoned for by his "salvation" of Maggie's career, liked that he could find meaning by pushing someone else into the spotlight, liked that he could show where the real talent was in guiding another's performance. His instincts were correct; audiences liked it too. Before its initial domestic release ended, it had grossed more than $220 million and Clint was Oscar-bound once more.

The film's cachet was helped immeasurably by the high level of the reviews it received—and by the curiously effective cross-genre performance of Swank, who had previously established herself as a major player in Hollywood with her Oscar-winning performance in Kimberly Peirce's *Boys Don't Cry* (1999). Similarly, in *Million Dollar Baby*, Swank played a very manly woman to amazing effect. She, too, was a shoo-in for the Oscars.

But it was those reviews that pushed the film forward and made people want to see it. Its biggest advocate was Roger Ebert, who both in his newspaper column and on his popular film-review TV show championed it as "the best of the year" and advised of a "spoiler" warning. That warning, echoed in numerous other reviews, gave the film a special "must-see" aura, much like that of Neil Jordan's *The Crying Game* (1992), that drove the film straight to the Academy Awards. Jordan had picked up an Oscar for Best Screenplay but lost Best Director to—Clint Eastwood for *Unforgiven*.

If this was finally going to be Clint's year to win it all—especially a Best Actor Oscar—the momentum appeared to be in his favor. Morgan Freeman and Hilary Swank were nominated for Best Supporting Actor and Best Actress, respectively. Clint was nominated for Best Director and Best Actor and, as producer, the would-be recipient for Best Picture.

One of the other nominees for Best Picture was *Ray*, a Hollywood biography of the legendary Ray Charles, directed by Taylor Hackford.* Charles's death earlier in 2004 had considerably enhanced the film's box office and helped catapult it into a Best Picture nomination. There was also Alexander Payne's charmingly out-of-nowhere sex comedy *Sideways*, about the misadventures of four middle-aged losers living in California wine country.†

On the direction front, the nominees included Taylor Hackford for *Ray*, Martin Scorsese for *The Aviator*, Alexander Payne for *Sideways*, and Mike Leigh for *Vera Drake*.

The ceremonies took place on the unusually warm Los Angeles evening of February 27, 2005, once again at the Kodak Theater on Hollywood Boulevard. Chris Rock began the evening with a series of interminably unfunny jokes. Despite the big box office that *Million Dollar Baby* had generated (it had outgrossed Scorsese's *The Aviator* by

---

*Hackford's previous biggest success was his 1980s faux-military fairy tale *An Officer and a Gentleman*, which made top-of-the-line box-office stars out of Richard Gere, Debra Winger, and Louis Gossett Jr. (who won a Supporting Actor Oscar for his performance).

†*Sideways* made stars out of its two male leads, granite-faced Thomas Haden Church (nominated for Best Supporting Actor) and longtime character actor Paul Giamatti. It also temporarily lit the glow of has-been, never-was Virginia Madsen (nominated for Best Supporting Acress) and brought Sandra Oh a leading role in the highly successful TV series *Grey's Anatomy*.

nearly $100 million, domestically), Scorsese looked unbeatable for Best Director. Scorsese's trademark was the idiosyncratic New York street drama, such as *Mean Streets* (1973), *Taxi Driver* (1976), and the grand *Raging Bull* (1980)—he'd lost both Best Picture and Best Director to Robert Redford for *Ordinary People*. The buzz was that this finally had to be Scorsese's year, as much as the previous one had been Clint's. The evening came down to a battle of the East Coast independent versus the western rebel.*

Clint was sitting several rows back with Ruiz—on the aisle, just in case—not far from where Scorsese had been placed, ready for his leap to glory.

The trend was set early. For Best Supporting Actor, the nominations included Freeman, Alan Alda for *The Aviator*, Thomas Haden Church for *Sideways*, Jamie Foxx for Michael Mann's *Collateral*, and Clive Owen for Mike Nichols's *Closer*. These were four strong performances, and although Church and Foxx were considered favorites, they likely split the vote, leaving not enough for Owen or Alda to overtake Freeman, who won it. The theater erupted. This was Freeman's fourth nomination but only his first win. Seated directly behind Clint, he got up and grabbed Clint's hand on the way up. Clint's grin lit up the room. "Heavens to Murgatroyd," Freeman said into the microphone under the noise from his standing ovation. "And I especially want to thank Clint Eastwood for giving me the opportunity to work with him again," he added, as Clint watched, slowly chewing gum and looking pleased and even a bit humbled by the moment.

The evening worked its way through the dozens of awards until it was finally time for the Big Three. The first, Best Actress, was given out by Sean Penn, the winner of the previous year's Best Actor award for *Mystic River*. The nominees were reviewed one more time: Swank, Annette Bening for István Szabó's *Being Julia*, Catalina Sandino Moreno for Joshua Marston's *Maria Full of Grace*, Imelda Staunton for Mike Leigh's *Vera Drake*, and Kate Winslet for Michel Gondry's *Eternal Sunshine of the Spotless Mind*. The only real challenger to Swank was Winslet, but her movie was indecipherable to the few people who had actually gone to see it. Penn opened the envelope and read aloud

---

*Scorsese had previously been nominated as Best Director for *Raging Bull* (1980), *The Last Temptation of Christ* (1988), *Goodfellas* (1990), and *Gangs of New York* (2003).

Swank's name. As she rose to head for the stage, she passed a black-tied Clint, put her hands on his face, and softly kissed him on the lips, all during her ovation. Wearing a dress with no back that cried out "I'm really a woman and a sexy one at that," she humbly accepted the award as "just a girl from a trailer park" and thanked everyone she could possibly think of. Then she stopped the music from playing her off to thank Clint, for allowing her to take the journey with him, for believing in her, for being her *"mo chuisle"*—the words she wore on the back of her robe during the film, which translated from the Gaelic means "My darling, my blood." Clint bowed his head gently in response.

Next came the award for Best Actor. The nominees included Clint, Jamie Foxx in the second of his two nominations for the evening, this one for the title role of *Ray*, Don Cheadle for Terry George's *Hotel Rwanda*, Johnny Depp for *Finding Neverland*, and Leonardo DiCaprio for *The Aviator.** During the recap, when Clint's clip was shown, and the TV camera found him, Ruiz had her arms linked around one of his, pulling him with excitement, while Clint stared ahead, unwilling or unable to show emotion. A radiant Charlize Theron opened the envelope and read the name of the winner—*Jamie Foxx*. The place cheered happily as Foxx ran up to the stage and accepted his award. As he did so, Clint's smile melted into a mask. His eyebrows raised slightly, and he applauded for Foxx.

Finally came the award for Best Director. After the nominees' names were read, the crowd hushed as Julia Roberts opened the envelope.

When she called his name, Clint showed little emotion as he loped on his long legs to the stage. Holding the Oscar, the white-haired, trim, and tanned actor spoke in his trademark low drawl, a guttural slide of sounds rather than a vocalized string of words. After thanking the usual roundup, he paid special tribute to the legendary studio-era production designer Henry Bumstead, ninety years old, who had worked on *Million Dollar Baby*. Clint thanked his mother, ninety-six, reminding audiences that she was only eighty-four when he had won for *Unforgiven*. "So I want to thank her for her genes. I figure I'm

---

*Interestingly, Clint's character was the only fictitious one. The other four were based on real people.

just a kid—I've got a lot of stuff to do yet."* At the age of seventy-four, he had become the oldest person to ever win an Oscar for Best Director.

"I'm happy to be here and still working," Clint said, with a smile, while in the audience a brittle-faced Scorsese slumped deep into his seat.

Clint was back again a few minutes later, when *Million Dollar Baby* won Best Picture. How a picture wins that award, Best Supporting Actor, Best Actress, and Best Director but not Best Actor is hard to explain. But one thing is clear: the Academy, as always, can be sadistically cruel in its reward-denial syndrome.[†]

This night Clint went home once more another actor's bridesmaid, this time to Jamie Foxx, as the remaining grains of sand ran ever faster down the hourglass of his life.

---

*Ruth Eastwood died a year later, at the age of ninety-seven.

†In 1997, at the age of seventy-two, Lauren Bacall, one of Hollywood's golden-age legends, had a one-last-chance nomination for her role in Barbra Streisand's *The Mirror Has Two Faces*, but she lost to Juliette Binoche for her role in Anthony Minghella's *The English Patient*.

TWENTY-THREE

My earlier work, I was a different person, the young guy with the brass ring. Things were going rather well for me, in the motion picture business as an actor, and I did what came along. Some of it was a lot of fun at the time. Would it be fun today if I were doing it? No, probably not. I've matured, I have different thoughts about things, as I think everybody should.

—Clint Eastwood

In 2005, at seventy-five years of age, Clint Eastwood was happily married to his second wife. His eight-year-old-daughter Morgan Eastwood had been named after his costar and good friend Morgan Freeman. He was a grandfather of two, Kimber's son and Kyle's daughter. And he was the head of a financial empire that included restaurants (the Hog's Breath Inn and the Inn Mission Ranch), real estate, the exclusive invitation-only Tehama Golf Club in Carmel Valley (with an initial joining fee of $300,000), part ownership in the Pebble Beach Golf and Country Club, whole or part ownership in the sixty films he had produced, directed, starred in, or all three, and Malpaso, the company that made nearly all of them. He had eight Academy Award nominations and five Oscars. And as the year began, he was deeply involved in not one but two new movies.

They were a related pair of World War II films that reached back to the days of his youth and held no star-turn roles for him. *Flags of Our Fathers* and *Letters from Iwo Jima* was a unique double package, separate films about the same battle told from the perspective of each side (both with musical sound tracks by Clint Eastwood). *Flags of Our Fathers* was based on the book co-written by James Bradley, the son of one of the flag raisers, and Ron Powers; the film uses flashbacks to tell the story of the Battle of Iwo Jima and the fate of the six men of Easy Company who raised the victory flag there.* Also known as Operation Detachment, the battle started on February 19, 1945, and lasted thirty-five days. It was one of the bloodiest and most pivotal battles in the Pacific Theater.

The historic raising of the flag on the fifth day would endure as a

---

*The six men were Franklin Sousley, Harlon Block, Michael Strank, John Bradley, Ira Hayes, and Rene Gagnon. The three who survived the battle were Bradley, Hayes, and Gagnon.

powerful symbol of victory itself. The moment was immortalized by photographer Joe Rosenthal, who won the Pulitzer Prize for it. (The one he captured on film was actually the second flag-raising.) *Flags of Our Fathers* tells how the three survivors of that photograph were exploited by the American government for propaganda purposes, to boost the morale of the American people during the war, and to help with the sale of war bonds. It also looks at what happened to the men themselves, how the battle affected them, and their difficulties dealing with guilt and self-worth in the years that followed the so-called moment of heroic glory.

It is a moving subject whose symbolic and political relevancies had, if anything, become even more vivid as the war in Iraq dragged on, while the administration that had forced it struggled to find ways to "sell" it to the American people. No one knew better than Clint Eastwood how much a picture could do to promote an image. Take a man with no name, for instance, and give him a poncho and a cigarillo, and you could redefine the iconic image of the gunfighters of the American West.

The project was the brainchild of Steven Spielberg, who, along with Tom Hanks, had become the self-appointed representatives of a peculiar niche of the baby boom generation: those who had never served in the military (and likely protested the war in Vietnam) but regarded the previous generation—their fathers, uncles, and older brothers—as "the greatest" for their service in World War II. (The "greatest generation" became the slogan for the uncomplicated heroism and patriotism of the Second World War, the "good war.") For Spielberg and Hanks, World War II became less the basis of real drama and more the ultimate boomer video game, something of a techno fetish in films like *Saving Private Ryan* (1998), an award-winning box-office smash loosely based on the true story of one family, the "fighting Sullivans," who lost five sons during the war. In the film, which begins with a violent re-creation of the Allied landing at Normandy, a group of soldiers are sent out to find the last remaining Sullivan son and bring him home. It is a noble gesture and a great theme for a film (if one disregards the huge body count that piles up to save the one last surviving Ryan). Spielberg had previously made *Empire of the Sun* (1987), *1941* (1979), and *Schindler's List* (1993), as well as the Indiana Jones films and TV series, all World War II–themed projects, and he would go on to do a ten-part series for HBO called *Band of Brothers*, co-produced by Tom Hanks. Perhaps wisely, this time Spielberg felt he needed to emphasize dramatic substance over stylized mythology, with a little more penetration and a little less envy.

Clint first came upon the project while he was in production on *Million Dollar Baby:*

> I ran into Steven [Spielberg] at a function, and he said, "Why don't you come over [to DreamWorks] and do something for me, you direct and you and I will produce it." I said okay, I was geared up and ready, he had a few scripts [adapted versions of the book], but he hadn't found anything he really liked. At the time I was working with Paul Haggis, on *Million Dollar Baby*, so I said, "Let me talk to Paul about it." He read the material, we had a few meetings, and he sat down and wrote a script.

Haggis's (and William Broyles Jr.'s) major cinematic leap was to tell the story in flashback, to keep the story pulsating and maintain a contemporary feel.

With Spielberg in place as one of the producers, Clint and Malpaso were able to bring Warner into the project. Filming began shortly after *Million Dollar Baby* was completed. In typical Clint fashion, the cast lacked a superstar—the biggest "name" in the film was Ryan Phillippe.

Then midway through production, as if to underscore the difference between himself and Spielberg, Clint made a decision to do something no one had ever done before.

> I started wondering, what about the other [Japanese] guys: What was going on in their minds? What were their lives like? I mean, it was pretty miserable for the Americans on that island—can you imagine what it was like for the other guy, who didn't have the same equipment, the same access to food and water—there was no water on Iwo Jima, the only water you get is from rain—so they were trapped out there, living on weeds and plants, worms, anything they could find. So they were an

interesting group of people. Now that decades had gone by, I thought it was important for the Japanese public to appreciate those men, even though it's not about winning or losing, who won or who lost. It's about the sacrifices they made for their country, rightly or wrongly—they made them.*

Thus was born the notion of making a simultaneous, or parallel, film, the same story seen from the other side, to be called *Letters from Iwo Jima*. Ken Watanabe would play the lead—he was a bigger international star than anyone in *Flags of Our Fathers*. Clint received permission from the Japanese government to shoot some scenes on Iwo Jima. (The property had been returned to them in the early 1960s.) But for economy and accessibility to mountains and underground tunnels, the bulk of both films was shot simultaneously on a volcanic island in Iceland, and they were released within weeks of each other.

After the war ended, it had taken decades for Japanese cinema to get art-house distribution in America because of the hard feelings left behind by Pearl Harbor. Marlon Brando (of all people) had been the first to attempt a sympathetic portrayal of the Japanese, during the postwar occupation at least, in Joshua Logan's Academy Award–winning *Sayonara* (1957). It was a daunting challenge to try to make Americans believe that the Japanese were human beings, let alone a cultured civilization capable of love, warmth, and dignity. Logan's and Brando's Academy Award–winning film opened the door to Japanese cinema's acceptance in the United States. But forty years later the industry still felt it was unlikely that any sizable audiences would go see *Letters from Iwo Jima*. Characteristically, even if Clint was aware of the whispers, he proceeded as planned.

"Between the two films together, I was trying to make an anti-war statement," he said. "It's hard to make any war picture and make it a

---

*A few other films had tried to show both sides, without much success. The biggest was Richard Fleischer and Kinji Fukasaku's *Tora! Tora! Tora!* (1970), about the attack on Pearl Harbor. The film, which had two directors, did not succeed at the box office and discouraged further attempts to show World War II from more than one point of view. No American film before *Letters from Iwo Jima* was ever made that showed any war issue completely and solely from the other side.

pro-war statement." Strong and perhaps surprising sentiments, indeed, from someone whose credentials were strewn with films of flagrant violence, messy bloodshed, and the twitchy pleasures of psychotic murderers, and especially along with the likes of Spielberg, whose vicarious-thrill movies were usually filled with fantasies of glory rather than realistic gore.

Flags of Our Fathers was released on October 20, 2006, amid high hopes it would be the big fall movie. Two months later, on December 20, *Letters from Iwo Jima* was put into limited distribution in the States, after having its world premiere and initial, highly successful run in Japan. Three weeks later, on January 12, 2007, it went into major nationwide distribution.

Shortly before *Flags* was released, Clint went on what was for him a PR spree, agreeing to sit for an interview with *Rolling Stone* magazine, whose resident film critic had, through the years, been up and down about him. But this time Peter Travers was unequivocal in his praise for Clint's decidedly nonconservative, non-flag-waving view of heroism and its inevitable fallout. He gave the film three and a half stars (out of four):

> The ambitious script . . . jumps back and forth in ways that could have been a jumble if Eastwood wasn't so adept at cutting a path to what counts. Eastwood's film is a fierce attack on wartime hypocrisy and profiteering, and also an indelibly moving salute to the soldiers who don't deserve to walk alone for following their own sense of duty . . . one thing is for sure, Eastwood will do it his way. As far as I'm concerned, that's the gold standard.

Richard Roeper, one of the sharper new multimedia critics, wrote in the *Chicago Sun-Times* that *Flags of Our Fathers* "stands with the Oscar-winning *Unforgiven* and *Million Dollar Baby* as an American masterpiece . . . but it is also patriotic because it questions the official version of the truth, and reminds us that superheroes exist only in comic books and cartoon movies."

Most of the major critics got it, and said that both films were among the best and most important movies in Clint's body of work— but neither clicked with audiences. *Flags of Our Fathers* earned about

$66 million, less than half of *Million Dollar Baby*, against $55 million in production costs. Using the standard formula that a film has to gross twice what it cost to break even, the film wound up losing a significant amount of money. *Letters from Iwo Jima* did even worse and exposed the huge miscalculation in Clint's overview; during one of the most vicious post–World War II wars in modern American history, audiences in this country simply weren't interested in a sympathetic view of the enemy—*any* enemy.

The films had their social critics, one of the most outspoken being Spike Lee, the African-American filmmaker, who had strong objections to Clint's take on the events of Iwo Jima. At the May 2008 Cannes Film Festival Lee was promoting his own World War II film, *Miracle at St. Anna*, about the exploits of the all-Black 92nd Buffalo Division, which fought the German army in Italy during the war. There Lee publicly criticized Clint and *Flags of Our Fathers* and *Letters from Iwo Jima* for not having "a single African-American character or actor. There were many African-Americans who survived that war and who were upset at Clint for not having one [in his two films]. That was his version: The negro soldier did not exist. I have a different version."

In response, Eastwood, who suspected Lee was trying to promote his films by criticizing Clint's, angrily told the *Guardian:*

> As for *Flags of Our Fathers*, he [Lee] says there was a small detachment of black troops on Iwo Jima as a part of a munitions company, but they didn't raise the flag. The story is *Flags of Our Fathers*, the famous flag-raising picture, and they didn't do that. If I go ahead and put an African-American actor in there, people'd go, "This guy's lost his mind." I mean, it's not accurate. He was complaining when I did *Bird* [the 1988 biopic of Charlie Parker]. Why would a white guy be doing that? I was the only guy who made it, that's why. He could have gone ahead and made it. Instead he was making something else.

Lee returned fire.

> First of all, the man is not my father and we're not on a plantation either. He's a great director. He makes his films, I make my films. The

thing about it though, I didn't personally attack him. And a comment like "a guy like that should shut his face"—come on Clint, come on. He sounds like an angry old man right there. If he wishes, I could assemble African-American men who fought at Iwo Jima and I'd like him to tell these guys that what they did was insignificant and they did not exist. He said, "I'm not making this up. I know history. I'm a student of history." And I know the history of Hollywood and its omission of the one million African-American men and women who contributed to World War II. Not everything was John Wayne, baby . . . I never said he should show one of the other guys holding up the flag as black. I said that African-Americans played a significant part in Iwo Jima. For him to insinuate that I'm rewriting history and have one of the four guys with the flag be black . . . no one said that. It's just that there's not one black in either film. And because I know my history, that's why I made that observation.*

After Clint publicly warned Lee to "shut his face," it was Steven Spielberg who finally got both sides to calm down, convincing Spike Lee to back off. "After game three, L.A. Staples Center, Lakers [vs.] Celtics, I'm going to the bathroom and Spielberg's sitting there with Eddie Murphy and Jeffrey Katzenberg," said Spike Lee. "And Katzenberg was getting on me about leaving Clint alone. I said, 'Steven, let me talk to you for a second.' So we talked. I conveyed a message and he said, 'I'll call Clint in the morning.' And it's hunky-dory. He said he was gonna make a call, he made it, squashed." A couple of months later, Lee even sent his new film over to Clint for a private viewing

Despite Lee's accusations (or possibly because of them—Lee and his films are not exactly laden with Oscars or nominations), the Academy found Clint's films good enough to nominate, even if its perception of *Flags of Our Fathers* was, inexplicably, one of *über*-patriotism rather than a profoundly vivid criticism of the Bush administration's war in Iraq.

---

*Clint was no stranger to public battles with other filmmakers. In 2005 he publicly vowed he'd kill Michael Moore if the documentarian ever showed up at his house, the way he had at Charlton Heston's in *Bowling for Columbine*.

On Sunday night, February 25, 2007, the seventy-ninth annual Academy Awards were held once again at Hollywood's Kodak Theater. This time television talk-show host Ellen DeGeneres hosted, in an attempt by the Academy to give a more modern look to its annual ritual of self-congratulation and to improve its ratings—the Oscars were a TV show, after all, and more often than not hosts were taken from that pool of talent rather than from the world of film.

There was a different feel in the air this year; for one thing, the Academy had moved up the presentation by nearly a month from the previous year to prevent declining ratings for the telecast. Awards programs were becoming a TV genre all their own, between the Golden Globes, the Screen Actors Guild Awards, the People's Choice Awards, and at least a half-dozen others related to film (and another dozen for music, TV, and theater), so the giving of the golden statuette was somewhat anticlimactic. And, by February, it was felt, a healthy number of the new year's films, were, at least theoretically, in theaters, making it increasingly difficult to look back at what was essentially old news.

This year's awards featured a rematch: Scorsese was back with *The Departed*, his sharp, return-to-form street-cred *policier*, a remake of Wai-keung Lau and Siu Fai Mak's Hong Kong original *Infernal Affairs* (2002); Clint was back as well with a Best Director nomination, but not for *Flags of Our Fathers*—it was, shockingly, for *Letters from Iwo Jima*.*

Scorsese's nomination was easy to understand, in light of his strong film, and that begins to explain why *Letters* was nominated over *Flags*. Clint had once been an Academy outcast, but ever since his explosive leap to prominence in the ranks of the Academy with *Unforgiven*, his public and industry images had melded into each other, and according to *Variety* editor Peter Bart, he had become Hollywood's elder statesman; meanwhile Scorsese continued to be the industry's aging and defiantly independent "bad boy." Like a film-without-a-film, the Oscar

---

Flags of Our Fathers received two nominations, for Sound Editing (Alan Robert Murray and Bub Asman) and Sound Mixing (John T. Reitz, David E. Campbell, Gregg Rudloff, Walt Martin). It lost the first to *Letters from Iwo Jima* and the second to *Dreamgirls* (Michael Minkler, Bob Beemer, Willie D. Burton).

presentations were moral stories as well as economic victories and almost always followed the standard rules that the villain rarely gets the girl, or in this case, the Oscar. This year, however, the feeling ran heavily throughout the industry that Scorsese had made the better film (better than *Flags of Our Fathers*). While television had taken over the crime genre as its own never-ending source of good triumphing over evil, Scorsese's movie transcended the usual laboratory-and-clues mundanity to spill over with the dynamics of the human moral condition. Clint, meanwhile, had made just another war movie. As good as it was—and few conservative Academy members thought it was all that good—in a nod of respect to Clint, they nominated his *other* movie, which *nobody* saw, thus ensuring that at least this time around, Scorsese could win. The other films in the Best Picture contest, all considered long shots by the pollsters and the pundits alike, were Alejandro González Iñárritu's *Babel*, Jonathan Dayton and Valerie Faris's *Little Miss Sunshine*, and Stephen Frears's *The Queen*.

Three of the most powerful directors in Hollywood, Francis Ford Coppola, Steven Spielberg, and George Lucas, assembled onstage to announce the winner of the award for Best Director. Coppola and Lucas had been part of the seminal 1970s San Francisco film movement that had helped to change the perception of American film from studio domination and toward larger independent films. The three titans gathered around the mike and did some obligatory and predictably goofy patented Academy Award blather ("It's better to give than to receive . . . no it's not!") and interminably back-patted themselves. Then they finally got around to reading the names of the Best Director nominees. When Coppola read Scorsese's name aloud, the audience burst into enthusiastic applause, at least twice as loud as they would for anyone else. When Coppola read Clint's name, the audience applauded dutifully. Ruiz, looking resplendent in a ruby-red dress with earrings hanging from her ears like giant shiny stalactites, smiled at her husband lovingly as she enthusiastically clapped. Clint, lips twitching as he chewed either gum or his lip, never broke his stare, aimed intently and directly at the stage.

Now it was Spielberg's turn to open the envelope. The tension in the room was negligible. "And the Oscar goes to . . . *Martin Scorsese!*" Scorsese threw his hands up in mock disbelief, like someone at a surprise party who was tipped off in advance, and then bolted toward the stage and his rendezvous with Oscar glory. Clint joined the standing ovation, his face frozen in a runner-up smile.

The Departed won four of the five Oscars it was nominated for that night, including Best Picture, losing only Best Supporting Actor (Mark Wahlberg). When the final award was handed out (to Graham King as producer), the long evening came to an end, as did Clint's latest, and perhaps last, chance to enter the pantheon of Best Actor Oscar winners. As the celebrity crowd left the building on their way to the various parties, with handshakes of congratulations flying through the crowd like a flock of birds madly flapping their wings, Clint and Ruiz quietly slipped away, unnoticed and unbothered, and headed home.

The next morning, back in Carmel, after breakfast and on the way to the golf course, Clint began formulating his next film.

Two more years would pass before another Clint Eastwood movie appeared. He was fast approaching eighty, and at last and inevitably, time seemed to be slowing his crank-'em-out pace. Increasingly, he spent his days on the golf course and looking after his business interests until, finally, he found two projects he wanted to do, one as director, and one more to act in—a last-chance effort to win that elusive Best Actor award.

The next one he chose to direct was *Changeling.** It was to be a joint venture between Imagine Entertainment, Universal, and Malpaso, making it the first film in fifteen years that a Clint project had no participation from Warner. In the aftermath of his double crash-and-burn Iwo Jima set, all sides had apparently agreed on a pause, if not a clean break, in the long-standing partnership.

The story of *Changeling* involves a woman who single-handedly takes on the corrupt L.A. police department over what she believes has been the kidnapping of her child by the authorities themselves. Stories of men (or women) alone who take on the system always appealed to Clint, and this one had some fresh angles he liked, not the least of which was that the hero happened to be a woman. He had had great

---

*A "changeling" is a being in West European folklore and folk religion, the offspring of a fairy, a troll, an elf, or other legendary creature, that has been secretly left in the place of a human child.

fortune with a female lead in *Million Dollar Baby* and was eager to revisit that setup.

Based on a true story, the film originated in the 1970s, in a telephone tip that had come to TV scriptwriter and former journalist J. Michael Straczynski. Someone had informed him that officials were about to dispose of several potentially incriminating documents concerning a city council welfare hearing involving Christine Collins and her son's disappearance. Intrigued, Straczynski did some research and wrote a screenplay based on what he had found. *The Strange Case of Christine Collins* was optioned several times but never got made. Twenty years later, in 1996, after a long and successful run in TV, Straczynski took another shot at the story. He wrote a new script in only about two weeks and got it to producer Ron Howard, who read it, liked it, optioned it through his Imagine Entertainment production, and fast-tracked it, intending to produce and direct it in 2007, immediately following the release of his *The Da Vinci Code*. But Howard opted instead to direct *Frost/Nixon*, then the prequel to *The Da Vinci Code, Angels & Demons*, so he and his partner, Brian Grazer, pitched *Changeling* to Clint in February 2007. He agreed to direct it, citing the script's focus on its heroine, Collins, rather than the "Freddy Krueger" story of the crimes as the reason why.

He changed not a single word of Straczynski's script and within weeks of the first cast reading, he was ready to shoot the film. Every available over-thirty actress had put herself up for the sure-to-win-an-Oscar-nomination part. Clint cast Angelina Jolie because, he later said, he thought her face was perfect for period films (as he had Swank's for *Million Dollar Baby*).

Production began on October 15, 2007, and was shot on location in and around Los Angeles, and principal photography was completed in just under thirty days. The atmosphere on the set was relaxed; Clint was in total and unchallenged control and able to easily guide his actors through their most intense moments. Angelina Jolie recalls how it was to work with Clint:

> My character, Christine Collins, came up against so much pain and hardship, and she fought hard and she became a real hero of mine and I wanted to tell people about her. Fortunately, I had someone like

Clint to work with who is such a supportive director and so economic with your emotions. He didn't drain me and he helped me through all the very difficult, emotional scenes.

Six months later, on May 20, 2008, Clint debuted the film at Cannes, where it was enthusiastically received. Its distributor, Universal, then scheduled it for its big fall 2008 release. Even before the film's spring French preview, a recharged Clint had already begun work on his next film, one that would bring him back to the front of the camera.

Like everything else in Hollywood, schedules are subject to a million different factors, any one of which can cause delays, sometimes interminable ones. Before *Changeling* had come his way, Clint had actually begun preproduction on another film, *The Human Factor*, a biography of Nelson Mandela, which, for one reason or another, had to be postponed for a year. After flying through production of *Changeling*, and with *The Human Factor* still delayed, Clint looked around for another project. *Gran Torino* came his way, and he decided that that was the one he would make to bring himself back as an actor.

The original script had been written by Nick Schenk, a popular TV actor (Butch the Janitor, on *Let's Bowl*), writer, and producer; *Gran Torino* was his first try at a screenplay. Schenk had actually written the script years earlier based on his experiences working at a Minnesota Ford assembly plant side by side with several Korean War veterans, who had returned from active duty loaded with prejudice and anger toward all Asians. While working and living in Minnesota, Schenk had discovered the Hmong, a mountain-based, migratory sect of Chinese, many of whom eventually relocated to Laos and fought on the American side during the so-called secret incursion against the Pathet Lao during the Vietnam War. After the Americans left in 1974, many Hmong wound up in Communist prison camps, while others came to America and set up communities in various cities.

Schenk (and his brother's roommate, Dave Johannson) developed the screenplay, which set a Korean War widower against the Hmong, who have taken over his neighborhood. He is at first bitter and prejudiced toward the Hmong, seeing in them the reflection of the North Koreans and Chinese he battled during the war, but gradually he begins to learn about their culture, helps rescue the daughter of the family next door from a violent street gang, and helps her brother resist being recruited by the same gang. In the end, the grizzled old vet makes the ultimate sacrifice to save the boy, in a top-heavy Christians-save-"savages" plot twist. The final scene is replete with crucifixion images that were affecting, important, and dramatic. But as Schenk found out prior to Clint's involvement, the studios considered it completely unmarketable.

The main objection had been the age of the lead character, Polish-American Korean War veteran Walt Kowalski. The youth-dominated film industry—not just the makers but the audiences for whom they made their films—felt that such a story would have no audience; the Chinese were not a huge factor in ticket-buying demographics, and the elderly rarely went to the movies.

After receiving turn-down after turn-down, Schenk sent his screenplay to Warner producer Bill Gerber, who gave it to Clint, knowing he was actively searching for a project to replace *The Human Factor*. In Walt Kowalski (with the name's distinctive echoes of Tennessee Williams's celebrated bear-man in *A Streetcar Named Desire*) Clint found yet another reluctant, one-last-time character who is not afraid to use force against those he feels are his enemies and to defend those he thinks are his friends. In many ways Kowalski was an amalgam of the Man with No Name, Dirty Harry, and William Munny, here aged and cynical but willing and able to fight on whenever the need arose.*

Using local Hmong on location in Michigan, where Warner, after green-lighting the film, had suggested moving the shoot to take advantage of tax incentives, Clint blew through the shoot in his standard thirty days, and *Gran Torino* made it into theaters by December 12, only two months after *Changeling* had opened. It had been rushed into limited release to qualify for the 2008 Oscar race, and went into wide release in January 2009. This step-by-step release pattern, known as "platforming," is used to build word of mouth for films that don't have an immediate and apparent appeal to a large audience; it was augmented here by a statement that was "leaked" to the press and that flooded the Internet, in which Clint was supposed to have said that this

---

*Age had taken its toll on Clint as well. His six-foot-four frame had "shrunk" to six foot one due to chronic back problems.

was his farewell performance as an actor.* Whether he said it or not—
and later he claimed he didn't say it *exactly* that way—the reason was
not hard to see; even if this film wasn't his last, it was almost certainly
his last chance to win a Best Actor Oscar, and to do it in highly dramatic fashion.†

Gran Torino received out-and-out raves, among the best of his
career. The *New York Times* said that "Clint Eastwood has slipped
another film into theaters and shown everyone how it's done." The
Wall Street Journal called Clint's work in the film "the performance of
a lifetime," and the *Los Angeles Times* called it "a move audiences are
wise to follow." Andrew Sarris, in the *New York Observer,* proclaimed
that "Clint makes my day as aging avenging angel . . . he caps his
career as both a director and an actor with his portrayal of a heroically redeemed bigot of such humanity and luminosity as to exhaust
my supply of superlatives . . . the result is a genuinely pioneering production very much worth seeing for the emotional thunderbolt that
it is." Dozens more were just as enthusiastic.

Audiences too responded to the film, and it, rather than *Changeling,*
became the sleeper crowd-pleaser of the Christmas–New Year season. Its box-office take grew every week until its wide release quickly
sent it over the $100 million gross.

In early January the Oscar nominees were announced, and to the
surprise of many and shock of some, both Clint films were all but
ignored. Angelina Jolie was nominated for Best Actress for *Changeling*
and Tom Stern was nominated for Best Cinematography, but there
was nothing for Clint's direction of either film or, even more outra-
geously, for his performance in *Gran Torino*. The film itself, like
Changeling, was left out of the Best Picture category, which included

---

*"Clint Eastwood, who has played strong, silent types on-screen for more than 50 years,
is done with acting. Eastwood, 78, says he has no plans to step in front of the camera
after *Gran Torino*, which he directed, and starred in . . . 'That will probably do it for
me as far as acting is concerned,' the Academy Award–winning director told Britain's
Sunday Express. 'But I've got no plans to stop making films.'"—Cathy Burke, various
newswires, December 15, 2008.

†In an interview in the *New York Times* to promote *Gran Torino*, Bruce Headlam asked
Clint about the persistent Internet and wire service stories that this was to be his last
acting assignment. Clint's reply: "Somebody asked what I'd do next, and I said I didn't
know how many roles there are for 78-year-old guys. There's nothing wrong with coming in to play the butler. But unless there's a hurdle to get over, I'd rather just stay
behind the camera." *New York Times*, December 14, 2008.

Steven Daldry's *The Reader*, David Fincher's *The Curious Case of Benjamin Button*, Danny Boyle's *Slumdog Millionaire*, Ron Howard's *Frost/Nixon*, and Gus Van Sant's *Milk*. None of these films held either the resonance or the grand career summation that Clint's *Gran Torino* did.* The cocktail parties and Internet debates started immediately— the Academy was too old; the Academy was too ignorant; Clint had passed his "darling" phase and returned to making movies that only the public liked; nobody went to see films about the Chinese; Clint was too old-looking; Clint was too old; the film's mood was anti–Obama's national sense of uplift; the film was too negative and prejudicial.

And on it went, the low din of whispers that had followed Clint around for his entire career, like Shakespeare's infamous sound and fury. It was all part of the game, he knew, but it never failed to prick his very tough if not always thick skin. But he couldn't let it bother him. As Robert Frost, one of Clint's favorite poets, expressed in his famous poem, "Stopping by Woods on a Snowy Evening," he felt that he too had miles to go before he slept. Already he had a half-dozen new projects dancing like juggler's balls in his head; the Nelson Mandela pic, with his buddy Morgan Freeman in the starring role; a biopic of Neil Armstrong, the first man to walk on the moon, tentatively titled *First Man*; a film for DreamWorks called *Hereafter*; a jazz documentary about Dave Brubeck, another one about Tony Bennett . . . there was even talk of yet another Dirty Harry sequel. That had made him laugh: *"Dirty Harry VI!* Harry is retired. He's standing in a stream, fly-fishing. He gets tired of using the pole—and BA-BOOM! Or Harry is retired, and he catches bad guys with his walker? Maybe he owns a tavern. These guys come in and they won't pay their tab, so Harry reaches below the bar. 'Hey guys, the next shot's on me.' "

While his career moves remained uncertain, Clint's personal life had settled down. Dina regularly organized huge weekend outings for all the Eastwoods. She had performed the mighty task of bringing the entire Eastwood clan together, the mothers, the sons, the daughters, even some of the ex-girlfriends, give or take an unforgiving one or

---

*Best Director nominees were Daldry, Fincher, Boyle, Howard, and Van Sant. Best Actor nominees were Brad Pitt (*The Curious Case of Benjamin Button*), Richard Jenkins (Tom McCarthy's *The Visitor*), Sean Penn (*Milk*), Frank Langella (*Frost/Nixon*), and Mickey Rourke (Darren Aronofsky's *The Wrestler*).

two. Even Maggie, who lives in the same area and remains Clint's business partner, often attends. Both agree they get along much better now that they're not married. Today the Eastwood ranch feels like a vast homestead, like the Kennedys' Hyannis Port, or the Bushes' Kennebunkport, or even Bick Benedict's Texas ranch in George Stevens's 1956 epic, *Giant*, released after James Dean, its star, was killed in a car crash. Clint had appeared in his first movie the same year Dean died. A lot of movies and movie stars had come and gone since then, but Clint was still going strong, willing and able to play the game. He was in no hurry to get to those woods, lovely, dark and deep.

Soon enough, but not quite yet.

SOURCES

Research Institutions

Margaret Herrick Library of the Academy of Motion Picture Arts and Sciences, Beverly Hills, California

New York Public Library, New York City

New York Public Library for the Performing Arts, New York City

Los Angeles County Court, public records, Los Angeles

British Film Institute

Cinémathèque, Paris, France

Library of the *Los Angeles Times* (librarian Scott Wilson)

Bibliography

Albert, James. *Pay Dirt: Divorces of the Rich and Famous.* California: Diane Publishing, 1989.

Bach, Steven. *Final Cut: Dreams and Disaster in the Making of Heaven's Gate.* New York: William Morrow, 1985.

Bingham, Dennis. *Acting Male: Masculinities in the Films of James Stewart, Jack Nicholson and Clint Eastwood.* New Brunswick, N.J.: Rutgers University Press, 1994.

Biskind, Peter. *Easy Riders, Raging Bulls.* New York: Simon & Schuster, 1998.

Bragg, Melvyn. *Richard Burton: A Life.* Boston: Little, Brown, 1988.

Clinch, Minty. *Clint Eastwood.* London: Coronet Books, 1995.

Duncan, Paul, ed. *Movie Icons: Clint Eastwood.* Los Angeles: Taschen, 2006.

Eliot, Marc. *Burt!* New York: Dell, 1983.

Engel, Leonard, ed. *Clint Eastwood: Actor and Director.* Salt Lake City: University of Utah Press, 2007.

Frayling, Christopher. *Clint Eastwood.* London: Virgin, 1992.

Haskell, Molly. *Holding My Own in No Man's Land.* New York: Oxford University Press, 1997.

Kaminsky, Stuart M. *Clint Eastwood.* New York: New American Library, 1974.

Kapsis, Robert E., and Kathie Coblentz, eds. *Clint Eastwood Interviews.* Jackson: University Press of Mississippi, 1999.

Kinn, Gail, and Jim Piazza. *The Academy Awards.* New York: Black Dog and Leventhal, 2002.

Knapp, Laurence F. *Directed by Clint Eastwood.* Jefferson, N.C.: McFarland, 1996.

Locke, Sondra. *The Good, The Bad & The Very Ugly.* New York: William Morrow, 1997.

McGilligan, Patrick. *Clint: The Life and Legend.* New York: St. Martin's Press, 1999.

Nichols, Peter M., ed. *The New York Times Guide to the 1,000 Best Movies Ever Made.* New York: St. Martin's Press, 2004.

Randall, Stephen, ed., and the editors of *Playboy* magazine. *The Playboy Interviews: The Directors.* Milwaukee, Ore.: M Press, 2006.

Reynolds, Burt. *My Life.* New York: Hyperion, 1994.

Richards, David. *Played Out: The Jean Seberg Story.* New York: Random House, 1981.

Rickles, Don. *Rickles' Book.* New York: Simon & Schuster, 2007.

Rose, Frank. *The Agency: William Morris and the Hidden History of Show Business.* New York: HarperCollins, 1995.

Sarris, Andrew. *The American Cinema.* New York: E. P. Dutton, 1968.

———. *Confessions of a Cultist: On the Cinema, 1955–1969.* New York: Simon & Schuster, 1970.

Schickel, Richard. *Clint Eastwood: A Biography.* New York: Random House, 1996.

Siegel, Don. *A Siegel Film: An Autobiography.* London: Faber and Faber, 1993.

Thompson, Douglas. *Clint Eastwood: Billion Dollar Man.* London: John Blake, 2005.

Verlhac, Pierre-Henri, ed. *Clint Eastwood: A Life in Pictures.* San Francisco: Chronicle Books, 2008.

Wallach, Eli. *The Good, the Bad, and Me.* New York: Harcourt, 2005.

Wiley, Mason, and Damien Bona. *Inside Oscar: The Unofficial History of the Academy Awards.* New York: Ballantine Books, 1986.

Zmijewsky, Boris, and Lee Pfeiffer. *The Films of Clint Eastwood.* New York: Citadel Press, 1993.

NOTES

Epigraphs and Introduction

ix "You go to an Eastwood movie . . .": Molly Haskell, *Playgirl*, November 1985.

ix "Clint Eastwood is a tall . . .": James Wolcott, *Vanity Fair*, July 1985.

ix "Eastwood has . . .": Robert Mazzocco, "The Supply-Side Star," *New York Review of Books*, April 1, 1982.

ix "People can know . . .": Quoted in John Love, "Clint Eastwood at 50," *San Antonio Light*, November 2, 1980.

ix "There is something . . .": Quoted in Haskell, *Playgirl*.

ix "I'm an actor . . .": Quoted in *Newsweek*, July 22, 1985.

1 "I grew up . . .": Interview by Charlie Rose, PBS, October 8, 2003.

Chapter One

11 "My father . . .": Quoted in Dick Kleiner, syndicated Hollywood columnist, collection of columns and notes, Margaret Herrick Library.

14 "Well, those were the thirties . . .": Interview by David Thomson, *Film Comment* 20, no. 5, September–October 1984.

14 "My father was big on . . .": Interview by Bernard Weinraub, *Playboy*, March 1997. This was the second interview Clint gave the magazine.

15 "I can't remember . . .": Quoted in Wayne Warga, *Washington Post*, July 8, 1969.

16 "I remember Gertrude Falk . . . she made up her mind . . .": Zmijewsky and Pfeiffer, *Films*, 9.

16 "dummy": Thompson, *Billion Dollar Man*, 19.

16 "When I sat down . . .": Ibid., 20.

17 "I would lie . . .": Weinraub interview, *Playboy*.

18 "I'd never seen a musician . . .": Quoted in Schickel, *Eastwood*, 40.

18 "really adrift": Quoted in Frank Thistle, "Filmland's Most Famous Gunslinger," *Hollywood Studio*, February 1973.

Chapter Two

21 "Basically I was a drifter . . .": Quoted in Frank Thistle, "Filmland's Most Famous Gun-slinger," *Hollywood Studio*, February 1973.

21 "You can only dig . . .": Quoted in Dick Lochte, *Los Angeles Free Press*, April 20, 1973.

25 "One of my auxiliary . . .": Interview by Michel Ciment, "Entretien avec Clint Eastwood," *Positif* 31 (May 1990).

27 Clint getting a Seattle girl pregnant: "Clint handed the money over to the woman and left for L.A." McGilligan, *Life and Legend*, 54. McGilligan cites as his source a story that appeared in the *Valley Daily News* in July 1993. Eastwood has never confirmed this story.

Chapter Three

29 "I had a premonition . . .": Quoted in Dick Kleiner column, Margaret Herrick Library.

32 Lubin taken to meet Clint: Clint Eastwood interview by Arthur Knight, *Playboy*, February 1974 (Clint would do a second interview for the magazine in March 1997, conducted by Bernard Weinraub); *Crawdaddy*, April 1978.

33 "I thought I was . . .": Knight interview, *Playboy*.

33 Mamie Van Doren: "[Clint] was always straight and direct—he always knew the most straight and direct path to my dressing room," said Van Doren, quoted in "Chatter," *People*, May 26, 1986.

33 "the first year of marriage . . .": Quoted in Clinch, *Eastwood*, 29.

34 "He is very much . . .": Maggie Eastwood, quoted in Tim Chadwick, "We Don't Believe in Togetherness," *Screen Stars*, July 1971.

36 "They made a lot of cheapies . . .": Quoted in Ann Guerin, *Show*, February 1970.

37 "Don't worry . . .": Burt Reynolds, quoted in Eliot, *Burt!*, 42.

41 "the lousiest western . . ." Quoted in Carrie Rickey, *Fame*, November 1988.

Chapter Four

47 "I was set to direct . . .": Quoted in Bridget Byrne, "Eastwood's Round 'Em Up, Move 'Em Out Film Making Style," *Los Angeles Herald-Examiner*, June 24, 1973.

52 "fairly open relationship . . .": Interview by Arthur Knight, *Playboy*, February 1974.

54 Leonard reportedly kept two sets of books: See McGilligan, *Life and Legend*, 105. McGilligan cites "unnamed sources."

56 PR tour of Japan: Clint told Japanese reporters, whenever asked, that Maggie did not want to come. But, in an interview with *Photoplay* magazine in 1961 entitled "Clint Eastwood: Hollywood Loner," he is quoted as saying, "I just didn't want her along. I felt like going myself."

58 Maggie never said anything and never complained: Tunis never publicly discussed her relationship with Clint, but Clint talked about the uniqueness of his marriage, both in *Playboy* in 1974 and in Tim Chadwick, "We Don't Believe in Togetherness," *Screen Stars*, July 1971. About his quite-rare interview with the Eastwoods, Chadwick stated, "The only way Clint and Maggie Eastwood have managed to keep their marriage alive all these years is by having kept their distance from each other most of the time. They have stayed together by staying apart." Maggie is quoted as saying, "Clint is definitely a loner . . . he holds so much back." And Clint said this: "We're not advocates of the total togetherness theory."

59 "I knew I wasn't . . .": Interview by Bernard Weinraub, *Playboy*, March 1997.

60 "Sergio Leone had only . . .": Ibid.

Chapter Five

61 "What struck me . . .": Sergio Leone, quoted in Duncan, *Icons*, 26. Unattributed.

65 British critic and film historian Christopher Frayling: See *The BFI* [British Film Institute] *Companion to the Western* (Deutsch, 1988). Frayling says Leone traced his plot back to Hammett. In *Spaghetti Westerns* (1988) Frayling quotes Leone saying, "Kurosawa's *Yojimbo* was inspired by an American novel of the serie-noire [*sic*] so I was really taking the story back home again."

66 "We were shooting some vast cattle scenes . . .": Quoted in Patrick McGilligan, *Focus on Film* 25 (Summer–Fall 1976).

66 "Finally, I asked Eric Fleming . . .": Interview by Bernard Weinraub, *Playboy*, March 1997.

68 "An American would be afraid . . .": Ibid. Clint's reference to a "tie-up" refers to the Hays Code prohibition against showing explicit scenes of murder: "Murder scenes had to be filmed in a way that would discourage imitations in real life, and brutal killings could not be shown in detail. 'Revenge in modern times' was not to be justified." A tie-up would be an explicit depiction of a murder. "Revenge in modern times" means that biblical depictions were acceptable.

70 "Every time they wanted a format . . .": Quoted in Dick Lochte, *Los Angeles Free Press*, April 20, 1973.

74 "Why should I be pleased . . .": Interview by Hal Humphrey, *Los Angeles Times*, September 16, 1965.

Chapter Six

77 "I came back . . .": Quoted in Thompson, *Billion Dollar Man*, 67.

80 "The stories . . . didn't mean . . .": Quoted in Tim Cahill, *Rolling Stone*, July 4, 1983.

81 passionate affair with Catherine Deneuve: McGilligan, *Life and Legend*, 151.

81 "If it goes on . . .": Ibid., 152. McGilligan's source is unclear.

82 "This will be . . .": Clint, quoted by Wallach in *The Good, the Bad, and Me*.

84 critics wasted no time: Bosley Crowther had written about the trilogy before their American release, in a "think piece" for the *New York Times* in November 1966, where he was more positive about *A Fistful of Dollars*. His enthusiasm waned somewhat when the advance word among critics was negative. Crowther, fearful of going against the tide and of losing his own relevancy, toned down his opinion for his official daily review. Judith Crist actually said the film "lacked the pleasures of the perfectly awful movie."

85 "When [Leone] talked to me about doing . . .": Quoted in Thompson, *Billion Dollar Man*.

87 " 'The burn, the gouge, . . .' ": *New York Times*, January 25, 1968.

88 "remains basically hostile . . .": Andrew Sarris, "The Spaghetti Westerns," *Village Voice*, September 19 and 26, 1968.

89 "I own some property . . .": Interview by Arthur Knight, *Playboy*, February 1974.

Chapter Seven

91 "I think I learned more about direction . . .": Quoted in Duncan, *Icons*, 134.

94 "She [Golonka] began to like him . . .": Ted Post, quoted in McGilligan, *Life and Legend*, 162; no attribution is given.

96 "I had signed with Universal . . .": Introduction to Siegel, *Siegel Film*, ix.

96 "one of the two or three . . .": Ibid.

98 "I learned a lot . . .": Quoted in McGilligan, *Focus on Film* 25, summer-fall 1976.

98 "I thought we did very well": Siegel, *Siegel Film*, 304.

99 "He and his buddies were like . . .": Jill Banner, quoted in Earl Leaf, "The Way They Were," *Rona Barrett's Hollywood*, circa 1972.

101 Burton's smoking habits: Burton discussed his lifelong cigarette addiction and his drinking with Ambrose Heron on British TV in 1977. (Details not available.)

101 "Clint and Richard . . .": Ingrid Pitt, interview by Rusty White, Einsiders.com, June 1, 2002.

102 "The script was given to me . . .": Quoted in Kaminsky, *Clint Eastwood*, chap. 7.

103 *When Doubles Dare*: This joke has many reported sources, including Bragg, *Burton*, 196.

104 "We don't believe . . ." and "By [the time . . .]": Maggie Eastwood and Clint Eastwood, respectively, quoted in Tim Chadwick, "We Don't Believe in Togetherness," *Screen Stars*, July 1971.

106 the two immediately began an on-set affair: The Eastwood-Seberg affair has numerous sources, most thoroughly McGilligan, Richards, and Schickel.

107 Seberg's heart was broken: Richards, *Played Out*, quotes several of Seberg's friends on her great disappointment after the relationship ended. In a French newspaper interview (quoted by Richards) Seberg referred to her affair with a man "who was the absolute opposite" of her husband, "an outdoor type." She said, "It's always a bit of a shock to discover that people aren't sincere." Schickel, *Eastwood*, speculated that Seberg's emotional and professional career declined as much because of her failed romance with Eastwood as her troubles with the FBI.

107 charitable reviews: *Paint Your Wagon* is "a big, bawdy rip-roaring Western musical of the gold rush in California," said the *New York Daily News*. It "will have an uphill fight to be a blockbusting box-office hit," said *Variety*. "Thought overproduced and sometimes a little weird, the movie is pretty interesting," said *Women's Wear Daily*. "Amiable," said Vincent Canby in the *New York Times*; "[s]toic and handsome," Charles Champlin said of Clint in the *Los Angeles Times*. Among the film's harshest critics was Pauline Kael, who wrote in *The New Yorker* that Clint "hardly seems to be in the movie. He's controlled in such an uninteresting way; it's not an actor's control, which enables one to release something—it's the kind of control that keeps one from releasing anything . . . [the film] has finally broken the back of the American movie industry."

Chapter Eight

109 "I feel Don Siegel is . . .": Quoted in Kaminsky, *Clint Eastwood*.

113 "There was no question . . .": Siegel, *Siegel Film*, 365.

114 "I think [the Leone films] changed . . .": Quoted in Frayling, *Clint Eastwood*, 61–67.

117 "I worked on *Kelly's Heroes* . . .": Rickles, *Rickles' Book*, 141–42.

117 "It was [originally] . . .": Quoted in Michael Henry, "Entretien avec Clint Eastwood," *Positif* 287 (January 1985).

118 "Why should I open . . .": Quoted in McGilligan, *Life and Legend*, 185.

120 "as another spaghetti . . .": James Bacon, *Los Angeles Herald-Examiner*, October 14, 1971.

121 "Eastwood films . . .": Siegel, *Siegel Film*, 356.

121 "Don Siegel told me . . .": Quoted in Kaminsky, *Clint Eastwood*. "[The studio] . . .": Quoted in Judy Fayard, "Just About Everybody," *Personalities*. (Further source information for *Personalities* is unknown.)

Chapter Nine

123 "After 17 years . . .": Quoted in Rex Reed, "Calendar," *Los Angeles Times*, April 1971, 50, 62.

125 "My father died . . .": Quoted in Cal Fussman, *Esquire*, January 2009.

126 "It was just an ideal . . .": Quoted in "Clint Eastwood," *The Directors: Master Collection*, AFI (American Film Institute).

127 "I started getting interested in directing . . .": Ibid.

128 "I was lying in bed . . .": Quoted in Peter Biskind, *Premiere*, April 1993.

128 "a good-luck charm . . .": Siegel, *Siegel Film*, 494.

128 "I was absolutely . . .": Quoted in James Bacon, "Entertainment," *Los Angeles Herald-Examiner*, May 15, 1972. The footnote is also based on this source.

130 "There's only one problem . . .": John Cassavetes, quoted in Duncan, *Icons*, 82. Clint repeats the story in the AFI *Directors* series.

131 "I've traveled all over . . .": Quoted in Tom Cavanaugh, *Mainliner*, September 1971.

131 "desultory romance,": Biskind, *Easy Riders*, 234.

131 "In Hollywood, . . .": Ibid.

132 "There are a million . . .": Quoted in Tim Chadwick, "We Don't Believe in Togetherness," *Screen Stars*, July 1971.

132 "Clint lives a double life . . .": Earl Leaf, "The Way They Were," *Rona Barrett's Hollywood*, circa 1972.

135 "Harry's pursuit of Scorpio . . .": Knapp, *Directed*, 43. Knapp elaborates on the doppelgänger aspect this way: "Harry embarks on a desperate crusade to rid San Francisco of a mad killer, only to discover that he is alienated from himself and the people he has ostensibly sworn to protect" (37).

136 "I was the one who hired . . .": Quoted in Patrick McGilligan, *Focus on Film* 25 (Summer–Fall 1976).

136 "exhausting and detrimental": Quoted in Joyce Haber, *Los Angeles Times*, May 3, 1972.

136 "Directing is hard work . . .": Quoted by the Associated Press, August 15, 1972.

138 The decision to toss the badge: Siegel, *Siegel Film*, 366, 375.

139 "The film . . . made the basic contest . . .": Pauline Kael's review of *Dirty Harry* appeared in the January 1, 1972, issue of *The New Yorker.*

Chapter Ten

141 "We live in . . .": Quoted in Cal Fussman, *Esquire*, January 2009.

144 "looking more like . . .": Richard Thompson and Tim Hunter, "Clint Eastwood, Auteur," *Film Comment* 14, no. 1 (January–February 1978).

148 "This was a small film . . .": Quoted in Patrick McGilligan, *Focus on Film* 25 (Summer–Fall 1976).

153 "People who go to the movies . . .": Quoted in Clinch, *Eastwood*, 66.

154 "Lenny Hirshan took a script . . .": Interview by Charlie Rose, PBS, October 8, 2003.

155 "I must confess . . .": Clint, in an article billed as self-penned, *Action*, March 4, 1973.

155 His disappointment and anger: This episode is discussed in McGilligan, *Life and Legend*, and Bach, *Final Cut*. Clint's swearing he would never work for UA again is from Bach.

Chapter Eleven

157 "I went into . . .": Sondra Locke, quoted in Marcia Borie, *Hollywood Reporter*, July 2, 1976.

161 "It was a very difficult . . .": Quoted in Michael Henry, "Entretien avec Clint Eastwood," *Positif* 287 (January 1985).

162 "the only time [Clint] ever . . .": James Bacon, "Clint's Cliff Hanger," *Los Angeles Herald-Examiner*, October 22, 1974.

162 Hog's Breath Inn: Some of the details in the description are from Phyllis Jervey, "Hog's Breath Inn Opens Without Fanfare," *Pine Cone* [Carmel-by-the-Sea], date undetermined, circa 1970s.

163 "There's nothing I can do about it.": Maggie Eastwood, quoted in Peter J. Oppenheimer, "Action Hero Clint Eastwood: I'm Just Doing What I Dreamed of as a Kid," *Family Weekly*, December 29, 1974.

163 "romantic Casanova . . .": Paul Lippman, quoted in Thompson, *Billion Dollar Man*, 89; unattributed. Clint's response is also from Lippman, also unattributed.

165 " 'So what have you been . . .' ": Locke, *Very Ugly*, 138.

165 "the worst thing that . . .": Philip Kaufman, quoted in McGilligan, *Life and Legend*, 261.

168 "What Kael says . . .": Dr. Ronald Lowell, quoted in Mary Murphy, "Clint and Kael," *Los Angeles Times*, April 12, 1976.

168 "I don't have any new . . .": Quoted in Catherine Nixon Cooke, "The Mysterious Clint Eastwood," *Coronet* (February 1975).

Chapter Twelve

169 "People thought . . .": Quoted in Larry Cole, "Clint's Not Cute When He's Angry," *Village Voice*, May 24, 1976.

172 The reason was simple . . . : Said James Fargo, "He wasn't even in San Francisco, basically because he was having the affair with Sondra." Quoted in McGilligan, *Life and Legend*, 275–76; the attribution is unclear.

175 Clint had inserted it: "[The script] was in very good shape. There was a minor amount of rewriting, a lot of deletions. I did it myself," Clint said, in an interview by Richard Thompson and Tim Hunter, "Clint Eastwood, Auteur," *Film Comment* 14, no. 1 (January–February 1978).

176 *People* magazine "scooped": *People*, February 13, 1978.

179 "In today's climate . . .": Richard Schickel, *Time*, January 9, 1978.

179 "In a modern society . . .": William Hare, *Hollywood Studio* (February 1978).

181 "The script . . . had been around . . .": Quoted in Charles Champlin, *Los Angeles Times*, January 18, 1981.

183 "it would be theirs forever . . .": McGilligan, *Life and Legend*, 303.

Chapter Thirteen

187 "I've been advised . . .": Quoted in Iain Blair, *Film and Video* 14, no. 3 (March 1977).

191 "I don't know": See "Clint Eastwood Talks About Clint Eastwood as He Stars in *Escape from Alcatraz* Film," unidentified interview, probably from Universal Pictures, circa 1979, Margaret Herrick Library.

192 "During [1978] Clint began . . .": Locke, *Very Ugly*, 162–63.

194 "When I was sent the script . . .": Quoted in Michael Henry, "Entretien avec Clint Eastwood," *Positif* 287 (January 1985).

Chapter Fourteen

197 "In the westerns . . .": *Inside the Actors Studio*, October 5, 2003.

199 "Eastwood is living proof . . .": Norman Mailer, in *Parade*, October 23, 1983.

199 "Clint Eastwood brought in . . .": Robert Daley, quoted in Army Archerd, *Variety*, November 12, 1979.

200 "We've done okay . . .": Quoted in *Variety*, July 28, 1980.

201 "reports are circulating . . .": *Us*, October 14, 1980.

202 "We meet as often as we can . . .": Henry Wynberg, quoted in Ansi Vallens, "Playboy Who Won Liz Taylor on Rebound Finds New Love—Eastwood's Wife," *Us*, October 21, 1980.

204 "Rarely did Clint acknowledge . . .": Locke, *Very Ugly*, 186.

206 "It was like an homage . . .": Quoted in AFI *Directors* series.

206 "Naturally, I talked about it . . .": Locke, *Very Ugly*, 184.

207 "When you point . . .": *Inside the Actors Studio*, October 5, 2003.

207 "It was just a whimsical thing . . .": AFI *Directors* series.

Chapter Fifteen

209 "Not until *Tightrope* . . .": Bingham, *Acting Male*, 186.

211 Megan Rose: Details of her affair with Clint are from interviews she gave McGilligan, as reported in *Life and Legend*, and by several friends who know them both.

214 Edwards had asked her . . . : The details of this story are from Locke, *Very Ugly*, 189–90.

214 "Before I knew it . . .": Sondra Locke, quoted in Reynolds, *My Life*, 3.

217 Locke as a director: "I began to explore the idea of turning to directing and mentioned it to Clint. 'That'd be a great idea,' he quickly responded." Locke, *Very Ugly*, 191.

Chapter Sixteen

219 "I've always considered . . .": Quoted in *Newsweek*, July 22, 1985.

222 "Maybe there were . . .": Quoted in John Vinocur, "Clint Eastwood, Seriously," *New York Times Magazine*, February 24, 1985.

222 "The Eastwood persona . . .": Ibid.

222 "Clint Eastwood is an artist . . .": Ibid.

224 "I enjoyed going there . . .": *Inside the Actors Studio*, October 5, 2003.

225 "*Clint Eastwood, depuis . . .*": From an article in French by Philippe Labro; the magazine it appeared in is unsourced.

227 "I don't need . . .": Quoted in *Pine Cone* (weekly newspaper of Carmel), February 5, 1986.

227 beat-up yellow Volkswagen convertible: Associated Press, April 9, 1986.

230 *"Heartbreak Ridge* [is about] . . .":* Quoted in Milan Pavlovič, "Kein Popcorn-Film [Not a Popcorn Movie]," *Steadycam* 10 (Fall 1988).

232 "I had known Fritz . . .": Locke, *Very Ugly*, 214–15.

Chapter Seventeen

233 "I went to a jazz concert . . .": *Inside the Actors Studio*, October 5, 2003.

236 "So this had become my life . . .": Locke, *Very Ugly*, 217.

238 a full 18 percent . . . : Clint's value to Warner is compiled from figures in articles and lists on file at the Margaret Herrick Library, and from Thompson, *Billion Dollar Man*.

240 "I would never have been able . . .": Quoted in *Los Angeles Times*, December 9, 1995.

240 Durk Pearson and Sandy Shaw:

> Hollywood insiders have a hairy theory about the pseudonymous actor whose medical history is chronicled in *Life Extension*, the best-seller that offers a "scientific approach" to retarding aging. Though the actor is called "Mr. Smith" in the book, "it's obviously Clint Eastwood," explained one acquaintance of the film star. "He's a friend of Merv Griffin, at whose house the authors say they met this Smith, and like Smith he was 50 the year the book was being researched and was also allergic to horsehair." In addition, authors Durk Pearson and Sandy Shaw were advisors on Eastwood's latest movie, *Firefox*, and are collaborating with the actor on a new biomedical film thriller. So, are Eastwood and Smith one and the same? "That will not be disclosed by me," said the actor's manager. . . . The history, by the way, includes taking a "life extension formula" of vitamins and drugs that not only have improved Smith's suntan, hair, and speaking ability, but allow him to ride a horse. (*New York*, September 27, 1982.)

Clint had always been allergic to horseback riding, which is why, in his westerns, he is rarely seen in close-up on horseback.

> Last year Clint Eastwood revealed that he was indeed the pseudonymous "Mr. Smith" (the professional movie star who increased his stamina and alertness and improved his tan) cited in the 1.5 million copy best-seller *Life Extension: A Practical Scientific Approach*, by Durk Pearson and Sandy Shaw. What he did not mention was that along with following the Pearson/Shaw health plan, he optioned the rights to their less-than-orthodox first screenplay, *Sacrilege*. (*Esquire*, July 1985.)

Chapter Eighteen

243 "There is only one . . .": Brainyquote.com.

246 "Well, I've divorced Maggie . . .": On the marriage confrontation between Clint and Locke, see Locke, *Very Ugly*, 231.

247 "Suddenly he'd want me to travel . . .": Ibid., 230.

251 Depositions: Details of the depositions are derived from Schickel, *Eastwood*, and McGilligan, *Life and Legend*, and publicly available documents. Most of the court documents remain sealed, but detailed portions of both depositions are in Locke, *Very Ugly*.

253 "A fellow by the name . . .": Interview by Charlie Rose, PBS, October 8, 2003.

Chapter Nineteen

259 "*Unforgiven* ends the trajectory . . .": Brett Westbrook, quoted in Engel, *Actor and Director*, 43.

261 "Warner barely released . . .": Locke, *Very Ugly*, 292.

261 "Does she want to . . .": Ibid., 293.

262 "I owe you nothing": Ibid.

263 "Why a western? . . .": Quoted in Thierry Jousse and Camille Nevers, "Entretien avec Clint Eastwood," *Cahiers du cinéma* 460 (October 1992).

264 "I started rewriting it . . .": AFI *Directors* series.

271 "Tired . . .": Quoted in Schickel, *Eastwood*, 469.

Chapter Twenty

273 "My feelings . . .": Courtroom testimony at the 1996 civil suit brought against him by Sondra Locke, Burbank.

277 "I don't know what's going on . . .": Locke, *Very Ugly*, 324.

278 Lance Young: Locke, *Very Ugly*, 325, and a source who must remain anonymous.

278 "We have no interest . . .": The Semel and Daley statements are ibid.

284 "I guess maybe . . .": Interview by Bernard Weinraub, *Playboy*, March 1997.

Chapter Twenty-one

287 "If I start intruding . . .": Interview by Charlie Rose, PBS, October 8, 2003.

289 Dina Ruiz: Background information on Dina Ruiz is from *San Francisco Chronicle*, April 9, 1996.

292 "The three or four . . .": AFI *Directors* series.

293 Fisher had pressured Clint unsuccessfully . . . : "[Fisher] would have loved to play the part Meryl played." *Playboy:* "Was that an issue?" Clint: "Enough said." Interview by Bernard Weinraub, *Playboy*, March 1997.

293 "The reason he can . . .": Streep, ibid.

295 "The fact that . . .": Dina Ruiz, quoted in Thompson, *Billion Dollar Man*, 229.

295 "I don't think about it . . .": Weinraub interview, *Playboy*, March 1997.

295 "She was feeling . . .": Interview by Gail Sheehy, *Parade*, December 7, 2008.

296 "With *Absolute Power,* . . .": Quoted in Blair, *Film and Video* 14, no. 3, March 1997.

298 "The characters . . .": Quoted in Pascal Merigeau, "Eastwood en son Carmel," *Nouvel Observateur*, March 1998.

Chapter Twenty-two

301 "Dina keeps me . . .": Thompson, *Billion Dollar Man*, 9.

303 "geezer squad": Source wishes to remain anonymous.

304 "At this particular stage . . .": Quoted in Thompson, *Billion Dollar Man*, 236.

305 "I've wanted to . . .": Quoted in *Daily Telegraph* (London), December 22, 2002.

305 "I knew of Dennis . . .": Quoted in Engel, *Actor and Director*, 218.

306 "absorbs the past . . .": Ibid.

306 "for his edge . . .": Rose interview, PBS.

307 "I think the most . . .": Sean Penn quoted in Mark Binelli, *Rolling Stone*, February 19, 2009.

Chapter Twenty-three

315 "My earlier work . . .": Interview by Charlie Rose, PBS, October 8, 2003.

319 "I ran into Steven . . .": Starpulse.com, July 23, 2008.

319 "I started wondering . . .": Ibid.

320 "Between the two films . . .": Interview by Charlie Rose, PBS, October 8, 2003.

321 "The ambitious script . . .": *Rolling Stone*, October 16, 2006.

322 "a single African-American character . . .": On the Spike Lee feud, see the in-depth interview Clint gave to Jeff Dawson that appeared in London's *Guardian*, June 6, 2008, to promote the release of all five *Dirty Harry* movies on DVD; Foxnews.com, June 6, 2008; and Nick Allen, "Clint Eastwood and

Spike Lee Row Over Black Actors," *Telegraph*, June 9, 2008. Additional information, including Steven Spielberg's acting as peacemaker, is from *Access Hollywood*, NBC-Universal Inc., 2009.

322 "As for Flags of Our Fathers . . .": *Guardian*.

327 He agreed to direct it: Todd Longwell, "United for 'Changeling,' " *Hollywood Reporter*, November 20, 2008.

327 "My character . . .": Angelina Jolie, quoted in "The Road to Gold: An Academy Award Preview," TV, syndicated, February 21, 2009.

331 *"Dirty Harry VI! . . .":* Clint jokingly did this mock-pitch on the occasion of the 2008 DVD box-set rerelease of all five Dirty Harry films. Geoff Boucher, *Los Angeles Times*, June 1, 2008.

332 Both agree they get along much better now that they're not married: interview by Bernard Weinraub, *Playboy*, March 1997.

CLINT EASTWOOD COMPLETE
FILMOGRAPHY, INCLUDING TELEVISION

All features are given with release dates; all TV shows, date of first showing. Clint's producer credits are individually indicated, as applicable. Also
included are Clint's musical recordings and a list of his awards.

FILM

As Actor

Revenge of the Creature 1955. Universal-International Pictures. Producer:
William Alland. Director: Jack Arnold. Screenplay: Martin Berkeley, from
a story by William Alland. With John Agar, Lori Nelson, John Bromfield,
Clint Eastwood (uncredited).

Francis in the Navy 1955. Universal-International Pictures. Producer: Stanley Rubin. Director: Arthur Lubin. Screenplay: Devery Freeman, from a
story by Devery Freeman based on characters created by David Stern. With
Donald O'Connor, Martha Hyer, Richard Erdman, Martin Milner, David
Janssen, Paul Burke, Clint Eastwood (the first time Eastwood receives screen
credit).

Lady Godiva (aka *Lady Godiva of Coventry,* aka *21st Century Lady Godiva*)
1955. Universal-International Pictures. Producer: Robert Arthur. Director:
Arthur Lubin. Screenplay: Oscar Brodney and Harry Ruskin, from a story
by Oscar Brodney. With Maureen O'Hara, George Nader, Victor McLaglen, Grant Withers, Rex Reason, Eduard Franz, Leslie Bradley, Arthur
Shields, Clint Eastwood (uncredited).

Tarantula 1955. Universal-International Pictures. Producer: William Alland.
Director: Jack Arnold. Screenplay: Robert Fresco and Martin Berkeley, from
a story by Jack Arnold and Robert Fresco. With John Agar, Mara Corday,
Leo G. Carroll, Nestor Paiva, Ross Elliott, Edwin Rand, Raymond Bailey,
Clint Eastwood (uncredited).

Away All Boats 1956. Universal-International Pictures. Producer: Howard
Christie. Director: Joseph Pevney. Screenplay: Ted Sherdeman, based on the

novel by Kenneth M. Dodson. With Jeff Chandler, George Nader, Julie Adams, Keith Andes, Richard Boone, Clint Eastwood (uncredited).

Never Say Goodbye 1956. Universal-International Pictures. Producer: Albert J. Cohen. Director: Jerry Hopper. Screenplay: Charles Hoffman, based on an earlier screenplay by Bruce Manning, John D. Klorer, and Leonard Lee, loosely based on the play *Come prima, meglio di prima* by Luigi Pirandello. With Rock Hudson, George Sanders, Ray Collins, David Janssen, Shelley Fabares, Clint Eastwood (uncredited).

The First Traveling Saleslady 1956. RKO Pictures. Producer: Arthur Lubin. Director: Arthur Lubin. Screenplay: Devery Freeman and Stephen Longstreet. With Ginger Rogers, Barry Nelson, Carol Channing, James Arness, Clint Eastwood.

Star in the Dust 1956. Universal-International Pictures. Producer: Albert Zugsmith. Director: Charles Haas. Screenplay: Oscar Brodney, from a novel by Lee Leighton. With John Agar, Mamie Van Doren, Richard Boone, Leif Erickson, Coleen Gray, James Gleason, Clint Eastwood (uncredited).

Escapade in Japan 1957. RKO Pictures. Producer: Arthur Lubin. Director: Arthur Lubin. Written by Winston Miller. With Teresa Wright, Cameron Mitchell, Jon Provost, Roger Nakagawa, Clint Eastwood (uncredited).

Lafayette Escadrille 1958. Warner Bros. Producer: William Wellman. Director: William Wellman. Screenplay: Albert Sidney Fleischman, from a story by William Wellman. With Tab Hunter, Etchika Choureau, Marcel Dalio, David Janssen, Jody McCrea, William Wellman Jr., Clint Eastwood.

Ambush at Cimarron Pass 1958. 20th Century–Fox release of a Regal Production. Producer: Herbert E. Mendelson. Director: Jodie Copelan. Screenplay: Richard G. Taylor and John K. Butler, from stories by Robert A. Reeds and Robert E. Woods. With Scott Brady, Margia Dean, Baynes Barron, William Vaughn, Ken Mayer, John Damler, Keith Richards, Clint Eastwood, John Merrick, Frank Gerstle, Dirk London, Irving Bacon, Desmond Slattery.

Fistful of Dollars (aka *A Fistful of Dollars; Per un pugno di dollari*) 1964. Released by United Artists. Producer: Harry Colombo and George Papi. Director: Sergio Leone. Screenplay: Sergio Leone and Duccio Tessari, adapted from *Yojimbo* by Akira Kurosawa. With Clint Eastwood, Marianne Koch, Johnny Wells, W. Lukschy, S. Rupp, Antonio Prieto, José Calvo, Margarita Lozano, Daniel Martin.

For a Few Dollars More (Per qualche dollaro in più) 1965. Released by United Artists. Producer: Alberto Grimaldi. Director: Sergio Leone. Screenplay: Luciano Vincenzoni and Sergio Leone, from a story by Fulvio

Morsella and Sergio Leone. With Clint Eastwood, Lee Van Cleef, Gian Maria Volontè, Rosemary Dexter, Mara Krup, Klaus Kinski, Mario Brega, Aldo Sambrell.

The Good, the Bad and the Ugly (Il buono, il brutto, il cattivo) 1966, Italy; 1967, U.S. Released by United Artists. Producer: Alberto Grimaldi. Director: Sergio Leone. Screenplay: Agenore Incrocci, Furio Scarpelli, Luciano Vincenzoni, Sergio Leone, from a story by Luciano Vincenzoni and Sergio Leone. With Clint Eastwood, Eli Wallach, Lee Van Cleef, Aldo Giuffrè, Mario Brega, Luigi Pistilli, Rada Rassimov, Enzo Petito.

Le streghe (aka *The Witches)* 1967. Released by United Artists in Europe and Lopert Pictures Productions in the U.S. (dubbed). Various producers around the world. Producer: Dino De Laurentiis. Director: Luchino Visconti ("The Witch Burned Alive"), Mauro Bolognini ("Civic Sense"), Pier Paolo Pasolini ("The Earth as Seen from the Moon"), Franco Rossi ("The Girl from Sicily"), Vittorio De Sica ("A Night Like Any Other"). Screenplay: "The Witch Burned Alive" story and screenplay by Giuseppe Patroni Griffi; "Civic Sense" story and screenplay by Bernardino Zapponi; "The Earth as Seen from the Moon" screenplay by Pier Paolo Pasolini; "The Girl from Sicily" screenplay by Franco Rossi and Luigi Magni; "A Night Like Any Other" screenplay by Cesare Zavattini, Fabio Carpi, Enzo Muzii. With Silvana Mangano, Alberto Sordi, Ninetto Davoli, Pietro Torrisi, Clint Eastwood (in "A Night Like Any Other"), Armando Bottin, Gianni Gori.

Hang 'Em High 1968. Producer: Leonard Freeman Productions (Leonard Freeman) and Malpaso Company, released by United Artists. Director: Ted Post. Screenplay: Leonard Freeman and Mel Goldberg. With Clint Eastwood, Inger Stevens, Ed Begley, Pat Hingle, Arlene Golonka, James MacArthur, Ruth White, Ben Johnson, Bruce Dern, Dennis Hopper, Alan Hale Jr.

Coogan's Bluff 1968. Released by Universal. Producer: Don Siegel. Director: Don Siegel. Screenplay: Herman Miller, Dean Riesner, Howard Rodman, from a story by Herman Miller. With Clint Eastwood, Lee J. Cobb, Susan Clark, Tisha Sterling, Don Stroud, Betty Field, Tom Tully, Melodie Johnson, James Edwards, Rudy Diaz, David F. Doyle, Louis Zorich, James Gavin.

Where Eagles Dare 1968. A Jerry Gershwin–Elliott Kastner Picture. Released by MGM. Producer: Elliott Kastner. Director: Brian G. Hutton. Story and screenplay: Alistair MacLean, from his novel. With Richard Burton, Clint Eastwood, Mary Ure, Michael Hordern, Patrick Wymark, Robert Beatty, Anton Diffring, Donald Houston, Ferdy Mayne, Neil McCarthy, Peter Barkworth, William Squire, Brook Williams, Ingrid Pitt.

Paint Your Wagon 1969. Distributed by Paramount Pictures. Producer: Alan Jay Lerner. Director: Joshua Logan. Screenplay (and lyrics): Alan Jay Lerner, an adaptation of the original Alan Jay Lerner Broadway production by Paddy Chayefsky. With Lee Marvin, Clint Eastwood, Jean Seberg, Harve Presnell, Ray Walston, Tom Ligon, Alan Dexter, William O'Connell, Ben Baker, Alan Baxter, Paula Trueman, Robert Easton, Geoffrey Norman, H. B. Haggerty, Terry Jenkins, Karl Bruck, John Mitchum, Sue Casey, Eddie Little Sky, Harvey Parry, H. W. Gim, William Mims, Roy Jenson, Pat Hawley.

Two Mules for Sister Sara 1970. Released by Universal. Producer: Martin Rackin, Carroll Case, Malpaso Company. Director: Don Siegel. Screenplay: Albert Maltz, from a story by Budd Boetticher. With Clint Eastwood, Shirley MacLaine, Manolo Fábregas, Albert Morin, Armando Silvestre, John Kelly, Enrique Lucero, David Estuardo, Ada Carrasco, Pancho Córdova.

Kelly's Heroes 1970. Released by MGM. Producer: Sidney Beckerman, Gabriel Katzka, Harold Loeb (uncredited). Director: Brian G. Hutton. Screenplay: Troy Kennedy Martin. With Clint Eastwood, Telly Savalas, Don Rickles, Carroll O'Connor, Donald Sutherland, Gavin MacLeod, George Savalas, Hal Buckley, David Hurst, John Heller.

The Beguiled 1971. Released by Universal. Producer: Don Siegel. Director: Don Siegel. Screenplay: John B. Sherry and Grimes Grice, from the novel by Thomas Cullinan. With Clint Eastwood, Geraldine Page, Elizabeth Hartman, Jo Ann Harris, Darleen Carr, Mae Mercer, Pamelyn Ferdin, Melody Thomas, Peggy Drier, Pattye Mattick.

Dirty Harry 1971. Released by Warner Bros.–Seven Arts. Producer: Don Siegel. Director: Don Siegel. Screenplay: Harry Julian Fink and R. M. Fink and Dean Riesner, from a story by Harry Julian Fink and R. M. Fink. With Clint Eastwood, Harry Guardino, Reni Santoni, John Vernon, Andy Robinson, John Larch, John Mitchum, Mae Mercer, Lyn Edgington, Ruth Kobart, Woodrow Parfrey, Josef Sommer, William Paterson, James Nolan, Maurice S. Argent, Jo De Winter, Craig G. Kelly.

Joe Kidd 1972. Released by Universal Pictures/Malpaso. Producer: Sidney Beckerman. Director: John Sturges. Screenplay: Elmore Leonard. With Clint Eastwood, Robert Duvall, John Saxon, Don Stroud, Stella Garcia, James Wainwright, Paul Koslo, Gregory Walcott, Lynne Marta.

Magnum Force 1973. Released by Warner Bros. Producer: Robert Daley. Director: Ted Post. Screenplay: John Milius, Michael Cimino, based on a story by John Milius, from original material by Harry Julian Fink, R. M. Fink. With Clint Eastwood, Hal Holbrook, Felton Perry, Mitchell Ryan, David Soul, Tim Matheson, Robert Urich, Christine White, Adele Yoshioka.

Thunderbolt and Lightfoot 1974. A Malpaso Company Film. Released by United Artists. Producer: Robert Daley. Director: Michael Cimino. Screenplay: Michael Cimino. With Clint Eastwood, Jeff Bridges, Geoffrey Lewis, Catherine Bach, Gary Busey, George Kennedy, Jack Dodson, Gene Elman, Burton Gilliam, Roy Jenson, Claudia Lennear, Bill McKinney, Vic Tayback.

The Enforcer 1976. Released by Warner Bros. Producer: Robert Daley. Director: James Fargo. Screenplay: Stirling Silliphant, Dean Riesner, based on characters created by Harry Julian Fink and R. M. Fink. With Clint Eastwood, Tyne Daly, Harry Guardino, Bradford Dillman, John Mitchum, DeVeren Bookwalter, John Crawford.

Every Which Way but Loose 1978. A Malpaso Production. Released by Warner Bros. Producer: Robert Daley. Director: James Fargo. Screenplay: Jeremy Joe Kronsberg. With Clint Eastwood, Sondra Locke, Geoffrey Lewis, Beverly D'Angelo, Ruth Gordon, Walter Barnes, George Chandler, Roy Jenson, James McEachin, Bill McKinney.

Escape from Alcatraz 1979. Released by Paramount. Producer: Don Siegel. Director: Don Siegel. Screenplay: Richard Tuggle, from a book by J. Campbell Bruce. With Clint Eastwood, Patrick McGoohan, Roberts Blossom, Jack Thibeau, Fred Ward, Paul Benjamin, Larry Hankin, Bruce M. Fischer, Frank Ronzio.

Any Which Way You Can 1980. A Malpaso Production. Released by Warner Bros. Producer: Fritz Manes. Director: Buddy Van Horn. Screenplay: Stanford Sherman, based on characters created by Jeremy Joe Kronsberg. With Clint Eastwood, Sondra Locke, Ruth Gordon, Geoffrey Lewis, William Smith.

Tightrope 1984. A Malpaso Production. Released by Warner Bros. Producer: Clint Eastwood, Fritz Manes. Director: Richard Tuggle. Screenplay: Richard Tuggle. With Clint Eastwood, Geneviève Bujold, Dan Hedaya, Alison Eastwood, Jennifer Beck, Marco St. John.

City Heat 1984. A Malpaso/Deliverance Production. Released by Warner Bros. Producer: Fritz Manes. Director: Richard Benjamin. Screenplay: Sam O. Brown and Joseph Stinson. Story: Sam O. Brown. With Clint Eastwood, Burt Reynolds, Jane Alexander, Madeline Kahn, Rip Torn, Irene Cara, Richard Roundtree, Tony Lo Bianco.

The Dead Pool 1988. A Malpaso Production. Released by Warner Bros. Producer: David Valdes. Director: Buddy Van Horn. Screenplay: Steve Sharon. Story: Steve Sharon, Durk Pearson, Sandy Shaw. Based on characters created by Harry Julian Fink and R. M. Fink. With Clint Eastwood, Patricia Clarkson, Liam Neeson, Evan Kim, David Hunt, Michael Currie, Michael Goodwin, James Carrey.

Pink Cadillac 1989. A Malpaso Production. Released by Warner Bros. Producer: David Valdes. Director: Buddy Van Horn. Screenplay: John Eskow. With Clint Eastwood, Bernadette Peters, Timothy Carhart, Tiffany Gail Robinson, Angela Louise Robinson, John Dennis Johnston, Michael Des Barres, Jimmie F. Skaggs, Bill Moseley, Michael Champion, William Hickey, Geoffrey Lewis, Bill McKinney.

In the Line of Fire 1993. A Castle Rock Entertainment Production in association with Apple/Rose Films. Released by Columbia Pictures. Producer: Jeff Apple, Bob Rosenthal. Director: Wolfgang Petersen. Screenplay: Jeff Maguire. With Clint Eastwood, John Malkovich, Rene Russo, Dylan McDermott, Gary Cole, Fred Dalton Thompson, John Mahoney.

As Actor and Director

Play Misty for Me 1971. A Malpaso Production. Released by Universal. Producer: Robert Daley. Director: Clint Eastwood. Screenplay: Jo Heims and Dean Riesner. With Clint Eastwood, Jessica Walter, Donna Mills, John Larch, Clarice Taylor, Irene Hervey, Jack Ging, James McEachin, Donald Siegel, Duke Everts.

High Plains Drifter 1973. A Malpaso Production. Released by Universal. Producer: Robert Daley. Director: Clint Eastwood. Screenplay: Ernest Tidyman (and Dean Riesner, uncredited). With Clint Eastwood, Verna Bloom, Mariana Hill, Mitchell Ryan, Jack Ging, Stefan Gierasch, Ted Hartley, Billy Curtis, Geoffrey Lewis, Scott Walker, Walter Barnes.

The Eiger Sanction 1975. Released by Universal. Producer: Robert Daley, Richard D. Zanuck, David Brown. Director: Clint Eastwood. Screenplay: Hal Dresner, Warren B. Murphy, Rod Whitaker, based on a novel by Rod Whitaker writing as "Trevanian." With Clint Eastwood, George Kennedy, Vonetta McGee, Jack Cassidy, Heidi Brühl, Thayer David, Reiner Schöne, Michael Grimm, Jean-Pierre Bernard, Brenda Venus, Gregory Walcott.

The Outlaw Josey Wales 1976. Released by Warner Bros. Producer: Robert Daley. Director: Clint Eastwood. Screenplay: Phil Kaufman and Sonia Chernus, based on the novel *Gone to Texas* by Forrest Carter. With Clint Eastwood, Chief Dan George, Sondra Locke, Bill McKinney, John Vernon, Paula Trueman, Sam Bottoms, Geraldine Keams, Woodrow Parfrey, Joyce Jameson, Sheb Wooley, Matt Clark, John Verros, Will Sampson, William O'Connell, John Quade.

The Gauntlet 1977. Released by Warner Bros. Producer: Robert Daley. Director: Clint Eastwood. Screenplay: Michael Butler and Dennis Shryack. With Clint Eastwood, Sondra Locke, Pat Hingle, William Prince, Bill McKinney, Michael Cavanaugh.

Bronco Billy 1980. Released by Warner Bros, in association with Second Street Films. Producer: Dennis Hackin, Neal Dobrofsky. Director: Clint Eastwood. Screenplay: Dennis Hackin. With Clint Eastwood, Sondra Locke, Geoffrey Lewis, Scatman Crothers, Bill McKinney, Sam Bottoms, Dan Vadis, Sierra Pecheur, Walter Barnes, Woodrow Parfrey, Beverlee McKinsey, Douglas McGrath, Hank Worden, William Prince.

Firefox 1982. Released by Warner Bros. Producer: Clint Eastwood. Director: Clint Eastwood. Screenplay: Alex Lasker and Wendell Wellman, based on the novel by Craig Thomas. With Clint Eastwood, Freddie Jones, David Huffman, Warren Clarke, Ronald Lacey, Kenneth Colley.

Honkytonk Man 1982. A Malpaso Production. Released by Warner Bros. Producer: Clint Eastwood. Director: Clint Eastwood. Screenplay: Clancy Carlile, based on his novel, *Honkeytonk Man*. With Clint Eastwood, Kyle Eastwood, John McIntire, Alexa Kenin, Verna Bloom, Matt Clark, Barry Corbin, Jerry Hardin.

Sudden Impact 1983. A Malpaso Production. Released by Warner Bros. Producer: Clint Eastwood. Director: Clint Eastwood. Screenplay: Joseph C. Stinson. Story: Earl E. Smith and Charles B. Pierce. Based on characters created by Harry Julian Fink and R. M. Fink. With Clint Eastwood, Sondra Locke, Pat Hingle, Bradford Dillman, Paul Drake, Audrie J. Neenan, Jack Thibeau, Michael Currie, Albert Popwell.

Pale Rider 1985. A Malpaso Production. Released by Warner Bros. Producer: Clint Eastwood. Director: Clint Eastwood. Screenplay: Michael Butler and Dennis Shryack. With Clint Eastwood, Michael Moriarty, Carrie Snodgress, Christopher Penn, Richard Dysart, Sydney Penny, Richard Kiel, Doug McGrath, John Russell.

Heartbreak Ridge 1986. A Malpaso Production. Released by Warner Bros. Producer: Clint Eastwood. Director: Clint Eastwood. Screenplay: James Carabatsos. With Clint Eastwood, Marsha Mason, Everett McGill, Moses Gunn, Eileen Heckart, Bo Svenson, Boyd Gaines, Mario Van Peebles, Arlen Dean Snyder, Vincent Irizarry, Ramón Franco, Tom Villard, Mike Gomez, Rodney Hill, Peter Koch, Richard Venture.

White Hunter Black Heart 1990. A Malpaso/Rastar Production. Released by Warner Bros. Producer: Clint Eastwood. Director: Clint Eastwood. Screenplay: Peter Viertel, James Bridges, Burt Kennedy, based on the novel by Peter Viertel. With Clint Eastwood, Jeff Fahey, George Dzundza, Marisa Berenson, Alun Armstrong, Richard Vanstone, Charlotte Cornwell, Catherine Neilson, Edward Tudor-Pole, Richard Warwick, Boy Mathias Chuma.

The Rookie 1990. A Malpaso Production. Released by Warner Bros. Producer: Howard Kazanjian, Steven Siebert, David Valdes. Director: Clint Eastwood. Screenplay: Boaz Yakin and Scott Spiegel. With Clint Eastwood, Charlie

Sheen, Raul Julia, Sonia Braga, Tom Skerritt, Lara Flynn Boyle, Pepe Serna, Marco Rodríguez.

Unforgiven 1992. A Malpaso Production. Released by Warner Bros. Producer: Clint Eastwood. Director: Clint Eastwood. Screenplay: David Webb Peoples. With Clint Eastwood, Gene Hackman, Morgan Freeman, Richard Harris, Jaimz Woolvett, Saul Rubinek, Frances Fisher, Anna Thomson.

A Perfect World 1993. A Malpaso Production. Released by Warner Bros. Producer: Clint Eastwood, Mark Johnson, David Valdes. Screenplay: John Lee Hancock. With Clint Eastwood, Kevin Costner, Laura Dern, T. J. Lowther, Leo Burmester, Keith Szarabajka, Wayne Dehart, Paul Hewitt, Bradley Whitford, Ray McKinnon, Jennifer Griffin, Leslie Flowers, Belinda Flowers, Darryl Cox, Jay Whiteaker, Taylor Suzanna McBride, Christopher Reagan Ammons, Mark Voges, John M. Jackson, Connie Cooper, George Orrison.

The Bridges of Madison County 1995. A Malpaso/Amblin Production. Released by Warner Bros. Producer: Clint Eastwood, Kathleen Kennedy. Director: Clint Eastwood. Screenplay: Richard LaGravenese, based on the novel by Robert James Waller. With Clint Eastwood, Meryl Streep, Annie Corley, Victor Slezak, Jim Haynie, Sarah Kathryn Schmitt, Christopher Kroon, Phyllis Lyons, Debra Monk, Richard Lage, Michelle Benes, Alison Wiegert, Brandon Bobst, Pearl Faessler, R. E. "Stick" Faessler, Tania Mishler, Billie McNabb, Art Breese, Lana Schwab, Larry Loury, James Rivers.

Absolute Power 1997. Castle Rock Entertainment/Malpaso. Producer: Clint Eastwood, Karen Spiegel. Director: Clint Eastwood. Screenplay: William Goldman, based on the novel by David Baldacci. With Clint Eastwood, Gene Hackman, Ed Harris, Laura Linney, Scott Glenn, Dennis Haysbert, Judy Davis, E. G. Marshall.

True Crime 1999. Malpaso-Zanuck Productions. Producer: Clint Eastwood, Tom Rooker, Lili Fini Zanuck, Richard D. Zanuck. Director: Clint Eastwood. Screenplay: Larry Gross, Paul Brickman, Stephen Schiff, based on the novel by Andrew Klavan. With Clint Eastwood, Isaiah Washington, Lisa Gay Hamilton, James Woods, Denis Leary, Bernard Hill, Diane Venora, Michael McKean, Michael Jeter, Mary McCormack, Hattie Winston, Penny Bae Bridges, Francesca Fisher-Eastwood, John Finn, Laila Robins, Sydney Tamiia Poitier, Erik King, Graham Beckel, Frances Fisher, Marissa Ribisi, Christine Ebersole, Anthony Zerbe, Nancy Giles, Tom McGowan, William Windom, Don West, Luci Liu, Dina Eastwood, Leslie Griffith, Dennis Richmond, Frank Sommerville, Dan Green.

Space Cowboys 2000. A Malpaso Production. Producer: Clint Eastwood, Andrew Lazar, Tom Rooker. Director: Clint Eastwood. Screenplay: Ken

Kaufman and Howard Klausner. With Clint Eastwood, Tommy Lee Jones, Donald Sutherland, James Garner, James Cromwell, Marcia Gay Harden, William Devane, Loren Dean, Courtney B. Vance, Rade Serbedzija, Barbara Babcock, Blair Brown, Jay Leno, Nils Allen Stewart.

Blood Work 2002. A Malpaso Production. Producer: Clint Eastwood. Director: Clint Eastwood. Screenplay: Brian Helgeland, from the novel by Michael Connelly. With Clint Eastwood, Jeff Daniels, Anjelica Huston, Wanda De Jesus, Tina Lifford, Paul Rodriguez, Dylan Walsh.

Million Dollar Baby 2004. A Malpaso/Albert S. Ruddy/Epsilon Motion Pictures Production. Distributed by Warner Bros. Producer: Clint Eastwood, Paul Haggis, Robert Moresco, Tom Rosenberg, Albert S. Ruddy. Director: Clint Eastwood. Screenplay: Paul Haggis, from stories by F.X. Toole *(Rope Burns)*. With Clint Eastwood, Hilary Swank, Morgan Freeman, Jay Baruchel, Mike Colter, Lucia Rijker, Brian F. O'Byrne, Anthony Mackie, Margo Martindale, Riki Lindhome, Michael Peña.

Gran Torino 2008. A Malpaso Production. Producer: Clint Eastwood, Bill Gerber, Robert Lorenz. Distributed by Matten Productions in association with Double Nickel Entertainment, Gerber Pictures, Malpaso Productions, Media Magik Entertainment, Village Roadshow Pictures, Warner Bros. Director: Clint Eastwood. Screenplay: Nick Schenk, from a story by Nick Schenk and Dave Johannson. With Clint Eastwood, Christopher Carley, Bee Vang, Ahney Her, Brian Haley, Geraldine Hughes, Dreama Walker, Brian Howe, John Carroll Lynch, William Hill, Brooke Chia Thao, Chee Thao, Choua Kue.

As Director Only

Breezy 1973. Released by Universal. Producer: Robert Daley. Director: Clint Eastwood. Screenplay: Jo Heims. With William Holden, Kay Lenz, Roger C. Carmel, Mari Dusay, Joan Hotchkis, Jamie Smith-Jackson, Norman Bartold, Lynn Borden, Shelley Morrison, Dennis Olivieri, Eugene Peterson.

Bird 1988. A Malpaso Production. Released by Warner Bros. Producer: Clint Eastwood. Director: Clint Eastwood. Screenplay: Joel Oliansky. With Forest Whitaker, Diane Venora, Michael Zelniker, Samuel E. Wright, Keith David, Michael McGuire, James Handy, Damon Whitaker, Moran Nagler, Arlen Dean Snyder.

Midnight in the Garden of Good and Evil 1997. A Malpaso Production. Released by Warner Bros. Producer: Clint Eastwood, Arnold Stiefel. Director: Clint Eastwood. Screenplay: John Lee Hancock, based on the novel by John Berendt. With Kevin Spacey, John Cusack, Alison Eastwood, Irma P. Hall, Paul Hipp, Dorothy Loudon, Anne Haney, Kim Hunter, Geoffrey

Lewis, Richard Herd, Leon Rippy, Bob Gunton, Michael O'Hagan, Gary Anthony Williams.

Mystic River 2003. A Malpaso Production in association with NPV Entertainment. Released by Warner Bros. Producer: Clint Eastwood, Robert Lorenz, Judie G. Hoyt. Director: Clint Eastwood. Screenplay: Brian Helgeland, based on the novel by Dennis Lehane. With Sean Penn, Tim Robbins, Kevin Bacon, Laurence Fishburne, Marcia Gay Harden, Laura Linney, Kevin Chapman, Tom Guiry, Emmy Rossum.

Flags of Our Fathers 2006. A Malpaso Production in association with Warner Bros., Amblin Entertainment, DreamWorks SKG. Producer: Clint Eastwood. Director: Clint Eastwood. Screenplay: William Broyles Jr., Paul Haggis. Story: James Bradley, Ron Powers. With Ryan Phillippe, Jesse Bradford, Adam Beach, John Benjamin Hickey, John Slattery, Barry Pepper, Jamie Bell, Paul Walker, Robert Patrick, Neal McDonough, Melanie Lynskey, Thomas McCarthy, Chris Bauer, Judith Ivey, Myra Turley, Joseph Cross, Benjamin Walker, Scott Eastwood, Harve Presnell, George Hearn, Alessandro Mastrobuono, Stark Sands, George Grizzard, Len Cariou, Christopher Curry, Bubba Lewis, Beth Grant, Connie Ray, Ann Dowd, Mary Beth Peil, David Patrick Kelly, Gordon Clapp.

Letters from Iwo Jima 2006. A Malpaso Production in association with Warner Bros., Amblin Entertainment, DreamWorks SKG. Producer: Clint Eastwood, Robert Lorenz, Tim Moore, Steven Spielberg. Director: Clint Eastwood. Screenplay: Iris Yamashita. Story: Iris Yamashita, Paul Haggis. With Ken Watanabe, Kazunari Ninomiya, Tsuyoshi Ihara, Ryo Kase, Shido Nakamura, Hiroshi Watanabe, Takumi Bando, Yuki Matsuzaki, Takashi Yamaguchi, Eijiro Ozaki, Nae, Nobumasa Sakagami, Luke Eberl, Sonny Saito, Steve Santa Sekiyoshi, Hio Abe, Toshiya Agata, Yoshi Ishii, Toshi Toda, Ken Kensei, Ikuma Ando, Akiko Shima, Masashi Nagadoi, Mark Moses, Roxanne Hart, Yoshio Iizuka, Mitsu, Takuji Kuramoto, Koji Wada.

Changeling 2008. A Malpaso Production in association with Imagine Entertainment. Producer: Clint Eastwood, Brian Grazer, Ron Howard, Robert Lorenz. Director: Clint Eastwood. Screenplay: J. Michael Straczynski. With Angelina Jolie, Gattlin Griffith, Michelle Gunn, Jan Devereaux, Michael Kelly, Erica Grant, Antonia Bennett, Kerri Randles, Frank Wood, Morgan Eastwood, Madison Hodges, John Malkovich, Colm Feore, Devon Conti, J.P. Bumstead.

The Human Factor 2009. A Malpaso Production. Producer: Clint Eastwood, Morgan Freeman, Robert Lorenz, Lori McCreary, Mace Neufeld. Director: Clint Eastwood. Screenplay: Anthony Peckham, from the book *Playing the Enemy: Nelson Mandela and the Game That Made a Nation* by John Carlin. With Matt Damon, Morgan Freeman.

As Producer Only

The Stars Fell on Henrietta 1995. A Malpaso Production. Released by Warner Bros. Producer: Clint Eastwood, David Valdes. Director: James Keach. Screenplay: Philip Railsback. With Robert Duvall, Aidan Quinn, Frances Fisher, Brian Dennehy.

TELEVISION

Allen in Movieland 1955. A one-time special to promote Steve Allen's upcoming role as Benny Goodman in Valentine Davies's 1956 *The Benny Goodman Story*. In the TV show, Clint plays an orderly. His character has no name, and he has no lines.

Highway Patrol 1956. One episode, called "Motorcycle A."

Death Valley Days 1956. Hosted by Ronald Reagan. Clint appears briefly in six episodes.

West Point Story 1957. Clint appears in one episode of this series, "The West Point Story."

Navy Log 1958. Clint appears in one episode, called "The Lonely Watch," as Burns.

Maverick 1959. Clint appears in one episode of this James Garner series, "Duel at Sundown," as Red Hardigan.

Rawhide 1959–65. Clint appeared in all 217 episodes as Rowdy Yates.

Mr. Ed 1962. Clint plays himself in one episode, "Clint Eastwood Meets Mr. Ed."

Amazing Stories 1985. Clint directed one episode, "Vanessa in the Garden." Steven Spielberg was executive producer and writer of this episode. An Amblin Entertainment Production for television. With Sondra Locke, Harvey Keitel, Beau Bridges.

The Blues 2003. Clint directed one episode, "Piano Blues," of Martin Scorsese's (and several other producers') multipart TV documentary about the blues.

AUDIO RECORDINGS

Albums

1963   ***Rawhide's Clint Eastwood Sings Cowboy Favorites***

Singles

1961   "Unknown Girl"

1962   "Rowdy"

1962   "For You, For Me, For Evermore"

1980   "Bar Room Buddies" (with Merle Haggard), *Bronco Billy* soundtrack

1980   "Beers to You" (with Ray Charles)

1981   "Cowboy in a Three Piece Suit"

1984   "Make My Day" (with T. G. Sheppard), *Slow Burn* album

2009   "Gran Torino" (as Walt Kowalski, with Jamie Cullum)

Clint also composed the score to James C. Strouse's *Grace Is Gone* (2007) and original piano compositions for *In the Line of Fire*.

ACADEMY AWARDS AND NOMINATIONS

(Boldface denotes wins)

1992—Best Picture—*Unforgiven*

1992—Best Director—*Unforgiven*

1992—Best Actor in a Leading Role—*Unforgiven*

1995—Irving G. Thalberg Lifetime Memorial Award

2003—Best Picture—*Mystic River*

2003—Best Director—*Mystic River*

2004—Best Picture—*Million Dollar Baby*

2004—Best Director—*Million Dollar Baby*

2004—Best Actor in a Leading Role—*Million Dollar Baby*

2006—Best Picture—*Letters from Iwo Jima*

2006—Best Director—*Letters from Iwo Jima*

OTHER NOTABLE AWARDS

Kennedy Center Honors, 2000.

Honorary degree from University of the Pacific, 2006.

Nomination for a Grammy Award, Best Score Soundtrack Album for Motion Picture, Television, or Other Visual Media, for *Million Dollar Baby*, 2006.

Humanitarian Award, the MPAA (Motion Picture Association of America) Award for *Flags of Our Fathers* and *Letters from Iwo Jima*, 2006.

California Hall of Fame (located at the California Museum for History, Women, and the Arts), inducted by Governor Arnold Schwarzenegger, 2006.

Légion d'honneur (the highest civilian distinction), France, 2007.

Jack Valenti honorary degree from University of Southern California, 2007.

Honorary Doctor of Music degree from the Berklee College of Music at Monterey Jazz Festival, 2007.

Best Actor Award from the National Board of Review of Motion Pictures, for *Gran Torino*, 2008.

AUTHOR'S NOTE AND ACKNOWLEDGMENTS

This biography continues my revisionist study of what is America's greatest and most original form of expression, the Hollywood motion picture, a nickel-and-dime novelty form of entertainment that became a billion-dollar industry even as it pushed its way into the pantheon of twentieth-century art. I study the lives of those in film I find most interesting, influential, and fundamentally responsible for defining the medium in which they have excelled. In doing so, I am reminded of Molly Haskell's belief, which is also my own, that there are many, many ways to talk about the cinema.

As a boomer, I grew up engulfed in the postwar media revolution that began with movies, black and white television, and, of course, rock and roll. I was a street kid from New York City, part of the working-middle-class mix in the West Bronx, and easily the most accessible forms of entertainment for my friends and me were TV, music on the radio, and 45s. Everyone my age was electronically weaned on *Superman, Howdy Doody, Andy's Gang*, the greatest, purest, most genteel cowboy figure of them all, *The Lone Ranger*, and singing the songs we heard on AM on street corners or learning a few chords on a guitar or how to bang the bongos like Marlon Brando. And, of course, our parents had Sinatra; we had Elvis.

If I came early to movies as entertainment, I came relatively late to movies as art, for two reasons: you had to pay to get into movie theaters, and I rarely had enough extra money for that; and on those Saturday mornings when I did have that spare quarter, it was just too hard to physically go to the Loew's Paradise or the RKO Fordham for the cartoon or sci-fi/horror marathons. The elderly, overweight, furious matrons used to drive kids crazy—they'd make us sit on the side, which meant watching the movie off the distorted edge of the screen, and then kicked us out exactly at three o'clock, to make way for the adults. At least in those days TV and the radio were free.

I remember the first film I ever saw—while I was still a toddler my parents took me to see Fred Zinnemann's *High Noon* (they didn't believe in babysitters). But only in college did I find the full emotional depth of that movie, and movies in general. It happened with two encounters that awakened my senses, changed my thinking, and ultimately altered the direction of my life.

As a drama major at the High School of Performing Arts, I was a little teenage Method actor in blue jeans devoted to "the theater." I knew very little of it—I didn't see my first live, on-Broadway show until I was a senior—and just talking about wanting to be on television or in the movies was almost enough to get you expelled for a "lack of serious commitment to your art." To the PA faculty, whom I loved dearly (and still do), and to whom I entrusted so much of my adolescent development, movies were about fake fame and corrupting money. No one ever discussed Alfred Hitchcock, for example, whom I already believed was the greatest director in the world. Instead, we were instructed in the art of sense memory, part of the "method" of acting that Stanislavsky had given the world. Sense memory? What was there to recall at the age of twelve?

A few years later, after a successful run as an actor on the stage and television, I attended City College (the City University of New York) for undergraduate studies. While there I participated in the usual run of student productions—Sophocles, Chekhov, Shakespeare, Miller, Williams. One semester I happened to take a film elective taught by Herman J. Weinberg, who had written a book about the film director Josef von Sternberg, whom I had never heard of. The title of Weinberg's course was "Sternberg and Dietrich." Each week we saw one of the legendary collaborations between the director and the star, and I looked forward to that class more than any other. In the darkness of that auditorium at City College on Convent Avenue, I first saw the full power of the magic flickering lamp.

For the first time, film was more to me than a surface experience. I was fascinated by Sternberg's "presence" in every film, even though he never appeared on-screen in any of them; seeing all eight films together, displaying the arc of Sternberg's and Dietrich's careers, energized me.

In 1969, a year after I graduated from CCNY, I went off to do a season of summer stock and fell in love with a beautiful young actress.

When we returned to New York City, we moved together into a small apartment in the Village so she could continue her college studies.

She was a student at the then-quite-radical NYU School of the Arts theater division and obligated to take an evening film survey course being taught by the relatively young and still mostly unknown Andrew Sarris. She came home quite animated one night after class and told me that if I really wanted to be an actor, I ought to go hear this man talk about movies. Somewhat skeptical, as I was about everything in those days (including love), I agreed to attend one class, more as a way of appeasing her than out of any real desire to hear someone else lecture to me on film, a subject about which I now believed I knew everything there was to know. But that Tuesday night, in a small classroom on Eleventh Street near Second Avenue, packed with students, a blackboard, a projector, and a pull-down screen, my head was completely turned around as Sarris spoke with great passion about his already controversial new critical methodology of film, the auteur theory.

An atomic bomb went off in my brain when he discussed how movies were not filmed theater, not dramatized novels, not acted-out historical re-creations, not moving pictures of paintings, but an art form unto themselves. It was an invisible art at that, or as he put it, "not a visual medium," meaning that the artist's personality—in this case, the director's—was not readily apparent but materialized in the force and style of his direction. He said that because film could stand alone, what a film was about was less important than how its story was told, and that story content was far less riveting than stylistic context. For that reason those American films that had been relegated to the bottom of the conventional critical bill needed to be reevaluated and reordered. The auteur theory was a critical evaluation rather than an artistic device—no director could ever start out wanting to be an auteur.

Sarris's words shook my creative soul. He had opened my eyes to what was great not only on the screen but within and beyond it. He was eloquent, beautiful, insightful, passionate, and profound, as inspiring to me as any song by Dylan or Phil Ochs or David Blue or Joan Baez or any of the other folkie idols of my teenage years. That night I was first awakened to what film really was and the power of what its art could do. Andrew Sarris was one of my primal influences as I shifted from performing the work of others to writing my own. (Five years later, when Sarris was my professor at Columbia University's School of the Arts, we would become mentor/student and good friends.)

While I was still sitting in on Sarris's classes at NYU, which I now attended religiously every week, a friend of mine from college, Joe Schneiweiss, showed up extremely excited about a film he had seen over the weekend. It was *A Fistful of Dollars*, and he literally pulled me by my coat sleeve down to where it was playing so I could see it for myself.

I saw it, and I got it. He was right; it was like nothing that I had seen in the movies before. Its "hero," the Man with No Name, played by Clint Eastwood, was the first tough guy I had ever seen on the big screen who was anything like the real tough guys I'd known in the Bronx. He wasn't prissy, he wasn't verbally poetic, he didn't ride a white horse like some knight in shining armor, and he didn't care who (or how) he killed. He could fight and ride; he was big, strong, and completely believable in a film that was, for all intents and purposes, otherwise, to me, incomprehensible. His character was new and different and original, and his face I could not forget. If I didn't yet understand what he and Sergio Leone were trying to do, I certainly experienced a visceral connection, both to the character and to the actor who played him. Not since James Dean in George Stevens's *Giant* (1956) had a screen actor and the character he played shown me so much about *me*.

Not long after I read Sarris's essay "The Spaghetti Westerns," which began to explain Sergio Leone and Clint Eastwood to me. Typically, Sarris was ahead of the curve. Whereas the rest of the critical pack disdained this and most genre films (and the actors who played in them), marking them as inferior to the standard Hollywood "product," Sarris could see them for what they really were. He reevaluated them and the men who made them, including Hitchcock, Welles, Chaplin, Ford, Hawks, Walsh, Capra, and all the rest, who would eventually find not just reinstatement but anointment in the pantheon of American movies and their directors.

I believe that Clint Eastwood, as a director (and also as an actor) is a legitimate auteur. His personality is imprinted on his characters and films like a signature indelibly written on a piece of paper, making them worthy of study and his life worthy of biography. That is why I have chosen to write about his work and his life.

It is always somewhat problematic, I think, to write about subjects who are still living. For one thing, their story has not yet ended. But a second and more difficult issue is cooperation. In my view "authorized" biographies (of which I have done a few) are really collaborations and should be called that, as I have called the ones I did with Barry White, Donna Summer, and James Brown, to name a few. The danger of cooperation is that the author may surrender editorial control in favor of providing so-called inside information (much of the time the truth turned into its most favorable limelight) and remove all blemishes and bad judgments and nastiness with the precision of a Photoshopped eight-by-ten. For this book, I decided not to contact Clint Eastwood, in view of his well-known aversion to public scrutiny; instead I chose to write the book from an objective distance. As a film critic and student of film history, I have always tried to write about filmmakers through the dual lenses of their lives and work, to see how one helps create the other.

When that subject is still alive, and is still a force in the industry he or she represents, getting people to talk about him or her on the record is nearly impossible. Hollywood is a place that operates out of fear more than any other emotion. Because I lived and worked there for so many years and have written extensively about the industry, I have many solid contacts. Several dozen primary sources did talk to me for this book, but because so many asked not to be named, early on I decided not to mention any of them. In the few places where this will be noticeable—"sources say," "according to someone who was there"—I regret I cannot be more forthcoming, but I must respect the wishes of some and the integrity of all. I believe that enough secondary sources can verify my account. I am telling the story the way I feel it should be told.

To keep a flow of continuity, I used two other biographies as guidelines. Both were originally published at least a decade ago and as such miss the best and I think the most interesting decade of Clint Eastwood's life. Richard Schickel's 1996 biography, *Clint Eastwood,* suffers from the problem of trying to be an insider and an outsider at the same time. It is hopelessly hagiographic, and I am not (by far) the only one who feels this way. According to Stephanie Zacharek, "Schickel hammers a little too relentlessly on his own enthusiasms—his championing of Eastwood, in particularly, sometimes approaches fetishization."* Too much of Schickel's work suffers from the problem of cross-over, of wanting to be in an industry for which he is also a critic. He and I have tackled similar subjects in the past; both of us wrote biographies of Walt Disney, and there too our approaches and our results were strikingly different.

As for Patrick McGilligan, he unfortunately comes from the "gotcha" school of buddy-buddy insiderism that is meant to pass as serious biography. His book reads like an attack on Schickel's and becomes, in the process, overly cynical and bitchily gleeful in pointing out Schickel's many critical omissions (as does much of McGilligan's biographical and critical work—of which I was a "victim" in the past for that Disney biography). He therefore errs on the other side of the coin of objectivity. Neither Schickel's book nor McGilligan's has a cinematically charged feel—they could have been written about a novelist, a painter, or a poet—but I found both useful and informative, especially in terms of chronology.

Sondra Locke's memoir was also helpful, although not well annotated (it has no index or list of sources), and naturally enough, it is a bit overly subjective. It nevertheless pointed me in several useful directions, especially in tracking down legal documents and court records.

Also important to me was the great availability of Clint Eastwood's movies. DVDs, videotape recordings, cable film channels, and other sources that eventually allowed me to see virtually every Clint Eastwood film. I thank all those who helped me find them.

I wish to thank the following people for their assistance and guidance: Mary Stiefvater, my wonderful sometimes assistant and researcher; overall good guy and researcher David Herwitz; my faithful editor, Julia Pastore; my publisher, Shaye Areheart; my agent, Alan Nevins; my photographer, and so much more, Xiaolei Wu; and all of the production and promotion people at Harmony Books.

To my readers, I thank you all, wish you the best, and know we will meet again a little farther up the road.

---

*Stephanie Zacharek, reviewing *You Must Remember This: The Warner Bros. Story* (Schickel with George Perry, with an introduction by Clint) in the *New York Times Book Review* of December 7, 2008.

INDEX

Italicized page numbers refer to photographs

ABOUT THE AUTHOR

MARC ELIOT is the *New York Times* bestselling author of more than a dozen books on popular culture, among them the highly acclaimed biographies *Cary Grant* and *Jimmy Stewart*; the award-winning *Walt Disney: Hollywood's Dark Prince; Down 42nd Street*; what many consider the best book about the sixties, his biography of Phil Ochs, *Death of a Rebel; Take It from Me* (with Erin Brockovich); *Down Thunder Road: The Making of Bruce Springsteen; To the Limit: The Untold Story of the Eagles*; and *Reagan: The Hollywood Years*. He has written on the media and pop culture for numerous publications, including *Penthouse, L.A. Weekly*, and *California Magazine*. He divides his time among New York City; Woodstock, New York; Los Angeles; and the Far East.

Visit the author at *www.MarcEliot.net*.